Playground

Playground. copyright© 2024
by Bradley Davenport

All rights reserved.
No portion may be reproduced without permission.

ISBN: 978-0-9997967-6-4

1st edition

Disclaimer

This book is a work of fiction. Any resemblances to anyone living or dead is purely coincidental

Also by Bradley Davenport

Brown Ridge: Shootin' Noise
Monster Fantastic
Days of Love and Crime

*For my family and friends,
thanks for all the support*

Playground

Part 1

1

Headlights broke through the darkness as a black SUV barreled down the lonely highway. The three passengers in the SUV were listening to AC/DC. The driver, Lex, a thirty-something with shaggy blonde hair and a pair of wire rims asked where they were going. The person in the back told him to get off at the exit they were approaching. The driver shook his head in compliance. He just wanted to get the trip over with. He didn't want it to turn into that big of a thing, and it started to look like it was going to be one of those things. The passenger, Charles, asked the guy in the back if it was the same house as before.

"Yes," the man said. "We're still there. We've just finalized prices with the contractors, nothing has been built yet. It'll take time."

The passenger nodded again. "Yeah, something like that you wanna take your time with. Don't want the thing falling apart on you. That wouldn't be good for anyone."

"You're right about that," the man said. "You put it so succinctly."

"Right about that, buddy."

The man in the backseat saw they had a suitcase with them. He told the guys it was a good thing they brought that along.

"We had to," Charles told the man. "How else are we supposed to do this deal?"

Lex said, "We're good people to be in business with, always pay our debts."

"That's good," the man in the backseat said. "Bad business, has a way of staying with you. Bad habits, can get you dead. I'd imagine you guys want to stay alive, am I right?"

Bradley Davenport

The passenger looked out the window into the night. "You don't have to worry about us, my friend."

"I have to say," Lex kept his eyes on the road, "you should think about a closer place. I mean, it's okay but a long drive."

The man in the backseat said he had his reasons. He told both of the men that the house and land enabled him to do what he wanted. "We get rowdy sometimes, and when that happens we don't want to be bothered by cops."

"That's what I need," Charles said. "No pigs snooping around. We can do without all of them. I don't like those pigs, never have. Guys think they are better than everyone."

They pulled onto a dirt road. They really couldn't see anything on the road as they drove. The only way they knew woods surrounded the area was due to the fact they'd been there a few times during the day. Lex commented on how he was good at navigating around. He made a sharp cackle and said what a great night it was for a drive. Lex asked the guy in the back if he had a particular music selection he wanted to listen to. Something told him the man didn't care for the music he was playing.

"Not right now," the man said.

"Because I can change it."

"Don't bother, we'll be there shortly."

"If you say so," Lex told him.

After a few minutes, they turned into the driveway of a big white house. On either side of the driveway, vehicles were parked with people scattered around. They were all drinking and having a good time, shouting into the night like crazed animals set loose to run a muck. A few people were seated in plastic chairs around a bonfire. Beer cans and bottles were being cracked open. The stress of

Playground
the day slowly faded with every drink and toke.

The driver nodded to the window. "Look, they started without us."

"The nerve of them! Bet there's a lot of single chicks here," Charles said. "It's like kids at a candy store."

"That's the fucking spirit!" the driver snorted. "Hope this will go on for awhile. They need to look out for us!"

The man in the back told the driver to pull up in front of the garage door.

Charles turned to the man. "We got the suitcase, what about the other thing? We good on that, too?"

No response was given.

Charles looked at him a bit longer and shook his head. He thought it was more than a little rude that he didn't say anything. Charles told himself they'd find out the answer soon enough. They were going to get everything they wanted. If the man in the backseat had a problem with it they'd make him come around to their way of thinking. The two were tired of getting the run-around from people. They were a team for good or ill.

As soon as the SUV was parked the back door opened.

"Luke, sir," a slender man wearing a black suit with long blonde hair said. "I assume everything is in order, yes?"

Luke thanked the man and said that everything was fine.

"Spectacular, sir. Good to know. I was hoping everything worked out."

Luke got out of the vehicle. "No problem here. Everyone inside?"

"Yes, they're inside, sir. They've been waiting for you to show up, asking when you were going to arrive. I told them I wasn't sure when you'd make it. Everyone except Layne is here."

"Where's he at?" Luke asked.

The man shook his head and said he didn't know. He called a few different places and they didn't know where he was. He suggested Layne might be at a casino or a local bar getting drunk.

Luke said, "That's right up his alley. Told him he needed to lay off the gambling for awhile. I'll give him a call tomorrow. Hope no one killed that freak. We don't need publicity like that. And that wouldn't be good for him."

"Of course, sir."

Luke closed the door behind him.

The other two got out of the SUV.

Charles looked at Lex. "Something tells me great things are gonna happen tonight."

"They better," Lex said. "We didn't come all this way out here for nothing."

"We should keep our eyes open, though. In the middle of nowhere anything can happen."

"Well, if things get crazy we always have our backup with us."

"That's true."

After talking with a few people hanging around they went inside. When they got inside more people were scattered in the kitchen and living room. Lex and Charles were offered all sorts of drugs. They turned everything down—which was ironic because one of the things they came there for was drugs. But they didn't want to get foggy before they made the deal.

Luke said, "Before we get down to it wouldn't you like to have a little fun?"

Lex shook his head. "We would, but we have a few other things to do after this."

"It's your call. Myself, I don't partake in any of that. There was a time, sure. But those things do nothing but

Playground
cloud judgment. Whatever a man wants to do, that's his own business. I honestly don't think very many of us are saints, you know? We all have something, an addiction we can't live without."

Charles said, "Dealing drugs, aren't you tempted to use your supply?"

Luke told them he used to have a strong addiction to cocaine and heroin. He overdosed and almost died a few times. The way he was, he had to keep his sights on the drugs to remind himself of what he didn't want to touch again. Luke explained one thing he learned over the years was that people can only change when they want to. You can't push it upon people; until that day, though, you had to take advantage of their weakness.

"You have to take what you can," Luke said. "We have to survive out here, right? I have people who depend on me. Can't let them down."

Lex said he understood.

People in the living room started to dance to music on the stereo. Lex liked how the girls looked grooving and swaying to the music. He wanted to go over to the girls and fall all over them.

Luke told one of the guys standing beside him they needed to move to the back bedroom to make the deal. There were too many people around. He couldn't take any chances of people getting any wise ideas and talk about what they were doing.

All of the men walked back to the bedroom. Three men were already in the room. Charles thought it was a bit odd because the room wasn't that big. But he just wanted to get the thing over with. The fact that the guys were already in the room made him a little nervous, but there was nothing he could do about it. He had plans later that night and just wanted to be done with it. The guys around Luke were intimidating, people you didn't want to mess with. Lex and his friend didn't know the guys nor did the guys know them. No one was going to back down. They didn't want to come off as weak. Lex and Charles didn't want to take their chances with the crowd.

Lex looked at the men standing beside Luke. "You guys have any names or should I give you some?"

One guy who told them to call him Hammer said, "This won't take long. Guys will be on your way in no time."

"Do I have your word on that?" Lex asked.

The other guys introduced themselves; one of them, a three-hundred-pound Scottish man said his name was Tick, another man who told them to call him Sway told them they were just a bunch of colorful characters. Luke's other guys, Bone, Riggie, Locke, and Zero introduced themselves. Everyone was getting along well, engaging in small conversations. The tension in the room was slowly fading away.

Lex asked Tick how he got his name. The man explained that when he was still in Scotland he put a car bomb in someone's car. Tick started his life of crime when he was twenty. The crew he was with at the time had a shoot-out one day, and when the smoke cleared he was the only one from his gang standing. He decided to come to America after a friend told him he was going and Tick should join him. Tick didn't have anything else going on and agreed to go. After going to a few places, and doing some jobs for people, they landed in Arkansas and got with a crew. A few years later they met Luke and started running with him. Tick's friend, Woody, was killed one night after a drug deal went bad. Tick always regretted the fact he wasn't there to back his friend that night.

Tick said, "You have to learn things on your own in this life. No one gives you a fucking book when you sign-up. Hell, some folks I've met couldn't even read the book if they had it."

"I get that," Charles told him.

"The weak have to fall sometime."

Lex looked at his friend and asked if their plans were still on for later that night. They were meeting some other people for another deal; they were going to buy a bunch of pills.

"Time and place for everything, my friend. Don't get into that shit right now."

Lex looked down at the suitcase he was holding, then handed it to Luke. "It's all there, every dollar. You can count it if you want, won't offend me any. We're honest people."

Luke told the man he trusted him, and then he handed the case to one of his associates standing beside him. Another person handed another suitcase to Lex.

"Why do you need all of that, just out of curiosity? Big banging party?" Tick asked.

"Something like that, sure," Lex told him, as he handed the suitcase to Charles. "It's the best way we think."

Tick laughed. "Everyone has their reasons."

Charles opened the suitcase. He was amazed at all the small bags of white powder. He'd never bought so much at one time before. As soon as he saw it he wanted to buy more.

"I promise it's all there," Luke told him.

Charles had a big smile on his face. "This should last awhile. Excellent, excellent! My dreams are in shades of white."

"There's a lot more where that came from," Luke told the two men. "We can make more deals whenever you want. It's good business."

They thanked him.

"My supplier assured me there'd be no problem getting as much as we wanted. Next time, just tell me earlier and

I'll make a note to get extra. He might want to meet you guys in person, but I'm sure that won't be a problem."

"Shouldn't be," Lex said.

"Good," Luke smiled. "He's a pretty solid guy. We'd been doing deals for years."

Lex and Charles started to tell one another how glad they were they made the deal with Luke and not one of their regular sources. They explained one of the regulars they bought from had a couple of guys track down the two and threatened to beat them up. Luke asked why they do that.

"I think they just wanted to see if they could pull it off, talk themselves into being tough. Figured if they wanted to play that game we'd just give them a pass. We don't fuck around like that, you know?" Lex said. "We talked it over, if they were going to start that shit all the time we didn't need to do business with them. They could've called the cops out of fear."

"That wouldn't have been good," Luke said. "Did they find out you went elsewhere for the candy?"

"Not sure."

"Well, if they find out then just act like it's not a big deal. In the end, if they're smart they'll see they can find cash anywhere. Sometimes you may have to reinvent yourself. Any good salesman should know when they need to branch out. Look at me, when I was a kid still in high school I started selling weed, little by little it grew, now look at me."

Charles said, "The money from this is a lot better than weed."

"You're right about that," Luke said. "When I first moved to this stuff it was crazy to me. But the bust risk is higher. You get busted with this and a lot of things nowadays, that's time I don't wanna do. I don't know anyone who'd want that sort of time. I have too many

Playground

things to do. I was in jail for six months a few years ago, that was enough for me."

Lex laughed. "I don't know anyone who'd want anything like that."

Luke looked at both men. "You guys leave here tonight, go down the road a couple of miles, and get pulled over by the boys in blue, you better not say my name. Yes, I have some cops in my pocket but not all of them. And it won't be anything for some new dip-shit cop who wants to make a name for himself."

Lex and Charles looked at each other, then told Luke that they'd never betray him or anyone else in the house. Luke told them if they ever did they may as well kill themselves because they'd end up dead no matter what.

"Fair enough," Lex told him. "We want a long-term business relationship. There won't be a problem."

Luke pointed his finger at him and said that there better not be. He wanted a smooth business relationship with no trouble. He told them about a couple of guys he used to deal with, and one day one of the guys put himself in a position with the law where he was going to give Luke's name up. When Luke found out he had a few guys pay a visit to the guy. Cops discovered the body a week later.

"You won't have that issue with us," Charles told the man. "We like life."

"Let's hope that's the case. Life is often good, it'd be a shame if you guys had to miss it. You always have ups and downs along the way. You just have to figure all of that shit out and put it in perspective."

All of a sudden some loud noises came from the front of the house. Luke told one of his guys to go check it out. They couldn't afford cops showing up. After a few minutes, the guy came back into the bedroom, saying it

Bradley Davenport

was some girl who started fighting with her man. She threatened to call some big fella she knew to come handle the situation. After she told the boyfriend about the big fella she threw a few glasses against the wall and fled. Luke asked who she was, and that someone needed to go after her and remind her about about not calling the cops.

"You'd think she'd know, but just to make sure," Luke told him. "I'm a nice guy but I can't have that going on. We all could get fucked."

The guy told Luke he'd take care of it, that he shouldn't have even bothered him with such a thing. Luke told him to take care of the problem and that it shouldn't happen again. The guy apologized again. After the guy left Luke turned to his other guys and said they needed to start checking people out before they came to the house. Too much was at stake for it to get ruined.

"You won't have to worry about a thing, boss," one of them said. "It won't happen again."

Another guy who worked for Luke came to the room and started saying there was a problem. These people who Luke made a bad business deal with were there to have a chat. Luke told him to tell the guys he wasn't home, and that no one knew when he would be back. He didn't want a fight at his house that night or any.

After the guy left Luke turned to the two men he'd just made the deal with. "Sorry about the interruption. As you can see I stay pretty busy around here. Everyone always needs me for something. It's hard being king at times. There's only so much I can do."

Charles said, "We aren't kings, what's that like?"

"It's not all it's cracked up to be, that's for sure. It takes a special type of person."

"Historically, that's something that hadn't worked out well. I mean, sure, there are a few out there but not many. I suggest you do your best to stay that way. I don't know, now and then someone comes along who wants to be in your shoes."

"I'll take that under advisement. Now, I have a bit of bad news for you guys," Luke told them. "I don't like giving bad news out but it's something that needs to be done. What can you do? I mean, I do my best, you know?"

"What would that be?" Lex asked.

"While I do appreciate your enthusiasm for our organization I regret to inform the two of you we can't make you members of Modo."

Charles said, "Why?"

"We're not accepting you guys as members. Feel free to try in the future, though."

"Why should we do that?" Lex asked. "You'll just deny us again."

Luke considered that. "We just feel at this time the two of you don't have the type of dedication we're looking for. Things like this happen."

"What the fuck is this?" Charles said. "Who the fuck are you?"

"I'm the one who calls the shots. If you don't like it I don't give a shit. Just the way things are."

Both men were speechless.

"But you have the drugs, be happy with that," Luke continued. "You win some, you lose some. Better luck next time. I have your numbers. I'll give you guys a call when something opens up."

Charles looked at him. "This is fucked. You're just another snake in the grass. I'm going to tell everyone I know about you, about what a fraud you are. This whole thing you have here is fucked."

Luke said, "You aren't going to tell anyone anything."

"Why's that?"

Bradley Davenport

"Because you guys aren't going to be leaving anytime soon."

"That's what you think."

"I know it for a fact."

"Fuck you."

They argued about the matter for awhile. Lex and Charles couldn't understand why they were being told they weren't good enough. Luke just shook his head and said they had to get used to it, and that he wasn't going to change his mind.

The other guys standing beside Luke told the two they needed to leave.

"I suggest you get on your way," Hammer said. "Guys said you had other business? Go and do that. Forget about this shit guys."

Charles said, "Now, you guys wouldn't be giving us the run-around, would you? We don't take kindly to that sort of thing."

"You got the blow," Luke told them. "Lots of people would be glad just to have that. You have the good shit there, not that stuff that's cut on the streets. Should last you awhile."

"But that's not all we wanted!" Charles started to get excited.

"You need to slow down, son," Luke raised his voice. "It'd be in your best interest just to leave. Get out while you can."

"I'm not your fucking son."

"That might be true, yes, but I'm the one who's telling you how it's going to fucking be. I'm the boss around here. I make the rules."

"That so?"

Luke continues. "You guys come into my house, try to get heavy with me?" he shook his head. "That might

Playground
work with others but not with me. You can ask around about me. I thought you boys were smarter than this. I didn't think I'd have to do this to you guys. This whole thing I'm doing, I'm not sure if you guys are familiar with my father, Harlan Reeves, but I'm continuing what he started years ago. This thing, Church of Modo, do you even know what it's about? It's more than either of you will ever be. But I'm sure I don't have to tell you guys about any of it. I mean, why would you want to join so badly? If I didn't know I'd say you guys were fucking crazy as two loons, always showing your ignorance. I'm going to wish you safe travels. Go out those doors and do good. You don't want this."

"Can't get rid of us that easy," Lex told him.

Luke and his guys laughed, telling them they needed to leave before something bad happened.

Tick said, "We don't want to see anyone get hurt. You guys just need to forget this. Some things just weren't meant to be. Now, we're asking nicely but that's wearing thin. Go outside this room and look around. There's a party going on. We don't feel like hurting anyone tonight. We just want to relax. We will if we have to, but we're not looking at getting rid of you guys."

Charles and Lex said the whole thing was pretty ridiculous, but there was nothing they could do about it. Was it worth it? What was so special about what Luke Reeves was starting? You would've thought Lex and Charles would've done their research on the Church of Modo and Harlan Reeves. Things didn't turn out well for him or any of his crew back then. But maybe they figured they had nothing to lose and didn't care what happened.

As the two men turned to walk out of the room Luke stopped them, saying they shouldn't discuss anything with anyone.

"Or what?" Charles shouted. "You going to beat us up?

Hurt us in some way? Get your big boys after us?"

Luke laughed. "We can't afford to have people run their mouths about what we do here. I have a reputation to uphold."

Charles shrugged his shoulders. "Listen, we can appreciate something like that, sure. But it doesn't negate the fact you told us something, now, you're telling us something else. What is that? Would you want something like that getting out?" It wouldn't put you in the best light."

"I'm sorry, guys, that's just the way it has to be. Now, we can do this the easy way or the hard way. I suggest you walk out of here before anything happens to you."

Tick said, "Guys better listen to him. I know you don't want things to go there."

Neither of the two men moved.

The big man on Luke's left pulled a knife from his pocket.

"I'm sorry, were you planning on doing something with that?" Charles eyed the knife. "Wouldn't be very nice."

About that time two other men walked behind Charles and Lex, blocking the doorway so they couldn't leave. They told the two they couldn't go.

"It ends here," Luke told the two. "I'm afraid you can't leave. I tried to be nice about it."

"What the fuck is this?" Lex shouted

The one guy grabbed Charles from behind, putting him in a headlock. The man with the knife reached out and stabbed him in the belly three times. As Charles fell to the ground Lex was tackled and stabbed a few times. Both men struggled to breathe before they bled out.

Everyone looked down at the bodies on the floor, moving around so they didn't step in any blood.

One of the guys said they had a big problem on their hands.

"You think?" Tick said. "We need to clean this mess up.

Playground
We didn't plan for it to go this far. We thought talking would help but it didn't."

Luke told everyone he couldn't have the dead bodies in the room. They were going to have to get rid of the bodies without any of the other guests knowing.

Tick said, "If anyone comes asking about these two, that won't be good. I just hope they didn't tell anyone they were coming out here."

Luke said he wasn't sure. He said if anything comes out about it they'll decide what to do about it then. It was too much to deal with at the time.

The guy with the knife, Bobby, said, "Goddamn, this is one of my good knives, boss. I should've brought another one. Now, hell, I'll have to clean this shit. It might rust."

Luke laughed and told him he'd buy the guy another knife.

Another guy commented that it was a good thing they didn't have carpet in the room.

Luke said, "I don't have time for any of this. I need this cleaned," he looked at all of his guys. "We can't have anyone out there knowing anything. You'll have to take them out the side door."

They nodded.

"You need to dump their car, too," he added. "We don't need wandering eyes around here. They may see something that doesn't make sense, call the cops, then we're fucked. It'll start a chain reaction, it would be very bad for us all."

They said they understood.

Their boss told them they'd have to dig two holes in the backyard when everyone left; until then, they were going to have to keep the bodies in the room. It was a good thing the bedroom was at the end of a long hallway, no one would disturb the room. They were told if anyone

Bradley Davenport

did start down the hallway to keep them away with force. They said they understood. Two guys left to take the car out into the middle of nowhere and torch it.

Luke told them he was going outside to mingle with the guests. He needed to get out of that room. Things were unsettling in there. He had to detach himself from the horrible event. He'd already killed his fair share of people, but that was too gruesome of a scene for him. He was used to just shooting people and being done with it, however, in this particular case, the only choice they had was to use a knife. Luke didn't want it that way, but they couldn't have risked it. They needed to make sure those two didn't talk. If they'd used guns people would have heard.

As soon as he stepped on the front lawn he encountered Reed Culp. Reed was dressed in a blue t-shirt and overalls. He had brown curly hair. He held out his hand for Luke to shake. The boss didn't care for the man that much. He tolerated him because his brother worked in the crew. Luke was considering getting rid of the brother for being a pain in the ass. He knew there were people in his crew who thought he was a pain in the ass, too

There were a few times Luke helped Reed get out of the jams. Reed got into a little trouble when he couldn't pay a drug debt. Word got out that some people were going to kill Reed. When Luke heard what was going on he had a meeting with the people, paid off the debt, and saved a life. When asked why he paid the money he just told people it was a gift to the guy who worked for him. Reed told him he'd pay him back but never did. Luke talked with him and put him to work.

"I just wanted to thank you," Reed told him.

"For what?" Luke asked.

"This party, for the night. It's been great. All the booze

Playground
and stuff, it's been insane. Ran into this girl, got a date with her tomorrow."

"What's her name?"

"Shauna," Reed said. "Didn't catch a last name. I'm sure I'll get it tomorrow."

"Good for you, buddy. I'm sure you will."

"Yeah, yeah! She wants to go to the fair. Probably talk me into getting one of those big stuffed bears or something. Girls, they like stuff like that, you know?"

"I do know. You have to get in her good graces if you want in her panties."

Reed laughed. "Think that'll do the trick?"

"Don't see why it wouldn't. Hell, she may tell her friends about it and they'll wanna fuck. You'll be knee-deep in a woman then, how about that?"

"That would be okay by me."

"Of course it would," the boss laughed. "We're only men with needs. Have to get it from somewhere."

"You're right about that, man. Good times were had by all. If she has an interested friend I'll let you know."

"You do that."

Reed smiled and told him that was the least he could do. Like every other time Reed saw Luke he thanked him again for getting him out of the jam with those guys. He told Luke that he didn't want that to happen again.

"Just pay your debts and it won't ever be a problem. If you want I could give you the name of a few money guys I know."

"Nah, I think I'll be fine."

"You sure?"

"I think so?"

They talked a little more before Luke told him he had to talk to a few other people. And Luke didn't care much for the guy anyway, so he wanted to get away as soon as he could. Luke told him to enjoy the rest of the night, and if he needed anything just say something.

As Reed drifted away to talk to other people Luke just stood there. He lit a cigarette and looked up at the dark sky. A shred of guilt about Lex and Charles crept into his mind. But he told himself it was their fault they ended up dead. He wasn't a bad guy. They shouldn't have threatened him like they did. Things were done and they should've let it go. All they had to do was say nothing. He told himself they should have just walked out and enjoyed the party. They would've liked it. They still would have been alive. While he stared into the sky a light from a plane glided through the night. For a moment he wished he was on that plane, off to a place where nobody would bother him. A guy could always use a vacation, a break from all of the stress. Being a boss is hard work.

Luke had to put the wheels back in motion, something he knew his father was proud of. He had promised his father, Harlan Reeves, that he would continue the Church of Modo. There was a time when Luke didn't want to have anything to do with his father or what he wanted. He had his own life to live. It wasn't his fault Harlan was locked away in prison. At the time he didn't know his father would ever be released. At some point he came to terms with his father and what he did. He made a promise he would start the church again. He knew the news was going to open old wounds. He figured the best thing he could do was downplay it, make it seem like the church was never going to open ever again.

2

In the summer of 1990, Harlan Reeves was sentenced to prison for a multitude of crimes, murder being at the forefront. When Harlan went away it was thought the Church of Modo was finished forever. The rest of Harlan's crew were also taken away for a variety of crimes; murder, rape, robbery, drugs, and battery. The whole situation hasn't been good by any means. After the followers were set free, they had scars and troubles for years to come.

In a series of visits to his father, Luke told him he'd do everything in his power to carry on the family message. But Luke told Harlan it was going to take some time. He didn't want to make the mistakes his father had. Luke knew as soon as the public caught word of the news there would be split reactions; some would welcome it, others wouldn't. They'd protest in the streets. Who knows how far they'll be willing to go? There was a two-year period where he got death threats from people because of things his father had done. The city would never forget its past.

Luke continued smoking as he looked at everyone drinking and doing drugs around him. Some people offered drugs to him but he didn't want any. They asked what was wrong. He told them he just didn't want any. He told them to have a good time, and if they needed they could crash at the house. There was plenty of room.

"My place is always open," he told them. "Life is a circus, have fun with it. Only have one life, might as well enjoy it, and live it to the fullest. You can't have any hang-ups about things. It's not worth it."

And he couldn't have anyone having an accident after they left his place. The cops would come and haul them

Bradley Davenport

all away. They'd lock him up and throw the key in the garbage.

They gave him a salute and went on with what they were doing. Luke liked the parties. He liked the fact he was able to bring joy to people, if only for a little time. He found himself asking if they treated him well because they wanted something from him. He'd tell himself that was okay, eventually he'd get them all back. If they wouldn't do what he wanted he'd make them.

To say he was a complicated guy would be an understatement. His mood could change in an instant. One minute he could be the nicest guy in the world, the next he could be meaner than a snake. If people didn't like him he could care less. He didn't give a fuck about what anyone said about him. The way he saw it, people could say what they wanted about him but at the end of the day, they were all jealous. They all wanted to be him.

He went back inside and all the ugliness from earlier was still being cleaned. Since the guests weren't going anywhere Luke suggested they take the bodies out the window of the room. The guys told him it would be a mess. Another guy suggested they could just tell everyone to go home, then they could have the whole space. After awhile of talking, they decided it was the best idea.

People kept coming over to Luke and asking about what happened in the bedroom. They noticed something was going on but weren't sure what was going on. A few people asked if anything criminal was going on. He just told them not to worry about it, that it wasn't their concern, just to go back and enjoy the night.

After a few hours passed most of the people had gone. Some passed out in the living room. They figured nothing would bother them. No one would be fool enough to break into Luke's house. They would've been met with a shotgun.

Playground

The bodies needed to be moved before the sun came up. They carried the bodies to an old truck that belonged to one of the guys.

"We need to get a move on it," one of them said. "Don't wanna get caught."

Another said, "Yeah, that wouldn't be good for anyone."

Riggie said, "The thing I can't get passed is the whole thing about how this didn't have to happen. I don't know, man, it's just some crazy shit. Stuff like that, hell, you can't even put it into words."

"You sure?" Tick said. "Sounds like you just said a bunch of words to me, brother."

"Yeah, something like that."

Luke said everything would be okay. He told them not to worry so much. He told them he'd buy them some beer later that day; they liked that idea.

They drove about four miles up the road to a secluded area that had heavy vegetation and trees. They asked Luke if he was sure it would be okay to put them there. He told them it was fine.

The two were buried in graves that weren't even six feet. The thought was they'd return the next night when they had more time. The sky slowly got brighter as they pulled away from the site.

They went back to Luke's place and fell asleep. When they woke up later that day they had some drinks with food. Luke retired to his office for the rest of the day. At some point, he asked his guys to go back out to the site where the bodies were and finish the holes. They had another party that night.

3

It was midnight when raindrops peppered the streets of Bancroft. Reports said rain and wind were going to increase throughout the morning hours.

Joey Ryder staggered through the double doors of the Redmond. The building was a twenty-story structure that stood beside Miller's Hall; one of the amphitheaters in the city. Earlier that evening Miller's Hall hosted the 2nd annual fall banquet. The event was started by Jeff Oaks as a fundraiser to help people in need, to help the shelters in the area. Everyone was free to donate whatever they could; money, food, clothing, household items, and toys for children. It seemed like the city took away funding every year. Jeff took it upon himself, with help from a few others, to start the donations. They did pretty well. It surprised Jeff how generous people were. The event also was a way they could welcome the fall to the fine people of Bancroft. Along with live entertainment, the locals sold homemade items. A few local restaurants catered for the event. Everyone had a good time. As the evening went on some homeless people came by, saying how grateful they were for everything. They were all happy and went about their way. A few of them mentioned it was supposed to rain overnight. Jeff told them if it did to stop by one of the shelters. They told him they would.

When Joey entered the building he gave the man at the front desk, Gary Johnson, a short bald guy in a black suit, a nod.

"Mr. Ryder, how's things in the world?"

"It's getting there."

"It happens to the best of us."

"That it does."

Playground

Gary said, "What about that weather out there?"

"Looks like it's going to be here for awhile."

"You can say that again," the man said. "Have a good one."

Joey walked over to the elevator and told Gary to have a good one. The first person he saw when he got off the elevator was Layla McConnell. She worked the front desk of the radio station, answering calls, signing for deliveries, booking things, and some of the more boring tasks of the station. She had light brown hair that was pulled back in a tight bun; it brought out her sparkling green eyes. He loved looking at her. She wore a long-sleeve black shirt with a pair of blue jeans. She smiled when they made eye contact.

"Whaddya say, Layla?"

"Hey, you!"

"How are things?"

She shrugged. "Okay, I guess. About the same around here."

"Just work, making that money, huh?"

She tapped a pen on a stack of papers. "Could always be worse. Not many people have called since I've been here."

"At least that's something," Joey said. "It's not every day that happens."

"It's a little eerie."

"I can see where it would be."

"But it's been a good night."

"That's the important thing," he said.

"That goes without saying."

"I know that's right."

She smiled. "How's the weather out there?"

"It started to rain when I was coming in."

"Yeah, I saw on the news earlier that it was gonna start about now."

"They were right about that," Joey chuckled. "The downpour hadn't started yet, so that's good."

"But I love it when I don't have to be in it."

"I'd have to agree," Joey laughed. "Good thing I'll be in here. I hope whatever it does it stops before I leave this morning. Driving in that mess isn't fun."

"You got that right. I always have this fear of my car breaking down in the pouring rain."

"It's happened to me a few times."

"A few?"

"I ran out of gas a lot."

"Sounds like you needed a full gas can in your trunk."

"It hadn't happened in awhile."

"I've never had that issue."

"Good thing."

She told him about how the homeless came out of hiding to stand outside the fundraiser. She surmised they heard it from one of the three shelters in the area. She asked if they posted a bulletin or something. Joey shook his head, saying he didn't know. She went on to say it looked pretty freaky seeing all those homeless people in one place, like they were going to riot or some other nonsense.

"If something like that were to happen they would have cops on them before they knew what to think. I'm sure they've thought about it before."

She said, "It's a strange place out here these days. Some people have told me I need to start carrying a gun to work."

"Really?"

"Our parking lot is usually dark when I get off."

He told her to ask one of the guys to walk her to her car if she ever felt unsafe, or, if he was there he'd be more than glad to escort her to her chariot. She told him he was awfully sweet for the offering. Joey told her that

Playground
was the right thing to do.
"I'd hate it if anything happened to you," he told her.
"The same goes for you, too. No one could do the show you do."
"Oh, is that all I am to you?" he smiled. "You're too kind to say that."
"When you know the truth it's easy to say."
"Well, that's nice of you to say."
"It's one of my better qualities."
Joey pointed to the hallway that led to the back. "How's it been back there? I wasn't listening when I was driving here."
"It's been the same old thing tonight. Not bad. Corey and Alexis are finishing up. They've had a pretty good show tonight. The other guys are here, too."
"Randy?"
"In his office."
"Sounds like a party."
"If you want to call it that, sure," she rolled her eyes. "I've just been out here trying to stay out of the way."
Joey laughed. "It's always like that around here."
"Seems to be a common theme."
They talked a little more before he headed down the hall. The first office on the left belonged to the station manager, Randy Nadeem. The two men acknowledged each other and nodded.

Joey loved his job in radio. He wanted to spend the rest of his life doing radio shows. He liked connecting with people, having an audience, and being somewhat of a local celebrity. He liked everyone he worked around. His ultimate goal was to start a station of his own one day.
As Joey continued down the hall someone called out his name. He turned and Randy was there. He let out a hardy laugh.

Bradley Davenport

"How's it going, Joey?" he asked. "It's going to be one hell of a night. Ready for the show?"

"No turning back now," Joe told him. "It's what keeps us going."

Randy gave a big grin. "You can't win 'em all. The world won't stop turning. We can only do our best. We're all sharks in a big sea. Don't worry, if you get fired they won't black-ball you around. I'm sure you can get on at another station."

Joey laughed. "You're a funny guy, man, anyone ever tell you that?"

"I've been here for fourteen hours, I'm about to lose it. Need something to laugh at."

"Why that long?" Joey asked.

The manager shrugged. "They still haven't found anyone to take Aaron's place. I've been having to do some of that shit. They have me running around this place like a damn madman. I can't go on like this forever. Something has to give."

"Need to talk to someone about that."

"I know, I know. The pay doesn't increase. I need to talk to them about that. They aren't going to screw me over this time, that's for sure."

"Sounds like a real problem."

"It's just one of those things."

"And the wheel keeps on spinning...."

"That's the kind of job we're in, you know?"

"I guess."

When he first started in radio Randy was full of energy. The first radio station he worked at, KPWX, in Landi, Texas, started with an afternoon time slot, which was a time he didn't care for but he had to make due. He'd worked at the station for five years before moving to Arkansas. After being in Arkansas for two months he landed a gig at a little radio station in the town of May-

Playground
berry. He started helping out with an evening show. After some time passed he got a morning gig with Ted Dull. They got along quite well in hosting the show. After some more time passed his boss offered him the job in Bencroft. Randy was going to take over for a guy, Jack Knight. Jack got fired for being a drunk. They gave him more than a few chances. Program directors were getting harder to come by, and they couldn't afford to lose those guys. But one day Jack came in drunk and got into a fight with the guy that did the weather report for the morning show. They couldn't have a loose cannon working for them.

Before Jack left he was told he could come back if he checked himself into AA and stayed sober. Since Randy took the job they haven't had any issues. Jack, on the other hand, only got worse. The day after he lost his job he was arrested for being drunk in a public park. His wife bailed him out of jail but divorced him soon after. A few days later he got into a fight at a bar, where he hit a man to the floor and slammed a beer mug down on the guy. A friend of the man on the floor stabbed Jack in the gut. After getting out of the hospital he was arrested. He moved out of state after serving his time. A couple of years down the road he was spotted by a friend in Maine. Everyone who used to work with Jack wished him well, but there was little expectation. Jack's story was a sad one.

As they continued chatting in the hallway Randy told him to remember to tell people that the fair was going to be in the city in the next few days, and that if anyone wanted to buy tickets they had a couple of boxes of them. Joey shook his head and told Randy it wouldn't be a problem, that he'd let it be known. Randy told him they got a call that day from Fred Mitts, one of the representatives from the FCC. Fred told Randy about a caller who called the station during Joey's show a few nights before. The caller, a girl named Linda, had called to share her opinion on the topic of conversation at the time. Joey and a few other callers had been talking about some of the eerie mysteries of the world. When Linda called they had been discussing whether or not aliens lived underwater. She told Joey that she had seen aliens come from the water, and if he wanted to she could take him to the spot where she saw it happen. When he declined the invite she became a little excited, saying he had to come and see it. He had to see it for himself. And after, he could report it on the radio show, alerting everyone about the truth, the truth they were trying to cover up. Linda had demanded it. She got so emotional about what she was saying. She started cursing at Joey and the other listeners, saying time was fucking running out and that they needed to get fucking moving if they wanted to make it out alive.

"They're fucking coming for us," she told them. "You guys are a bunch of blind sheep being led by people who want you to believe what they want you to. Mark my words, everything will come out one day. All of you have to open your eyes and look around. Don't be like everyone else. Don't bring shame to any of us. If you want to live your life with your head in the sand, please don't come around me."

He tried to calm her down.

She told him it was her right to say what she was.

He told her it was his show, and she needed to show some respect.

She went on to say that if they had important things to do they needed to do it fast, that everything was going to end. She started calling out some of the others who had opinions that differed from hers. Joey told her she

Playground
couldn't talk like that on the radio. She ignored him and continued, telling him he needed to remove his head from his ass and wake-the-fuck-up. They needed to start praying to God. If they didn't they'd all be sorry. They'd all be sent to Hell when everything was done. He finally had to cut her off. He didn't want to be rude or anything, but he had to do what he had to. He couldn't have anyone talking in that manner. Joey knew he might get in trouble because of it. But he told himself he couldn't control what people say, and they can't edit everything. When they asked about it he would just tell them he can't control everything, plus, he felt like that being his show starts at midnight they could let a few things go. Little kids shouldn't be listening to the radio during that time.

Randy told Joey that Fred told him if they get another violation they'll have to raise the fine an extra thousand dollars. Joey was the one who was going to have to pay for it. Randy went on to tell him that while he understood it wasn't solely his responsibility, he and his team should have cut her off sooner than they had.

Randy said, "Between you and I, I think we should be able to say any fucking thing we want on the radio. But until that day comes we have to bow down to the powers that be. We all have to play nice with each other. Just do me a favor and not let it happen again, okay? You do good numbers and I'd hate to have to fire you. And I'm sure you wouldn't like that."

"Understood."

"It could be worse," Randy patted him on the shoulder. "I know you'll do good. I have faith in you."

"Thanks for that."

"You keep with it and you can go far with this," Randy said. "I don't listen every night but when I do I enjoy it. You have a way of grabbing people and making them listen to everything you say. The things you discussed during the show, it's all interesting," he looked Joey in the eyes for a minute. "Tell me, have you given any thought to how long you want to do radio? I mean, you do what you love for too long it starts to feel like a job, you know?"

Joey told the man he hoped to be in the industry for at least ten years or so. He didn't have any plans of going elsewhere any time soon. Joey went on, telling him how much he loved what he did. He liked the fact he didn't have to look at his listeners. It made things easier when he would go on his rants.

Randy said life was a crazy thing and you had to expect the unexpected. He stated again how good of a job Joey was doing.

"Thanks," Joey nodded. "That means a lot. People keep listening, that's the important part, right?"

Randy had a big smile on his face. "You should teach a class on the subject."

Joey laughed. "I'd have to pass on that. I don't like teaching things to people."

"That's a shame. You'd be good at it."

"Something tells me that's not true. When I first started college I was going to teach, that's what I went for. But the more I sat in classes, the more I turned away from the idea of it."

"Oh, don't say things like that. I'm sure you'll change your mind as time passes."

Joey looked at him funny. He couldn't figure out why Randy was so insistent on him teaching.

After some more talk, Randy said he had to go home to his wife. If he was late she'd kill him. His wife made some burgers he couldn't wait to eat.

When you work from midnight until the early hours of

Playground
the morning you start to adopt strange hours. While most people are asleep you're up and moving, getting stuff done, talking about the things that ponder minds, being heroes of the day. And by the time you get out of work, the only thing you can think about is resting. When most people are eating breakfast you're eating dinner. You darken your windows so the sun doesn't shine through your bedroom. You feel like a vampire after awhile, a vampire that doesn't suck blood. Even on your days off one finds it hard to adjust to normal times.

Randy turned and continued down the hall to the door, telling Layla to have a good one when he passed her.

Layla peeked around the corner of the hall at Joey and smiled. She walked over to him. He liked the way she moved.

She said, "He's an asshole."

"I get that," Joey told her.

"Think he's mad because he's on his way out."

"Is he?"

"That's what I heard the other day."

"From whom?"

"Alexis. We were at lunch when she said something about it. She said he was getting canned."

"Why?"

She shrugged. "She didn't know why, just said it was going to happen. Figure it wouldn't hurt anything. It might get better around here. Change can be good."

"Interesting," Joey said. "He hadn't let anything slip. He was just telling me about the cutbacks they were doing, that's why he was working."

"Oh, really?" her eyes got big. "Maybe he doesn't want any of us knowing?"

"I just hope they don't get to me, I can't afford that," Joey told her.

"Know what you mean. If they do I'll have to go on an-

other job hunt. That's something I don't like doing."
"Does anyone? I dread the day I'll have to do it. They'd be fools to get rid of you, Layla. You're one of the best around," he took her hand in his. "You're a blessing to the world, girl."
She giggled. "That's sweet of you to say."
"I can't tell a lie."
"Thanks. It's hard being me sometimes."
"I can relate."
"Yeah, you're a pretty good guy."
"Well, thank you."
Another smile.
He loved it when those smiles ran across her face. It was like they were dancing for everyone to see. He told her he liked the way she smiled and laughed. She thanked him. For a moment he thought about leaning over and kissing her cute lips. But he didn't. He didn't want to take the chance of destroying the friendship they had. He figured if they ever came to that bridge they'd deal with it. He knew what he wanted, and he wanted more than just to remain friends. He told himself they'd be good together. He could see a clear future. He was going to have to plan how he was going to confront her about his feelings. He didn't want to mess things up and lose her forever.
 She said she was going down to the lobby to wait for her ride. She had to take her Honda to the shop. She didn't know much about cars, so she couldn't say what the problem was. All she knew was that it wouldn't start one day when she had to get to work. She had to get a ride from a friend.
 "I should know more than I do about cars," she told him. "It just makes me feel stupid."
 "Don't feel bad, there's a lot to remember."
 "That makes it better."

Playground

"See."

"I still need to study a book on it or something."

"Maybe just a little."

He watched as she hopped on the elevator. They told one another to have a good morning, and she blew him a kiss. He blew her one back.

4

Joey continued down the hall. When he got to the big window that looked into the studio he knocked on it. Alexis looked up and gave him a nod and a thumbs-up. Alexis had black hair and wore a black AC/DC shirt with red lettering. She had tattoos on both arms that trailed up and continued under the sleeves of the shirt. She wore a pair of dark thick frames. She looked tired. Corey was looking down and didn't see Joey. They were just finishing up their show.

When they signed off Joe entered.

Corey took his headphones off and said he thought that the show went well.

"Better than yesterday," Corey announced.

"Oh, stop that!" Alexis told him. "You have to take into account that yesterday wasn't today. Vibes change all the time, it's nobody's fault, just the way of the world."

"I never thought about that," Corey replied. "You make a good point. I need to think more like you do."

"You do."

"I try."

Alexis patted him on the shoulder, telling him he'd get there eventually.

Corey, even though he wished he was, wasn't her boyfriend. They talked about it a few times and decided it would be best if they just remained co-workers; mainly, Alexis decided that for the both of them. She wanted to make it seem like it was something they both decided. She was nice and didn't want to hurt his feelings. But she knew he probably thought she was a bitch and everything else. He wanted more than she was willing to give.

Playground

Corey was a big guy with a soft voice. He had long stringy hair with a thick brown beard. He had been in a few local bands around the city. One of those bands, Circle Gang, recorded an album. One of their songs was a minor national success for about two weeks. The band broke up shortly after. All the members went their separate ways; two of the guys went on to other bands, one moved to Florida, and Corey got into the radio business. He tried for awhile to get another band going but things never worked out. People told him he just needed to go solo for awhile. He wasn't too sure.

A lot of people said he was one of the nicest guys you'd ever meet. He was a nice guy but you wouldn't want to make him mad. His size intimidated some people. He'd worked in the industry for almost three years. His partner, she had two years. In the beginning, they didn't get along, however, as time passed they grew to like one another. And after some more time, Corey started to really like Alexis. He made his feelings known at Night Owl one night. She didn't exactly share the same feelings. He told himself that if he just gave her time she'd come around. Sometimes that is all it takes.

Alexis looked at Joey, ran over, and hugged him. She loved giving hugs. If it was solely up to her she'd love to get him in bed. What girl wouldn't? He had a lot to offer the opposite sex. She knew he'd like that but she was going to have to wait until the moment was right. One night when they're out at the bar she'd get too drunk and have him give her a ride home, then, she'd get to ride him.

"Have a good show?" Joey asked.
"You didn't catch it?" She asked.
"Not the whole thing. Caught a little in the car."
"Went without a hitch."
"That's good," he told her. "Better than a bad show,

makes the time go by."

"Who you work with, that plays a big part of it."

"It does."

"Makes you thankful for co-workers," she told him.

"That's true."

She glanced over at Corey. "I owe it all to him. You wouldn't believe it, man, he's boss. He gets it done, that's for sure. I wouldn't have had lunch if it wasn't for him. I forgot my money when I left my place earlier. He offered to pay."

"Oh, how nice," Joey told her. "Yeah, he's one of a kind. They're gonna write books about him one day. If only we could all be like him, you know? He could teach people a thing or two."

"I know. He's such a gentleman. I know lots of people would buy that book."

"You can always count on him," Joey gave her his smile.

"You can," she shook her head. "It's nice to know people like him are around."

Corey came over to see what they were talking about.

"You guys talking about me?" he slapped Joey on the shoulder. "You always talk about the greats."

Joey said, "We could learn a few things from you."

"Like how to fuck your life up?" Corey said. "I wrote the book on that one. I have more material for sequels."

"Among other things," Joey laughed. "Come on, man, I wouldn't expect less."

"Yeah, yeah, yeah, I know. I just look at this place, think where I would be if it wasn't here."

"That's the best way to look at it."

Corey shrugged. "Don't want to work at a damn burger place."

"Me neither."

"Although," Corey went on, "if you were to work there

you'd probably get free food. I'll take that."
"Free food is something I'll never argue about."
"You can say that again," Corey said. "Speaking of food, did you hear we're going to be grilling burgers at the fair?"
"Really?"
"Randy asked if I wanted to do the cooking, but I didn't answer. Not sure if I want to spend time over a grill like that."
Joey laughed. "You don't think Randy is going to do it, do you? He doesn't want to do anything like that, it'd be too much like work. He could get Alexis to do it."
"Very funny," Alexis said. "I won't be anywhere near that fair. I'll tell him I have plans."
They laughed.
Corey walked over across the room and grabbed his jacket from a hook on the wall. He asked Alexis if she wanted hers.
"Saw it was supposed to rain for the next few hours," he handed Alexis her jacket.
Joey said, "It started as I was driving up here. Just as long as it stops when we get ready to leave."
"You might get lucky," Corey put on his jacket.
"Hope so."
Corey said, "With the weather like this, I'll be able to sleep well. It's nice and peaceful."
Alexis agreed with her co-host. She was going to go home. make a nice cup of coffee and finish the book she'd been reading. She loved reading. She could devour a big book in about four days. She loved fiction, of all kinds, it didn't matter. She liked stories, telling and reading them. She liked the idea of being taken away to a place, a place of imagination, an escape from reality. She used to tell the guys she worked with about how she always wanted to write a book. The thing was, she never

took the time needed to write one. People always told her she had to make time.

Corey patted his pants pockets, then clapped his hands. "Just another day at it, you know how that goes? I need a smoke. Sucks we can't smoke in here."

"I know what you mean,' Joey said. "We should talk to someone about that. Guys, have a lot of crazy callers today?" Joey asked.

"Not today, no. I don't know, guess those guys had better things to do. You have to wonder what goes on in their heads. They think they're so funny."

"One never knows," Joey said. "The interesting times are when they come up here. They always get so mad when we tell them about calling the cops."

"They always love that."

"They have to learn somehow."

"If they were smart they'd be out working. I mean, if they contributed constructively... Most times that shit's just annoying."

"Got to make that fucking paper, buddy. It keeps the lights on," Joey replied. "Something everyone needs."

"Got that right," Corey said. "Just wish I didn't need to do so much of it."

"Work?"

"Need my own business, that's what I need."

"What would you do?" Joey asked.

"I hadn't figured that out yet. Get into the vending machine business, something like that. The music thing seems to be out."

"Vending machines?" Joey gave him a funny look. "That's an idea."

"Hell, yeah. You know how much money you can make?"

"All in coins and small bills?"

Playground
"Your bank account doesn't care."
"Good point," Joey told him. "Well, you can have all of that. Sounds like a lot. Nah, you can have all of that while I get my station."
"Could I come work for you?"
"I'd think about it."
"You better. I have some mad skills right here, son. I know you want to be like me. But there can only be one pimp at this motherfucker!"
Joey gave a dismissive wave. "Yeah, yeah, yeah, I hear you talking that mess."
"We'll see," Corey told him. "You see our latest numbers?"
"Guess I missed that."
"Well, they're pretty damn good, buddy."
"I'll have to take your word for it."
"They're up from last week."
"Really? That's good. You don't want to get canned."
Alexis said, "If you're doing your station you have to give me a job."
Corey laughed.
She continued. "I'm the reason we received the good numbers. You boys, you guys wouldn't know what to do if we weren't here. They all say I have a soothing voice. I look at our website every few days and people are always commenting, and saying nice things. Check it out if you don't believe me."
Joey told them he hadn't visited the website since he started. He said he needed to check some of that stuff out. Alexis asked him what the hell was wrong, that he should've been looking at the site the whole time. How was he going to know what was going on in the city or the station? He'd be lost if he didn't know where to look.
Alexis told Corey he owed her dinner to celebrate their numbers. She told him they'd have to go some night

when they were both off. Corey wondered to himself if he should take her out or not. After all, it wasn't like they were an item or anything. He didn't want to devote much time to her, knowing she told him they'd never be a couple. He didn't want to put himself in that position. He was a nice guy, but at a certain point, you have to put down your foot. He said he'd buy her dinner, saying she could get whatever she wanted. She told him she wanted to go somewhere with nice burgers and fries, no fast food junk. She didn't want to put any of that garbage in her body.

"Your wish is my command," Corey told her. "When you're in a hurry that stuff is okay. But you don't want to eat that shit all the time. You need fuel that stays with you."

"I agree," she shook her head. "That stuff is just garbage."

"Want to check out a movie, too?"

"Sure, depending on what's playing."

They talked more before leaving. On their way out they told their friend to have a good show.

5

Joey needed coffee before he put in his time. It was tiring sometimes hosting the radio show. He had to keep his energy up doing the show. Even though he loved the job and couldn't imagine doing anything else, at times some of the callers were boring or got on his nerves. He was always polite about it and never dropped any of the calls, even though he'd love to do so from time to time. As far as callers he disagreed with, he just listened to what they had to say and said nothing. He never wanted things to get too heated in the air. There were ones who would call to heckle and try to spread their hatred like butter on bread. He'd just tell himself it was something he had to put up with. There are a lot of people out there, odds are you aren't going to agree with them all. You just have to laugh and go on about your business.

When he first started he was doing the evening show. A few months later Corey and Alexis, who were doing the overnight at the time, wanted to switch things up. They knew none of the afternoon guys would change. Joey agreed to the change. At first, he was a little worried about his numbers. But as weeks passed it became clear everyone liked what he was doing. The show dealt with all things odd and mysterious, everything dealing with the macabre. He would start with some stories, then, he'd open the show up to callers. They would make comments on what Joey was ranting about, or, they would tell their tales.

The producer of the show, Bruce Yunni, was a long-haired, slender guy with an eye patch on his right eye. He lost his eye in a car crash in 1998. He had been drinking and slammed his red Honda into the side of Waves mini-mart. He spent a week in the hospital. Despite efforts by his doctors, due to the severity of the injuries, they weren't able to save the eye. When Bruce got out it took him a long time adjusting to life with the use of only one eye. After years of drug and alcohol abuse, he finally came to terms with being disabled.

He worked all sorts of jobs over the years. One day a friend of his, Reggie Gibbs, offered him a job at the station. The job wasn't much, cleaning floors and toilets. As time passed he got a few promotions. Eventually, he got to be a producer. He had to get some schooling before he got the title. But he did it. He proved everyone wrong, everyone who told him his life fell to pieces when his car slammed against the brick mini-mart, and everyone who told him the world would leave him behind because he only had one eye. He was a nice guy and treated everyone the way he wanted to be treated. Bruce was liked by pretty much everyone he met.

"How's it going, Bruce?" Joey said.

He shrugged. "Okay, I guess. You?"

"Can't complain. Just gearing up for this thing. It's going to be a good time."

"Hope so, man. I want it to. It always makes the time go by," Bruce told his friend. "I'm ready to go over here."

"Sounds good. I need a little something before we start."

"Like some blow?"

"No, not that."

"Oh, man, that'd be a good time."

Joey laughed. "Yes, indeed."

"I could ask around, get some for later if you want?"

"No, I'm fine."

"Okay, then."

Joey asked Bruce if he wanted any coffee. The producer said he did. As they drank their coffee they discussed some details of the show. They always wanted to do their best.

Playground

Joey put on his headphones and said, "It's that time again, people! It's my favorite time! I get to hang out with all of you exceptional humans for a few hours. Time to wander with me down the eerie, shadowy road. You'll hear strange things, matters of the macabre, things that may make you examine what you thought you knew. There's something for everyone here. You need to keep your eyes and ears open. One never knows what is creeping around the corner. You pass a guy walking the street who tells you to be careful around parts unknown. Look out for sharp turns and cracks along the way. Enjoy the ride! Things may get a little creepy, a little haunting, a little insane. You may be surprised by what you find. Things aren't always as they seem. Everything will be understood in due time. Life is a maze, an amazing life. Joey Ryder here again, my friends, to guide you through the prism, gliding through transparent levels of imagination. Keep calm, and relax. I'm just a rider, a passenger in this life that's inching away with every breath. Thank you so much for joining. Might as well brew some coffee and have some fun. This is going to be an assault on the mind," Joey sighed. "We spend a lot of time trying to figure things out just to realize we know nothing. But we do what we need to. We have to survive out in these streets. When I checked, the weather was supposed to stay like it was for a good chunk of time. But how long will that be? I'm afraid I don't have the answers you seek. We'll just have to power through it together. The streets are piling up out there, piling up with dreams and broken souls."

He talked into the microphone awhile longer before he looked at the producer. Bruce squinted at him. Joey shrugged his shoulders and gave a grin. He told the listeners that they had to take a quick pause to pay some bills. In a perfect world, he wouldn't have any ads. He didn't like being told he had to do things at a certain time and have parameters for things. But his bosses said he had to do it.

Three advertisements: The first one was an ad for cheap health care called Inveratint. This guy, Dr. Bill Hopterson, was talking about when life has you down and you get hurt or have an illness, you don't have much money, you should give him a call. He rattled off the number of the place and said their staff was very understanding when it came to those matters. He said that by making the call you will already be taking steps in the right direction. Their people are eagerly waiting to help you. Dr. Bill went on to say how the business is legit, and they've been in the business of serving people for two years.

The next advertisement that played was for Simportan North: A guy by the name of Judd Simportan opened a used car lot, and he was telling the listeners that he was slashing prices on his cars, slashing them so low people were calling him a fool. He didn't care. It was important to him everyone had a car or truck they could depend on. Being without transportation, as he put it, isn't fair to anyone. With everything out there it was sad to see someone go without. He ended the ad by saying that if you had financial problems things could always be worked out.

The third advertisement was for a funeral home called Pine Glover. The guy, Malcolm Palina, said if you want to have a lovely farewell for your loved one you should give him a call. When someone in your life passes on it's hard on everyone. Malcolm and his crew are just a phone call away. Life can end in a blink of an eye, and they know how to handle the situation. The guy said to give him a call whenever the time came. He gave out the information on the business and told everyone to have a

Playground
great day.
  When they came back from break Joey started to thank the listeners for being a fan of his and what he does. The people, they never let him down. They knew how to support what they liked.
  "And if you're a new listener, thanks for joining. For anyone who doesn't like me, it's okay. Hey, man, I get it. Not everyone's on that same groove, the same reality, the same wavelength, the same road. I understand it, brother, it happens. How can I get mad at you? You guys are one of the big reasons I still do this. You guys crack me up. The differences bring us together. Who wants to be the same as everyone else, right? When you look out the window, you look at reflections, manipulating others about what they see. The world is a crazy place, what can I say? If any of you out there want to call, or discuss your experience with something crazy feel free. I'll be here for awhile. We'll get through this. The gentle night calmly waits in the shadows anticipating greatness," Joey said.
  Early on he found that in the radio business, you had to constantly repeat yourself, letting people know current events, telling them the weather, reminding them of the festivals and fairs in the area, and being their entertainment guide. There were always worse ways he could spend his time. Hell, he was still lucky enough to have a job. The way people come and go you can never be too sure what's waiting around the corner.
  He said, "Before I came down here I was at home watching the idiot box, flipping channels and I came to a show where they were talking about parallel dimensions. It looked interesting, so I wanted to see what it was all about. That stuff always intrigued me. This guy, Donald Cane, was telling his theory to his friend, John. He was saying things like the Bermuda Triangle is one of the

Bradley Davenport
gate-keepers to this other dimension. He was saying when all the ships sank or planes crashed there, they went into another dimension, a parallel universe. He said there is an invisible gash in the fabric of the Earth in that area. He went on to say there are a lot of these gashes, cuts in space and time. I guess he had gone on a few other shows and talked about a lot of that stuff. According to him many of the mysteries of the world can be attributed to these dimensions. He rattled off a list of examples. I'm not going to list them all, but things like the whole D.B. Cooper thing, even the JFK shooting," Joey looked at Bruce, who gave him the signal that they had to take another break.

While they were waiting to come back from break Joey asked Bruce how his day was. Bruce told him it was a pretty good one, and that he had wild sex with his wife before he got there. Joey asked how his wife, Mary, was doing. Bruce said things couldn't be better. They were very happy together. They'd been married for ten years with no kids.

"I don't know what I'd do without her, man. She was the best thing that ever happened to me. That girl there, she saved my life. She's a keeper."

"Glad to hear it," Joey said. "Those women, we owe them a lot."

"I only wish she looked as good as she fucked."

"That's funny. Don't let her hear you say that. She might cut you off for good. Not only would you have to start cooking for yourself, but you/d have to start dating again or buy hookers."

"No, no, I don't have a death wish."

"Can't say as I blame you."

"Wouldn't want anyone else."

"That's good."

Bruce said, "Yeah, I need to keep her around. And also,

Playground
what woman would want me? Have nothing to offer anyone new."
"Shouldn't sell yourself short like that."
Bruce told him they were coming back from break.

Joey said to the audience. "Welcome back, guys! I hope you didn't turn the station on me. Of course not, not any of you. You guys would never do something like that to me," he let out a smile. "Well, I'd forgive you. Sometimes I want to change the station on myself," he took a drink of coffee. "Back to what I was talking about before the break: This guy, Donald Crane, he was all about this stuff with parallel dimensions. When asked if he had any proof of any of this, he said he was walking down the street one day and some guy from out of nowhere started running toward him. He was startled and started running away. Well, as he was running, he said the guy ran in front of him and disappeared. The people who were around, he asked them if they had seen the guy and no one had. He started to think he was going crazy. Said the guy was as real as could be. Strange. Donald swore the man running after him was running to another dimension. Something like that would freak me out. I'm not sure if I believe his story or not. There's been a few of those stories going around, they always end up being crazy. But I wasn't there, so I don't know if it was true. Anyway, they talked about this for awhile. His friend, the guy he was telling this to, asked if he thought that's where spirits are. Donald said he did. Said he thought anything paranormal was other dimensions brushing against ours. They can't communicate the same when they are in that state. Interesting stuff. They spent the rest of the show telling ghost stories."
Bruce sat back in his chair and looked at the ceiling. He sighed as he looked at the lights. It was going to be an-

other long one. He liked Joey's personality. Even though they rarely did things outside of work Bruce thought the man was a good friend. Joey's feelings about his producer didn't run that deep. He was okay, sure, but as far as Joey was concerned Bruce was just a co-worker. He liked their conversations at work but that was where it ended. He wasn't interested in being friends with Bruce. He didn't mean to sound like an asshole or anything, but it was just the way things were. He had his own life.

The host continued. "So, if you guys have any interesting stories to go with this topic feel free to call in. I'd love to hear your story. We can talk about anything you want. I'm all ears. I can talk about anything. I learn a lot from you guys. The things we get into at these hours. Something about it, the time just opens that special door in your mind. Been in this industry for awhile and this is my favorite time."

He proceeded to tell the listeners that you couldn't use foul language when calling into the station. He understood how one could lose control in the heat of conversation, but they'd had to reframe from using those bad words. When they got off the air he'd be the first one to turn back on his sailor vocabulary, but until that time came he'd have to wait. He told them if they do cuss they would have to pay a fine. He hoped by telling them that they'd get the message.

A few people called to tell Joey how much they enjoyed the show, and that they hoped he'd never give up the radio show.

"I don't plan on going anywhere," he told them. "I love what I do and you guys love what I do. The world would have to end to make me leave."

They broke again. Joey asked Bruce how much time he had. Since he couldn't smoke in the studio he ran to the bottom floor and went outside. On his way back he got

Playground
coffee for himself and Bruce.

6

A few minutes later a man named Harry Munn called. He told Joey he believed in the alternate dimension theory. He looked at it as a world on top of another world. He said he thought those rips were everywhere, that they're probably made all the time.

"I wouldn't be surprised if one of those rips is where your building is," Harry told the host.

"What makes you say that?" Joey asked.

"I'm a firm believer in that stuff. Read books about it. I don't know much, but I'd like to think I'm really on to something with this stuff. I'd get lost for hours reading and thinking about everything."

"That's interesting."

"I'm not sure if any of your listeners believe the same way I do. I'd like to think they do."

"I'm sure there are."

"It's not for everyone. Some people go throughout life never questioning things."

"That's one way to look at it, sure."

The guy went on to tell Joey that his brother was the one responsible for getting him interested in those things five or six years ago.

The guy pressed on. "I think when someone dies they go to the other side. When people claim to see ghosts, it's just that person trying to communicate with them."

"I have to say, Harry, that's an interesting thought. Have you ever seen a ghost or anything?"

"I never have. I'm still holding out hope. I figure my time is just around the corner."

Joey said, "I've never seen any. I'm not saying they aren't out there, I've just never seen them. I have to see it to believe. You know, people can say what they want but it doesn't make it true."

"You're someone who wants facts, proof of something?" Harry asked.

"It goes a long way toward someone's argument, sure."

"Nothing wrong with being a skeptic. If you ask me the world needs more people like you. You ask questions, questions some people don't take time to ask. They might not get the answer they seek, that's beside the point. At least you ask. I commend you, sir. It's important to ask about things we don't know about. As humans, it's natural to get all the information we can. Where would we be without knowledge? I want to live among those who want to know truths. Tales are for those fiction books."

"Let me understand you correctly, even though you have never seen a ghost you still believe in them?"

"That is correct," the caller said. "You hit the nail on the head there, Bubba. And I think if I do see a ghost or spirit, that would give me nothing but Joy. I want to know there's something else out there, something beyond what I can fathom."

"You think you've seen one and didn't know it?"

"Anything's possible," Harry said. "They say sometimes they look like everyone else. Some folks, when they hear you say that think of a transparent spirit. From what I understand that's not always the case. I think if I were to see one I'd ask if they could see into my future. Why not?"

Joey said, "I have a feeling if you knew what the future held you'd subconsciously try to curve things in that direction. I'd rather be surprised."

"I can see that. I mean, yeah, I'd like both. I know, it's a strange thing to think about. When I would start talking to my friends about this stuff most would look at me like I was crazy, like I should be locked away in some crazy

house. I don't know, you think they should?"
"No, not at all. It's not like you're hurting anyone. You just have questions."
"I guess you're right."
Harry told Joey he had thought to write his book about the subject. Joey told him that sounded like a great idea. The two went on for a bit longer before the man got off the line.

The next caller was a man named Luke.
"How are you, sir?" Joey said.
Luke said, "Greetings. I'd like to first express my gratitude for what you're doing. This show, your show, it's a great thing you're doing. A lot of people I know, like what you do. We've been listening for quite awhile. Your insights about the human condition are fascinating. People, they respect you. They listen to what you have to say. You have worth, my friend. We applaud you, a man who gives so much and asks so little. You're a man of the people. A friend of mine told me about your show awhile back. I listened to a bunch, trying to decide when I should introduce myself. It's good to get through to you."
"Thanks," Joey told him. "I just do what I do. Just trying my best to make it in this maze of chaos, trudging through this blizzard of insanity."
"I hear that, brother. I'm holding it down out here. Someone has to do it. It can't be all fun and games, know what I mean? I take comfort in the fact I do the best I can every day."
"That's a good way to be."
"It can turn into an overwhelming task at times. When you oversee people, no matter their age or gender, you become powerful. You can take whatever is thrown your way. I can take it, give me what you have. I'm afraid of

Playground
nothing."
"Interesting way to look at things. What do you have for me this morning? What's on your mind?"
"Oh, not a whole lot. About the same as anyone else in this crazy place," the man said. "I'm just trying to get this thing of mine going. I' 'm a man of the people, just trying to get my message out there any way I can."
"What is that? A business of some kind?" Joey asked.
"I want to discuss my family. Are you familiar with the Reeves family?"
"I've heard a few things, sure," Joey said. "Most people in this area have heard, I'm pretty sure."
"I see," the caller continued. "We've been around for years. We hide in plain sight. Our numbers are good. They may increase, or decrease as the days pass. It depends on how this conversation goes. Back in the late 70s and 80s we were flourishing. We're getting back to how things once were."
Joey thought about it. "What are you talking about?"
"Some call us a cult, but we're just a family. We've been slowly coming back. It has been difficult. When things ended in the early 90s we weren't looked on favorably. People were quick to deionize my father. They would say he was a cult leader. What's a cult? People are quick to put labels on things they don't understand. They don't take time to try to understand, to gain knowledge one needs to make themselves not look foolish. We can't help how others act in everyday life. It's not up to us to decide how people view us. We're a family. Yes, we may roam but we always come back. It's been a long road to get to this point. You have to leave the past where it is. We're not violent. There are people out there who say I'm nothing but bad news. These people, they don't even know me. They hear what my last name is and think I'm like my father. I'm nothing like him."

"Who's your father?" Joey asked.

"Harlan Reeves."

Silence grew on the other end.

Joey said, "Luke? Luke, you still there?"

"Yes, I'm still here. My apologies. What we do, Joey, we're here to raise awareness. A lot of people, almost everyone not in our family, don't know what's around the corner. All those poor souls with blind eyes, marching like sheep. They're so misguided. It's a shame, truly unfortunate. It's time. Time is running out! It's all about to end. It's vitally important we get the word out."

"What would that be?"

"We have a mission: inform all about the impending doom and the love of God. We are at war, Mr. Ryder."

"At war?" Joey said. "What sort of war are we talking about here? Do we need to get our guns, and start blasting on the streets?"

A laugh. "No, no, nothing like that. See, that's another misconception people have about me, they think because my dad was quick to pick up a gun I'm the same way."

"I didn't mean anything by it," Joey told the man.

"The Devil and his followers, they creep around everywhere. They need to be stopped. I can see where it's hard to see those evil people out there. They do whatever it takes to try to not be seen. It's a messed up place out here. You have to be careful what you do. They watch everything."

Joey said, "I've heard of people joining you guys. But for anyone out there who doesn't know, tell them all about it."

"It's the Church of Modo," Luke said. "You have a choice, everyone does, about what direction to go in this world. I'm here to save souls. For those who want to live a pure life come to the Church of Modo, and see what we're all about. We all have sins, all of us. But it's about

Playground

repenting. God forgives you if you have done wrong. We've all done wrong. Everyone has their little secrets. I'm not perfect, no one is. People who claim to be perfect are fools. They think everyone else is stupid."

Joey said, "Does Harlan still run things?"

"He just wants to put the past behind him. He's turned it all around. I'm proud of him."

"That's good when someone can change like that."

"He told me he was never going to go back. I mean, sure, he's had a history of being in jail but this time is going to be different. He promised this time he was going to stay out. Things went sideways for him a few times, but he's straight as an arrow now. He just wants a quiet life. He doesn't want any trouble."

"That's good," Joey said. "I think a lot of people out there won't be so welcoming to him. He affected so many people and families. A lot of damage was done on his watch."

"Listen, I know a lot of people still see him as an evil man but he's changed. His time locked away, he's had time to think about his life and how everything went sideways."

"He's out? I thought he got life?" Joey asked.

"But as luck would have it they let him out."

"Why?"

"I can't get into that right now. All I can say is that he's out and won't be harming anyone. But he's on a very short leash."

"I see."

"For anyone listening who doesn't know anything about Harlan Reeves, you need to look him up and see what he did or ask someone who was around here then. I'm sure people can tell you what happened. I don't want to get into any of that now. Time and place for everything, you know?"

Joey thought for a minute. "And what did you think of everything that went on?"

"I was young at the time and didn't know what was going on. All I knew was they came and took everyone away, including my dad. As the years went on my mom told me things about what happened. Some stuff I heard from kids at school. I guess their parents didn't want them hanging around me. Guess they thought I was going to beat them up, something crazy like that, you know? I'm not a monster. Now that I know what happened there, I still don't know what to think. If everything was true, I don't condone it. Sure, some of it but not all. Everyone there, from what I can recall

Joey said, "That's an interesting way to put it. I'll have to interview with you sometime. We could get you and your dad in here for a whole show. I'm sure there's a lot of areas to cover."

Luke went on to tell the host that his father would love to get on the radio and speak about all of this. He told Joey and everyone listening that the Church of Modo was back, and it was going to be more structured. He explained that when his father first started the church, the vision wasn't that clear.

Joey asked about the whole thing being a con. A few papers and reporters stated that when the church first started it was nothing but a way for people to part with their money, a con. But as time marched on the message changed. He wasn't sure if it was a con or not. He knew about his father's life before the church, but he didn't know what prompted it. Luke asked that question once, and he gave a speech on how they were spreading God's word. He and his friends weren't frauds. But Luke didn't know what the truth was. He'd heard so many stories over time.

Luke made it clear that his father wasn't what he once

Playground

was, and that if he got in trouble again he was gone for good. If anyone was interested in what Luke had to say and wanted to join the cause, he told them to be at a certain address at a time he gave.

"You were asking about my father's intention like it was a fraud or something?" Luke said. "I'm here to tell you that I'm legit. We are here as servants. We just want to bring the word of God to everyone. Across this country we have churches that like to preach to you about everything, what they think is wrong, what they think is right, and the whole time they're committing the biggest sins. There's so much hypocrisy," Luke cleared his throat. "There will be none of that with us. We realize nobody's perfect."

"I'd agree," Joey said.

"And anyone who wants info on us, we've been putting flyers all over the city. I'm sure you've seen them around."

"Yeah, I've seen them at a few places. Are you going to have a compound like Harlan had?"

"It's in the works. Construction is going to take awhile. I mean, it's going to be a huge place. I think when it's built I'm still going to keep the place I'm at now."

"That's good."

The two talked for another twenty minutes. Luke went on to explain that they welcomed anyone, no matter someone's background.

When Joey asked the caller about his mother he said she was somewhere in Europe, but she'd be back in a few weeks. Luke went on to say she'd been over there for about ten years. When Luke told her about his father getting out of prison she said that she had moved on, that she wanted better things. Why didn't Luke go to Europe? Luke was an exceptional student in high school, so much so that he got a free ride when it came to college,

Bradley Davenport

everything paid for. He got a business degree and planned to open a little retail place with a friend—that never happened. The friend met some girl and moved to Ohio. He thought about just getting another business partner but no one was that interested.

 Before Luke got off the line he told everyone that if they got a flyer they should call the number on it.

7

Luke Reeves hung the phone up turned the radio back on and walked to his kitchen window. He was going to call the radio show back but he knew Joey Ryder's show was about to be over, and he didn't want to talk to the host of any of those other shows. He figured they would just hang up on him anyway. He thought he would get through to Joey. He would just have to wait and see how things went. He told himself just to forget about it and shut the radio off. For a moment he thought about smashing the machine against the wall.

Rain was still splashing to the ground outside. He glanced down at his watch and started to make coffee. He was putting coffee into the filter when footsteps came behind him. He turned to see his beautiful girlfriend, Mindy. Her wet brown hair dangled around her white bathrobe. She wore a smile as she brushed strains of hair from her eyes. He reached out and touched the tattoo on her neck.

"I thought the rain was supposed to quit by now," she said.

"Afraid not," he said. "Still coming down pretty good. Not sure when it's going to end."

She looked past him to the window. "That brings a certain comfort to the morning," she looked at the coffee machine. "And look, you made coffee! I knew there was a reason you were still around. You know what I like."

Luke chuckled as he turned to get some cups from the cabinet.

"I love the smell of coffee in the morning," she walked across the kitchen to the fridge. She asked if he wanted eggs. He told her he did. When the coffee was ready he poured some into both cups.

"Got a long day?" she asked.

"Yeah, a few things I need to take care of. I have a meeting later."

"A meeting?"

"Yeah, some things the other guys and I are going to work on."

"I see," she looked over at him. "How long should that take."

"Not sure."

"I hope it doesn't take long."

"Me, too," he told her. "It's not up to me, though."

"Who decides that?"

"The person we have the meeting with."

"That makes sense."

He walked over and kissed her on the lips. "Sleep okay?"

"I guess."

When the eggs were done they sat at the kitchen table and started eating.

They were talking when a commotion came from outside the front door. Luke started toward the door when Tick and Bobby walked in; they were both wet and looked tired.

"How'd it go?" Luke asked.

Tick shrugged. "About what we suspected."

"We took care of it," Bobby added.

Luke said, "Where'd you guys put him."

"Same place as those guys from the other night."

"Yeah, about that place, I don't think we need to use that anymore. Have enough buried out there. The rain makes problems for you?"

Bobby shook his head. "Not really. We thought at first it might but it worked out. It'll take more than a little water to keep us from doing what needs to be done."

"Weather waits for no man," Luke chuckled. "No fear, that's the game we have to play, boys. We've come a long way to lose it all."

Tick said, "You can say that again, brother. I think everyone in the crew would agree that prison can't happen. My goal is to stay out."

Mindy's voice came from the kitchen, telling Luke to offer them eggs and bacon.

Tick called out to Mindy. "No, thanks, hon. Thanks for the offer but we need to get going," he looked back at Luke. "We just wanted to come by, and let you know it was done. He won't be a problem for you from now on."

Luke gave a little smile, "Sounds good. I'd hate to see him hanging around, see what shit he'd come up with."

"He was a problem," Tick agreed.

Bobby said. "When were you wanting to do that one thing?"

"I'll have to get back to you on that," Luke told him. "Hadn't decided if I wanted to do it or not. I'll let you know."

"You got it. Anytime, just make the call and I'll be there."

"Thanks for that," Luke said. "Before I forget, you guys deliver all of those flyers around?"

Tick said they had a few more to go. He told his boss not to worry, that they'd all be gone before the sun came up. If things went as planned Luke would have tons of people calling, asking about the church and what they were all about.

"Good work, guys," Luke told them. "I owe you. Couldn't have done all of this on my own."

Bobby said, "We look at it as an honor. Well, I do at least. Can't speak for anyone else. But you have some good guys on your side."

"And will for many years," Tick added.

Bobby and Tick said they'd let the two get back to their morning. They didn't like bothering their boss no matter the time. It was hard at times to gauge whether or not Luke was going to be in a good mood or not. They all, at one time, had seen him at his worst. They knew when they shouldn't press their luck. The two left and Luke went back to his breakfast.

"What did they want?" Mindy asked. "They giving you a wake-up call?"

"Something like that," Luke said. "They were just letting me know some things were done I asked them to do."

"Like what?"

"Things you don't want to know about."

She raised her brow at him. "Now, how could you possibly know something like that? Are you in my head? In my thoughts? I tell you, it's full of insanity."

Luke laughed. "You aren't that bad. You don't want to have that picture in your mind. You want to have a good day."

"Oh, honey, you don't need to worry about me. I can handle it."

"Nah, there were a few complications we needed to get rid of."

"Was it the only way?"

"Afraid so."

She took a drink of coffee. "Well, I guess you had to do what needed to be done."

"It was them or us," Luke said. "I don't like to do that stuff. I'm not a monster."

"Of course, babe, it's just one of those things."

He lit a smoke. "Are you sure you're okay?"

"Sure."

And she wasn't bad at all, nothing Luke couldn't handle. Throughout his life, he dealt with more than a fair share of crazy women. He was attracted to crazy. He

Playground
liked the excitement it brought; it kept him alert and on his toes. He had to keep up with her, match her at every jagged edge. People often said they were a perfect match.

He and Mindy met one July night back in 2001 at a beach party. He was amazed by her. But at the time she was dating a guy who was much tougher than Luke. He knew if he tried to fight the guy he'd lose. A few weeks later she broke things off with the guy when he went to prison. Luke and Mindy started dating a few days later. They had nothing but lust and love for one another. They couldn't get enough of each other. Their souls became one. They got matching tattoos to symbolize their love. About a month after they got an apartment he asked for her hand in marriage. She told him she wasn't ready. They revisited the conversation a year later and she said she wanted to get married. The news made Luke very happy. He told all of his friends they were invited. He told his father the next time he went for a visit. Harlan told his son he was proud of him but couldn't attend. Harlan told his son he couldn't because the law said he was a bad man. It was something Luke had to deal with, but it was nothing new.

At a pretty early age, Luke got used to the fact his father was never around. He had problems with it, but there was no one he could turn to. His mother was in the picture but she had her issues to deal with. Tiffany Reeves, after she got out of prison for her part in what happened, left the country. With her girlfriend by her side, she went to Europe. She couldn't deal with how people in Bancroft looked at her. Everywhere she went people looked at her, whispered behind her back, and made jokes about her. She'd always say how people were so rude. They didn't know the whole story. They didn't know what she had gone through, the pain she felt when it all ended. Actually, at one point they had a petition going around, wanting to kick her out of the city. She left on her own, though. She would write to Luke, keeping him updated on where she was and what she was doing. She told him to come over for a visit once. He stayed for about a month then came back to Arkansas. Tiffany wanted him to stay but he had things he had to do. It wasn't for him. He didn't want to start life over. He had nothing to run from.

Luke took a drink of coffee. "Good eggs."

"I do what I can," Mindy said. "I have that magic touch, what can I say? Not many girls have it. Lord knows I didn't learn how to cook from my mother. The only thing she cooked were drugs."

Luke smiled. "That's something you could've gotten into."

"Not me, babe, too much risk."

"What, a little time in jail? You could do that, no problem."

"It's not a matter of me being able to do it, I don't want to. Hell, if I wanted to go to prison I'd just take a gun from the safe and kill you with it."

Luke said, "Oh, baby, it's too early in the morning for that."

"If you say so."

"I mean, I know how crazy you are but it'll have to wait. Got things to do today."

"Sure, you do,"

"Really, why would I lie?"

"Like what? What's your big business today?"

He lit a cigarette from a pack on the table. "We still need to figure out how we're going to get the rest of this money together."

"I still say we rob something."

"Like what, a bank?"

Playground
"What could it hurt?" she said. "Those things are full of money."
"They do. If we do one of those we have to plan shit down to the smallest detail."
She said she understood.
"I wouldn't count it out completely," he said. "Anyway, we can get it is good in my book. I mean, I just have to insist we plan it out."
"Of course, you don't just want to walk in without looking at things. I'm not getting killed."
"Well, I'll float it passed a few of the guys."
"That's a good idea."
He said that he hoped people would respond to the flyers they had been sending out. They had a few people, sure, but they needed a lot more. His father told him at one time that they should go cross-country like he and his friends did, getting more people as the days passed. Luke didn't want to do that. He didn't want to just be a copy of his father. He had to make his mark on the world. His father was going to be proud of him. Luke laughed and said maybe they did need to rob a bank, if nothing else so they could pay for the big party they were going to throw for Harlan on his birthday. Luke wanted it to last three days
She said, "What did you think of the guy on the radio?"
Luke shrugged. "On the radio, he sounded okay."
"Do you think he was interested?"
"Seemed to be more interested in my father more than anything."
"Really?"
"He said he wanted to interview with us."
"That should be fun."
Luke sighed. "It would be good for his ratings. I'm sure all those people working in that fucking building would love to hear that. They'd give him an award for the most

dangerous, shocking exposé of the year. We'll make him famous. The guy will be thanking us before it's over."

"Do you think he would?"

"Probably not."

She gave a smile. "You can't count on anyone these days, what's the deal with that? People judge without even knowing you."

"That's the harsh truth of it."

When they finished eating they took their plates over to the sink. Luke kissed her on the cheek. He needed to jump in the shower. As he was walking away he suggested she should join him for some lovemaking.

"Maybe when you get out," she told him. "I need to get these dishes done."

"Oh, forget those. You can do them after."

"After? We might spend the whole day in the room."

"Sounds like a good time to me," he told her.

She looked at him. "You have a point. Can't argue with that logic. I don't know, that's something we can do later."

"I'd like that."

He walked over and kissed her on the lips. She followed him into the bathroom.

8

It was after 5 am when Joey stood from where he'd been sitting. He was tired, ready to get back to his place, ready to get something to eat and fall asleep. He gave a big stretch, throwing his arms in the air. After telling Bruce goodbye, he grabbed his jacket.

He met the morning crew as they were coming in, Toby Vine and Samantha Russell. The two were a comedy duo, or, at least that's what they told themselves. Joey liked the two. They liked him. They had good numbers and that's all the bigwigs cared about. They'd only had the spot for a few months, but they were informed two days before that they could keep the spot for another six months. As far as Joey was concerned they could keep it. He never liked the mornings. The only reason he saw the mornings was because he was still up from the night before. He was a night owl and never wanted to change.

Toby said, "You look like you had fun."

"Always," Joey laughed. "Wouldn't have it any other way."

Samantha said, "When are you going to let us steal you away? We can use you, you know?"

"You guys don't need me on the team. I'd just get in the way. Think you guys have it covered. The night's my time to shine."

"We can always put a good word in for you. We can do a trio thing."

Toby nodded. "Hey, double the trouble! Our fans would love it! We can have a lot more fun. You've been around so long you can ask for a raise when you come over."

"I can?"

Toby said, "Might as well try, never know until you do, man. You've earned it."

Joey patted Toby on the shoulder. "Well, actually, that

wouldn't be doubling anything. Where'd you go to school? What did they teach over there?"

"Get the fuck out of here with that shit," Toby replied.

"We can see what happens," Joey told him. "I have people all over who are counting on me. I have a good thing going with my show, why would I change that?"

"You have a good point," the girl said. "But we'll have a great fucking show."

Joey waved her off. "Nah, I'm good. No offense to you guys or anything."

"None taken, loser," she giggled.

"Oh, is that the way it is now? I see how it is."

They chatted a little more before parting company. As he approached his car he noticed a piece of paper on the windshield. He grabbed the paper and realized it was a flyer for the Church of Modo. The paper said how Luke Reeves would like to invite everyone to a meeting, a talk about what the Church of Modo was all about. It gave an address and said that refreshments would be served. Honestly, he didn't know what to make of Luke. He knew he shouldn't judge him based on his father, but that's all he knew about the man. And he wasn't overly enthusiastic about getting to know the man.

It was too early to care about any of that stuff. He tossed the flyer into a nearby trash can. He didn't want to have anything to do with that bullshit. But something told him he'd hear from Luke again, that someone like him wouldn't let it go. He was one of those guys who wanted to make sure you understood every aspect of something.

When he got in his car he lit a cigarette and turned some music on. It was going to be a Guns n' Roses type of morning. He started to sing with Axl Rose, as he was welcoming people to the jungle, the jungle of life. In a

Playground
lot of ways, that song could be used to describe a lot of cities, an epitaph for America.

He felt good being in his car. He was free to do what he wanted. He'd be home in a few minutes. He stopped at a gas station to fill his tank and grab two packs of cigarettes. When he pulled into the parking lot of the apartment complex he saw a tall man with long blonde hair was messing with something in the trunk of his car. Joey told his empty passenger seat that the guy was nothing but boring. Joey pulled into a parking space, got out of his car, and called over to the man.

"Hey, Hank!"

The man stopped what he was doing, looked up, and gave a nod.

Joey wondered what the hell the man was doing at that time of the morning. But it was none of his business, he guessed.

"Oh, hey, Joey, what's up?"

"Just getting home from work," Joey walked over to the man.

"That's where I'm headed."

"You don't say?"

"Afraid so," Hank said. "Hadn't won big at the casino yet."

"Me, either."

"Shame for us both. Until that day comes," Hank looked back at his car, "I'll be driving that thing to the damn job."

"Yeah."

He looked at Joey. "Things could be worse, I guess. I just hope it'll be a slow day. Think they might fire me, though. Just another fine day in my life. I'll just have to wait and see how things go."

"Why would they fire you?"

"To prove a point. Their way of telling me they can do

Bradley Davenport

whatever the fuck they want. One of the managers claims to have a video of me taking a case of beer the other day. They told me they'd decide what they wanted to do. So, I might be home earlier than normal today."

"Do they have a video like that?" Joey asked the man.

"Hell, I don't know what they have. I assume they have cameras in that place. If they happened to have had those cameras running that night, yes, they may have evidence to their claim."

Joey lit a smoke. "All you can do in cases like that is just take the hit and keep going. Whatever happens, was meant to be. Have to look out for yourself these days."

"Ain't that the damn truth?" Hank said. "Nobody else is going to do the job. We haven't been little kids for a long time. I'll just have to face the music and take what's coming to me. We all do things we don't want to do."

"That's life for you."

"Yeah, it's always messing with my plans."

"You just have to do what you have to."

"That's an understatement."

Hank looked down at the trunk of his car. "Damn, I don't know what I'm doing with any of this anymore."

"Oh, come on, don't beat yourself up too hard about this."

"You want to do it for me?"

Joey laughed. He asked the man what he was putting in his trunk when he pulled into the complex. Hank explained he needed to mail a few things back. He bought a grill that broke. He planned to get all of his money back. He said if he didn't get it all back he'd sue. He told Joey that you can't go through life compromising with everything. Sometimes you have to take what you want. You have to beat injustice in the face. Don't ever back down. You have to take a stance.

"They still have you doing the overnight thing?" Hank

Playground
asked. "That must get tiring?"
"No, not really. I like what I do. I have fun with it."
"It's good you like it. Wish I could say the same. If you like what you do, it makes all the difference."
"I mean, don't get me wrong, sometimes I walk in there and it's nothing but dread; those times I want to leave as soon as possible."
"I can relate."
"Well, if you get fired I can probably talk to my bosses about getting you something at the station."
"You'd do that?"
"Sure," Joey gave a smile. "They have a lot of jobs that don't require you to be on the radio. And if you ever want to be on the radio, well, you just take a few classes. Some there have gone that route."
The man took a cigarette from his pack and lit it. "Thanks for that. I'll let you know what happens. For me, I don't care either way. If I do get the boot I can always find something else, know what I mean?"
"Things are always on the other side of the corner."
Hank chuckled. "That's a good way to think about it after they kick your face in the mud."
"I'm sure they could use you at the station."
"I can do whatever they want."
"I'll let you know."
Hank exhaled a stream of smoke, then it floated away in every direction. "What the hell has this world come to, you know? Seems things are always getting worse before they get better. It's a crazy place out there, buddy."
Joey asked how Hank's girlfriend, Raven, was. Hank said she was doing fine. But he asked Joey why he was asking, teasing that Joey wanted to get her in bed.
Joey laughed. "You're crazy, Hank."
"You're welcome," the man replied. "Never a dull moment with me, that's what the old lady says."

"That's something, buddy. I was asking because I hadn't seen her around in a few weeks."
"Yeah, she has been working a lot. They got rid of a few people. Had to catch some things up."
"I see."
"Yeah, it's messed up over there."
"Sounds like it."
"Seems that's going on a lot."
They talked a little more before parting ways.

Joey lived in an apartment building called Bay Point. He'd been living there a few years. He was kicked out of the last place he was at, kicked out for something that wasn't his fault. This girl he'd been dating came over one night and started a fight, throwing dishes and glasses. The neighbors called the cops. The landlord thought it would be best if he and Joey parted ways. Joey found the new place the very next day. And luck was on his side, rent wasn't too high. He enjoyed the place.

He lived on the second floor of one of the buildings. It wasn't much but it would do. He had another six months on his lease, then, he wasn't sure where he was going to go. He was never one to plan too far into the future. He liked moving to different places in the city. He wanted to get a house, but he'd just have to see what his money looked like when it came time.

He loved where he lived. He'd lived in the city all of his life. He couldn't imagine being anywhere else. He had all he needed, good family and good friends. His brother, Mike, and sister-in-law, Kim, lived in a house up the street with their two kids. Joey liked they lived so close. He could drop by their place whenever he wanted. They enjoyed each other's company. Family is very important.

Joey's place had a living room, kitchen, bedroom, bathroom, and a few closets. When he moved in they told him not to have loud parties. If that was something he

Playground
wanted to do he'd have to find a new place to live. He walked into his place and threw his keys on the little table beside the door. He walked over to the fridge, and grabbed a beer and stuff to make a sandwich. He ate, drank the beer, and fell asleep on his couch with the TV on.

  The girl he was talking to earlier at the station, Layla, lived two doors down. She'd moved in about a month after he did. He always wondered why she chose to move where she did. He thought it was because she had a thing for him. But he learned that it wasn't the best idea to get romantically involved with a co-worker, because things could go bad and you'd be forced to see them every day. He liked her a lot. The two had a good connection. He'd just have to take things slow. You can't rush into things.

9

Later that day he woke, got ready, and went to hang out with some of his friends. They ended up at a place called Electric Sun, where they drank and told stories until the place closed. The two friends, Doug and Quinn, had been friends with Joey since their high school days. Those days seemed so long ago. As much fun as it was, he never wanted to return to those days. He had a good thing going on and never wanted to ruin it. Their other friend, Ethan, moved out to California a few years before to work in the movie business. They were going to go out there to see him.

"What's the plan?" Doug blurted. "We need to keep this party going. You only live once, you know? I think at this point in the chronology of our history we should get some burgers."

Doug had always been a crazy and wild soul. He liked to push limits with things just to see how far he could go. He was someone who knew how to have a good time. A lot of times he'd overdo it and have to get some help coming back from the edge. The way he saw it, you only have one life to live, so you may as well get the most out of it as you can. Life should be an adventure. He told his friends when they got to California they needed to find the craziest parties.

Quinn said, "I can get behind that, sure."

Joey said, "You guys won't get any argument out of me."

"It's set!" Doug howled. "We have a good plan."

They drove to Red Bench. The burgers were juicy and the fries were the best, which were two important things a burger joint could offer. Doug also liked one of the girls who worked behind the counter. She was a redhead curly fox with pale skin. Doug promised the guys he'd ask her out if she was working that night. She was. Quinn joked that maybe she was a vampire because she was so pale.

"You're fucking crazy," Doug told him. "However, man, you make a good point. Hell, that might be what we're dealing with here. Who knows? Don't know until I find out. Need to take that shot."

Joey said, "Go for it, Bubba! Spin the wheel, and see where the chips fall. She could very well be the one for you."

"Enough of that talk," Doug snapped. "Don't take it there too fast. I don't know what the future has in store. Don't judge me, man. If you want that, go see something for yourself. Don't worry about me, I'll get there in time."

Quinn said, "If you don't ask her you know we'll make fun of you forever, right? We'll make fun of your dumb ass until the end of time."

"Fuck that shit," Doug waved off the comment. "In due time, my friend. And, hey, she might have a friend for you. I'm just looking out for my boy, you know?"

Quinn said, "That would be nice. I'd have to make sure she isn't a whore or anything."

"I know what you mean. I mean, you can never tell with that stuff until you know."

Joey said, "Just don't think too much about it."

Doug said, "And the best part, if she is a vampire she could turn me into one. How cool would that be? That's not something that happens every day. Her and I, we could live forever."

"You sure you'd want that?" Joey asked.

After more conversation, Doug ran over and started with the redhead. After awhile he came back, telling the guys she told him to give her a call the next day. He was pretty impressed with himself. They left the burger place and went to Blue Flame for some drinks. Joey told his friends they still had to get home. He told them he couldn't afford to get pulled over and arrested.

Doug looked at him. "Man, we can just get a fucking cab. That's their whole reason for being, to pick up drunks like us, you know? I don't want to get in a crash or anything. A night of being dead doesn't sound like a good time to me."

"That's an idea," Joey said.

Quinn said, "Let's do it. Come on, let's all put in some money."

They ordered more beer and shots.

Quinn looked at Doug, "So, you have any plans, you and the redhead?"

"Not really. I just figured we'd hang out, and get to know each other. Might fool around if she wants."

"What's her name?" Joey asked.

"Lexi," Doug said.

"That's a nice name."

"I thought so. Never met anyone with that name."

"First for everything."

"She seems like the sort of girl I need."

"You just need a girl," Joey laughed, as he patted Doug on the shoulder. "It looks promising for you."

Doug took a drink. "It does. I have to say. Once we get to know each other more I'll know for sure, then, I'll see about a girl for you. I wouldn't want to give her the wrong impression from the start. She may just think I'm just after her friend or something, you know how that goes? Women always seem to compete with one another. They all just love fighting over me. Can't say as I can blame them."

"I don't know," Joey told his friend. "You amaze me, man."

Playground

Quinn laughed.

"Laugh it up, fools," Doug said. "I think I hear a bit of jealousy there, am I right?"

"Well, whatever helps," Joey said.

"Fuck you, bitch," Doug pointed his finger at him. "You'll see."

"I'll believe it when I see it."

They laughed as they went back and forth, ribbing one another, enjoying the night.

As far as Joey was concerned these guys were the best friends anyone could ask for. Since his friend, Ethan Bursott, went back to California, Joey made sure to spend more time with Doug and Quinn. Wayne, who was Ethan's brother, also hung around the guys. Wayne saw Ethan more because he was able to fly out more. Wayne was poor until the day he won the lottery. He was able to do what he wanted for awhile. He didn't buy anything too flashy, a few things here and there. He did keep his job as a bartender for awhile, but after a few months, he was able to start his own business. He had a few people working for him at his landscaping company. Joey and the others worked on the crew for awhile, but Joey had to stop during summer. Things got too hot, plus, he was finding it hard to do the job after putting in nights at the station. He hated to let his friends down. He took them out drinking one night and explained him leaving the landscaping gig. They understood. He still felt bad, like he had betrayed them or something. Even though they understood he still felt bad.

10

Joey got home around 2 am. When he got inside he turned the TV on and drank a few beers until he passed out.

When he woke he got a shower and something to eat. After awhile, a knock came to the door. He wondered who it could be. He found the beautiful Layla standing in front of him. She looked amazing in a black miniskirt and white blouse. How did he get so lucky to live by a beauty like her?

He invited her inside and offered her a beer.

He went to the fridge and grabbed two beers. He cracked both open and handed her one.

"Thanks," she said.

"Hey, what are neighbors for?"

She smiled, then took a drink. "I liked the show the other night."

"Really? Thanks."

"What did you think of it?" she asked.

He shrugged. "It was okay, I guess. I mean, yeah, we can always do better. When you sit there and examine what you do, it's something you think about. Had a few crazy people call in, but stuff like that always happens. It was just another night. I do what I can," Joey said.

"I was entertained."

They walked into the living room. She sat on the blue couch, he sat across on a black leather chair.

"How have you been?" he asked.

She sighed. "Okay. Could be worse."

"Like everything else, ups and downs."

"About right. It's the same old story."

"It's just the way of things."

"It sucks," she said.

"It does."

Playground
"But things get better, that's how it always works. Just keep saying things will get better and eventually they do."
"That's a good way of looking at it," he smiled at her.
"It's the only way for me."
"That's a good outlook, that's one thing I've always liked about you."
"You mean there's more stuff you like about me?"
"Of course, don't be crazy. If I gave you the whole list we'd be here all day."
"That's nice of you to say."
"The truth is easy to say."
She told him about the guy who lived next door to her, Layne, and how much of a creep he'd been. The day before, as she was leaving her apartment he met her outside her door. He lived across from her. In his sleazy voice, he asked how she was doing and how he couldn't wait to take her on a date. She looked at him, gave a smile, and told him she was seeing someone; a lie. He told her that as long as they weren't married it didn't matter. She wasn't under any obligation to anyone. She took his meaning but still passed on the offer. She politely walked away and got into her car. He stared at her until she drove away. He had done that sort of thing a few other times. She guessed that he had a mental illness and didn't understand she didn't want to have anything to do with him. Joey told her he'd talk to him and try to get him off her back. If talking to the guy didn't work Joey would have to resort to other tactics—that was something he didn't want to do, but sometimes you have to use force.
"Thanks for that. I didn't want to be rude to him or anything, but he's strange."
"I've heard that from a few others."

Bradley Davenport

Layne Wallhone was a creep. He came from a whole line of oddballs. Over the years Joey had more than his share of run-ins with various members of that tribe. They were all the same. Layne was a skinny guy with puffy brown hair and tattoos all over. He wore clothes that were too big for him and always had a long necklace hanging off him. Despite his age, he always wore his ball hat backward. Layne always had this strange look in his eyes, like he was planning some evil deed. He was one of those guys you always had to be on guard when they were around. You never knew quite what he was going to do. Layne had a long history with law enforcement—reckless driving, being drunk in public, shoplifting, fighting, and drugs were things he'd been arrested for.

"Don't worry about him," Joey told her. "He just wants attention. Nothing to lose sleep over."

"Do you think he's dangerous?"

"Anything's possible. He may talk big, but when it comes down to it he's all bark. I'll have a little talk with him, and see what the deal is. That whole family, I don't know what goes on with them. Everything he knows he learned from his dad."

"He thinks I'm cute," she said. "It's a little flattering. I mean, I'd never go out with him no matter how much you paid me... just nice to know people notice."

"Oh, you attract the crazy people, that's nice," Joey smiled.

"They love me, what can I say?" she replied. "It's my charm."

"Yeah, that's it."

She laughed.

Joey said, "Well, I'd have to agree with him that you're cute, who wouldn't? That's one thing we have in common."

Playground
"Hopefully that's the only thing."
"As far as I know."
Layla took the last swallow of beer. She asked if she could have another.
He got some more beer from the kitchen.
"Thanks for the beer," she said.
"Think anything of it."
"I don't want to drink your whole inventory."
"Nonsense," he said. "I make sure that never happens. It's a staple at my place."
"I like the sound of that, mine too. I have to have my alcohol and cigarettes."
"Right on."
He asked about her car. She had to take it into the shop a few days earlier. She couldn't figure out what was wrong with it. The only thing she knew was that it wouldn't start. She was going to pick it up the next day.
"If you need a lift I can take you," Joey said.
"Awe, thanks, hon. I'll take you up on that. Are you sure it won't be a problem? I can arrange something else."
"Trust me, it won't be any trouble. I'd love to help."
"I'll buy you dinner or something."
"You don't have to."
"I need to pay you somehow."
"Don't worry about it."
"Well, that's super sweet of you."

She mentioned that she was starving. Joey tossed out the idea that they should order a pizza. She told him that was a great idea.
Joey dialed the pizza place on his cell. Awhile later the food was delivered. They spent the afternoon eating, drinking, watching TV, and getting high. The perfect way to spend a day, the both of them thought. They en-

joyed the company of one another.

"This is nice," Joey told her. "When you're at work there's only so much you can learn about someone. Most times you don't have much time to talk."

Later that evening she told him she needed to get back to her place, saying she had a good time and they needed to do it again. She kissed him after he walked her to the door. He wanted it to be more but he'd have to wait.

He went back to work later that night. It was the same story, crazed lunatics calling the station to rant about whatever-the-fuck. Joey would patiently listen, and then, offer his advice; it worked sometimes, but other times he wasn't as lucky.

After he went home and got some sleep they went to pick her car up from the shop. One of the guys there tried to get her to go out with him. He was an older man, about sixty. He had thinning silver hair and wore overalls. He was about forty pounds overweight.

He said, "Hey, baby, you want to ride somewhere? I can take you wherever you want to go, pretty girl. We can go back to my place. Get that sort of party going on. You'll love it!"

Layla stared at him. "Oh, no! That's never going to happen. I'm good. Thanks."

"You sure? I like it when you girls play those games. You'll come around, just wait. I'm not as old as I look, lady," he nodded at Joey. "You can drop him right now. I can show you things you've only read about in dirty books."

"Like I said, that's never going to happen," she said, "You're a creep."

Joey told him to leave her alone, and if he didn't he'd be sorry.

"Like what?" the old man asked.

"Believe me," Joey said, "you don't want to be any-

Playground
where around here when that happens. Things could happen to you."

"Like what?"

"I'm connected all over."

The old man chuckled. "That a threat? We don't like those around here. Think you got a few things fucked around here. See, no one threatens me. All I have to do is make a little phone call and your ass is in a dumpster."

"What, you can't handle things yourself?"

The man stepped closer to Joey. "You don't want to go down that road. You'll be in a world of hurt if you continue like you are," he raised his brow. "You two get the hell out of here and don't come back. If you have car issues in the future I guess you'll have to go across the city. I don't care," he snorted. "And I may call the cops, say there was a couple punks in here threatening me. I'm sure they'd love to hear something like that."

Joey said, "Call them. They'll beat you, take you to jail."

"Fuck you, boy," the old man said. "That little whore of yours, she can stay if she wants. I'll fuck her good."

Layla said, "You're gross. Honey, one night with me and you'll die from a heart attack halfway through."

The man laughed. "Just go back where you came from. I'm tired of talking to you guys."

They left and went back to the complex. Joey invited her to his place for a drink and a good conversation. Four shots of whiskey and four beers later, the two found themselves in bed.

11

Layne Wallhone sat in a booth at Monky Jack's as he looked out the window. A waitress walked over and asked if he wanted to order anything.

"I'm waiting on some people."

"You going to want to order when they show?" she asked.

"Not sure."

"Well, sir, my name is Betty and when the rest of your group gets here just call me over if you need anything."

He told her he just wanted coffee.

When she brought the coffee she asked if he wanted anything else.

"Maybe later," he told her.

"Well, if you do decide to eat something, We have homemade apple and cherry pie."

"Those sound good."

"They are good, sir," she said with soft eyes.

He had a feeling she was trying to get with him. He wasn't interested at all, but it was nice she tried.

He asked if she made the pies. She laughed and said she couldn't cook if her life depended on it.

"I'll keep that in mind," he said.

After she walked away he continued to look out the window. Traffic zoomed down the road. A few people walked the sidewalk; it was a nice day for it. Layne thought he should've walked to the diner from his place. He always told himself he needed to start getting back in shape. People told him he looked good, but he told himself he could do better. He told himself he could get that girl, Layla, who lived in his apartment complex. He told himself she'd like him or else he'd have to get mean with her.

He stared out the window for another ten minutes when

Playground
the waitress came back over to ask about more coffee. "Yeah," he told her. "I'm not sure where the people I'm meeting are."
She got the coffee and said maybe they got stuck in traffic. He told her that must be it, that there must've been a wreck or something somewhere. An hour passed and he was still staring out the window. he started to think they weren't showing when a black SUV pulled into the parking lot. Four people emerged from the car. The first guy to walk through the door was Tick, followed by Bobby, Hammer, and then Luke. Layne nodded to them as they approached. He was glad to see them. He looked at his watch and nodded at the men again.
 Tick and Luke sat across from Layne. Hammer sat beside Layne while Bobby pulled up a chair from one of the other tables.
 "Hey, Layne," Luke said. "Where the fuck have you been? Have you been hanging around here all day? The coffee must be good."
 Layne chuckled. "What do you mean?"
 "What, do I have to be a good-looking girl for you to show up? The party the other night? I started to think someone had shot you or something. We waited for you. You were missed. And before that, there was that other thing."
 "Come on, Luke, what are you talking about? I'm the one who's been sitting here almost two hours waiting."
 Tick said, "You have a problem with our timetable? You need to forget that shit, yeah? We had business to conduct."
 Layne shook his head. "Sure. I mean, it's okay with me. Do whatever you want. I'm not going to stop you."
 "Sounded to me like you were complaining?" Tick said.
 "No, I was just saying."
 "Just saying, just saying what?"

Layne folded his hands on the table. "I didn't mean anything by it."

"That's what I thought," Tick said.

"So, what do you guys want?" Layne asked.

Bobby said, "The boss, he was the one who wanted you here. We were just along for the ride, okay?"

The waitress came over and asked if the newcomers wanted anything. They said they just wanted coffee. After she got them their coffee she tried to get them to order something to eat.

"We're fine, hon," Bobby told her. "We don't need anything. It's okay, I can speak for all of these guys."

She let out a small chuckle and said if they changed their minds to let her know.

"Thanks," Tick told her.

She walked over to one of the other tables.

Luke gave Layne a menacing stare.

Layne nodded. "Oh, that. Yeah, I took this girl out that night. We went back to her place, and got down to a little business, know what I mean? Just figured I'd catch up with you guys in a day or so."

"You hear of a phone? And what the fuck happened to the night before that? People don't see you around for a few days, they start getting the wrong idea."

"Sorry," Layne told him. "It won't happen again. I didn't think it was a big deal. Who did you think killed me?"

Luke shrugged. "The fuck do I know? I don't know what bullshit you have going on. Just don't do the shit again or I'll kill you."

A lump started to form in Layne's throat. He said how sorry he was. He didn't know how many times he had to say the same thing. He fucked up. When he first got mixed up with those guys he was told what was expected of him.

Playground

Luke told the guy he had a surprise for him.

"For me?" Layne said. "You didn't have to do anything like that. What is it?"

Tick told him they'd have to take a drive. They didn't want to spoil anything. They'd made a special trip just to tell him.

"I don't know," Layne shook his head. "That's funny. Here, I thought I was in trouble."

"Why would you be in trouble?" Luke asked.

"Not sure. I just figured it was going to be something. It's all fun and games until it's not, you know? A lot of times you don't even get the pleasure of knowing if you're in trouble or not, just get a bullet to the head."

"Well, I hate to disappoint. Something like that can be arranged."

Everyone at the table laughed.

Layne said he'd have to pass on that type of fun.

Bobby patted him on the shoulder. "Come on, man, you'll want to see this. It'll be good for you. Think of it as therapy."

Layne looked at him. "How so?"

"You'll have to come and see. We don't want to spoil it."

Layne let out a sigh. "Okay."

"Let's go," Tick said. "Don't be an asshole."

They were joking earlier but something in the back of Layne's mind told him they might kill him. It was just something you had to learn to accept when you entered a life of crime. Your time could be around the corner and you wouldn't know it.

After they finished their coffee they walked out to Bobby's car. Layne asked Hammer if everything was okay. The guy told him he had nothing to worry about, that everything was fine. They piled into the car and

Bradley Davenport

went about four miles down the road. The whole time they were joking and laughing. They got the sense they gave Layne an uneasy feeling; that wasn't their intention at all.

Along with a few houses in the area Luke owned a set of storage units. He used the storage whenever he needed to hide something or somebody. He'd always try to tell his associates about the benefits of owning property and not just renting. If you owned whatever it was you could use it however you saw fit. It was perfect if you needed to hide something.

They pulled into the parking lot and got out of the car.

"The fuck are we doing here?" Layne asked.

Luke turned to him. "Why, you nervous about something?"

"Nothing like that, just asking."

"Don't worry about anything. We told you it's a surprise. Just take it easy."

"I just don't want any surprises."

Tick slapped him on the back. "You need to learn to calm down. We're not all bad."

"You aren't?"

Tick waved the comment away. "I'm offended you'd say something like that."

Layne laughed.

They walked to the last storage unit on the first row. Luke took a key from his pocket and popped the lock open. "They're still working on getting electric in some of these," he opened the door. "This one is already done."

After they walked in Tick flipped on the light switch. A chair with a man tied to it sat in the middle of the room. The guy had streaks of dried blood on his face. Tick told Layne he'd been tied to the chair for a couple of hours. Luke turned back to them, saying they were going to be

Playground
there for awhile. If they needed to go buy any food or anything they needed to do it then. Bobby and Hammer left to get some food and drinks. They said they'd be back in a bit.

"Don't worry," Luke told them. "I had some guys work on these doors so you can close them from the inside."

When the two men walked out of the unit Bobby slammed the door down.

Tick nodded to the guy in the chair, then at Luke. "Think he'll say something now?"

"He needs to for his sake," Luke said. "If he doesn't we'll have to get rid of him."

Layne asked who the guy in the chair was.

The guy in the chair was Larry Scott. Larry and a few guys he knew stole drugs and money from some people who worked for Luke. When he found out what happened he did some investigating and tracked Larry down. Luke and his guys were trying to get the man to come clean and tell them who put him up to the crime.

Luke looked at the man in the chair. "See, my friend, I don't think you fully grasp the position you're in. There's no play for you but to tell the truth. You can't go to the cops now. You can't do anything, friends, family, girlfriends, you can't reach out to anyone. If I take that gag off, are you going to tell me what I want to hear? You going to tell me who told you to steal from me?"

The man in the chair nodded.

Luke walked over and took the gag off. "If you say anything mean I'll crack you in the face, you got it?"

The man looked at the floor, then at Luke. "I didn't mean for this to happen, you have to believe me."

"You didn't mean to get caught, that right?" Luke said. "People don't start to feel bad until they're caught."

"It wasn't like that."

"What was it like, then?" Well, let me tell you something, not everything you stole was mine. Some of it belonged to associates of mine. I'll go to each of them and they'll decide what they want done."

The guy shook his head.

Luke continued. "See my friend standing over there? Layne is his name, and some of that shit you guys took was his. Now, if someone has a problem with me we deal with it, but don't drag others into it. As far as I know, Layne didn't do anything to you. As it turns out he got into trouble because not all of his was for personal use. He caught a beating because of you."

The man looked at Layne. "I'm sorry. I didn't know. I have no problem with you, you have to believe me."

"That so?" Layne said.

"I don't even know who you are. Trust me, if I had known I would've never taken the stuff. I wasn't told anything about you or anyone connected to you."

"You sure about that?" Layne said.

"Of course. I don't want any trouble."

"It appears you found some."

"Yes, it looks like it."

Layne walked closer to the man. "You stole the stuff. I get it. Hey, we are all in that life. Lord knows I've done my share of stealing over the years, however, you knew the risk. I imagine you've been doing this awhile, am I right?"

The man shook his head. "A few years."

"Thought so," Layne continued. "Well, because of what you did I caught a beating. These guys, believe me, you don't want them knowing you were the one who stole it. If I tell them there's no doubt in my mind that they'll hunt you down and kill you, leave you in a ditch somewhere. Today is your lucky day, I'm not going to let that happen to you."

"Thank you," the man muttered.

Playground

"All you have to do is tell me who told you about the stuff. You had to have known somehow. Someone must've told you."

Larry caught his breath. "It means a lot that you won't let them kill me. I made a mistake. I'm sure you made a few in your time. Truth is, I don't know the guy's name."

"You don't know the guy's name, you expect me to believe that?"

"Believe what you want, I'm telling the truth. A friend of mine told me about this place he knew where drugs were being stashed, and hidden until someone could come and get them. Now, he told me that some guy told him about it."

Layne said, "With everyone talking it's surprising no names were mentioned."

"That's all I know."

"You know more than that, come on? You expect me to believe no one gave details other than that? Do you take me for a fool?"

Larry kept insisting he didn't know the name of the guy his friend talked to. He wouldn't even give up his friend's name. After Layne smacked the guy around a little he asked Luke what they should do with the guy. It looked as if Larry wasn't going to give anything up. They couldn't just let him go. He could go to the cops, and where would they be if that happened?

After they talked about it for a bit the best course of action was to kill the man in the storage unit. They couldn't just let the guy go. Layne thought they should torture the guy first to try and get the information they needed. Luke said they didn't have that sort of time for that, that they'd find out sooner or later. A gun was all that was needed to get the job done.

Bobby and Hammer stepped outside to make sure no one was around. They told the guys it was safe, and without hesitation, Layne took out his .45 and put two into the man.

Luke looked at Layne. "Make you feel any better."

"Not really. It's just part of what we do."

Luke nodded. "Some things are just duty. When something is in the way you have to. That feeling, you get a little number everyone you do. Just have to block it out."

The group spent the next couple of hours getting rid of the body along with the evidence. After they detailed the storage unit they took the body to the woods where they buried the others.

Layne told them it felt good getting that out of the way. He just wanted to put the whole thing behind him.

"We just have to move on," he told them. "This whole thing has made me hungry. Anyone else want to eat?"

They went to a spot for burgers and fries.

Luke and the guys had another party that night. Things didn't settle until the early hours of the morning.

The whole thing with Larry started about a month earlier when he robbed a house that was holding cocaine. The guys who told Larry about the cocaine helped Layne haul it. They were supposed to meet up with the contact at a different location, a drugs-for-money deal. The guy buying the drugs, a man named Flynt, when he discovered the product had been stolen, with help from a few other guys tracked down Layne and gave him a beating outside of a bar. Flynt thought Layne had taken him for a fool. The whole time he was getting beat Layne swore he had nothing to do with it, saying he didn't know who stole the drugs. But he told Flynt he'd find out who took the product. After some more convincing Flynt let him go.

Layne had a mission. He had to find who the hell stole the drugs or he was going to be killed. Layne spent the

Playground
next few weeks trying to get all the information he needed. After he talked to almost everyone he knew who dealt in that world word started to leak about Larry. Layne talked to Blue, a man who helped Larry steal the cocaine. After finally getting what he needed Layne knew who to look for. The thing he would regret was not killing Blue that night, because Blue told Larry he was being hunted. Another two weeks went by with Layne trying to find Larry. He let everyone know there was a manhunt for Larry. In those two weeks, he went back to Blue and shot him to death. As much as he didn't like doing so he told Luke what the problem was, that he couldn't find this guy.

"Don't worry," Luke told him. "I'll get some more people on it. We'll get to the bottom of this."

It only took two days. They found Larry at a friend's house. At first, he denied it, but that didn't last long. When they first brought him to the storage unit Tick threatened to take a torch to his face. Luke told him no, saying they should let Layne decide what his fate should be—and that was that, the rest was history. In the end, Layne didn't get to decide what happened to Larry. But it was all probably for the best. He didn't want that type of thing hanging over his head. He had more pressing things to worry about.

The party that night lasted until 5 am. They all told Luke what a great time they had. They were all glad they didn't have to end up killing someone at the party.

Later that day Luke called the guys back to the house for a meeting. Mindy made a big lunch for all of them.

Luke said, "We have plenty of booze if you guys need any."

They got what they wanted to drink and sat around the kitchen table. After they were done eating they just sat at the table talking and joking. Among the things that were joked about, they started teasing Bobby about getting a girlfriend. He had a history of women leaving pretty quickly. Bobby told them to go to Hell.

Luke said, "I just wanted to thank all of you for showing up," he looked around at everyone. "The future is nothing but bright for us. Are you guys with me or not? If you guys are with me, that's great, I couldn't ask for anything more; those that don't want to be with us, I understand, you can exit now. No one will think any less of you."

Everyone said they were staying.

Luke continued. "I must tell you that this could get dangerous. We're already going to have the cards stacked against us. As you may know, my family doesn't have the best history."

For those who didn't know he explained the history of his family and what the Church of Modo was all about. He was quick to tell them that he wasn't going to turn into his father, that he wasn't going to murder people just for the hell of it. He understood that not everything that happened back then was good.

"With everything there are exceptions," Luke told them. "You have to take things on a case-by-case basis when it comes to that. I mean, come on, folks, I'm not an evil person or anything. Sometimes you have to do things you don't want to. I'm all about peace and love."

For the next few hours, they discussed ways they could raise money for the business. They'd already spent a great deal of money on flyers and posters. Luke told them he could always call up Joey at the radio station and advertise that way. A few of the other guys and girls threw out some ideas. He wrote everything down and said they were all good ideas.

After most of the people left Luke told a few of his key

Playground

guys to join him in his office. They needed to talk over some things.

12

The phone broke the silence, making Joey's eyes pop open. After four rings he took the phone from the nightstand.
"Hello?" he muttered.
"Hey, man!" the voice on the other end said.
"Hey," Joey responded.
"I wake you?"
Joey recognized the voice as Ethan.
"Nah," Joey said. "I was just taking it easy. I was doing some stuff earlier, got caught up."
"I bet."
"You know how it is, you have to take what you can when you can."
"Heard that," Ethan said. "Hey, I'm not going to fault you for anything. I'm right there with you, good buddy. If it gets you through the day, what can it hurt?"
"What's new in sunny California?"
"It's cool," Ethan told him. "Nothing much here, same old stuff."
"That bad, huh?"
"I just do what I can. It's all pretty crazy. Just all the booze and ladies I can stand. It's been nothing but work here, always busting my ass. Making that money. Someone has to pay the bills around here."
"Yeah, it sounds rough," Joey told his friend.
"Someone has to do it," Ethan told his friend. "I know it seems like nothing but fun and games here, but it's a lot of work. You'd be surprised what goes into it. Not as simple as everyone thinks."
"I bet."
"When I write my memoirs I'll let them all know how much work it is."
Joey laughed, as he grabbed his pack of cigarettes from

Playground
the nightstand. "You want my sympathy? I know you, you got it under control."

"Thanks for that."

"What are friends for?" Joey looked over at the beautiful figure in his bed.

"Some days are better than others, what can I say? It's a business that takes awhile to understand. Joey, you guys ready for some California action?" Ethan asked. "That's the main reason for the call. I've been telling some people out here about you guys, about what good friends we all are. They can't wait to meet you guys."

"You know we are. We were just talking the other day about it."

"I miss you guys. It'll be like the good old days. The clubs they have here are a lot better than anything they could ever come up with there."

"I can believe it."

"We need to tell the architects here to head over there, polish that fucking place up, make it look brand new."

"That'd be a miracle," Joey told him. "Maybe that's what it needs, who knows? I have a few things I should run by them."

"You should. Wouldn't hurt anything."

"Probably wouldn't listen."

"Never hurts to try."

"The fuck do I care about this shit for? Let them do whatever-the-fuck they want."

Ethan laughed. "That's the spirit. Tell them what you think."

"Someone has to."

Ethan said, "You guys should just move out here. One of the best parts is all the sexy women around. Have your pick! They're all up for grabs. It's like a fucking candy store. You can be with a different one every night. I know all of you guys are single these days, so that shouldn't be a problem."

"I'm sure that would make for some interesting times," Joey told his friend. "Yeah, Doug and Quinn are still single. And I think I'm about to be off the market."

"Really? Damn, man. Who's the lucky girl? I know her?"

"Her name's Layla. You don't know her."

"That's nice."

"She works at the station."

"Oh, a little work romance, huh?"

"Something like that," Joey laughed.

"Nothing wrong with that. The only thing, if something goes wrong one of you will have to get a job somewhere else. That's nothing but drama."

"I don't plan on that being the case."

"Good for you."

Joey asked if he could bring Layla along. He thought it'd be rude if he didn't ask.

"Sure," Ethan said. "There's plenty of room. It's all good with me. And she won't be the only girl. Heather's still coming too, right?"

"Yeah."

"Well, it'll be a great time had by all."

Joey said, "I'm sure when I ask her she'll be more than willing to come along."

"Just tell her what a nice guy I am. It's all fun over here. Before you know it she'll be wanting you to buy a place out here."

Joey laughed at his friend. "Maybe?"

"You never know. With women, it's always a mystery. They like it that way. Be prepared to spend a good chunk of money on a house. Oh, man, these are exciting times we live in. And, I'll tell you this now, she'll thank you beyond anything you could think of."

"I'm all for that. I'll ask her when I get off the phone."

Playground
Ethan snorted. "She'll jump at the opportunity. It'll be something you can tell your kids."
Joey laughed. "I wouldn't go that far just yet."
His friend continued. "Nothing quite like fresh love. The fond memory you guys can look back on. You'll thank me later."
"I'm sure I will," Joey said. "What's been new over there?"
"Just been busy."
"Really?"
Ethan told his friend about some of the things he was working on. It all sounded fascinating to Joey. He always thought it would be neat to work on a movie. As he talked to his friend he remembered the first time Ethan asked him about promoting his first movie, Monster Fantastic, on his radio show; that seemed so long ago. Joey was proud of everything his friend had done since then. Ethan told Joey about a woman he'd been dating, and how it was turning into something great. Joey told him it was good to hear. He was glad his friend found someone. They talked a little more before ending the call. Ethan said he had to get back on the set or the actors would get pissed.

Layla got out of bed and wiped her eyes. "What a night!"
"I hope you had fun," Joey exhaled a stream of smoke.
She smiled. "I did."
"Good."
"You?"
"Yes, indeed. I've always been told I was a good lover."
She giggled. "The best, what are you talking about?"
"Thanks for saying that," Joey said. "You're pretty good, too."
"I'm glad you liked it."
They kissed.

Bradley Davenport

She told him that his bed was a nice place to be.

He thanked her.

Layla lit one of her cigarettes. She asked who was on the phone. He told her, and he explained the whole story behind Ethan and what he was doing in California. He told her all about their friendship. She asked what he said about bringing her along. It didn't occur to him when he said it, but he should've asked her about it first. The thought just came to him and he ran with it.

"Guess I should've asked you."

"I think it'll be fun," she told him. "I've never been there before. Once when I was a teen my parents were going to go and bring me with them, but then they had to cancel the trip. Mom found out Dad had a woman on the side."

"Oh, that's not good."

"It turned into this whole thing. They split for awhile."

"Sorry to hear that."

"They got back together two years later. Guess mom figured the grass wasn't greener on the other side. Sometimes it takes a lot for people to see that."

"That's the thing about that, you think it will be but sometimes it doesn't work out. There are things you have to learn on your own."

"Yeah."

"They still together?"

"No," she said. "They gave it another three years, but then after all sorts of fights, they called it quits. They found other people to spend their remaining days with. I'm happy for them."

"I see."

"But, yes, I'm all for going. It'll be a lot of fun."

"It will be."

"I can't wait."

He was glad to hear her say that. When he told her that

Playground
they'd be able to go on movie sets she got excited. She's never known anyone in the movie business before.

"And everyone else will love you."

"Promise?"

"Just like I do."

"Exactly like you do?"

"I think if it was like that we'd have a problem."

"Oh, would we? I'd hate to be a problem. I can't help it if I'm attractive."

"Oh, boy!" Joey took another drag of his cigarette.

"I'm just stating a fact."

"I'd have to agree with you," he told her.

Layla walked to the bathroom. When she came out she asked how long they would be in California. He said they'd probably be there a week or so. It would take twenty-eight hours of strictly driving time. But they were going to have to make stops along the way, so it would most likely be two or three days. He said he was going to use his vacation, and she could take off time, too. He told her the bosses wouldn't mind. There were enough people at the station, they could find people to fill the spots. And if they had issues with it they could go kick rocks down a dirt road. Joey didn't give a damn. He told her they'd have no problem getting another job.

She worked hard and was due a vacation. Layla started at the station about a week before Joey had. She was a fast learner and got comfortable with her role at the station fast. For awhile, she wanted to be on the radio, but some things were never meant to be. She was told by her bosses that she didn't have the voice for radio and that the station would lose listeners if they put her on. Who the fuck did they think they were, dictating who's ready for what? She said that the fact they said she didn't have a voice for it was subjective. She was more than a little offended by that. So, she didn't care about the job. She thought about quitting because of it. The same people who told her they wouldn't put her on the radio told her that maybe in a few months, they'd give her a chance.

  Before she came to the radio station she held a position as a waitress at the Stone Grill. She'd gotten the job when a friend of hers put in a good word. She didn't mind witnessing. The most appealing thing about the job was the tips—some days were better than others.

  Joey went into the kitchen and made some coffee. After making some breakfast he regaled her in stories of his friends and himself.

  They laughed and continued to eat.

13

Joey and Layla joined Quinn, Doug, Wayne, and Heather for drinks that night. They all laughed, joked, and had a good time. Heather was glad Layla was going. Heather wouldn't be the only girl on the trip.

The group filled Layla in on stories about Ethan. They assured her he was a very pleasant person to be around, that they all trusted him, that they'd known him for years and he wasn't some sort of crazy psycho or anything.

Instead of taking cars, they decided to rent a van. The thought was that they didn't know how many trips they would be able to take. As they were all talking Joey floated the idea of all of them moving out there. Wayne and Heather had thought about it, but they decided they'd miss Arkansas too much. Joey laughed when he heard that they would miss Arkansas. As far as Joey was concerned Arkansas was a shit-pit. Doug and Quinn loved the idea of moving. There was nothing for them in Bancroft except shitty jobs. They said they'd have to think about it. Joey remarked that if Doug thought about it too long his head would explode.

"Fuck you, buddy," Doug spat. "I'll beat your ass for saying that."

Joey said, "You and what army? You'll need a lot of guys to pull that one off. I don't think you have it in you."

"You're a funny guy."

"I know."

"I should smack you."

Quinn joined in. "Kids, can we ever take you out?"

Wayne laughed. "Some things never change around here. You guys will always be crazy as shit."

"That's the way we like it," Doug said. "Have to keep you guys on your toes. Can't have you going around

Bradley Davenport

thinking I'm normal or something."

"You are far from normal, my friend."

"Fuck that shit, man."

"You can't deny it."

They continued talking and drinking the night away.

When Joey told his bosses they'd be out for over a week they didn't care.

They started on the road at 5 pm. Joey calculated how long it'd take to get there and how much gas it would take. They didn't need to stop until they got to Smith, Arkansas. They had plenty of music and grass for the trip. Everyone was excited to be getting out of town for awhile. They weren't even a mile down the road when the first joint was lit and passed around.

Doug howled. "This is going to be an amazing trip, I tell you, something magical is in the air, who can feel it? We're taking this shit to the next level."

"I hear that, brother!" Wayne said. "We should do this more often."

"Well, I'm all for going across the world. It's nice to see everything."

"Exactly."

Everyone agreed. They also agreed, while the joint was being passed around, that they needed music. Nothing quite like good rockin' music to go bombing down the road. They had a whole galaxy of music to choose from. The first selection was Radiohead, Doug's pick. He always loved that band. The others in the van didn't care for the selection, but they told themselves that everyone didn't like the same music. And it would be their turn to choose soon enough. When it got to Wayne, he made them listen to a handful of Bob Dylan tunes. Quinn said that a lot of Dylan's lyrics were great, but his singing needed work.

Playground

"He sounds like one of those damn hillbillies who took his sister in the woods and did the dirty deed with her. When he got done he probably did the same thing to his mama."

They laughed.

They played a few more songs and smoked another joint. Awhile later they pulled into a gas station that wasn't too busy. An older man walked out of the station and waved to them, before getting into his yellow Volkswagen Beetle. Joey and Layla waved back. After some discussion, it was decided Doug would cover gas the first time.

"Do you have my Dinner?" Doug asked Joey.

"I don't know. Ask Wayne about that one, buddy."

"Something tells me he's not going to come through," Doug replied. I mean, he could but I'm doubtful."

"You never know what's around the corner," Joey laughed. "We can see what can be done about that. Don't hold out hope. You have money. Focus on the matter at hand. You don't want to get your mind too fuzzy, do you? We can all plainly see you're already fucked, been like that for a long time."

"But I want you to spend your money, brother. I need mine for what I do."

"Good luck trying to do that. Just worry about the gas for now."

"You're no fun," Doug told him.

"Guess that's the way it is."

"I see how it is."

"Good thing you're not blind."

"Yes, that is good."

The others took their turn at giving Doug the business. They enjoyed each other's company. They were family, a tight circle. They made jabs but in good fun. They couldn't imagine it any other way. Whenever new people would come into the fold they were given a test to see if they would push through, some made it, others didn't. Doug got out of the van and walked inside to pay. While he was inside he bought everyone cigarettes and snacks.

Later down the road, they decided to stop at Loon-A-Lance, a burger place. They were hungry and needed a break from the road. They still had a long way to go. But first, they needed dinner.
Quinn barked. "Burgers, burgers, burgers, old buddy! I can eat a whole fucking dozen. Get a fuck-load of soda. We need all we can get."
"Fuck yeah, dude!" Doug joined. "I'm all about that, sure. Those are my thoughts exactly. Well, we don't want to drink too much, you don't want to be pissing all the time."
Quinn laughed. "You make a good point."
"But you get enough food in you, that'll make for a good sleep, you know?"
"That's another good thing about it."
"Sure is."
As they were waiting Doug looked around at their fellow patrons. Everyone looked bored, soulless people eating tired food. He thought maybe they needed live music to spice up the place.
They ordered, got their food, and sat in a booth. Joey and the others told Layla more stories about Ethan and the adventures they had. She thought he sounded like a fun person to be around. She'd never met him before, but it felt like she'd known him for years. She asked if he had a girlfriend out in California.
"Her name's Emily," Wayne told her. "We met her the last time Heather and I were there. We liked her. I just hope he hadn't run her off with his bullshit. He didn't

say anything about her when we talked last week."
"But that doesn't mean anything," Heather commented.
"I think they'll be together for awhile, if not forever."
"Why do you think that?" Joey asked.
"Just the vibe I got from them. I looked at the two and I saw that sparkle in their eyes, how they looked at each other. I have a feeling before too long we're going to be at their wedding."
Doug gave a hard laugh. "That'll be the day! I mean, I guess it would be cool if it happened but it's not going to. You can't tie someone like Ethan down. That guy was made to hunt, like me. Some can be tamed but not us. We have to have something new. I can't explain it, it's just this thing we have inside."
"That's interesting," Heather said. "You guys think highly of yourselves, huh?"
"That's right."
Heather flipped him the bird.
Layla asked more about Emily and Ethan. She wanted to know what she was getting herself into. She loved Joey and all his friends. When she asked why Quinn and Doug were single they just shrugged it off, saying it was just one of those things, that they were both tired of all the baggage that comes with relationships and didn't want to deal with it anymore, that they just want to have fun now. They continued chatting and carrying on.

14

They decided to take a break after they crossed into Oklahoma. The day was in full force and traffic was everywhere. They found a hotel that looked good. Joey told them they were leaving the next day, they weren't going to stay for good or anything.

The Waterfront Hotel was next to Lake Ridley. The lake had small bridges on either side. People were all around doing things; walking the bridges, swimming, walking the trails, lying along the water's edge, and having lunch on blankets or at one of the tables. Layla mentioned to the guys how lovely the lake was, and she thought it would be nice to take a swim. Joey told her she didn't pack her bikini.

"I don't need my suit to do that," she smiled at him.
"That's some cold stuff," Joey told her.
"Bet you'd enjoy the show, huh?"
"Might be right about that."
"That's what I thought."
"I could see where that'd be fun."
"Yes, it would."

Quinn and Doug were in the back working on another fatty. Joey turned and said they'd smoke themselves silly. Doug laughed, saying he was one to talk. Joey smoked more than the both of them. When they were in high school they used to sell weed to anyone who'd buy. It was easy money for them. The only thing about it they didn't like, they didn't like the guys they had to buy it from. Those guys were a lot older, and they didn't mess around. The guys got to the point where they got tired of selling weed. Even though they made good money the risk of getting busted was always a thing. About eight months after they got out the older guys all got busted. They guys never gave up on Joey and his friends.

Playground

They parked and the driver killed the motor. Heather told Wayne how nice it would be to own a hotel like the one they were at. She told him how lovely it would be to have something next to a big body of water.

"Got that kind of money, babe?" Wayne asked her.

"Don't look at me. If you stick around here awhile you could find someone."

"Don't tempt me," Heather told him. "I'm certain I can find my millionaire around here."

"If you did I'm sure they'd give you back after an hour, after they got a fill of your nonsense."

"You'd be surprised."

"Hell, babe you are going to spend that sort of money you might as well buy a house."

"I was thinking we could make some cash out of it. We could always reinvest it into a house if we wanted."

"That's smart thinking," Wayne said. "I always knew there was a reason I was with you. Got to get it where you can. No one can fault you for that."

Heather gave a smile and tapped the side of her head. "This isn't just a pretty face in front of you."

"I can see that."

"See, aren't you glad you kept me around?"

"I count my lucky stars every day."

She laughed. "You know you love me."

They got their bags and went into the hotel. People were lingering around the lobby, some sat in chairs watching the big flat-screen television. Doug pointed at the television and said the girl on screen looked a lot like the woman who lived in the apartment across from his.

"Really?" Wayne said.

Doug said, "Her name's Candy something... She doesn't have a guy."

"There you go. She was made just for you, buddy. Give it a shot."

"I'm going to have to look into that when we get back. That's interesting. I never knew that about her. Come to think of it, I don't know much about her. I always wondered, you know?"

"Never know until you find out."

"I'd show her a time she'll never forget."

"I'm sure she won't," Wayne muttered. "You're one of a kind, my friend."

"Yeah, thanks for that. Well, with women you can never tell, you know? They are all different. Just when you think you have them figured out, look out because they'll change things on you."

"That's the truth. Just have to take the punches as they come, I guess."

Doug shrugged. "It's always something."

Heather looked at Doug. "You have a lot to learn, buddy."

"That right?" Doug said. "Well, you have a lot to learn. You just don't even know."

"Yeah, whatever you say."

The guy working the front counter greeted them. He introduced himself as Gabe, Gabe Tutor. He was a big man with a little voice. He'd worked ten hours and was exhausted. The last thing he wanted was to have to welcome new guests. He told himself he would be brief and try like hell to make it go fast. There was a bed waiting for him at home, and that was all he could think about. He didn't get much sleep because he got called to replace someone at the last minute. He was a team player and didn't want to leave his boss hanging. He enjoyed doing his job and the extra money was good. He thought about getting beer and frozen pizzas when his shift was over. He was single and never wanted to spend a lot of time preparing meals. He was fine with it. The only time

Playground
he made anything from scratch was when he had people over for a visit, and even then he always made the same things. People never complained to his face. Who was going to bitch about a free meal? After the person left, they probably dragged the meal through the mud, calling it every bad name in the book.

Gabe said, "Welcome to Water Front. Hope you guys are having a lovely day. How may I be of service to you?"

Joey and Wayne told him they needed some rooms.

"You going to pay for our room, man?" Doug looked at Joey.

"Hadn't planned on it," Joey told him. "You have your own money. I'm not your damn mama. Guess you'll have to go begging for cash."

"I'm not going to walk the streets like some homeless fuck. I don't know my way around this place. I'd get beat up."

Quinn said, "If he was he would've already been pushed into oncoming traffic."

"Fuck you," Doug hit Quinn on the arm. "Keep that up, I'll beat your ass. I'll take all your money, retarded bitch. I'll get you, buddy."

"You and who else?"

"Bitch, I don't need any help."

"Huh-uh. You know, having too many delusions isn't good for you, you know? They'll put you in a patted room."

Doug gave him a dismissive wave. "Get out of here with that."

Wayne threw his hand up. "Kids, do you guys have to do this every time we take you out? Don't fight. I'll pay for your room. We'll have to get cages for both of you."

They paid for the rooms, and then Gabe told them they do breakfast in the morning if they were interested. They thank him. Before they walked away Layla commented to Gabe about how the lake looked peaceful.

"Yes, it's nice," Gabe said. "It's been good for us over the years."

"How so?" she asked.

"Selling point," he said. "People like to take walks around it in the mornings, at night, whenever they feel the need. Whole families spend the whole day over there."

"I can see why, it's beautiful."

"Funny how water can do that, am I right?" Gabe chuckled. "I get a joy out of seeing people like the view. That picture speaks volumes."

"Took the words out of my mouth."

Gabe said, "We get all sorts of lovers who want to celebrate whatever. That's what we have to offer to those who visit our great state. But, yes, you can still live here and appreciate it. It's for everyone. We aren't in the business of turning people away. Money makes the world go around, I'm afraid."

"That's good," Wayne told the man. "Sure you guys would hate if someone gave you a bad review for that."

Gabe told them he hoped the group enjoyed their stay as he handed them the keys. He told them it was their mission to make sure every guest had a nice stay.

They gave him a nod and went to their rooms. A little while later Layla talked Joey into going down to the lake. She said it'd be okay if Doug and Quinn came along. Heather and Wayne were already walking around out there. When they got down to the lobby Gabe was standing at the front desk punching keys into his computer. Layla approached him.

"And what can I do for you?" he asked her.

"Nothing," Layla said. "We were just going to check the lake out."

Playground

Gabe shook his head. "What a fine choice."

"Yeah, we don't see stuff like that every day. We'll be gone tomorrow."

"It's nice," he stopped typing. "Are you guys familiar with this area at all?"

"Just passing through," she said. "We're on our way to California. We're going to see a friend of my boyfriend. Should be fun."

"I know a few people who just moved there. Where are you from?"

"Arkansas."

"We may not have much in the area, but the things we have are impressive. There's just one thing we always have to warn people about."

"About what?" she asked.

The others in her party gathered around the counter.

"Well," Gabe sniffed the air. "I don't mean to alarm you but people claim the lake is haunted."

"Haunted?" Layla said. "That sounds interesting."

"That's a whole other story you don't want to hear about. And I don't want to spread an ugly past."

"No, no, no, you aren't getting off that easy. You started to dish," Layla slapped the counter. "If you don't tell I'll let everyone know you're a fraud. Your business will be a memory."

"We wouldn't want that," Gabe said from behind the counter. "Oh, come on, don't do that. This is my livelihood. Not sure how much I should tell you. It tends to give people the creeps. I don't want to run anyone off, it's not the way of the service industry. We want people to stay and enjoy the amenities we have to offer."

"Tell us," Joey said.

The desk clerk nodded to the lake out the window. "There used to be a drive-in there. They got rid of it years ago. Back in the late 70s sometime. Can't recall the year off-hand. You can probably look it up."

"They shouldn't have closed it down," Joey said. "That would've been good for you guys."

"There was a murder one night," Gabe told them. "The guy came up to two people in their car and shot a few times. Killed them both and walked over to some other folks and shot them, too. People who were there didn't know who else was going to be killed. There was a panic, of course. I guess they thought they were next. I don't know what happened out there that night. Have my guesses. People who were there have told their tales, and others still won't talk about it. The whole thing is sad. Something like that, I couldn't imagine what it was like being there."

"Shit," Joey said. "That's quite the story. Never heard about that. Well, I guess it wouldn't be something you'd want to advertise. Red flag for the state."

"And, actually, that night, the drive-in was showing that movie Star Wars, it had just come out that day. I guess it shook things up for awhile. Hell, people were afraid to go out at night. I was a teen at the time, so I'm a little fuzzy about some things. Now, why was the killer picked that night? That, my friends, is the mystery. The cops never found out who it was. Over the years it was rumored that the guy who did the killing was a serial killer, and he was taken down by the Church of Modo guy."

"Who?" Joey asked.

"You know that cult leader guy from the 80s?"

"Harlan Reeves?"

"That's the one," the guy shook his head. "Damn, there were a lot of those clowns around during that time, how can you keep up?"

"You got that right," Joey said.

"Never heard what happened to that freak."

Playground

Joey said, "I host an overnight radio show and his son called the other night."

"Really? A radio show? That's pretty cool. Maybe I can convince you to advertise this place on there."

"Maybe," Joey said. "I'm always looking for new stuff to put on."

"Surprisingly, they never killed him."

As they continued talking Wayne and Heather came back from their walk. Wayne asked what they were talking about. They filled him in.

Wayne said, "That wasn't a good thing at all. I used to work with two people that lived in the compound. They said it took awhile to get back to normal. Sad story."

"That's understandable," Gabe said. "That whole thing had people on edge over there. Hell, people here were worried. They were on the lookout, thinking some of those folks would come by. They never did. I was a door-to-door salesman at the time."

"What did you sell?" Heather asked.

"Cleaning products. I got out of it, though. Wanted something more for myself. Got a job in computers. After I got fired from there I came to work here."

"What did you get fired for?" Joey asked.

"Oh, I was late too many times. They gave me a warning, but I didn't pay attention. It caught up with me. I've gotten better since I've been here. I was someone else in those days, that's for sure."

"That's good."

Gabe went on to tell them that the area where the drive-in stood was haunted by those who were murdered that night. They had all sorts of reports, guests hearing and seeing strange things on the grounds

Layla asked if the hotel had always been there.

The guy gave a nod. "Yes. It was built back in the early 60s. They've done a few remodels since then, but yeah...

Bradley Davenport

I guess the idea was when you and your sweetheart were done watching the movie, it would be too late to drive home. There's a bed here for a small price. You know, you'd have a young couple who would give fake names and stuff. I guess they didn't want people finding out their real names. Their nosy parents can be stopped in their tracks if they ever wondered—nobody wants to deal with that."

"Why'd they tare it down, because of that?" Doug asked.

"Money," Gabe told him. "Attendance started to drop. Time passed and people wanted something else. They didn't want to keep pumping money into it. The hotel never loses business. They've talked about putting a few new things in

but nothing has been settled on. Honestly, I think they should put in an arcade. A few fast-food places would be nice, too. They had a vote a year ago. But the city planners put things on hold. A lack of funds, that's why things haven't started."

Layla asked if they were ever going to continue the matter. The clerk told her he didn't know.

Joey and Wayne wanted to be nice to the man, but they didn't care to learn about a place where they didn't live. They were just being polite. It wasn't like they'd ever be back to the place. What did they care?

Doug asked more questions about the area.

They didn't know why their friend continued asking questions. He kept on and on with the guy. The other people in the group thought Doug was blazed out of his mind. He couldn't be that interested in the stuff, could he?

Quinn looked at Doug. "How much did you smoke, man? You're out there beyond the universe. Why didn't you share it with me? You need to come back to us. Stop

Playground

talking to all those people in your head, man. If the wrong person sees you, they'll lock you up faster than you can blink. You're crazy."

"We all are, aren't we?" Doug smirked.

Joey said, "What did I tell you guys? Before you know it both of you are going to be taken away, thrown in a padded room somewhere."

"They laughed.

The girls told them they were stupid.

After Gabe finished he told them he was going to his house, to his place of peace. They thanked him and trampled outside. After hanging out by the lake for awhile they decided to go back out when it started to get dark, to go ghost hunting. When they got back to the room they smoked a joint and watched TV until they came back down.

15

They went to the edge of the lake and started down the bridge to the other side. The bridge had all fresh wood. High weeds and rocks were at the mouth of the bridge. Nothing was in the weeds that would get them. They were halfway to the other side when Doug lit a joint. Quinn turned to him and said that he'd better share. Doug joked that he would think about it. When Quinn threatened to throw him in the water Doug passed him the joint. A few people were walking from the other way. When the two groups passed each other one of the women from the other group said she needed to call the cops on Doug and his friends.

Doug barked. "When they're out here they can haul you away, too. There needs to be a law about minding your fucking business. This is a free country. Get over it."

"You just need to stop it," she pointed her finger at him, "You're boring."

The woman turned her nose up to him. Doug went on to tell her if she didn't have anything nice to say she shouldn't say anything at all. The woman asked if he had a girlfriend.

"No," Doug said.

The woman said, "That makes sense. No girl with any respect for herself would be caught dead with you."

Doug told her that kind of talk wasn't nice at all, and he told her if she wanted to do the world a favor she should jump into the lake, go to the bottom, and never resurface. She didn't like that sort of talk and told everyone in her company that Doug was nothing more than an evil demon. After some more unfriendly words the woman and the people she was with left. Doug said he was glad she left,

Quinn said, "Maybe she needed to smoke, you think? It

Playground
would calm her ass down."
"See, it can be used for good. It's not as bad as people make it out to be."
"That's the sad story behind it."
"And the people who have the most problems with it have never used it before. It's nothing but a crock of shit. It's all about money."

    Layla and Heather were the only ones who thought there was something to the ghost stories. The others thought the whole thing had been concocted by the people of the town to promote tourism. How many suckers can they get to buy the lie? To profit off of a crime? What kind of person would do such a thing? The guys just knew something had to be at work there. It must have been someone's idea to make up a story like that, like on Scooby Doo when people would give things scary back stories and they had tricks to keep them away from someplace. What was really on the other side of the bridge? Had something been buried there that wasn't supposed to be uncovered? Many thoughts swirled in their minds that evening.
    When you looked beyond the lake to the tree line on the other side, traffic hummed and buzzed down the highway. The sun was fading away with its bright rays piercing as birds were chirping to one another about the events of the day, praising the comfortable weather. Joey turned his head to the right and looked into the water. He was saying how calm the water was when a white ball floated passed. He told himself the ball must've belonged to a kid from one of the families that were around the area. Whoever the kid was, he or she was going to have to jump in the water to get it. Joey wasn't going to do it for them. He didn't want to get his clothes wet.
    "Do you guys think it's haunted?" Doug broke the si-

lence. "Myself, I don't think it is. I think people just want it to be. They see what they want. It's all craziness, I tell you. They smoke their shit, snort whatever-the-fuck, come out here, and look at the stars. They stand around dreaming about what they can't understand. Man, you know how that stuff goes? A little thing, a little of that. Buddy, that's what it's all about. But I don't believe in any of that afterlife shit. It's amazing what goes through people's minds. Too much of that stuff, you have to watch it."

Layla asked him why he didn't believe.

"Not sure," he said. "I've just never believed in any of that stuff. I guess if I see something I'll believe in it. I've never seen anything like that before. I remember hearing once how only certain people are perceptive to things like that."

Layla told him she'd heard that, too.

The others agreed with their friend.

Joey said, "Tell me, ladies, if you saw a ghost what would you do? Would you be scared? Do you think they'd hurt you?"

The two girls said they wouldn't be scared or anything. They would welcome whatever, and try to connect to it with love and understanding.

Heather explained. "If we do that then there won't be any confusion anymore. Our worlds can be as one. You know what I'm saying? Can you grasp that concept? I'd like to see something tonight, yes. That would be neat."

"Neat?" Wayne said. "I don't know if I'd agree with that."

When they got to the other side of the bridge they scattered. Joey took Layla by the hand and they walked to the mouth of the water. They smoked a cigarette as they talked. She told him that on their way back from California they should stay at Water Front again. They'd have

Playground
more time to spend at the lake.
 Joey said, "They have lakes everywhere."
 "But I like this one."
 "Why?"
 She licked her bottom lip. "It's just beautiful. And I like the area."
 "That explains it," Joey said. "We'll see how things go."
 "That's all I ask."
 "Glad you understand," Joey told her. "You know, I'm glad we took this trip together."
 "It's nice," Layla said. "We just need to get away sometime. You just have to stop and reflect on this beautiful planet sometimes. There's beauty all around. It's bigger than you can imagine."
 They looked at each other and kissed. As they were embracing one another she told him she was very glad they finally got together. She told him that she had secretly wanted to be with him for awhile. He told her that was funny because he thought the same. She got a big smile on her face and told him she wanted to grow old together.
 "That would be nice," he told her.
 "But we'll have to figure something out. When we get back to Arkansas I don't want to go back to the radio station. I need a change."
 "What would you want to do?" he asked.
 "Not sure. I'll need to think about that."
 Joey laughed. "Don't you think you should figure that out?"
 "Eventually, yes. But if I didn't go back to work I have enough money to last a few months."
 "How long would that be?"
 "Five or six months."
 "Not bad," he told her. "It's good to have a little some-

thing set aside. You never know when it'll come in handy."

"That's what I was thinking."

"You could take a nice vacation," he told her.

"That'd be nice. I'd want to go in the summer, so I could go to the beach."

"Can't beat that."

"You'd be there, of course."

He told her that would be perfect.

She went on to tell him how she'd like to be a bartender. She learned fast. And with her looks, she'd get great tips. But there would always be those drunk assholes who'd try to do something, touch her, grab her, say dirty things to her. Even though she'd never think of going home with anybody like that she'd have to set personal rules, what types of things she'd put up with and those she wouldn't even tolerate. There were a lot of places she knew of, and she did not doubt that they'd hire her on the spot. Joey told her he'd help in any way he could.

They waited around until it got darker out. The wind picked up and it got cooler. Quinn thought he heard faint cries at one point, but it could've been the wind. The girls started talking to the night, hoping they'd hear voices. They told the air that they knew all about the story, and how lost souls could still be roaming around. It was silent. Distant howls came from somewhere in the night. The highway beside started to die down for the night. They walked around the area more, seeing if they could feel or hear anything out of the ordinary. They got nothing.

Doug laughed. "There's nothing here, guys. It's a scam. They do this to get more business."

"And you know this for a fact?" Layla asked.

Playground

"Well, no. It just sounds like something someone would say to get more people to spend money. You see it every day. They all want to get your money. Look around, the middle of fucking nowhere, they have to get people to stay."

"What about the newspaper he showed us?"

"I won't deny the murder took place. I just don't think any ghosts are lurking around. Too many people are on drugs or something."

Layla said, "I think it'd be interesting if there were. Don't they say the reason they hang around is because they can't let go, can't go anywhere due to what happened to them?"

"I've never heard that. I think you just made that up. You're just saying crazy stuff just to get some sort of reaction from me. I don't believe you," Doug said.

"Think what you want. I heard that long ago. Sounded interesting. That would explain a lot."

Joey said, "But we're still alive. We don't know anything about that. If you see one you should ask."

Quinn said, "I thought I felt something a bit ago. Then again, it could be the weed. Sometimes it has me talking all kinds of stuff. Hell, I don't know what I'm going to do. Things just go like that now and then. We all march to our drummer."

Doug nodded at his friend. "See, I'm not the only one."

Quinn kicked at the ground with his shoe. "My mom claimed she saw a ghost once. Not sure if you'd want to believe that. She said she was drunk at the time."

Doug said, "So, she must see ghosts all the time. Lord knows she's always sloppy drunk," he laughed. "Oh, man, Quinn, you know I'm just fucking around with you. The thing that concerns me, when I'm gone I hope your mom doesn't go crazy. I don't know, going all that time without sex with the king, know what I mean?"

Bradley Davenport

Quinn gave him a strange look. "You have problems. If I were you I'd get someone to help. You need to pay someone to listen to your whole story. Maybe they can figure out what the hell is wrong with you, you think?"

"No way that's happening," Doug got wild eyes. "You get someone walking around in my mind, they'll come running out screaming. They'll need an asylum when they get done. They might never get out. Things have ways of getting twisted, spun around so tight you don't know what way to think."

Wayne shook his head. "I don't quite know what to say about that. That imagination of yours always cooks up outstanding things."

"I'll take that as a compliment," Doug said. "That's big of you to say."

Quinn told all of them it wasn't nice to make fun of someone that wasn't there. He said just to think of what people would say about them if they weren't in the room. Doug told his friend to shut up. Doug flipped him the bird. They shoved one another a little. No matter how much they teased one another they were good friends. If they were in a war they would be on each other's side—and whatever side that would be, it would be the winning side.

They all looked out onto the body of water. Layla said how amazing it was that a simple thing like water can be so mesmerizing.

They waited around a bit more but nothing happened. Doug went on a rant about how he felt robbed, that he wanted that time back. But he wouldn't ever be able to get that time back.

"Oh, just go smoke a joint and stop it," Heather told him. If you bitch about everything in the world, that won't be good for you at all. It'll give you a heart attack. Nobody wants that."

Playground
"Thanks for that."

The next morning everyone in the group met down at the lobby. Everyone helped themselves to eggs, bacon, sausage, and all the coffee they could drink.

When Layla saw Gabe she rushed over and told him about how they didn't see any ghosts.

Gabe said, "Are you implying I lied to you? I don't know what to say. Sorry, you guys couldn't witness that. Maybe tonight? Maybe they didn't like something they heard?"

Joey shook his head and told him they were leaving. They had to hit the road. Joey told the man they still had a lot of miles to go.

Gabe said, "I hope it's not because you didn't see a ghost, is it? You need to stop on your way back, might have better luck then. It could still happen to you."

"Sadly," Layla said, "we won't be back. It was a once-in-a-lifetime thing for us."

"I hate to hear that. If it's just the ghosts, if you want we can have somebody hide in the bushes out there and moan?"

"You're a funny guy. No, that's okay," Layla laughed.

"I see," the man said. "Well, if you change your minds you know where we are."

"Will do," she smiled. "On our way back through we might stop. It'll all depend."

"We will be here."

Doug told the man the next time they come through they better see a ghost out at the lake. If they didn't he was going to sue. Gabe laughed, saying he needed to bring the issue up with the ghost. Why should Gabe or any of the others have to pay?

They piled into the van and went on their way. They

were a few miles down the road before they stopped again. When they were getting gas there was a man telling people a new burger joint around the corner was having their grand opening that day. The guy was a portly man with buzzed hair and a long beard. He told everyone they needed to come over and check it out. The first week they were giving a discount on burger meals.

The crew begged Joey to stay. In the end, they had a discounted meal. All of them said it was pretty good. Doug told him the food was good. When the guy started to thank him Doug said if he wanted his business to stay alive he needed to offer something different, something the other places couldn't offer. The owner said he'd give it some thought.

"You should buy part of the store," Wayne told his friend.

"No, thank you," Doug told him. "I'll have to pass on that one. I already have a job back home. I wouldn't want to deal with this stuff, know what I mean?"

"You could change the industry. Doors open and close all the time. Move out here, get a good spread going on."

"Think if I had big enough land I'd grow weed."

Wayne raised a brow. "You could do that, too. Nobody can tell you how to make a living. If they do they need to be paying something of yours."

Doug said, "You make a good point, my friend. That's why I don't want any of their help. You have people saying what they think you should do, all of that bullshit."

When they were in Nevada they stopped at a place, Cutting Board, for a meal. The place was nice. They needed to get off the road for awhile. Heather and Layla started to discuss how nice it was that they were getting to see some amazing parts of America on their road trip.

Layla said, "It's not every day you get to see so much of the landscape like that."

Playground
"It's sad to me when you talk to someone who has never experienced life outside the state they live in," Heather said. "I just think it's crazy."

"It is," Layla agreed.

Joey was thankful the girl he brought with him was able to get along with his friends. They accept Layla for who she is, and that means a lot to Joey.

They were enjoying the time they had together.

They ordered some fried food. As they were sitting at their table talking, a couple of guys with drinks in their hands approached the table. The guys were friendly and wanted to know if they were in town for the races.

"What races?" Joey asked.

"Dog races," the one man said. "We do them every month."

"We're just passing through. We've been on the road for awhile and we stopped for a bite to eat."

"Oh, I see," the man said. "Well, if you guys were staying I was going to say it would be a good time. And the best part, is you can win big. With me, I do okay. It's all a gamble. I go to the casino after winning a bunch of cash, lose it the more I drink."

Quinn said, "I'd been there before. Hadn't ever bet on dogs, though."

"Oh, man, you need to try it out," the man said. "I can teach you how to do it right. There are a lot of things to consider when dealing with dogs."

"I see."

The two men said they could take them to the track if they wanted.

"Thanks, but we need to get back on the road," Wayne told the man.

"Sure you want to do that?" the man asked. "We always go out and party afterward. We get pretty drunk."

"Maybe on our way back."

Bradley Davenport

Doug asked the man how much they bet. The man looked at him and said if he had to ask he most likely didn't have enough and walked away.

"Don't have to be rude about it," Doug said.

The one guy stopped and looked at him. Doug thought the man was going to cause a scene but he didn't.

16

About noon they pulled into Ethan's apartment complex. It had already been quite an adventure and there was still a lot more to come. They were all weary from the road and were glad to be at their friend's place. It was time to relax for awhile. All the stress and hassle of Arkansas was going to have to wait.

Ethan came out of his front door and gave the van a wave. Joey killed the engine, turned to everyone, and said it was time to have some fun. Everyone got out. The sky was clear and fresh. Joey looked at his friend and gave a big laugh.

"Look who finally made it!" Ethan bellowed. "I was afraid you guys might have gotten lost. Large place out here."

Joey chuckled. "Us? Never. It'll take more than something like California to get me."

"That's what I like to hear."

"You figure with all of us someone is bound to have a clue what the hell's going on."

Doug said, "Look at it, guys, it's a nice day out. It's a great time to be alive. The universe is a wondrous place. If you weren't here you couldn't imagine the depths."

Ethan threw his arms in the air. "Welcome everyone! Make yourselves at home."

Everyone hugged and shook hands.

Joey introduced Ethan to Layla. After some conversation, they made their way inside.

They told Ethan how nice and fresh everything looked. They didn't know why they'd never come out before.

The layout of the apartment was that of a small house; living room, dining room, kitchen, three bedrooms down the back hallway. Everything still looked brand new. The high ceiling and wood floors were just what their friend

Bradley Davenport
wanted. He didn't say the price, but he told them he got a pretty good deal on it. He said it might've had something to do with the fact he was in the movie business. The place swallowed them in the space.

"It's someplace you have here," Joey said.

Ethan said, "It's been a good spot. Nice and relaxing."

"Good, good," Joey said to his friend.

"And it's not too far away from places."

"That's always a plus."

"Yeah, it comes in handy when I have to keep late hours."

"How often is that?" Quinn asked.

Ethan shrugged. "More than I'd like. I'm in the middle of a production right now, and after that, we have two more to do."

"Damn, that's a lot. Well, you have to make that money, right?"

"Of course."

Everyone got a drink. Ethan told them to drink as much as they wanted, he had more than plenty to go around. He told them he had good connections, and that he could get any amount of drugs they wanted.

Doug rolled a joint and passed it around.

They asked where Ethan's girl, Emily, was. She'd gone to the store and would be back shortly. She had to stock up on supplies.

Quinn leaned back on the leather couch. "I take it things are going good for you here, yes? Oh, it looks like it to me."

Ethan nodded. "Things are good. No complaints. I've just been doing my stuff. They keep me pretty busy out here."

"Keeping you out of trouble?" Doug added. "Warn all the ladies, tell them your boy is in town! They'll come running just to gaze upon my glorious face."

Playground

"Of course, man," Ethan told him. "I have to keep that secure. Can't lose this gig. I have to keep bread on the table. Early on I learned when the time to party was. All of that, it's all window dressing. This is a hard business to stay in. It can eat you up and throw you out. You don't want to get lost in the shuffle."

"Didn't think of that," Quinn told his friend. "I just watch the movies when they come out. I don't know anything about that business. I couldn't even begin to think about how those are made."

"And that's fine. I was fortunate all those years ago with Monster Fantastic, but there are a lot that aren't. You'll get someone who'll have success the first time out and then fall off the map. In some cases, they give up, in other cases, people stop returning calls. It's a fucking mystery sometimes, why things happen as they do, who the fuck knows? I don't want anything like that happening to me. I still have stories to tell."

"Can't blame you for that," Joey said. "You need to make sure nobody's at the table who shouldn't be there."

Wayne took a swig of beer. "Oh, brother, if you have any problems like that just kick their asses. I know you can do it. We always have your back if you need it."

"I don't think that'll be an issue, but I'll keep that in mind. Thanks," Ethan said.

Heather added. "You don't want to go to jail, do you?"

"Hadn't planned on it," Ethan said to her.

"Just don't beat the shit out of anyone and that won't happen," Heather said.

"I'm not planning on beating the shit out of anyone, you guys brought that up. Ever heard about people in gangs out here? Shit, they probably are working together."

"Well," Doug said, "if you encounter anyone like that we'll be glad to help you fuck them up. We don't play with that type of shit."

Ethan thanked him but said there would be no need for that type of thing. Ethan got everyone a fresh drink as they laughed more.

A few minutes later Emily came through the door with an armful of groceries. She was a thin blonde with baby-blue eyes. As soon as she came in she told Ethan there were more bags in the car, that if he wanted her to cook anything he needed to help bring the load in. She was so happy to see everyone and gave them all hugs and kisses.

Ethan told her they were coming, but she didn't know quite what to expect. They laughed as they drank and told stories. There was nothing but good vibes everywhere.

The host told his guests it was perfect to grill burgers outside, so that's what they did. They drank and ate like kings and queens. Ethan said he'd take them to the movie set.

"You guys will love it," Ethan told them. "We don't have a title yet. We're thinking over a few names but nothing stuck yet. It's about this guy who discovers his neighbor is hiding from the mob. The neighbor started this whole new life with a new name and everything. When his true identity is found out it turns into this thing of both of them having to hide out from the mob. It's a little dark comedy."

"Sounds interesting," Heather told him.

"Oh, yeah, it's pretty cool," Ethan told her. "The whole process has been unbelievable. Doing this, lets me do things that I would've never gotten a chance to do, you know? I love it. I helped write it. They'd hired a guy to write it but he ended up getting arrested and thrown in jail. The studio bailed him out and they got into a fight. After they took him off of the project they asked if I wanted to finish it. Told them I'd give it a crack. Had to

Playground
start from scratch, and couldn't work around something someone else did. A few weeks later I handed them a finished script. A few weeks after that they brought this one guy in to do rewrites."

"That had to hurt?" Heather said.

"No, not really. As long as I get paid I don't care what they do. They can put it on the shelf and never make it for all I care. I always have things in the works. And in this business that's a big plus."

"That's good. I hope nothing but the best for you," Heather told him.

"I appreciate you saying that."

Wayne said, "Look at the, my little brother doing good. He makes us so proud."

As Ethan told them more about how he spent his days, the guys told themselves they could do the same thing. They could each make a movie and have it be a huge success. What would they have to lose? Anything is worth a shot. You never truly know unless you do it. You only have one life, might as well live it to the fullest and enjoy what you do. Doug asked now that his friend was a rich movie maker if he does cocaine all the time. Ethan just laughed and told him not to believe everything he read in the papers. He went on to tell Doug that even though he made movies it didn't make him rich. True, he was making a lot more money than he had in Arkansas, but he wasn't rich. He told his friend he was rich when they were around.

"The more money I get, the more people swear they want to be my friend. I don't buy it. You have to watch yourself out here."

The next day they went to the movie set. They were all excited about everything they saw, everyone coming and going, everyone rushing around, making calls, talking wildly, and getting things done.

"And it's like this every day?" Joey asked.

"Pretty much," Ethan told him. "All of them want to act like whatever they're doing is much more important than the job they're supposed to be doing. Big ego bullshit, if I can be fair."

"Sounds about right," Joey looked at a group of people chatting away in a circle. They were discussing a movie that was about to go into production. He didn't catch the name of the movie, but he thought it was a little more than rude they were discussing their next project, disrespecting what they were working on. But it was like Ethan said, nobody seems to give a shit about the thing they're working on. It didn't make much sense to Joey. He figured it was none of his business what they did.

Doug hit Ethan's shoulder. "You think you could talk to your agent for me? I need to get into one of these movies. Get some of that fat money."

"I can see what I can do," Ethan told him. "Do you have any credits to your name? You need those."

"I don't have anything like that."

"Sorry, with most agents that's what you need."

"I mean, I have some money if that'll help anything."

"Not that kind of money, my friend."

"How much?"

"They deal in the millions out here."

"Really? Damn. I don't have that figure."

"Told you."

Doug muttered. "Fucking rich people with all their bullshit," he looked at his friend. "You rich like that?"

Ethan shook his head. "Hadn't got that lucky yet. I'm just glad I've made it this long."

"Yeah."

"And if it gets bad I can always move back home."

Doug laughed as he agreed with his friend. Ethan's

Playground
friends wanted him to come back to Arkansas, but they knew he wanted to continue with the business he was in. Ethan was making his dreams come true and that was a good thing. But when you're successful in your dreams there's nothing to search for anymore. You always need something to help propel you forward. The crew walked by the catering table. Some of the guys who were putting out trays of food explained that everything was free. The crew got plenty to eat. The crew asked Ethan who paid for the food.

"The studio does."

"That's insane," Doug said. "Don't they care how much it costs?"

Ethan shrugged. "Hey, they have lots of fucking money, more than you and I will ever have. They don't care how much the shit is. They put millions into projects all the time. When they take a loss, it's something they just roll with. Figure they'll make it up with the next one."

"That's a lot of risk."

"It depends."

"On what?"

"There are lots of things you have to factor in."

"Tell me."

Ethan sighed and told him all about it, all of the boring stuff about making movies, and the money it takes to make it all happen. He told him he thought the budget for his first movie was a lot, and then he found out that they didn't consider that to be big money.

The next day they went to the movie set. It was a big production. Everyone was rushing around, talking wildly to one another about the business at hand. Some of the actors in the movie were approachable, others weren't. One of the actors with slick-back black hair was yelling into his phone while he was smoking a cigarette.

Bradley Davenport

The person on the other end must have been his agent or something because he was saying that he needed to get a bigger project going with a bigger paycheck. And he wanted to get the person on the ball as soon as possible. Another one of the actors walked over to the guy and told him to tell the person on the phone to have sex with his sister and mom.

The first actor got off the phone. "That guy has always been a piece of shit. I should go over there, kick his fucking ass, burn down the house, and steal his car. The first thing I'd do would be go over to his house and fuck his girlfriend for a few hours. She'd love it."

Actor number two. "And she might have a sister, get a little party going on. Get some stuff, get fucked up some."

"He has it coming to him," the guy said. "Karma is a fat bitch."

"Shit, you don't have to tell me how it is. I have so much stuff, it'll make your head spin."

"I don't want to hear your story."

"I'm just saying."

"Please don't."

Ethan introduced the crew to a group of people who were discussing some of the finer points of the movie they were making. They were sucking down their coffee and smoking cigarettes as fast as they could. You'd think they had truckloads of the stuff. They were bragging to one another, telling each other how good they were at doing their job. For the most part, everyone was friendly, everyone except this guy named Drawnsey, Blake Drawnsey. As everyone was friendly, laughing and joking, getting to know each other, Blake was in the corner mad. Someone asked why he was mad. He told the person that he just found out his wife was sleeping around on him. Plus, he thought Ethan's friends were actors who

Playground
were going to take his job.
"You have it all wrong," Ethan told him. "These guys are my friends from back home. They have no interest in acting or taking your job. Just calm down. Do you need some weed?" he looked around. "Can someone please give Blake some weed? If he doesn't get some I think he'll kill someone."
Blake cocked his head to the side and looked at Joey and everyone else. "You guys wouldn't make it doing this."
They asked him why.
Someone walked over to Blake and handed him a joint. The actor thanked the man.
"You gonna share that?" Doug asked him.
Blake said, "Well, a lot of it has to do with who you know. I hate to say it but you guys don't know anyone around here. And I can tell you guys aren't here to meet anyone of any importance."
"That's a pretty rude thing to say," Quinn told him. "We're all friends here, man. Don't know why you have a bug up your ass. Don't blame us you're mad."
Blake took a hit off the joint. "Words hurt sometimes. You need to face facts in this world. It may not be what you want to hear, but it's something you need to hear. Don't get me wrong, I'm not perfect but I know the truth when I hear it. I'm just saving you time. This isn't for you. Think about it, think about whatever it is that makes you happy, it's not this."
Doug gave the man a strange look. "Are you okay? Is there anyone home in there? You're off on some other kind of trip, my friend."
They talked more and Blake shared some of the joint with Doug. After a bit, Blake just walked away.
They thought he was an odd guy.
When everything was ready Ethan told his friends they

could stay for a few of the things being filmed. They just had to be quiet. If they made a noise they'd get kicked out and not invited back; they were sure never to do that. They knew bad behavior would fall back on Ethan and he would have to explain and apologize for whatever they did.

The scene that was being shot was one in which the guy, Nicholas Watts, discovered the true identity of his neighbor, Stan McHenry. Stan, when he lived in New York, went by the name Jimmy Shore. Jimmy started his life of crime at the tender age of sixteen. He started gambling and breaking into houses. He started doing bigger and more dangerous stuff for the mob; hijacking trucks, giving people beatings, and murder. Everything was going well until he found out his people wanted him dead. They thought he had done something he didn't do. But he figured if they were willing to turn on him they weren't friends. He went to the police station and spilled it all. After a few trials and people behind bars, they relocated him. By that time his wife left him, so he was the only one who went. For awhile, he needed to get moved every six months or so. Just when he was ready to settle in a place he'd have to pick up and move again. The mob was getting closer to catching him. And once they caught him he'd meet a painful death for being a snitch. When Jimmy started his new life in the last place they moved him to he told himself he wasn't going to run anymore.

He stayed inside for the most part, not socializing with anyone. Now and then people would see glimpses of him coming and going. They never thought much about it, just figured he liked to keep to himself. One day his neighbor, Nicholas, invited him to dinner at his place. The guy just started dating this girl he wanted to impress. Dinner was great and they all had plenty to eat.

Playground

Since they'd just started dating the girl left, telling them to have a good night, saying if she did stay the night she most likely would have sex with Nicholas, and she wasn't ready for that sort of thing.

After the girl left the two men started to drink heavily. After some conversation, Jimmy let slip who he was. At first, neither man said anything. Jimmy thought Nicholas must've been in shock. After a cigarette, he asked Jimmy if he was in any sort of danger. As it turned out the mob was on his trial again, and they came face-to-face a few days later. Things got interesting.

Anyway, they were filming the scene where the two men were drinking and Jimmy told his secret.

Everything got off to a good start until the guy who played Jimmy, Ray Otio, started flubbing his lines. It took sixty takes just to get a few lines of dialogue right. At one point the director pulled him to the side and asked if he even bothered reading the script. Ray assured everyone he had. When it happened three more times they told everyone to take a break, and they had a chat with Ray. They threatened to fire him if he didn't get it together.

"See, they make it look so easy," Quinn said. "It's one thing seeing it on TV, but it's another to see it in person."

"That's the magic of it all," Wayne told him. "It's always something to see, that's for sure. Makes me rethink things."

"I can see that, sure. Anyone would love to do this for a job."

"Wouldn't you?"

"Better what I have going on."

After they shot another chunk of dialogue they called it quits for the day.

17

They went to a little bar called Frog. They all had good beer and food. They wanted to celebrate their friend's movie. Ethan thanked them but said it was just a job. Someone had to do it, why not Ethan? He told them they didn't have to make a fuss about it.

"But it's a great accomplishment," Wayne told him. "Take the time, enjoy this for awhile. None of us here have made a movie, my brother."

"Speaking of which, how much do they pay you for that, if you don't mind me asking?" Doug said.

"That's not polite conversation," Ethan told him.

"I just have to know if it would be worth it. I might stay out here."

"It all depends on who's paying you. Sometimes it's better than others. If you were to just get into the business I'd suggest always trying to get the studio to pay for it all. Even when you're making a passion project of yours always get someone else to pay. Don't ever pay with your own money. They say you're a sucker if you use your own money. When I first got here I thought using your money was a smart way to go about it, that's what I did with the first one. After I got an agent and started talking about my next movie I realized what I'd done wasn't the proper way to go about it—but I didn't know, that was my first time out. Basically, around here money does the talking. If the money is right anything can happen. They all just want to look good here. They are so scared to think people will look down on them, and stick their noses in the air when they walk by. It's all a bunch of bullshit. The public imagines they think it's so important. They get into this business for the right reasons, but as time goes on things change, some think the popularity contest is everything."

Playground

Doug said, "I don't know about all of that. Sure, making movies would be great but I couldn't deal with all the other stuff."

Emily said, "But all of that aside it's pretty exciting. Don't get me wrong, there are times when it can be a pain but the benefits make it worth the time. And it's better than other things. It keeps a roof over your head and food in the fridge."

"I'm sold," Doug said. "Give me a pen and I'll sign whatever I have to. All that other stuff, I guess I can put up with. I look at the TV and all those magazines, and I'm not so sure about the press. But all those guys writing words, pounding away on their laptops have to eat too, I guess, like everyone else. I don't have anything going on back in Arkansas so I could give it a shot."

"What about us?" Heather asked.

"In terms of a job?" Doug asked.

"You just going to toss us aside like garbage?"

Doug laughed. "Not at all. I wouldn't do that. You guys are my family. I would move you guys out with me."

"Really?" Wayne took a drink of beer. "That's a generous thing. I'd buy the moving truck."

"Sounds good to me."

"Right right, right, we're all just a big family here. It's just a big party, you know?"

"That's the way it should be," Doug exclaimed. "Nothing is more important."

They continued talking over another round of drinks. It felt like old times again. They enjoyed being around Ethan again. Layla asked if the stories she'd heard about Ethan were true.

"It depends on what you heard," he told her. "I have a feeling, not everything you heard is true. I don't know what was said but these guys are known for telling long tales," he nodded toward Doug. "That one, one time he told this girl I was seeing I was cheating on her with the best friend, so there's no telling what he told you."

Layla said, "I imagine that didn't go well?"

"It didn't."

Layla looked at Doug. "And why did you tell her that?"

A shrug. "I was just fucking around. She took it seriously. I tried telling the truth. I told her I love joking around with people. She didn't want to hear it. I guess there was already an issue there or something. I'm not sure what her problem was."

"She already had trust issues," Ethan said. "That sort of joking wasn't in her vocabulary."

"I see," Doug said. "How was I supposed to know? The girl never said anything about it. Just got pissed at me and that was that."

"Yeah, she didn't appreciate that. Looking back on it, I'm glad that happened when it did," Ethan continued. "I'd thought for some time she'd be the one for me."

Doug smiled. "See, it all worked out! Whenever any of you have a problem in your relationships just give me a call, I'll ruin it no questions asked. I need to open a business. I can just see it now, all the cash will come rolling in."

"You think?" Ethan asked.

"Don't see why not. I bet you a lot of people out there want a good reason to get rid of their spouse."

"I don't know about that."

"Well, here I am, I'm ready for duty, sir. It could be a lucrative venture."

Ethan said, "I guess you could try it, I guess. Not sure how that's going to work out for you."

Emily said, "I'm glad it didn't work out. I mean, I hate that happened but it worked in my favor. We might not have ever met if it weren't for that."

"That's true," Ethan looked at Emily. "It worked out

like it needed to. And I've never looked back."

"I bet she was heartbroken?" Layla said. "I mean, I know it was just a joke but I couldn't imagine what ran through her mind."

Quinn asked the two how they met.

"It was at a bar," Ethan told him. "Some of the best things come out of bars, am I right?"

"I know all about that," Quinn laughed. "It's a good mixture of the two, good and bad."

"Anyway," Ethan pressed on. "It was a Friday night. We'd just finished filming for the week on a project we were doing. It had been a long day for everyone and we needed drinks, a lot of them. There were about ten of us. We were all chatting and talking about whatever, good times. At some point, a group of girls came in. We started talking. Emily was one of those girls. When I saw her I was amazed. She was a ray of sunshine in my shattered life. We started talking, just us. I fell in love with her smile and voice. I asked if she wanted to go to dinner sometime. The rest is history. She moved in a few weeks ago."

Doug chimed in. "Next thing you know you guys will be walking down the aisle."

"Could be," Ethan said. "I just have to play my cards right."

Emily said, "You better believe it, buddy. It'll be one of the best days of his life."

Ethan shook his head. "You know it, babe."

"That's what I thought, dear," Emily smiled. "It's a good way to get new kitchen appliances."

Doug told them that was what he needed to do to get a new knife set. Quinn asked who would have him. They liked to tease Doug for being single at the age he was. Doug told his friends to go fuck themselves.

They laughed.

Bradley Davenport

Layla and Heather told the couple how sweet of a story they had. Layla said it was a great thing when a new love walked into your life. You might be at the point where you are ready to give up on love, then, something happens, something you were never expecting. A burst of sunshine creeps over a dark canvas, and you do everything in your power to keep that sunshine. You don't want it to fade into the dark.

As drinks flowed the conversation went to crazy places. Quinn and Doug caught the attention of some waitresses; one of them was a redhead, and the other was a blonde. Doug loved redheads. He told his friend he could have the other girl. Doug approached the redhead but things didn't work out the way he wanted. While they were talking her boyfriend came up to the bar.

"What's all of this about?" the boyfriend asked. "I don't think I've seen you before. You new here, partner?"

"Something like that," Doug told the guy. "We're a few states from home. Arkansas, you ever been there?"

The guy said he hadn't.

Doug said, "You should check it out sometime. Might be good for you. But if you don't mind I'm talking to this girl, I'm sure you understand. I'll get back to you in a bit. I hate to be rude to the girl, I'm sure you can understand?"

The guy asked the girl who Doug was. Doug realized the guy was her boyfriend. Things got heated for a few minutes. Doug told the guy he thought she was just another foxy girl, that if he wanted to he could have her and there was nothing the guy could do about it.

"And this is what I'm thinking," Doug said. "I think the fact that she was even talking to me meant she's not happy with you. I suggest you go out and find another desperate girl, you stupid piece of dog shit."

The guy laughed. "That wasn't very nice, friend.

Playground
Sounds to me like you want your ass beat. yes?"
"Try it."
The guy laughed. "Man, there'd be no contest."

Quinn and Wayne stepped in. At first, it seemed they were going to fight with their hands because some of the boyfriend's friends walked over. They needed to get Doug out of there. After some more harsh words, they went to another place down the street. The whole time Doug was telling his friends how they all could've beat their asses. They agreed.
　Gilbert's was a little place with very few people. There was no loud music to distract from people around you—just what they needed. They ordered some drinks from the bartender and walked over to a table.
　"This is a lot better," Doug told his friends. "Now I'm thinking the guy from the bar might come after me."
　Wayne told his friend not to worry about the guy. "I'm sure that was the booze talking. He just needed to sleep it off. You'll probably show up tomorrow and have a friendly conversation over whiskey."
　Quinn said, "With that said, you're lucky we got over there when we did. That guy, he would've kicked your ass. It's hard to reason with a drunk."
　"You're right about that," Doug said. "I don't have that kind of patience. I know there's been times I've been the one you've tried to reason with," he laughed. "I can't help it, just the way things are. I'm bull-headed when I get drunk, and from what I've seen a lot of people get that way. We can't help it, that's just the way it goes."
　"Is that what it is?" Wayne asked. "That's an interesting way to look at it. I'm glad you know what the problem is."
　"Think he'd let me fuck his girlfriend?" Doug asked. "I'd show her a real good time."

"I don't think so," Ethan said. "You'd have to go behind his back. And I wouldn't recommend it. But if he's cool with it you should. I highly doubt he'd be into it."

Doug said, "It could happen?"

Ethan laughed. "That's funny. I don't think that would work in your favor. But who am I? I'm just trying to look out for you."

"Don't have to worry about me, brother. I can handle myself."

"I'm sure you can, I'm not saying that. I'm just thinking it'd be nice not to have my friend in a fight every time I turn around. You guys are on vacation. Sit back, relax, enjoy yourself. Might be awhile before you get another one. If it were up to me I'd have you guys out here all the time. You guys could get things going for yourselves. I just want you guys to have the same thing I have. We could start our own production company."

The conversation turned to movies. One of their pastimes back in Bancroft was going to the movies. Throughout the years of living in that city in Arkansas, they saw a lot of movies together. There was nothing quite like seeing a movie on a big screen. After the movie, they'd go eat someplace and talk about what they'd seen. When Ethan left Bancroft the movie nights ended.

When Ethan came back to Bancroft the group would resume movie nights. When Ethan returned to California the group would dissipate a little. They were still good friends without Ethan, but it wasn't the same. Ethan was the glue that kept them together. If you were to ask them to describe their friend, most likely they'd tell you he was one of the nicest people they'd ever met. He'd do the best he could to help those who needed it. He was one of a kind.

Ethan had always been an outgoing person. He liked

Playground

most people and they liked him. Doug recalled a night they went to a favorite bar of theirs, as soon as they got in they went to the bartender and Ethan said the next two rounds were on him. Everyone drank for free—two drinks at least. Everyone at the bar thanked him and most of them returned the favor. He did that type of thing all the time. He wanted everyone around him to have a good time. He believed life was a party and you had to enjoy it while you could. You only live once. You never know when your days are going to be up, so you need to enjoy it while you can.

18

Luke Reeves and his friends loved to gamble. When they couldn't make trips to the casino there was always a card game going on at Luke's house. There would be twenty or more people playing depending on the night. Mindy and the other women they hung around with were responsible for making the food. When you've been playing cards for hours on hand you have to keep your energy up somehow.

Some took the games more seriously than others. When someone would get upset at someone due to the game Luke would always tell them to calm down. He didn't want to get too loud. He couldn't afford for the cops to show up and break everything up. They'd more than likely haul everyone away.

It was a Saturday night and eight guys were seated around Luke's big circular table in his kitchen. Other guys were in the kitchen and living room waiting for a turn. As guys were making their bets the room was getting more smoky by the minute. They were all laughing and joking. When Bobby threw his bet into the pot on the table one of the other guys, Patrick Munro, claimed Bobby didn't put in all the money he should have.

"What are you talking about?" Bobby asked the man. "I can show you it, man. I didn't fuck anything up, buddy."

Patrick looked at the money in the middle and still swore Bobby didn't put in enough. The two men started to argue. The man told Bobby he was getting tired of listening to him and pulled out his gun. He told Bobby to say his prayers because he was going to die. He was going to put two in his face. Layne was across from Patrick and told him to lower his weapon. The guy didn't lower the weapon. Patrick didn't notice Luke was standing behind him before it was too late. Luke put him in a choke-

Playground

hold from behind and pulled him onto the floor. Luke pinned the man's head against one of the legs of the table and stomped on his head a few times. Layne and some of the others asked if they needed to take the guy to the basement. They didn't need to get the kitchen messy.

"I need to," Luke said, as he pulled the guy to his feet. "You were wrong, you know that?"

Patrick shook his head. "It'll never happen again."

"You know, you're a stupid motherfucker, you know? When you bring a gun into my house, think about it first. I'm the only one who gets to tell you when to use it. You don't get to decide that when in my house."

"I understand."

"That's good. You were very close to not being able to walk out of here. I'm trying to work on my anger, so I'm trying to be cool about this whole thing."

"Thank you."

"Now, I think you owe someone an apology."

"You serious?"

"Do it or I'll get rid of you right-fucking-now."

Patrick apologized to Bobby. They shook and the game resumed. Luke let out a sigh and made everyone drink. He wasn't in the mood for any of that mess that night.

He already had enough on his plate. He looked at the time displayed on his phone. His father, Harlan Reeves, was due back at his house at any time. Harlan had gone to see a friend of his for a few days. Along some of the terms of his early release from prison, Harlan had to be someplace where others could account for his whereabouts, and he had to stay out of trouble. The smallest infraction could get him sent back behind bars faster than he could blink. Even though Luke didn't care much for cops he didn't want to see his father get into trouble. He looked at his phone again. He didn't quite know when his father was returning but he hoped it was fast. One of the guys earlier was telling him that he heard a lot of police were supposed to be out that night.

Luke asked if anyone wanted anything to eat. A few of them wanted sandwiches.

"Okay," he told them. "You got it, guys. As boss, I need to keep my men happy. Already pay you guys enough, so I can't give you more money. Well, I guess I can but I won't."

"Why?" Bobby asked.

"Bobby, I should've let Pat kill you."

"Hey, that's not nice."

Luke laughed. "It's true, what can I say? But back to what you just asked, if you want a raise you need to show a little more initiative. You give me more of that then we can talk. But you're on the right track, don't worry. It'll happen one day. Just don't get killed."

"I understand."

Awhile later, after they were finished eating, they talked over a few business matters. Anyway, to make a buck was good with all of them. Some of the guys were talking about whether they should take down an armored truck that they knew would be making a money delivery to Bushmeire, one of the local retail stores in the area.

"Sounds good to me," Layne said. "We need to stake it out, make sure there won't be any surprises. I've seen them deliver a few times, but every time the number of guys in the truck changes. Some of the time they've had three, others only two. We need to make sure they have the same amount of people on the day we decide to do this."

Patrick said, "You know how much they bring every day?"

"That's something we need to figure out. It would be nice if we could get some sort of man on the inside."

Playground

Luke said, "Something tells me that won't work out that well. Don't get me wrong, I like the way you're thinking. Maybe we should just go in there, and bust up the manager, you think? I'm just tossing out ideas."

Luke said that as a joke but they liked the idea. They figured if the armored truck thing didn't pan out they could just get the safe. They needed to hit the place later in the night so there wouldn't be as many customers.

"No customers would be perfect," Luke told them. "But yeah, we can look into that. What does anyone else have?"

They went around the table offering ways of getting money, scams they could run on people, and ways to survive in a world of crime. Luke found himself telling his men that all of this, the rough life, could end in an instant. Even if they'd never planned for it to ever happen, in time it would. If you were smart you would stash cash away in different places, so when your day finally came your loved ones would have something to get by on.

Luke, when he was younger, he was headed down a completely different path. But a couple of bad discussions and struggling nights led him down the life of crime. Over time he'd amassed a pretty good livelihood. After all, someone told him years ago that you needed to do the best at whatever you do, good or bad. But Luke never looked at himself or his friends as bad people; they were just a couple of people who were trying to get by, trying to get through the day. Luke liked everyone in his crew. He thought of them as family. He'd do anything for them and he hoped they'd do the same for him. Yes, he had bad days, arguments, and fights with his friends, but everyone had those moments. Truth was, he'd pick his guys over anyone else any day of the week. He trusted all of them and he hoped they trusted him. He wanted to provide the best for his men. He knew they respected him.

"It all sounds good," Luke said. "We just don't want to fuck things up."

The doorbell chimed. The sound echoed through the big house. Whoever it was rang the doorbell two more times. Mindy jumped up from where she was sitting, asking if everyone else in the room was dumb because they didn't answer the door. She shouted something about how she wanted to rip the bell out because it was too loud. She opened the door to find Harlan Reeves on the other side.

"Oh, hey there, we were wondering when you were coming back," she smiled.

"Yes, of course," he told her. "With the long hair and beard, I must look like a homeless man standing out here."

"Oh, don't be crazy."

He chuckled as he passed through the doorway. He walked into the kitchen and greeted everyone. They looked at Harlan as a king of sorts. They had nothing but respect for him. Luke filled his father in on what they were talking about. Harlan reminded them all he couldn't take any part in what they had going on. He had to keep his nose clean or he had a one-way ticket back to a cell.

Harlan looked at the guys around the table, "And I can't do that again. It'll be a cold day in Hell before I go back. Don't know if you guys realize this, but when I went away I lost everything. When I got out it was clear I had to start over. Hell, I didn't know what I was going to do."

"Have any idea now?" Layne asked.

"No clue," the man said. "I had a few thoughts. I don't know... I'll figure it out."

"Damn, I don't want that to happen to me."

Playground

"You're the only one who can decide that. I don't blame you for that at all. Just need to make sure you don't get into a situation like that."

"I don't plan to."

"Well, don't take this the wrong way, as long as you're with these guys you're going down the wrong road."

Patrick told him not to worry, they were smarter than that and wouldn't end up in any prison.

The rest of the night was spent with Harlan telling stories about his old crew and the things they got up to in those days.

The next day Luke and his friends started the task of getting all the information they could about the retail store. Everyone was on board. As they started to watch the store from across the street Layne said that if they had enough balls they should just walk over to the store and just open fire on everything.

Patrick said, "That's the stupidest motherfucking thing I've ever heard. What, you plan on catching a charge afterward? That's what is going to happen fuck-stick."

"Nah, it's not going to be like that at all, brother."

"That so? I'd like to see that."

both men laughed.

All of the guys in Luke's crew always knew what they were getting into. They understood that they could die any day. The way some of them looked at it was this, everyone was going to die one day, they might as well die in an exciting and legendary way.

A few hours after watching the store Layne said he was hungry.

"What do you want to eat?" Patrick asked.

"Oh, I had some leftover chicken earlier. Think I'm in the mood for tacos."

"Tacos?"

"It's pretty hard to mess those up," Layne told him. "I

could go for three or four of them."

"Man, I guess you are hungry."

"Yes, sir. What were you planning on? Is that okay with you?"

"It's fine with me. I'm not too picky."

"Good, let's go."

"Well, wouldn't you want to wait a little longer?"

"No, it'll be okay."

"You sure?"

"What did I just say?"

Patrick shrugged.

Layne started the car and pulled away.

Two miles down the road they stopped at a little place that served tacos. Layne promised Patrick they'd go back to the staking store after they were done eating and made a stop at the gas station.

After they finished eating they stopped at the gas station for cigarettes and sodas. Layne drove the car back to where they were parked before, across from the store. They waited another hour without incident, then, two guys started fighting in the parking lot. For a minute they thought they'd have to involve themselves. The guys got a kick out of the guys yelling at one another. They were two white guys in their mid-twenties. The argument ended with the one guy jumping into his Blue Jeep and pealing out of the parking lot. Layne and Patrick laughed wildly.

"That was some funny shit," Patrick said.

Another hour came and went without anything going on. They started to talk about the fact that they wasted their whole day watching this store.

"Maybe they don't get a money truck today, you think?" Layne suggested.

"We hadn't seen one since we've been here. Could be."

"So, what? We just going to come back every day to

Playground
watch the place, see what happens?"
"That's the idea. That's how it works. You haven't done this much, have you?"
Layne shook his head, "I've done this type of thing two other times. In both cases, it didn't take long."
"I see."
"Yeah, one of the times I was watching the house of this scumbag drug dealer. He'd ripped one of my friends off and needed to pay. I was waiting for the perfect time to hit the guy."
"How long did you have to wait?"
"About eight hours," Layne told him. "Well, eight hours, and then I got tired of waiting. I'd been watching the place, watching cars come and go. But this one car sat there the whole time, and I knew that was the guy's car. No other cars stayed, just that one. Anyway, the guy, Ben, knew who I was so I just walked up to the door. I told him I wanted to buy some shit."
"That's the best way to go about it."
"Anyway, I pulled my gun on him. Just as I was about to pull the trigger a bedroom door opened and a woman and her little son came out. The kid was probably three or four."
"Damn, man, that's a hard one."
"Tell me about it," Layne continued. "I was in a bad situation. I could have just left and that would have been that, or, I had to kill all three of them. I didn't want to do it but I killed them. I used pillows to muffle the sound of the gun. After I made sure they were dead I trashed the place, looking for anything of value I could take. Found a bunch of drugs and two thousand in cash."
"That all you take?"
"I wanted to get the TV but it was too big."
"Yeah, that's the thing about those."
"Thought about going back later that night with a truck.

Glad I didn't because the bodies were discovered that night."

"I take it nobody saw you when you went over there?"

"Not that I know of," Layne said. "If they did I never heard about it."

"Oh, well, hell, you did what you had to, right? Couldn't have the woman turning you in."

"Right about that."

"Get a charge like that, you're gone for a long time. Might as well kiss everything you know goodbye."

As time went on they shared more stories about some of their past crimes. Patrick told Layne a story about how he killed his best friend. The guy was going to the police about drug trafficking and money laundering Patrick was involved with. The information he would have given them would have sent Patrick away for a long time.

Patrick said, "I couldn't have that. Sort of like the thing with you I couldn't do that time. I never plan on going to that place."

"Had you ever been inside?"

"Only been to jail a few times, never prison."

"Good for you," Layne told him. "Hope that never happens."

"It won't if I have anything to say about it."

Layne told Patrick about this girl, Layla, who lived in his apartment complex and how he liked her. He didn't know if she liked him or not, but something told him eventually she'd fall in love. And if she didn't he'd make her. When his friend asked how he planned on getting her to like him he looked at him and said if she didn't want him he'd have to hurt her.

"You can't do that," Patrick told him.

"Why?"

"If you do that, what would be the point?"

"If I can't have her nobody will."

Playground

"Oh, I see," Patrick said. "Well, you need to shit or get off the pot. Someone may come, and sweep her off her feet. Time is ticking away."

"I hope."

Patrick told him he wished him nothing but luck. Layne thank him. Patrick went on to tell his friend that he was never much of the romantic type. Yes, he has had a lot of one-night stands in his time but that was about as far as it went.

"I've never been that guy," Patrick told him. "People I used to hang around, they could put their lives together like that. I could never do it. I mean, I wish my friends well and everything... I don't know. I almost got married before but things didn't work out."

"What happened?"

"She found someone else."

Thirty minutes later, as the sun faded away, a white armored truck pulled up in front of the store. Two officers got out of the truck and went to the back of the truck. One of the guys unlocked the back door. The other guy jumped into the back and came out with a cart. They piled ten bags of money on the cart and then went into the store. A third man stayed behind the wheel. About ten minutes later the two came out, got in the truck, and started down the street.

Layne looked at his friend. "How much do you think were in those bags?"

Patrick shrugged. "Not sure. Maybe ten grand? I guess it depends on how much business they get."

"Would we want to hit the truck every day if it shows up?"

"Have to wait to see what Luke says about it. Before they left Layne wanted to go inside to get some stuff. His friend told him not to take long. Twenty minutes later Layne came back to the car with four bags.

Bradley Davenport

After he got in he lit up a cigarette. "I was thinking about it, if we do decide to steal the money in the store we should take everyone to the money room."

"Like a counting room?"

"Something like that," Layne said. "When I was in there I saw people coming and going from that room. Everyone had a key. It'd be easy."

"Sounds good. Well, we'll see what Luke says about it. Everything is his call."

"Yeah, I don't understand that shit."

"That's just the way it is."

Layne told his friend that he needed to get his crew going. He told Patrick that he could be second in charge.

When they got back to Luke's place they filled him in on everything they found out. Layne also told him about the money room and the keys. The boss said they'd sit on it for awhile, and see what the routine is. When Layne complained Luke told him that he needed to calm down, that he was getting paid no matter what. His job for the next few days was just to sit in a car at a store and take note of everything that happened. If he had a problem with it he could just leave and never return. Of course, if he did that someone would follow him out the door and get shot.

"You're the boss," Layne said. "Whatever you say. I live to serve you."

"Glad to hear you say that," Luke said. "We'll figure out what to do when it's time. Don't worry."

The next day they did their recon work. That night Luke had a big party at his place. Everyone liked his parties. Layne managed to find a woman for his dad to sleep with. Even though Harlan was on probation it didn't stop him from drinking and doing some drugs. He knew that

Playground

he had enough time to get the stuff out of his system before he had to do a drug test.

Everyone loved Harlan. Those people looked at him as a legend. They worshipped him and would do anything he told them to. Someone asked him for his autograph. He didn't understand why it was important for someone to get him to sign something.

Luke and his father were in his office talking and drinking beer. Luke didn't want to let his father down, and at the same time, he didn't want to follow the exact steps Harlan took.

"I have to say, son," Harlan said, "I'm proud of everything you've done here."

"Thanks."

"You're the boss. You've built something that's going to last."

"That's what I hope for," Luke sat at his desk. "I'm making good money. In the event I get killed I want to make sure Mindy is taken care of."

"That's something that every man wants, for his family to be safe. Tell me, have the two of you talked about having kids?"

"I wouldn't want to bring a kid into this."

"Wish I would've thought about that more. I told your mother when you were first born that I wouldn't let my two worlds collide. Sadly, that wasn't the case. Things happened that I didn't plan on."

"Oh, you don't have to go there," Luke took a drink of beer. "I get it. Things happen. I don't blame you for things that went down. Like I used to tell people, at that age I thought it was normal. I didn't know anything else."

"I'm glad to hear you say that, son," Harlan looked at Luke. "I spent a lot of time over the years trying to figure out how I went wrong. Everything just got so fucked up. I know your mom still blamed me for everything. And honestly, she had a point at the time."

"Yeah, but she wasn't completely innocent either."

Harlan said, "I know, I know. There were a lot of drugs going around back then. I'm not saying that was right or anything, I'm just saying that was what was going on."

"I get that. We're all good. Let's just leave the past where it is. I know how much things can get fucked up when drugs are around."

"Glad you understand. Hell, I have a new lease on life, I don't want to make the same mistakes. I'm older than all of that shit from back then. I just want to relax now. When you get my age you'll understand better."

Luke gave a nod. "Yeah, I understand. Well, you can stay here as long as you want. Mindy won't mind you being around."

"That right?"

"Of course, you're family."

"Good thing I have one."

Luke asked about Tiffany. Harlan told him he didn't know. She visited him in prison one day and said she had enough. She needed to get away and start over. She thought the best thing was to not have anything to do with her son. She had fallen out of love with Harlan. The good thing was when she sent Luke that letter, saying she was coming back. But he didn't know when she'd be back.

The two continued talking for some time. Mindy came into the office and asked if they wanted lunch. She made some burgers and they had a nice meal. Harlan told them both he wished they had many more meals.

19

Two nights later in California Joey and his friends went to a place, Dragon Moon, where a friend of Ethan's, Jude Upton, invited them. There was a ten-dollar cover charge at the door. groups of people were coming and going, all wild and loud. Doug took issue with the price, and the bouncer told him they had a band. If he didn't want to pay he could go elsewhere for the evening. They always had to charge when they had a band playing. The guy told Doug they had to pay the band somehow. It wasn't like he was going to go into his wallet and pay them the cash. Doug told the guy it would be okay, that he didn't have to get himself into a fit, that he'd pay that one time. If he wanted to have fun he had to pay. There were no two ways about it.

The bouncer looked at Doug. "You and your friends, you guys better not start any shit. You'll be out of here faster than you can blink. We have a nice place here. You guys from out of town, you need to stick to your place."

"Don't threaten me," Doug told him. "I can make a call to a few people. We know how to get the job done right. Now, I don't feel like making that sort of statement."

"Tell me why I shouldn't fuck you up right now?"

"You need to learn to calm down, man," Doug told him. "Just go with the flow. You have my word everything is going to be cool."

"It better be," the man said. "You guys don't start any trouble in here."

Doug said, "Me? Well, my friend, you don't seem to have much faith in the common decency of humans, do you? If things get crazy you can beat my ass."

"Is that a promise?"

"I never break those."

"Better not, for your sake."

Doug slapped the man on the shoulder. "I knew you were a good guy. See, sometimes you have to test people to see what they're made of."

"That you do."

"You have to show people who's boss sometimes."

The guy laughed at him and said he was a funny guy.

The crew went straight to the bar and got drinks. Everything was loud and busy. There was an energy in the air, an electric snake slithered through the place. People were laughing, drinking, dancing, and having a good time. The loud music crept through souls like a surge in the night. There was something magical about that moment, about that night.

Jude came over and introduced himself to everyone. He told them the private party was in the back room. They followed Jude. There were more booze and people. They were celebrating the birthday of some guy named Steven Barnassbie. Jude didn't even know the guy that well but anyone would use any excuse they could to party. As they got drinks Jude introduced them around. There were so many they wouldn't remember who everyone was the next day. At one point Doug asked Jude if he knew anyone who had some nose candy.

"Of course, of course," Jude told him. "The stuff is a food group around here. Don't know what I'd do without the stuff, you know?"

"That's good news. I've been needing to get my hands on some since we rolled into town. I should've got some before we started the trip."

"How long have you guys been in town for?" Jude asked.

"Two weeks or so."

"Right on, man! There's so much to do, so much to be. You guys have to see all there is. There's so much, so

Playground

fucking much. Have to open your eyes, and taste the sky, my friends. You guys known Ethan long?"

"Since high school," Doug told him.

"That's a long time."

"It is."

"That's good," Jude said. "Friendship is an important thing. In a fucked world like this friends are all we have. They're the life of the party. The good ones stay. You need people like that with you. Now, you can stand there and say it's all about style and it might be true."

Doug asked the man if he was in the movie business.

Jude said, "Most everyone you meet around here is in the business one way or another. It's something that's more accepted around here than anywhere else."

"I get that."

Jude told the two men if they wanted to score some good cocaine they needed to follow him to an apartment above the club. He said he used the apartment from time to time when he was in the area. He sold the big house he had because he didn't need it, traveling all the time like he did. Jude talked to them some about the movies he'd worked on over the years. He was proud of some, others not too much. He told them if they wanted to get into the movie business they needed to remember that everyone thinks their opinion matters more than others. Ultimately, at the end of the day, you have to decide what you think is best. And the other thing is everyone is a critic and they'll do everything in their power to let you know what they think. They might be wrong, might be right, who cares? Everyone is a fast talker.

The apartment wasn't anything lavish by any means; it was just your standard apartment, two bedrooms, one bathroom, dining room, living room, and a kitchen. Jude told the guys to make themselves at home. Jude told them it wasn't the best-looking thing around but it does the job.

"Yeah, boys, it's about that high life. Need to keep up appearances if you're going to live up here, you know?"

Quinn told the man they might move out there, that they might get into the movie business. They liked everything about it they'd seen.

"Hope it works out for you guys," Jude told them.

Three blondes had been waiting on Jude. They said they could hear the party downstairs.

One of them, Maggie, said, "We were going to come down."

"Why didn't you?" Jude asked. "Plenty of fun. We're still going at it hard, baby. We just dropped by for a few. My boys here were interested in purchasing some of that fine nose candy. They want to be somebody."

"How much did you want?" another girl, Sue, asked.

"Just a bag," Doug told her. "Whatever size you have. We aren't too picky."

"That's good. We don't like a lot of demands. We have a simple operation here and that's the way it's going to stay. We don't take requests. We aren't a radio station. If you have a problem with it you can go someplace else. Not going to ruin my day."

"Hey, I have a friend downstairs, he has a talk show on a radio station."

"Good for him. What the fuck that gotta do with anything?"

"Nothing," Doug said. "Just thought I'd throw that into the conversation."

Sue snorted. "You one of those retards, one of those goofy fools? You want to put me on the radio, something like that?"

Quinn laughed. "I like this girl."

She looked at Quinn and brushed her hair from her face.

Playground
"Want to get to know me better, stranger? Go to the bedroom?"
"Maybe later," he told her.
She blew him a kiss.
Quinn chuckled.
The girl told them it would be three hundred for the bag. They tossed her the money. One of them went to a suitcase for the bag.
Before they could leave, one of them, a blonde, Katie, walked over to them and asked if they wanted to stay and have a good time. She explained that they wanted to have some fun.
Jude stepped in. "We don't have time for that now, baby. There are people downstairs waiting for us. I'm sure you can appreciate our time constraint."
She shook her head. "Your friends will still be there later."
Jude looked at Doug. "She has a point. It's up to you."
"How much?" Doug asked her.
"I'm not a fucking hooker!" Katie snapped. "Just thought you looked like someone who wanted to have a good time."
"Well, I do like a good time."
"Oh, baby, you'll want more."
"Maybe."

The next thing Doug knew he was in a room with Katie. She told him everything would be okay and tore off his clothes. He ripped hers off and they went at it like rabbits. They were about to finish when a gun blast rang through everything.
"What the fuck!" Doug shouted.
The world became silent for a minute or two. Doug and the girl quickly threw their clothes on and rushed out of the bedroom. When they got to the living room Sue was

lying naked on the floor with a bullet hole in her head. Jude was over the body with a gun in his hand.

"What the fuck happened?" Doug yelled.

Quinn and the other girl, Maggie, rushed in. They were in shock, not knowing what to say or do. Maggie started yelling at Jude, asking what he did to her friend. She started to cry.

Quinn said, "The fuck did you do?"

Jude just looked at all of them. He was dripping sweat. "I don't know," he said in a calm voice. He turned back to where the body was.

Pounding came from the other side of the front door, and someone in a loud voice asked if everything was okay. The voice was going to break down the door if someone didn't open it. Jude, still over the body, didn't move. He was dazed. He finally looked at everyone around the room.

"Put the gun down," Quinn pleaded with the man.

"It was an accident," Jude muttered. I didn't mean to do anything. I just wanted to show her. You need to believe me."

"Why should I do that?" Quinn asked.

A tear rolled down his face. "I'm a good man."

The front door came crashing down. Two big African American guys came bursting in. They tackled Jude to the ground, breaking the gun from his grip. The guys were bouncers from the club downstairs and they ran up when they heard the gun. They knew the blast didn't come from anywhere in the club. The bouncers told the guys they needed to get rid of the cocaine in the apartment before the cops got there. If the cops found any powder it would be bad for all of them. The two girls each grabbed a suitcase. They told the guys there were a few other big garbage bags with bricks of the stuff in a bedroom closet. After they retrieved all of it Quinn

Playground
asked one of the bouncers what they should do with it all.
"Do you have a car?" one of them asked.
Quinn said, "No, we came with some other people."
"Well, you'll have to put it in their car. Can't leave this shit in the club. Cops, they'll search this whole motherfucker from top to bottom. Can't have it here, no good. Can't flush it either, man. Who is your friend you came here with?"
"Ethan," Quinn said.
The man shook his head. "Something like that would be good. You need to get him, tell him what's going down. If he has a problem tell him to come see me."
"Why me?"
"You guys are here. You know, we have to think fast on this. I'm sure more people are friends with the owner, but time isn't on our side."
Quinn nodded toward Jude. "What about him?"
"Can't say what's going to happen to him."
"I can do that."
The other bouncer looked at Jude. "What the fuck? Tell me what happened."
Jude looked confused.
The guy told him he wasn't in the mood for any of his mess.
"I...I...I...don't...I don't know what happened. I didn't mean anything... It was an accident. I was showing her the gun, didn't check to see if it was loaded."
"You didn't think to check? That should be instinct. Come on, man, how long have you been around guns?"
Jude looked at the floor. "I'm sorry about this. I can't get in trouble. You have to help me."
"And why should I? Why should any of us? Who the motherfuck are you? You own the club so you think people should just do what you say, huh? Sooner or later this

is going to come out. The truth may not help you, you know?"

"It all happened so fast. Please, I'll give you guys anything you want. I can't go to prison."

"Should've thought about that before."

"Don't judge me."

Both bouncers told Jude they should toss him out the window. If he wanted out of trouble they could just kill him, then, he wouldn't have any problems. Jude didn't like that idea.

Two other people raced up from the club. They said a few people had called the cops already. The rest of the crew found their way up to the apartment. Quinn and Doug told Ethan they needed to store the cocaine in his car.

"Why mine?" Ethan asked. "I'm not the only one with a car."

Doug raised his brow. "If you have a better idea I'm all ears. We can just give it back later."

"Any car but mine."

"Oh, come on, just do it. Look at it this way, he goes down for this he won't be in the picture."

"What?"

"Yeah."

"What's your point?" Ethan asked. "You want this club or something? What?"

Doug nodded at one of the suitcases. "We could get a lot of money for this stuff. Think about it."

"What about the girls?"

"Shit, nobody will believe them."

"I don't know about that," Ethan said. "We aren't drug dealers. We'll end up in the cell beside Jude."

Doug said, "Come on, man, we can do this. Just until we get this shit sold."

One of the bouncers walked over to Ethan and ex-

Playground
plained the situation. The guy told Ethan he didn't trust the girls. They were junkies who'd use it themselves or sell it for little money. It was worth more than they knew. The bouncer told them if they got through the situation without fail they'd go out the night after and get drunk.

"I know this isn't the best situation ever, man. But this is what we're forced to do," the one man said.

After some more convincing the guys took the cocaine and fled to Ethan's car. When they got to the car Ethan told his friends somebody would probably be after them for stealing the drugs. He explained that the girls most likely would get some guys to go after them.

"If that happens," Doug said, "then we'll deal with it."

Ethan said, "We've been friends for a long time, we have your back."

Doug said, "It's all about teamwork. If it comes down to it just blame Jude, yeah?"

"Really?"

"Why not? He's already going down for what happened."

The rest of the crew were all on board. They couldn't just stand by and do nothing. All they had was each other. They didn't want to get thrown into a prison cell somewhere. They had a lot more life to live.

Ethan told his friend that Jude probably has friends all over the state that could cause problems for them.

Jude yelled over. "You bet your motherfucking ass you're going to have a problem! You don't know who you're messing with."

Doug told him it was their word against his, and they were just helping him out.

Jude said, "I'm going to beat this. I'm not worried about it."

"I think you should be worried," Ethan told him.

"There's a bunch of witnesses."
"We were all in separate rooms. They don't have proof. This whole thing is fucked. And things started so damn good. I feel sorry for that girl, though. I bet she didn't think that would happen to her, you know?"

The bouncer told them they'd better leave. A few minutes after they left the cops showed up.

It was said Jude went peacefully and didn't put up a fight. When they got him down to the station he confessed, telling the cops he shot her after they got into a little argument. Jude told them they were alone when it happened, that there was no one else there. He didn't want to get anyone else in trouble. He'd already done enough harm for one night. He told the officers he was sorry about what happened.

Ethan explained to his friends that Jude getting in trouble could very well impact him. Jude fronted Ethan's company some of the money for future projects. With Jude being in trouble he might have to pull some of the money for a legal team. Doug suggested they sell the cocaine and put the money in the company.

"I'm sure he's not the only one with money," Doug said. "Jude strikes me as the type of guy who has himself covered."

"You're right about that," Ethan told them. "He's been in the business a lot longer than I have. His movies have always gotten a warm welcome."

Doug said, "Don't get me wrong, he seemed like a good guy. It'd be nice to party with him again."

"Oh?" Ethan said. "Well, we'll just have to see about that. Who knows what the future holds?"

As it turned out Jude did have money for good lawyers. He made bail. He went to Ethan's place and got his cocaine back. He let them keep one of the bags and told

Playground
them everyone should always have access to candy. "We all need it," Jude told them. "Don't know where I'd be without it. And I have to thank you for what you did. A lot of people, they'd just sell the shit. Truth is, there was no way I could've trusted those women. There were a few things from before that knocked them off the list of people I trust. Those girls are just a bunch of whores. They're no good. I can make a call and get how many I want at any time."

Doug said, "Sounds like a good deal to me. When you get tired of them, call and get some more. Don't see a problem with that."

Jude sighed. "If that was all it was. You were there and saw those three girls. They always have some type of drama going on."

"Yeah, I can see where that can be a problem."

The girls in the room objected to what the two men were talking about. Heather started to tell them about how mean and disrespectful they were being. Jude apologized but said he wasn't talking about them.

Doug asked Jude if he wanted to stay and smoke a joint. He told Doug he'd have to pass, that there were a few things he needed to tend to before he went home for the night.

Before he left he told them about another party. They told him they'd be there. He assured them he wouldn't be getting arrested at that one.

"That's good," Quinn said. "You don't get that kind of pass a lot in this life."

"Thanks for everything," Jude said. "That had me freaked-the-fuck-out. That was a good wake-up call. I'm sorry that happened to that poor girl but shit happens sometimes."

Quinn asked if the charges disappeared.

"We'll see," Jude told him. "I have a pretty good feeling

they will. They were last time."

"Last time?"

"About two years ago at this party. We were all drinking and things got a little out of control. This girl and I got into an argument. She told some cops I assaulted her and that was it for me. They put me behind bars faster than I could blink. Was in there a few days before they turned me loose. We gave her some money and went our separate ways."

"Was it true?" Quinn asked.

"Hell, I was so drunk I'm not sure if it happened or not. Some friends told me she'd only said that to get a big payday. I just wanted to move on."

"I see."

20

They went to the other party Jude had. They had to have it at a different club than before. Someone started a fire and burnt the other one down. It turned into this whole thing. No one knew for sure who started the fire. There were a few names thrown around like pennies in a lake, but no one knew for sure; it was a mystery.

They got to the place a little after midnight. Everyone was drinking, laughing, just having a good time, escaping the day, and finding joy under neon lights and loud music.

Someone came over to where the crew was, introduced himself as Rock Sid, and said he was going to buy everyone three rounds. They thanked him and asked why. He just told them that was what you did at parties. He asked if they'd put in a good word about him to Ethan.

Joey shrugged. "I guess."

It seemed Rock wanted to be in this movie Ethan was going to be a part of, a movie that was supposed to start its pre-production after Ethan's current movie was finished being shot.

Ethan came over and shook hands with the guy. Rock asked about the movie.

Ethan said, "If it was just up to me I'd have you in it like that before you knew what happened. But there are a few other things to take into consideration with this one. You have to get in good with the suits."

"I can see that," Rock said. "It just sucks that's what goes on in this business. I've been doing this for a little more than a decade, I should be able to get into any project I want."

"I know."

"And all those fools down at the studio know that. Think I should bring my lawyers in on this?"

Ethan shook his head. "I wouldn't go that far."
"Well, I feel like I need to do something."
"Like what?"
"I need to go up there and beat some ass."
"That's all you need, to get thrown in jail. It's not worth it. We'll hopefully get it on the next one."
"You think?"
They talked about it some more. Rock asked Ethan about Jude, and if what he heard was true.
"I wasn't in the room when it happened," Ethan said. "Can't say what happened."
"But he killed the girl, right?"
"That would be a safe bet. But I'm not one to spread rumors. There were a few others in the apartment but they didn't see what went on."
"That's a damn shame."
"What are you going to do? It's a crazy life out here."
"Tell me about it," Rock said. "I hear about dark stuff like that going on all the time. They all think they're entitled."
"That's the way it's always been."
"Yeah."
They looked across the room at Jude, as he was greeting and talking to people. He looked happy. Rock said it shouldn't have been that way, that they shouldn't have let him out. Rock knew a few things about Jude, and they weren't good. But if you have enough money you can get yourself out of any trouble. He told Ethan about a time he went over to Jude/s place for lunch to talk about a movie script. While at the house, Rock witnessed him verbally abuse his help. He even went so far as to threaten the girl he was dating at the time. He told her if she didn't mind her own business and get out of their conversation she'd be very sorry. He had a gun and bullet with her name written all over them.

Playground

"Damn," Ethan said. "That's fucking crazy."
"Yeah, as soon as I could I got out of there. I didn't want him to turn on me. As it turned out I did get that movie."
"Well, that was good."

Everyone was drinking and having a good time, not a thought of tomorrow anywhere. They just wanted to be there in the moment. Who knew how many parties were in the future? Some thought the host was on his way out, to spend the rest of his days in captivity, to spend it in a steel cage. Ethan and Joey overheard a few people discussing whether or not Jude pulled the trigger, ending that poor woman's life.
One of the men said, "We all know she was nothing but a whore, but that's no reason to kill someone."
"Of course," another said. "Those girls, there's a few of them, they were never good news. If I had to guess I'd say that she was running her mouth about something, said the wrong thing, pissed him off."
"I'm afraid we'll never find out," another man said. "The truth might come out in the papers, who knows?"
A little woman who wore too much makeup said, "She was always nice to me. I don't like to put labels on people, but I always wondered how she made her money. I thought it'd be rude if I just came out and asked. I remember this one time, she told me if I wanted to make extra money come see her. At the time I just thought she wanted to start a business. Well, I guess she was in a business, just not something I wanted to be a part of."
They continued talking about it.
Joey asked Ethan why they were going crazy over Jude. Despite what people might have thought about Jude he was regarded as being an important person in the movie industry. Joey thought it was crazy they'd give so much

praise to just one person. He told Ethan they'd have to get another guy in Jude's position if things went sideways for him.

"I'm not sure," Ethan told his friend. "It's just one of those things, people around here kissing each other's asses. It's just a popularity contest out here."

"What about you?"

"I've had to play their stupid games a few times, yeah. They make it so that's the only way."

Joey told his friend that was the reason he wouldn't make it in the business. But Ethan reminded him about the money and the nice things he could buy with money.

"Everyone likes that paper," Joey said. "And you have to make a lot of it to stay out here, cost of living and whatnot. You have to be on top of things."

"That you do, my friend. It's not like that back home."

Joey laughed. "You got that right. It's just another mess over there."

As people trickled away from the party the crew congregated at the bar for one last drink. Jude walked over to them with a girl on each arm. He asked what they wanted to do once the place closed. Half of them had the idea of continuing to drink someplace else, the other half voted they go to a place to get food. It didn't take long to convince those who still wanted to drink that they needed something to eat. They all had their share of booze and they needed to relax. They found an all-night diner about three blocks away. They ate and told many tales, as the dark sky faded to blue.

Filming wrapped on the movie Ethan had been working on. When he told the crew they were all invited to the wrap party they got excited. Doug asked if other actors and directors were going to be there, or if it just was going to be the ones who worked on the movie.

Playground
"Typically, yes, just the people who worked on the movie," Ethan told him. "But anyone could drop by. Why? You want to try to break into this business?"

"Think I have a chance?"

"Anyone does. You just have to believe in yourself."

"I don't need validation from anyone."

"That's a good start. Part of it is not giving a fuck what people think. Let them think what they want. Fuck them. You aren't living for what they think, you know?"

Doug nodded. "I pick up every word you're saying, every syllable comes down like slicing rain. I dig it all. It's something I've been thinking about for awhile."

Ethan chuckled. "In a lot of cases, the movie doesn't have to even be good. I mean, hell, just look at some of the movies I've been involved with. I came close to losing future deals because of it. Now, it all wasn't my fault but I caught a big part of the blame. The higher you get in the industry, it comes down to you and a bunch of talking heads. Everything is a fucking negotiation. They just need to be made to think you haven't screwed them over."

"They get screwed over a lot?" Doug asked.

"I wouldn't quite go that far. It happens more than it should."

"That's gotta suck, no?"

"Well, yeah, it does. All that fuss over a movie. In the big picture of things this isn't much. You have those who think it's everything, living or dying in the papers. It's all bullshit. They just love bragging to each other. From the outside looking in it's just entertainment. With certain people around here it's just business. There isn't a creative bone in their body."

"I see," Doug said. "So, you think it's for me?"

"It's a good way to make money, sure. You should go for it," Ethan lit a cigarette from his pack. "You have any good ideas?"

"A few."

"That's all you need."

Doug hadn't thought about that part. He just saw the money and told himself that was what he needed. "I had an idea or two, nothing solid. crime movies, those are my favorite. Guess if I'm going to make a movie it would be in that genre."

"There's a lot of good movies there," Ethan exhaled a cloud of smoke. "You'd want to put a unique spin on it."

"I see," Doug lit a cigarette of his own. "Yeah, I'd like to do something nobody has ever done before. Have to plant a flag."

Ethan said, "If you want I can talk to this guy I know about it. He'd be able to help you with funding and things."

"What's the guy's name?" Doug asked.

"I've worked with him a few times. He's a great guy. He's had me over to his house before, met his family, had dinner and everything. His name is Jeff Atona."

"That'd be great."

Ethan made the call to Jeff. After explaining the situation Jeff told him he couldn't work with Doug for another few months. He had a lot on his plate and couldn't spare any time. Ethan thought Doug would be pissed when he told him, but he wasn't. The way Doug looked at it, nothing was lost. He told himself that it was the universe telling him it wasn't the right time. He didn't have the kind of money he'd need to make a movie, anyway. He knew he'd never get back from a studio until he had a little experience.

21

They went to another club, Dizzy Way, for the wrap party. Emily told all of them she knew the owner, Matt Zane, and everything was free.

"We let him know about two weeks ago we were going to have the party here. We told him we'd pay, but he insisted that he'd pay for it all," she said.

"That was pretty nice of him," Joey told her. "You sure he won't mind us being here?"

"He's fine with it. He has a reputation for being a generous person."

"That's a good way to be."

"The best."

Layla said, "Most of the people around this town seem to be nice."

"Yeah," Emily said. "From the outside, it looks good but some of these people just want something."

"That's a little shady."

"Yes, it is. I don't understand it. That's just how things go here."

"Interesting."

Matt came from the back of the club and introduced himself to everyone. He told them to have fun and drink all they wanted, but he didn't want any fights. He told them if anyone got into a fight he would be forced to kick them out at press charges. He had a reputation to uphold. He didn't want to ever give anyone the wrong impression of him.

Doug said, "We wouldn't do anything like that around here. Don't want to fuck up what you have going on. We aren't like that."

"I appreciate that," Matt gave a big smile. "A lot of important people in the industry come here. I have to make sure all of them are kept happy. I have my heart and soul in this place."

They understood.

"That's good," Matt continued. "I want everyone to have fun, just don't spoil it for others, you know? One of the many missions I have for this place is to have repeat customers. I mean, I first got into this business on a whim. A friend of mine said it'd be a good idea. We opened the place and he bailed, leaving me in the lurch. Heard from him a month later. He told me I can go fuck myself and said I could have the whole club. He moved to New York and got killed at a bar one night. With all of that said, let's have a great night tonight."

They stood and talked for awhile. They asked how Matt got into the nightclub business. Twenty minutes later after Matt finished explaining why and how he got into the industry Doug got a bored look on his face. He didn't care for the story. After Matt left Doug told the others he bet when most people hear that story for a second time they go running.

"He must get that from you," Heather chuckled.

"You're a dumbass!"

"Get the fuck out of here with that," Doug started over to the bar. "When are you going back to Arkansas?"

"I'm afraid you're stuck with me for good," Heather smiled. "I'm your shadow."

"Oh, man, I don't need any of that. Just don't write a report on it."

"Hadn't planned on it."

"Good to know."

The rest of them took a stool and the bar and got a drink. Wayne held up his glass and toasted his brother, then, he gave a speech about how proud he was.

Wayne said, "Ethan is great at what he does because his heart is in it. You're an inspiration to us all, my brother. We all wish we could reach the success you have. We all

love you, man. You should be proud of yourself."
Everyone else told Ethan what a fine job he had done. It was a night full of good drinks and great friends. The conversation that night went to some ridiculous places, as they often did with that crew.

Layla liked how the girls and everyone else had been so warm and inviting. She was a little intimidated by everyone at first, being the new one to the group. But seeing how close everyone was she became comfortable. She told Emily that when she and Ethan came to Arkansas she was going to have to cook for them, any dish they wanted. She loved to cook. Heather told Emily that Layla knew what she was talking about.

"Sounds like I'm in for a real treat," Emily told them. "I need to cook more. I used to all the time but got a little tired of it. Ethan does a lot of the cooking. I was surprised the first time he invited me to his place, and told me he was going to cook. We had chicken, mashed potatoes, and mac n' cheese; it was so good."

"Sounds good," Heather told her. "I guess that's something he picked up when he moved away."

Ethan said, "No, no, no, I cooked before I left. I'll admit it increased when I moved out here."

"Oh, I see."

"You do what you need to."

They laughed.

Quinn told Doug. "Think you can get some action going?"

"Here?" Doug asked. "You know it, buddy. I'd be a fool not to. You only live once. You want to make a contest out of it?"

Quinn waved away the thought. "Not tonight. Maybe tomorrow. Can't have all the joy at once. Need my rest."

Doug laughed. "You're talking like you're an old man."

Bradley Davenport

"I'm not fresh out of the egg."

"You aren't old and crippled. You're still young. You know, you can always teach those young girls a thing or two."

"That's true."

"That's the way to look at it," Doug said. "You know, all of these women out here want us to look at them in a good light. They know it's all a game. They like to see how things play out."

Quinn looked out on the dance floor. Some people had a partner they were dancing with, others were scattered around talking amongst themselves.

Doug told his friend to pick out a girl, any girl. He just wanted his friend to have a good time. Doug was always looking out for his friends. He knew they always did the same for him. He knew how priceless friendship was, and that it could vanish if not nurtured properly.

"Girls are fun," Quinn stood from where he was sitting. "They remind us that the world is still beautiful."

"That's what the story is all about, buddy."

"Of course."

"We have to make sure they know how we feel."

"We do."

Doug took a drink of beer as his friend went over to a lovely girl with pale white skin and black hair. She was with two other girls. Quinn introduced himself to her. Her name was Janet White. She had a date but he never showed. Janet thought it was her like there was something wrong with her and he didn't want to tell her the truth. It turned out the guy got arrested on the way to the club. He got pulled over for a little traffic violation. When they were getting all of his information he got loud and tried to fight the cop. Backup was called and things didn't go well for him.

Quinn took the woman by the hand and started dancing.

Playground
She moved well on the dance floor. After two songs Quinn took her up to the bar for some drinks.

A girl came over to where Doug was sitting. She had wavy blonde hair, blood-red lips, and a great smile. Her blue eyes looked as though they were made from a million seas. She wore a soft blue blouse with a black mini skirt and stockings. She told him her name was Pinky and asked if she could sit. He welcomed the company.

"It's a good night, isn't it?" he asked.

"I guess," she said. "Just like any other night. Nothing different about it."

"We just met, that's new," he lit a cigarette. "It's good to stop now and then and meet new people along the journey of our lives. It's all about the journey."

She looked at him. "You're right about that shit. Never know what's going to happen."

"So, tell me, are you here alone?" he blew smoke across the table.

"A few friends of mine were going to another place, and asked if I wanted to join but I didn't go. I had a business meeting earlier with a few people here but they left."

"Here?" he asked.

"Me and five others."

"I hope things went well."

"They did."

"I'm sure that was a load off the shoulders."

She smiled. "It was, you have no idea."

"That makes it worth doing."

"Can't argue with you there."

He wondered what kind of business has a meeting at a nightclub. By the look of her, he didn't think she had an office job. He didn't want to ask for fear of upsetting her. After they got a drink he forgot all about it. They talked and drank. He offered her a cigarette but she had her own. As she put one to her lips he was there to light it.

"Thanks," she told him.

"I'm a gentleman like that."

She laughed. "Do you tell all the girls that?"

"Just the pretty ones."

"Oh, you don't have to say anything like that. I know you don't mean that, honey."

"How do you know what I mean? I'm being honest with you."

"That so?"

"You have my word."

She told him she'd give it a shot and trust him. It wasn't every day someone came along and gave her a compliment like that. She was used to guys telling her what they thought she wanted to hear to get sex. She kept telling herself how she needed to change that about her life, about how she conducted herself. But she had a good feeling about Doug. She had a good feeling. She wanted to get to know him.

"What about you?" Pinky asked. "You here by yourself?"

"A few friends of mine are around here."

"I see," she shook her head. "It's a good night to enjoy the club. You never know who you'll meet, that's why I like these places. I've found people change depending on the environment they're in. In a place like this, for instance, people are more relaxed. They get a few drinks in them, start grooving to the music, and forget all about the world outside that door. Their everyday problems vanish in a glass of liquor or speaker. People just need to shut-the-fuck-up and have a good time. I'm not the smartest person in the world or anything, but I know when someone has a good thing going. It's all a surprise, just waiting for someone to see it."

Playground
Doug smiled at her. "Never thought that much about it. But, yeah, I like everything you just said."
"I've been coming to this place for a few years. I like to see people come and go. The real annoying ones, I'm glad to see them go. A few guys have been banned because of me."
"Really? No shit? I knew I saw trouble in you."
"Well, those were my good days."
"Impressive."
She explained that she had been involved with a few guys over the years which made it tough sometimes for her to be seen around the place. They all used her and tossed her aside like garbage. She was better than that. She was going to make something of herself. She wanted more out of everything. When Doug asked what she wanted to do with her life she didn't know. He told her there was still time for her to figure it all out. She told her it wasn't healthy to plan every single moment out, doing that just drives someone crazy. You have to allow yourself to stop and look around now and then, plus, if things didn't work out the way you wanted it would save you from being disappointed.
"Let's go someplace else, would you like that?" she brushed hair from her eyes. "It's the same song in here tonight. A bunch of the same crowd, all trying to drink their problems away. You know what? It never works no matter how much they drink. Yes, they can say it helps all they want but it's a bunch of shit."
"That's what I hear."
"Your hearing must be good because it's true."
"That's funny," he told her. "Both of my parents were bad drunks. They broke up when I was a kid."
"That's too bad."
"It was a long time ago. I've had time to adjust."
"Good for you," she told him. "So, tell me, how many

sexy girls have you seen tonight?"

"Where?" Doug asked. "Well, this is my first time here but I can tell you it's not a boring night. You're the only sexy one I see here."

"Oh, come one. You don't mean it."

"I do."

"Why do you say that?" She took a drink. "Don't get me wrong or anything, I just don't get compliments like that."

"I understand," he told her. "That's a shame. You need to have people tell you that all the time."

"Thank you. You're sweet."

"That's just the truth. I'm not one for telling lies."

"Great to know," she said. "That's a big plus in my book."

22

Doug nodded to Ethan, sitting on a stool at the bar talking with a few people. "That guy right there, Ethan Bursott, he's celebrating finishing a movie today. I can't just leave the party."
"Why are you sitting here?" she asked. "Why aren't you sitting with your friend?"
"I was about to go back over," he told her. "I just needed to take a break from all of that for a bit."
Pinky said, "You can always come back inside."
"Where are we going?"
"Just come with me."
"Where?" he asked.
"It's a surprise."
"I like those."
"Well, let's go, buddy. I don't bite."
He looked at her. "Let's boogie, baby!"
They got up and walked to the door. The bouncer told them if they leave they'd have to pay another cover if they wanted back in. The bouncer grunted at her. She gave the man a dirty look and they walked out the door. Doug asked himself what that exchange was all about. He figured they must know one another. He told himself that she must have had an affair with the guy at some point. He was going to ask but didn't. He figured her past wasn't any of his business. And he'd be right, it wasn't any of his business. When they got more comfortable with one another they'd discuss all of that stuff.
When the two got outside they turned down the alley beside the club. He asked where they were going.
She pushed him against the side of the building, pressed herself against him, and whispered. "Do you want me?" her breath floated on his shirt.
"Of course," he told her.

"Two hundred bucks and I'm all yours."
Her breasts were against his chest.
"Are you a hooker?" Doug asked.
"I'm a businesswoman."
"Is that business being a hooker?"
"You're a funny guy."
He gently pushed her away. "I don't pay for sex. Never have, never will."
"There's a first for everything, baby," she told him.
"I'm good at what I do."
"Good at sex? That's not a hard thing to do."
"What are you waiting for?" she raised her brow at him.
"I want to get with you. Do you not want to get inside me?"
He said that he didn't pay for it no matter the case.
"Oh, come on, baby," she continued. "I'll do whatever you want. I don't care."
He told her to back up.
She didn't.
He pushed her. She fell to the ground. A man from across the street jumped out of his car and raced to the both of them. The guy was in a long black jacket and black hat.
Doug looked at the guy.
"The fuck you doing?" the man hit Doug on the side of the face. "You stupid motherfucker!"
"What the fuck?" Doug hit the man back. "Why'd you do that?"
The man shook his head fast and pointed at the girl. "That's my bitch! She's one of my finest pieces of pussy," he helped her to her feet. "Show the woman some respect."
"She started it," Doug said.
The man said, "You have a problem with her, you have a problem with me. I can't have people fucking with my

Playground
shit out here."
She looked at Doug. "You could've just walked away. Go fuck yourself," she turned to the man. "The bullshit I have to put up with. You said it was going to be different with you. You're nothing but a liar. I don't know why I even fuck with you."
The man held his hands up. "Hey, now, I can't control what everyone does. Baby, I always have places to be. I have to treat all my hoes right. Now, you saw I was parked across the street, didn't you? Shouldn't that tell you something? Why's everything my fault, girl? You need to stop blaming others all the time."
She frowned. "I can't even depend on you."
The man looked at Doug. "Allow me to apologize, I'm Jagged," he extended his hand to Doug.
They shook.
"Jagged?" Doug said. "What kind of name is that?"
"The streets gave it to me."
"The streets?"
"I've been running all types of things for years. Started dealing with women a couple of years ago, after I saw how good a friend of mine was doing at it. Shit, I ended up stealing some of his bitches. Hell, this one here, I fucked her three days straight before I told her I'd be her sponsor. And let me tell you, she's into all that freaky shit. She would let me fuck her in the ass while we watched TV. She'll let you unload all over her. She's a freak."
"That so?" Doug shook his head.
Jagged nodded. "Oh, yeah, she doesn't care a bit."
"You have to earn that money somehow," Doug said to her. "I mean, you can do whatever you wanted but chose this? Should be proud of yourself."
"Fuck you, asshole," she said.
The man told Doug he had to give him a warning. Be-

fore he could say anything Jagged punched him in the belly. Doug fell to the ground, clutching himself. He asked Jagged why he did that.

"I had to teach you a lesson. I believe there's a lesson that can be learned in everything, good and bad."

Doug got to his feet. "Well, there's better ways to go about it."

"Maybe, but I had to put the hurt into you. I need to make you learn."

"Thanks."

"You can't be out here saying those things to females. Would you like it if someone did that sort of thing to you?"

"Can't say as I would."

"With that being said, I believe in giving good customer service. Since things went down the way they did you get one on me. Free of charge," he turned to the girl. "You're going to fuck him right here."

"No!" she shouted. "I'm not going to do it."

"Yes, you are!" he demanded.

"No."

Jagged pulled a gun from his jacket, and pointed it at her. "Bitch, I'll blow your motherfucking head clear off if you don't."

She got a terrified look on her face. "I don't want to die."

"Well, if you don't want your brains splattered all over I suggest you get to fucking."

Doug looked at the man and asked if he was sure. The man said he didn't care. If he had to he'd pull the trigger and end her life. He'd done it before, he could do it again. He said he could always get another woman.

Doug even told him he'd pay what she would've made. The pimp told him it was okay, that she had told him already she was going to have sex with him. Why should anything change?

She ripped off her clothes and did the same to Doug. After they had sex she started to cry. Jagged told her not to cry and smashed the gun in her face.

The man gave Doug his card. "Anytime you want a girl, just put a call in. I have ten girls."

"Really?"

"And I'm always seeking out more."

"I see," Doug got a surprised look on his face. "I need to get that type of thing going."

"I'm partnering with a friend of mine. He has a few girls. We plan on opening a club soon with a motel on the side."

Doug said, "All of that sounds good. Where's it going to be?"

"A few blocks away. We got a pretty good deal on the place. It's a good building. When we get up and running you need to check it out."

"I'll have to do that."

The pimp let out a laugh. "Hopefully when you come down there I won't have to punch you in the belly, you know? That's one thing I don't like doing. But sometimes you need to get your point across, you dig?"

Doug shook his head.

"Good, good. There have been some I couldn't reason with. Those guys, you can't talk to them. I guess you can, but you'd have to go to the graveyard."

"Doesn't sound like a good deal for them."

Jagged turned to Pinky and told her they needed to get going. He told her how sorry he was for everything he did, but it was something that needed to be done. He told her they needed to go before the cops came by. They'd both been busted a few times before and couldn't afford to get another charge. Jagged told Doug that no matter what they did the cops could never stop the business they were in. As soon as they shut someone down, a few others were there to take their place.

"No one has a right to tell anyone how to make that paper," he told Doug. "Hell, if they want to give us some of their money I'd be okay with that,"

"That's a good point."

The pimp told him that the good thing about his business was the fact that women would always come along. There were always ones out there who wanted to get their hands on some of that money.

Pinky said, "What else is going to happen tonight? Man, it's a strange thing."

The pimp told her she was one of the crazy ones.

She told him to eat a pile of shit and shut up.

Awhile later Quinn and the others walked out the door, saying they wanted to go check out another place. Jagged and Pinky introduced themselves to everyone and said they had to go. After they were gone the guys turned to Doug.

"What was that all about?" Joey asked.

Doug shrugged. "Just some people I met. The guy was telling me how he was opening a club in a few weeks. Didn't say what the name was going to be."

"From the looks of it, I think he was a pimp and she a hooker, am I right?"

Doug laughed. "I don't know where you get this stuff. I didn't see that. Maybe you need to get your eyesight checked? I'd never get into that stuff."

"My eyesight is perfect."

"Well, I didn't pay for anything."

"Sure about that?"

"Of course," Doug told his friend. "I'm not one of these sorry suckers you see who have to pay for it. If anything, they come begging me for a good time."

"Just keep telling yourself that."

Playground

Doug told him if he didn't watch it he'd pay a visit to his mother. Joey just patted his friend on the shoulder. "Only in your dreams, buddy."

Doug laughed.

While they all lit cigarettes Ethan thanked them for coming to the party. It meant a lot to him that his close friends could be a part of that moment with him.

"We have to thank you," Joey said. "Let's face it, if it wasn't for you we'd have no reason to come out here. I think everyone would agree you're the nucleus of this crew."

Everyone else said they agreed.

Emily wrapped her arm around Ethan. "Can't wait to see where else that'll take you, babe."

Ethan kissed on the cheek. "I wondered about that, too."

"We'll see, I guess."

"Indeed. I just do what I do."

She let out a smile.

Ethan turned to his friends to tell them he thought of them as Family. He'd known them for a long time. He didn't know what he'd do if something ever happened to one of them.

23

They got back to Ethan's place at about 5 am. They all passed out. When they woke a few hours later Ethan made them a big feast—chicken, burgers, fries, and steak. He told his guests it had been good having them visit. It had been a great adventure that none of them wanted to end.

They were all sitting around eating and drinking when Doug said, "It all comes together, boys and girls. Only have one life to live, live to the fullest. I can't speak for everyone here but I try to do that very thing. It all could be over in the blink of an eye, man."

Heather said, "When the pot smoke fades away he has in sight. There's genius in there."

They laughed.

Doug said, "Yeah, yeah, if you say so. It takes one to know one, loser!"

"Oh, I'm the loser?" Heather said. "I'm not the one who has to buy hookers."

"I didn't buy a hooker."

"Don't think anyone's buying that story."

"But it's true."

"No one here can verify that."

"You can't either."

Heather laughed. "You got me there, I guess. I wasn't there. Guess that'd be one of life's many mysteries."

Doug told her he would go to her mother's house for a good time.

She flipped him the bird and told him to go sleep with a farm animal.

They laughed and joked awhile longer.

Ethan invited a few other people over to his place. A lot of memories were made on that trip, memories they'd carry with them for the remainder of their days.

Playground
They stayed another two days. Joey said they had to get back. To be honest, he didn't want to, none of them did. Before they left Ethan and Emily took them out for dinner.

Ethan told them. "I hope we can do this again soon."

"That'd be nice," Wayne told his brother. "You should bring Emily back sometime. Show here what it's like back home. And I'm sure some others want to see you, too."

Emily said, "I've never been there. Seems fun. I'd heard a bunch of stories before you guys came out."

"We'll have to change that. You'll like it."

"You think?"

"Everyone does. Don't get me wrong, this is good out here, too. But you have to experience Arkansas. It's a pretty nice place with nice people. We might convince you to stay."

Emily laughed. "Might be pretty hard to do."

Ethan slapped his brother on the shoulder. "Something tells me you aren't going to let this go, are you?"

"Nothing like that. We understand. You have to do your business out here. We just like to fuck with you, that's all. We don't mean anything by it."

Ethan nodded. "I get it. I'm thinking about going back after these next few movies get done filming."

"Really?"

"Yeah, I kind of feel like I've done everything I can do out here. I want to get back to writing novels."

Wayne said, "I'm sure they'll be good. You've already made one hell of a living writing movies."

"I like both forms of wring, don't get me wrong. It's just they're so different from one another."

They talked at great length about what Ethan said. He told them how he didn't think he had any friends in California, that everyone wants something from you. The

Bradley Davenport

minute you can't give them something they're nowhere to be found.

24

Luke and Tick were sitting in Marcus Bishop's office. Marcus was a lawyer who took care of the legal needs of Luke and his crew. Luke had the idea of asking Marcus if he could help him out with Funding for the Church of Modo. Before Luke was able to contact his lawyer about the church he had to meet with him about other matters, matters he'd just found out about earlier that day. It seemed that the guys who were going to knock off the armored truck at the store got busted. They didn't even get out of the parking lot before they were caught. The day before when they tried to pull off the robbery they didn't realize that a few undercover cops were sitting in the parking lot. There was a small shoot-out and Patrick and one of the officers were fatally wounded. As for the others in Luke's crew that were there, they were arrested. They used their phone call to contact the lawyer, the lawyer called Luke.

Things had fallen silent for a few minutes after Luke stated his case.

"So," Luke said, "what's the next course of action? They need their day in court, yes? They might be seen as bad guys, but they still have rights."

"Of course," the man said.

Tick asked how much time the men would get.

The lawyer laid everything out for them. He explained all of them except Layne would be held without bond until their day in court. Since Layne was only charged with being the getaway driver he'd be able to get out until his court date. The others could get ten to twenty years for their crimes. The man told Luke he'd get Layne out as soon as he could. He knew how important Layne was to them.

"We need to make sure he won't say anything," Luke

said. "It could be bad for a lot of people if he turned. We'd all be fucked, no doubt about it. And to think, everything I've done for him over the years... It could all come crashing down."

Marcus stared at Luke from behind his desk. "How would you want to handle that? He's been with you guys for awhile, I'm sure you can trust him. I mean, look at all the things he hasn't talked about. He could've turned on you guys many times but never did. I think that says something."

Tick said, "I think one of the things that concerns us, is if they try to still get at him, what then? They can always find something to try to bend him. I've seen it many times with people."

"Understood," Marcus told him. 'I can see where that can be a problem. That's why I need to get him out and make sure things don't go sideways. You've come this far, don't want to throw it all away, am I right?"

"I agree," Tick said.

Luke told them they always had the option if they felt the need to get rid of Layne. Luke told them they had to do things they didn't want to sometimes. That was just a part of the life they chose. Everyone knew it when they signed up. You had to do your best to stay alive. If it was going to turn into a fight between Luke and Layne, Luke was always going to come out on top. He had to. It was the only thing he knew how to do. But the lawyer told them he didn't think Layne would be a big problem.

"So, I'll head over and get him out," Marcus told them. "I'll take him out for lunch, explain the concerns you guys have."

Luke and Tick said they liked the sound of that.

"That's fine," Marcus said. "I'll get over there after we're done here."

"How much will it cost?" Tick asked.

Playground

"Won't know until I get there. Thirty percent of whatever it is."

"Oh, I see. Thought you might've already known what that would be."

Luke told Marcus he was a good man, and he owed him a lot.

Marcus pushed the conversation towards the matter of why they tried to pull off the robbery in the first place. Luke had to figure out ways to fund the resurrection of the Church of Modo, to build the building, to pay people off, and the list went on. He had to keep his father's dream alive.

"I have to tell you, Luke, I don't know what you want out of me," Marcus lit a smoke, and sat back in his chair. "I mean, it sounds really good. I'm sure your father is proud. Last time I saw him in that place he told me what a fine human you turned into."

"He is," Luke said. "I'm the only thing he has left. My mom, she doesn't want to have anything to do with him anymore."

Marcus exhaled a cloud of smoke. "How is Tiffany these days?"

"Oh, she's okay, I guess," Luke said. "She's still over in Europe last I heard. Told me she was coming back in a couple of weeks."

"When did you see her last?"

"A couple of months ago Mindy and I flew out there. It was nice, but I prefer it here."

"I'm sure she just needed time away," the lawyer said. "After they all got their sentences back then she was devastated. I remember she kept saying how she didn't know how she was going to make it in that place. Being apart from the love of her life, I know it killed her. I saw her a few times while she was in there. They didn't have an attorney at the time, so the court asked me to step in.

The rest was history. Boy, she was glad the day she got out."

"Yeah, I remember that day," Luke said.

"But she was still at odds with the fact your father was going to be locked away forever—at least, he was at the time. She tried to go back to living in Bancroft, but people wouldn't let her be. They never believed for a minute she didn't kill anyone. All of it made her sad. When she got off parole, she came and told me she and Laralyn were living in the country. She needed time to heal. I hope you never had any ill feelings towards her for that. Hell, she didn't leave until she knew you were in good hands."

"Well, I was grateful for that," Luke told the lawyer.

Tick said, "I've been making sure he's been doing the best. You guys have nothing to worry about on this end, that's for sure."

Marcus told the two he appreciated that. He went on to tell Luke that even though he thought the world of Luke and his family he couldn't get mixed up in what they were doing. If certain people found out he gave money to help Luke he could lose his ability to practice law, and if that were to happen it wouldn't be good for any of them.

"And I think I have to remind you, if your father gets involved again he'll be sent back to prison," Marcus warned. "I won't be able to help if that goes down. It'll be over for him."

Luke said he understood.

Tick asked if there was someone else they could talk with about investing. Marcus shook his head and said he didn't. Marcus did know a lot of people with big money that were always looking to invest in something new, but, those people wouldn't want to have anything to do with Luke or his friends. Given the history with the fam-

Playground
ily, Marcus knew that eventually, Luke would be up to no good. And Marcus couldn't subject his friends to that. If, and when, things turned sideways he wouldn't be able to show his face around town anymore; no more lunches, no more golf outings, no more rich parties, he'd be out, ostracized by the community. Marcus said he couldn't move, or relocate, he had clients that depended on him in Bencroft. After another twenty minutes of talking the lawyer told Luke and Tick he wished them a good day, and said they needed to do lunch sometime.

"And bring Mindy with you," he said. "I know she doesn't like me, but I still enjoy her company. She's a good girl."

"She likes you," Luke told him. "She just has her moments," he laughed. "I think sometimes she wished I was six feet under. No, no, she just has different moods as we all do."

"I see," Marcus said. "Well, tell her it'll be on me. I can put it on my card. I don't know anyone who'd turned their head to a free meal."

"I'll let her know. I'm sure she'd be glad to hear from you."

Tick said, "They'd love to see you up at the house, man. It's been way too long. Don't seem like a ghost, you know? You need to be in the light."

Marcus took out a file and opened it on his desk. He told them there might be a few people on that list they could talk with. He told them when they were finished to his office. He didn't want to know about anything. He told them he needed to go and use the restroom.

"So, what now?" Tick asked when they got back in Luke's car. "He's changed, hasn't he?"

"It could be stress. He has a lot on his plate these days. People depend on him every day."

"I get that, I guess. I'm just saying there could've been something he could've done. Hell, we all know he's always been a criminal first."

Luke said they got what they needed, they got a name from Marcus' list.

Tick told him they were lucky they got that. Tick didn't trust the lawyer all that much. He thought the guy had another agenda.

The name they got was Seth Carman. They were going to contact Seth after they got something to eat. They decided to go to a place up the road for tacos. While the two men ate they talked about their day-to-day lives. Since they'd met years ago their friendship had grown stronger, stronger than any of the other men in the crew. They had a great respect for one another. There was nothing they wouldn't do for each other. One of the things Tick was proud of was the fact he was able to save Luke's life on two occasions; the first, about two weeks after they met Luke had Tick riding with him for backup when he needed to meet some people who owed him money and refused to pay. An argument broke and Tick killed the man before he killed Luke, the second, a few weeks later, it was the same scenario, except for the fact the guy had a knife and Tick had to get up from the ground after being beaten down. When Tick got to his feet he pulled his handgun out of his coat and killed the two men they were confronted with. The one guy had Luke's head in a lock with a knife against his throat.

Tick told his friend he was glad the guys didn't have guns. They could've been done for. Tick always said it was best to bring a gun instead of just a knife. A gun versus a knife, the gun would always win. He knew of people who'd use booth in a fight, but he thought that was overkill. With a knife, things got bloody.

When they were walking out of the restaurant two guys

Playground

were talking in. One of the guys hit Tick with his shoulder.

Tick shouted at the man. "Hey, what the fuck is the deal?"

The guy who hit his shoulder turned around. "You talking to me?"

"Yeah, I'm talking to you."

"And?" the man said.

Tick threw his hands to the side. "An apology, maybe?"

"Whatever," the man scoffed.

Tick stepped closer to the man. "We going to have a problem here?"

"I don't have an issue with you."

"You must," Tick said. "You shoved me like you have a problem with something."

"I have no problem with you, but if you want one we can take it there."

Luke said, "Okay, no need for any of that."

The guy's friend said to Luke. "You need to check your boy. Don't want to have him fucked up, do you? It can be done. We have no problem with turning things that way."

Luke nodded. "No, we wouldn't want that."

"Good. We suggest you leave."

"It's a free country."

The man laughed. "Sometimes. Depends on what you're doing," he walked over to where his friend was standing. "Now, we don't want to have to teach you guys a lesson."

"What would that be?" Tick asked. "If anything we should teach you guys a few things. Just think of it like school."

"That's funny. I can tell you this, that's not going to happen."

"That right?"

"Oh, you better believe it."

Luke said, "Hey, it's fine. We don't want any problems. I'm sure you guys don't. Let's just part ways."

The two men turned to walk inside the restaurant. Before they got to the front door Luke and Tick grabbed them from behind and threw them to the ground. Tick picked up the guy who shoved him and ran the man through the front bay window. Luke picked the other man up by the collar and hit him in the jaw a few times. He threw him back to the ground.

Tick said, "Think you'll show some respect next time?" They walked away.

As people started to converge to see what the situation was the two were already down the road in their car. Tick asked what they should do if the guys tracked them down. Luke said not to worry. If it became something they'd deal with it. They had other matters to tend to.

Luke contacted Seth and they set up a meeting for that day. It had to be that day because Seth had to go out of town for business later that night. Luke told his friend he'd rather not do things like that, but there was no other way. If they didn't get anywhere with Seth they had to go back to square one. And they didn't want to do that.

"So," Tick said, "have you ever heard of this guy before?"

"I've heard of him. Never met him. Hope everything goes well."

"Me, too. I don't want things to turn into what they did back at the restaurant."

"I know what you mean. I just knew the cops were going to stop us at some point."

Tick laughed. "We don't need that sort of thing. Hell, we have things we still need to do."

"Got that right."

Playground
It took them thirty minutes to get to the address Seth gave them. They parked across the street. They didn't know the guy and didn't want to just pull into his driveway, plus, they wanted to hang back a little so they could observe the residence while they came up with the strategy. An hour passed and they walked to the front door. Luke was about to knock when the door opened. A heavy guy with no hair filled the doorway.

"Seth?" Luke asked.

The man looked at him. "Is he expecting you?"

"I'd say so."

The man shook his head. "What does that mean?"

"Of course, he's expecting me. I just talked to him on the phone."

"Why didn't you say so, man?" the man said. "I was about to hit you in the belly."

"Well, I thank you for not doing that. It wouldn't be good for you."

"Why would that be?"

"Do you know who I am?"

the man shook his head slowly. "Think I've seen you around town."

"I see," Luke continued. "I'm Luke. This guy beside me is Tick. Nice to meet you."

The guy told him his name was Hank. He asked what their business was with Seth.

"No offense," Luke told the man. "That's our business. I'm not at liberty to say."

"Understood."

Tick added. "If we told you we'd have to kill you."

The man laughed. He walked them to the living room and told them to wait. Seth was on a call and would be out in a few minutes. Hank said he needed to leave and get some things ready for another meeting later that day.

"You sure about this?" Tick asked Luke.

"Not sure. Hope it works out."

"If it doesn't?"

"We'll cross that bridge when we get there."

"That can be easier said than done, man. But I have your back whatever you decide."

"Thanks."

"Hey, what else am I going to do? Have to keep an eye on you, make sure you don't go crazy out here."

Luke said, "It's just crazy how things go sometimes."

"You don't have to tell me. Hell, I'm thankful for every day. I should've been dead long ago."

Luke chuckled. "Yeah, it's been a time."

About twenty minutes later Hank came in the room with a short guy with a pale face. He introduced himself as Seth. He told Hank it'd be okay, that he could go back to what he was doing.

"I'd feel better if I stayed here."

"It's okay," Seth told him. "If I need you I'll holler for you."

"If you insist...."

"I do."

Hank shuffled away. Seth offered the two men a drink. They didn't need anything. All the men sat in chairs around the room. Luke applauded Seth about the look of his place. He went on to tell Seth that he didn't want to waste any of his time and that he'd get to the point.

"I assume you guys want a loan of some sort?" Seth asked.

"If it'd be okay," Luke said. "We'd also be open to going in business together."

Seth laughed. "The fuck you talking about? Is it legit? I can't afford to get mixed up with any more criminal business. Cops are already itching to throw me in prison for life. I have to tell you, the only reason I agreed to meet with you guys was because we share the same at-

Playground
torney."

"We can appreciate that," Luke said. "And we know you must be a busy man, and with that, we thank you for the meeting."

"I'm all ears," Seth said.

Luke told him about his father and the history behind the Church of Modo. He told him that his father was out of prison but couldn't have anything to do with the business.

"Business?" Seth muttered. "I don't know, sounds more like a cult to me."

Luke said he understood where he could get that from.

"I don't know," Seth told him. "I'll have to think about it. Not sure how much I could put into this. I'll have to sit down with my bank book."

Tick told him he could even live at the compound after they got it built. Seth told them he'd have to think about it. He wasn't sure. But he told the two that it'd be a good idea if they tried to get some more investors.

"Yeah, that's the thing," Luke said. "The thought was to try and launder money. We're guys who can't exactly go to the bank. Marcus said you were good and laundering money."

Seth laughed. "Marcus said I was good at it? Shit, he has never told me that in all the time I've been with him."

Tick said it was for a good cause.

Seth told them he'd call them later and let them know. Some of the people who worked for him might be interested.

Seth heard about Harlan Reeves and the church from back then, but he didn't fully understand what they did. Seth thought they must've been up to something. He didn't want to be part of anything like murdering people just for the hell of it. But still, if he made an investment he could profit from the business, whatever they decided to do, or, the church could work as a perfect front for things. But he told them he'd think about it. He always told himself it was best to wait at least two days to make a big-money decision. He wasn't the type you could bribe easily.

When Luke and Tick got to the car they asked each other how many people they could talk with about investing. When they got back to Luke's place they made a little list of people. neither of them knew whether the people they thought of would even be interested.

Later that day Luke got a call from Seth. He thanked Luke but told him he didn't think he could be part of what they were doing.

Seth said, "I wish you guys luck, really I do. But there are some other things I wanted to get into."

"I appreciate you getting back to me," Luke told him. "I understand. No worries."

They talked for awhile longer before Luke ended the call. Mindy asked what he was going to do. He didn't know. Everyone he'd asked turned him down. After the run-around he got from those guys it became clear to him they didn't want to be associated with him or his father, even after he'd explained to them that Harlan wouldn't even be involved.

After a few drinks Mindy said, "Honey, your guys will follow you anywhere, you know? They look up to you and respect you. They don't care what you get into. They'd blindly follow you into Hell. Shit, baby, why don't you just open a club or something?"

"A club?" Luke said.

"And what would be wrong with that?"

"Nothing. Those are fine. I just wanted to do something different, something I'd never done before."

"You've never had a club before."

Playground

"True."

"And you already have some of the money and the land."

"That's true."

"And people will be more open to investing in a club. It can be the hottest place in town."

"It all sounds good. Damn, babe, where would I be without you?"

She laughed. "You want to know?"

"I wouldn't be any place I'd like."

Luke told her that he'll get into it. If Luke opened the club he could use it as a cover for his illegal activities.

Luke told himself he needed to tell his father what he was going to do. He didn't know what Harlan was going to say. He didn't want to be a disappointment. He and Harlan went out for burgers and fries when he broke the news. Luke figured if you have to break bad news to someone the best thing is to do it on a full stomach. They went to a place called Flippin' Cow; it wasn't crowded, which was perfect.

"Thanks for lunch, son," Harlan took a drink of his soda. "Burgers and fries are one of the best combinations there are. You'd have to be a fool not to like it."

Luke took a bite of his burger. "I couldn't agree more."

"After I got out of prison the first time I wanted to open my burger place, you know that?"

"Really? Why didn't you?"

"Looking back on it, I'm not sure. It would've changed how things went for me, that's for sure. I was too into fucking things up for myself to get in that business, I guess."

"Damn."

"But everything has a reason. It was my fate to go to prison. I don't know why."

Bradley Davenport
"That's something to think about. If you hadn't you could've been a millionaire."
"Just what I always wanted," Harlan laughed. "Nah, honestly, I was too damn lazy for any of that. I think that was really why I wanted to get the church started when I did. I just needed to pass the time somehow. And if I made a few bucks along the way, it wasn't the worst thing that ever happened. In the end, I was a stupid motherfucker, you know? If I could go back in time I would've never done that. When we first started it was about one thing, then, after some time passed it became about something else. I was too fucked up on drugs at the time to know anything."
Luke said, "I have some news you may not like."
"What is it?"
"We won't be able to continue with plans for the church."
"Why?"
"Well, it seems all the people we reached out to invest don't want to be a part of it. It still a dark cloud over the area. I'm sorry. I know you must be disappointed."
"No, I'm not disappointed. I was afraid something like that was going to happen. It's not your fault."
"Thanks for saying that."
"But you already bought all that land, what are you going to do with it?"
"Well, Mindy and I were talking and I think a club would be the answer."
"Sounds like a great idea," Harlan told his son. "If you need any help with it just let me know. I'm still connected everywhere."
"I'm going to have a meeting with the contractor next week and talk over some things, layout and whatever. I'm thinking of making it a sort of club/ movie theater combo."

Playground

Harlan said, "I could get behind something like that, sure. I'd imagine you'd have an easier time getting investors if you just have a club."

"That's what I thought. And I thought we could build a place to live above the club, like an apartment or something."

"That's good thinking."

"Got a name for it?"

"Not yet."

"That's the easy part," Harlan said. "It could be hot!"

Luke went on to tell his father that the club isn't an illegal thing and that he can be around it without the cops snooping around like crazed junkies. They continued their lunch, hyping one another up on the possibilities of the club. They were excited. Luke was finally getting to connect with his father in a way he hadn't thought. It was all falling into place.

Harlan said, "If you need help along the way I know people to talk with. It's always good to know people when you're in a tight place.

Luke looked at his father and laughed. He told his father how funny it'd be if he became a bartender.

"I'm up for it, son," Harlan told him.

25

The sun slowly crawled into the sky as Joey and the crew rolled out from Ethan's place. It was going to be a long ride but it had to be done. It was more of the same pot smoking and laughter from before. When they crossed into Arizona they stopped at Big Ed's for gas and supplies. The only person in the place was the clerk behind the counter, an old man in a floppy hat. He nodded when he saw the crew. He told them if they needed anything to let him know. They got the previsions they needed and approached the counter. He asked where they came from and where they were going. They told him.
"Oh, never been to Arkansas," the man said. "Never really had a reason to leave my home."
"That so?" Joey said. "You need to check it out sometime."
The old man looked at everyone in the crew and shook his head slowly. "Nah, I'm fine where I'm at. Don't have any reason to poke my nose around there. Don't have a reason to go into those parts. All my family is here. I know a guy who went over there a few years ago, though. Had some friends that way. Think they moved as soon as they could. I guess they liked it okay, though. Me, hell, I'm fine right where I am. Don't see a reason to go elsewhere."
"That's nice," Wayne said.
The guy told them they'd better be on their way if they didn't want to get stuck in traffic.
"Seems like it lasts about an hour," he said. "All those folks, they just want to get home after a long day at work," he glanced over at the time on his computer screen. "My time will be here before too long. It's been one of those days, know what I mean? Within the first

Playground

two hours of my shift had to call the cops. Someone stole someone else's car. It turned into this whole big thing."

Joey said, "You don't say?"

"Afraid so. Things around here aren't like they used to be. Time changes things. People are too busy getting ahead of themselves, you know?"

Joey and Wayne agreed with the man, even though they didn't care to carry on a conversation about such matters. It was the polite thing to do.

The old man rattled on for a few more minutes, telling them that the crime rate had grown in the past five years. They wished the man a good day and walked out the door of the gas station.

Doug said, "That guy was a little chatty, wasn't he?"

"You would be too if you had to work in a place like that for eight hours a day," Layla said to him.

"You make a valid point."

They got in the van and started down the road. They were having the time of their lives, being with one another, on the road, without a care in the world, making memories as the minutes passed. Their bond could never be broken. As they passed fellow motorists the music and laughter continued. They weren't in a big hurry to get back to Arkansas.

When they entered Oklahoma they stopped at a place for a bite to eat. When they finished they were talking in the parking lot when a slender man with a brown mop on his head and a big black backpack walked up to the group.

"How's it going?" he asked everyone.

They told him they were fine.

"Nice day out, wouldn't you say?" the guy said.

"Not that bad," Joey looked him up and down. "You been out here long?"

Bradley Davenport

"You have to love nature, you know?"

"It's quite a sight," Joey told him.

The guy looked at everyone standing around. "I'm Chris, by the way."

They introduced themselves to Chris. After some talk, they discovered Chris was on his way to a concert on the other side of Oklahoma.

"We're headed that way," Joey told the guy. "Going to Arkansas."

"Oh? Well, look, would you guys mind if I tagged along? I have gas money, among other things."

"What would those be?"

"Weed and pills."

Doug and Quinn looked at one another, shook their heads, and told the guy he'd fit right in. They had things they could share with him, too.

Joey told Chris they were headed that way anyway, and that he could ride with them.

"Thanks," Chris told them. "I knew the minute I saw you guys you were good people. It's just one of those things, you know? Sometimes you just have a feeling about people. It's all about good times, right?"

They agreed with the man.

Chris looked tired and worn out like he'd been walking for a day or two. They felt that they needed to help the guy out. It was the least they could do. You never know when the tables will be turned.

As Chris got in the van the driver hoped he hadn't made a mistake picking this guy up. He'd heard horror stories of people picking up hitchhikers just to be killed later down the road. You can never really tell with some people. Joey figured if something happened he had the power of numbers on his side.

Chris Harts was in his early thirties. As they went down the road they found out the concert he was going to was

Playground
a two-day affair with a bunch of bands. Everyone seemed to like the new passenger.

"Thank you guys for the lift," Chris told them.

"Think nothing of it," Joey said. "Glad we could help. I do what I can. It's always nice to meet new people. We're just all about having a groovy time."

Chris went on. "You have no idea what that meant to me. I'd been trying to get a ride for awhile. Guess people get a little skittish about picking you up, thinking you'll hurt them in some way. I tell you guys, I'm not like that at all. But you have to be careful, some people you pick up might be crazy. You can never tell nowadays."

Joey laughed. "I think we can defend ourselves. They'd be fools to mess with us."

"Yeah," Doug said. "If it comes to it we can fuck a bitch up. We don't play that shit. Don't be fooled, we're nice but we can be twisted when we want. Cross us, you don't want to see what happens. We've always been tight."

"I hear you loud and clear, buddy," Chris said. "Nothing wrong with that. You have to keep it all together, man. Make sure everything is right with the universe, know what I mean? Never know what's lurking around the corner."

"Yeah, yeah, I know," Doug shook his head. "It's all about preserving the quality of human existence, you dig?"

"Of course."

"Good."

"I like the sound of that. Guys are my kind of people."

"We do what we can," Doug told the guy.

Quinn added. "That's the truth, buddy. We wouldn't have it any other way. If you find something better, go for it. But you won't, we're the best."

The driver, from the front of the van, told Chris he was

in good hands, that he was with a good bunch of people. Joey told him that he'd trust anyone in the van with his life. Joey would always pick them to be on his side in a fight.

Chris reached into his bag and pulled out a bag of weed. "Just a little thanks for the ride. A bag of goodness. There's enough for everyone. Feel free to indulge."

They told him it wasn't a problem.

He rolled a joint and lit it. They passed it back- and forth as they chatted away.

Quinn said, "You say that show's going to be good?"

"Hope so," Chris told him. "A few people told me about it. They do it every year. They said that it's been really good every year they've gone. This is the first I've gone. I'm hoping to get wild. I've heard of some of the bands, some I haven't. Guess I'll have to see. No matter what it is, it's going to be a great time. And you can never go wrong with live music."

Joey said, "I'm sure it'll be a hoot. You have people meeting you there?"

"A few," Chris took a hit off the joint. "I was supposed to get a ride with them, but things didn't work out in the end. It's all good, we'll meet up there somewhere. I'm going to be in it for a few days. It'll be crazy when I meet up with my friends. And I'll more than likely be meeting new people, that's what it's all about. The experiences you have, that's one of the things that makes you who you are. We could all be gone tomorrow, we don't know. What the fuck? It has to be right now, it all does. We're all just particles floating around this planet, always learning, never knowing. Wish you guys could join the concert. Hey, man, we can go and then afterward you guys can continue on your way home. It'll be a riot. The road will still be there, that's for sure. Look at it this way, you'll have something new to talk about, a new adventure. Memories, something nobody can take from you."

Wayne said, "You make a valid point."

They continued to pass the joint until it was gone.

Layla, who was looking out the window at the passing traffic, turned her head to the backseat. "What bands are going to be there?"

Chris said, "Do you know who Mask Face is?"

"Heard of him," Layla said.

"Flemington?"

"Never heard of it."

"What about Stanley Bob and Runner Row? Maxwell Sicko?"

"I know those," Layla told him.

"That's good. And there's going to be a few more there."

"Runner Row is good," she told him.

"They are."

"They put on a pretty good show. I saw them last year. They played for a few hours."

Chris opened his bag, dug out a flyer, and handed it to her. "Got this from a friend of mine."

The flyer, along with a list of music groups, had a section devoted to all the vendors that were going to be there. She handed it back to him.

Chris said, "I was hoping I'd meet a girl there. That would be great. With all the people who are going to be there. I'm bound to get a girl. I know everyone there will be up for a good time."

Doug looked at him. "Just broke things off with the chick I was with."

"Sorry to hear that, my man," Chris nodded. "That happens a lot, more than it should."

"It was for the best. She was going to bleed me dry before it was over with. Nothing ever seemed to be good enough for her. But she had no problem with me buying her things."

"Yeah, that happens. You're singing my song. They can be like that. It's hard to tell if things are going to turn into something like that or not. Shit, man, you should hang around with me at the show. We can get crazy drunk, and be each other's wing-man."

Doug shrugged it off. "I would probably do it if we weren't on our way home. Just ask anyone in this van, I can party with the best of them. I'm a crazy fuck when it comes down to it. I just like to have fun. You only live once, better enjoy it while you still have time. We never know when it'll all disappear."

Chris started to roll another joint. "We're all human, you know?"

"That's what I try to tell people all the time."

Chris lit the joint. "I've seen a lot of things over the years, been to a lot of places, and it amazes me the people you meet and the stories they have to tell. Take you guys, I'll bet each of you has led an interesting life before I came by. I'm just a little paragraph in your book of life," he laughed. "It might turn into a chapter. I'd buy it. I've always been a reader. Not a big fan of long books. I want to get in, get out as fast as possible."

They talked for awhile about books. Chris told them they needed to write a book about their trip. He said people would pay good money to read something like that. He told them they could all contribute chapters, and that the chapters could be from their point of view. If it it was good enough they'd make it into a movie.

Wayne said, "I don't know how well something like that would sell."

"We can figure all of that out when the time comes," Doug told him. "I always thought it'd be cool to get my voice out there, to tell my story. I have a lot to tell, you

Playground

know?"

"That's interesting," Chris said.

Joey asked if anyone was hungry. Everyone was, so they stopped at a small burger place to get something. They spent about an hour there before getting back on the road. The more they got to know the guy they picked up, the more they thought it'd be a good idea to attend the concert he was going to. They could make sure he didn't get into too much trouble. They'd feel bad if they found out something happened to Chris.

Layla decided to listen to the radio. After flipping through the stations she stopped on a classic rock station, stating how important it was to have good tunes on a road trip. She asked the others why they didn't have the radio on beforehand.

"Well," Heather told her, "you're the co-pilot, silly."

Layla laughed. "Good point."

"But Joey is right there, too," Wayne added. "Who listens to the radio anymore? That's why we have the playlists."

As they continued down the road they started to tell stories to each other. When they got bored with telling stories they started singing songs they made up. There was a lot of laughter and joking around. Chris felt like he met some special people. He knew he'd made friends forever. He thanked them again for picking him up.

When they got to the other side of Oklahoma, in a town called McMurray, they stopped at a gas station for more supplies. When they all got back in the van they told Chris they decided to go to the concert with him. It wouldn't hurt to go and see what it was all about. After all, one of the best things ever is live music.

26

The concert was held in a big field. People from all walks of life descended onto the field, all hollering and laughing crazily. People were selling drugs out in the open. A few people with shaggy hair were passing out drugs and water. They said it was important to stay hydrated. You never wanted to go without. You don't want to die just from a lack of water. As soon as Doug saw what they were selling he ran over and bought some. He came back with acid for everyone. It was like Christmas morning for him. The look on his face said it all. He gave everyone in the group a little treat.

"Don't spend all of your dough, man," Quinn told him. "You'll need to buy other things. Pay attention to what you're doing."

Doug gave him a look. "You aren't my parents. You know I always share. Don't worry, buddy, you'll get some."

"Because if they were here they'd kick your ass."

Doug waved off the comment. "Shit... They might take some for themselves. Could you blame them?"

"Guess not."

"They'd probably take it all, leave us with nothing. We'd have to buy more."

"You'd have no problem with that," Quinn said. "You'd take it all."

"You're right about that."

"After that, you'd buy more."

"You never want to run out. Whenever you're in a social situation you never know what's going to happen. You need to be prepared for anything. Get in what you can."

Quinn said, "That goes without saying."

"Never know when something will happen. The world

Playground could blow up at any minute."

Some people said the first act was about to hit the stage, so they needed to find a spot to settle in. The place was packed with people, eager concert-goers who just wanted to have a good time. Some of them were talking about the bands they didn't know, and that they didn't care as long as it was live music. A tall man who wore a white shirt smashed a beer bottle on the ground, then, he started to jump up and down in his black boots. Someone who was with him said he'd had too much of the good stuff. After he finished jumping he started running in circles.

"The fuck's wrong with that guy?" Wayne asked. "Someone should help him."

"Too much of that stuff," Doug said. "You have to know your limits, got to keep it cool. Can't freak out around people. No telling what might happen. You might do something, mess up, or find yourself in a fight. Doesn't sound like something I'd want to do."

"Got that right," Quinn said. "You have to be careful with some of this."

After the first band took the stage they took the acid and things got a little blurry. Lots of booze and drugs were had. The next thing Joey knew he was lying on a blanket with Layla, both of them were naked. They had sex. It wasn't until a few minutes later that they realized there were people all around them. They didn't give a fuck. She told Joey that if they wanted to see a show they should give them one, and told him to lick her pussy and she'd suck his dick; both happened. They got cheers when it was all over. Two guys wanted to have their way with Layla but Joey wasn't going to have any of that business. They got into a fight over it. In the middle of the fight, some guy who didn't have anything to do with anything got his face bashed with a rock. A few others

Bradley Davenport
got knocked around. After about twenty minutes the situation died down and everyone went back to enjoying themselves. The injured went to a medical tent that was close by. Things could've been a lot worse. One of the guys that got hurt started talking about suing people, everyone who was fighting, and the people who put on the concert. Somebody told him it wouldn't be wise of him to get the courts involved. Something very bad could happen to him, and he didn't want that at any cost. After awhile everyone made up and everything was cool again. No one wanted to get the police involved, and the people who put the concert on didn't want any part of that scene. It was supposed to be peace and love. In a lot of ways, it was their version of Woodstock.

Some people decided they'd had enough and left after the first few bands. The crew went over to one of the vendors to get something to eat. Wayne struck up a conversation with the guys, asking if the business was worth getting into. They told him not to waste his time.

"At first," one of the men said, "it was pretty good. No problem. After a month or so things started to slow down. We have so much debt because of this thing that it's not even funny. Got into it with the best intentions, but things faded fast. We got into every event we could but it wasn't enough. If things don't start looking up we'll have to close shop.

"That's a shame," Wayne said.

Both men shrugged.

Wayne went on to tell them that maybe they should look into expanding. They told him that was a good idea, that they'd look into it when they got back to normal business. They were based out of Cron, which was about four hours from where they were. Yes, it may have taken awhile for them to get to the field but the money was worth it.

Playground

The other guy said, "After doing this you get tired of dealing with drunks all the time. They always want something for free. I mean, if I could do it I would. They're trying to bleed me dry every time I turn around. I can't have that. Why the fuck we in business? You'd think people would understand but they don't want to."

"I can see where that can get to be annoying," Wayne told him. "I guess it comes with the job."

"You can say that again," he handed their order out. He told them if they needed anything else to come back. They'd be there until the end.

When they got back the crowd was hooting and hollering, laughing at the night with the right kind of energy. The stage lights illuminated the faces. Everyone was bright and ready for anything. The singer, a guy named Rob Lamers, told everyone how pleased they were and everyone came out to support them. They played another nine songs before leaving the stage. The next group on the bill was Runner Row, a band with five albums under their belt. A big reason a lot of people were there was to see them. Their set lasted almost three hours. The next band to take the stage was called Mitten Grithern; they had a few good songs, but mostly people spent their set getting high and conversing with each other. This guy, Rick Jones, came on after they left. He did about four songs before he said he couldn't go on any further. No other explanation was given.

When the morning greeted them a couple dozen people decided to leave. They had all the fun they could take. A few asked Joey and the others if they wanted to join. Joey thanked them but said they were staying to see the other bands. The guys told them to have a good one and were on their way.

Chris came over a little while later with a few people. A girl hugged him. He said they'd just met twenty minutes before. They were all drinking and talking fast.

"Everyone having a good time?" Chris asked.

They all said they were having a good time, that it turned out to be a fantastic time with a lot of surprises.

"Glad to hear it. That's what it's all about, man. Live it up. I just like this, a music festival, everyone dancing and having a good time, just grooving to the music, you know? Things like this make me think what Woodstock must've been like, the one in '69 not the others."

"I dig it," Doug told him. "I wanted to go to those but I didn't. Had the money but no ride."

"I'm sure that sucked for you."

"At first, but it all worked out. I still had lots of fun that weekend. Hooked up with this girl I was wild for."

"Good to know."

"Yeah, man, it was all good. I still wish I could've gone to the show."

"I know what you mean."

"Well, shit happens. You can't think about past things too much."

Everyone continued drinking and doing drugs. Joey told all of them that they'd always remember the past few weeks they'd shared. At one point during the madness, they went backstage and hung around with a few of the bands. Doug and Quinn even convinced two girls in one of the bands to have sex with them.

At the end of the concert, while the last band played, Wayne and Joey asked Chris if he wanted to go with them to Arkansas.

"Thanks, but I'm fine," Chris told them. "We'll have to do that another time. We can make a weekend of it."

He went on to tell them he was going to Utah with the girl.

Playground

They asked if he was sure, and that it'd be no problem to give him a lift. He told them he was fine and wished them safe travels. When they got back home they were all tired of the road. As they went their separate ways Joey asked Layla if she wanted to come to his place.

27

Layla went back to her job a few days later. The shift went without incident and everyone loved to have her back. She had her doubts. She wasn't sure about the people she worked with. She wanted to quit but wasn't sure what she wanted to do.

Joey walked through the door as she was gathering her things to leave. She came from behind the desk and kissed him.

"How'd it go?" he asked.

She sighed. "About as good as can be expected."

"At least it wasn't too bad."

"Yeah."

"It could always be worse. Could always be homeless, living at my place."

"I pretty much live there already."

Joey laughed. "How can you argue with something like that?"

She smiled. "That's just how it goes."

They talked some more before she walked out the door.

When Joey got back to the studio Bruce said how thankful he was to see him. He said he had asked the other guys about him, but they didn't know when he was coming back.

"Well, I'm back now," Joey told him. "Have to get back to work sometime, right? Need to make more of that money."

"For a minute I thought you might've decided to stay over there."

"I thought about it, but I couldn't do that to you guys. Plus, this place would probably fall apart without me."

"Thanks for that," Bruce said. "You might be right about that one."

"Not a problem."

Playground
Bruce ran through some things with him as they got ready for the show. As the show unfolded Joey got relaxed in his role. It'd been a nice vacation away but it was time to get back to work.

Joey opened the show how he always had, telling his audience who he was and what the show was about. He always opened the show by giving his name out, because he could never tell when he'd get some new listeners.

Joey said to everyone. "My vacation was nice, but I had to get back here to you guys, to see what's been new with you. I'm sure some of you were awaiting my return. If you were one of those people I have to thank you. You guys will never what what that means to me. I mean, let's face it, you guys are the only reason the station keeps me around," he let out a laugh. "I'm sure they'd find something else for me to do. Anyway, that's how things go in this crazy world of ours."

Bruce gave the signal that they had to run some ads.

When they came back Joey launched into the topic of ghosts, and how crazy it was that so many people had encounters. He never had any but that didn't mean he didn't believe in them. Something was out there, he didn't know what it was. He told the story of Water Front and what happened there, that people had said they'd seen and heard things that can't be explained. things that aren't of this world. He added he and his friends went out there and didn't encounter anything.

The time came for him to open the show to callers. The first caller of the night was a woman who talked all about crime in the city. Her name was Gina and her brother was robbed at gunpoint a few weeks earlier.

"That's very unfortunate," Joey said. "They catch the guy?"

"No, he's still out there somewhere. He's probably robbed a few others. Cops searched but nothing came of it. Well, they claimed they did a full search. Not sure if they did or not. They were beside the highway when it happened, and the cops said the guy probably sped away and never looked back. The case is still open."

"Did your brother get hurt?"

"He was in shock."

"That's understandable," Joey glanced at Bruce. He didn't want to have a conversation about how her brother got robbed one night. He had to find the right time to ease her off the line. You can't just be rude to someone and tell them to shut up. They'd get pissed and complain. Joey couldn't afford to complain. His bosses might've kicked him to the sidewalk.

After entertaining the conversation for another ten minutes or so she got off the line.

"Thanks so much for joining us if you're just tuning in," Joey told the listeners. "We'll be here for a couple more hours. You're in safe hands, guys and girls."

This guy who said his name was Clay was the next person to call into the show. Clay had an interesting story. He started to talk about this one time he had a full conversation with a ghost. At first, he just thought it was a normal person but he soon learned what it was. He'd always been a non-believer before that happened.

Clay said, "When I first told friends about it they'd thought I'd lost it, like I was off my rocker or something. I think they wanted to check me into a house for goofy people. After awhile, I thought I was going crazy."

"Have you had anything happen since then?" Joey asked.

"No, it was just that one time."

"Well, that's good."

"I keep wondering if it'll ever happen again. I always hoped it would."

"Why?"

Playground
"After I found out what it was I thought it was pretty cool."
"That's interesting."
"I take it you've never talked to a ghost?"
"No, I haven't. What did the two of you talk about?"
"Nothing major, weather mostly. It had just rained."
"Oh, I see."
They talked a little more before taking another ad break. They ran three ads and came back.

"Welcome back all," Joey said. "This world is a crazy place sometimes. You always have to remember that you can't think too much about it. You only have one life, might as well live it to the fullest. I think it's important to have that kind of mindset. It's all about having fun with the circus. I was in California for about two weeks and I saw a lot of crazy things. My friend, Ethan, he's in the movie business over there. That was the first time I'd ever been on a movie set," he scratched his arm. "If any of you have been out there and have a story feel free to tell us all about it. I love hearing from you guys. It's the strange world of the rich and famous, that's what it amounts to. It just seemed to me, for the most part, they are so out of touch with reality. Well, it's a world where imagination runs free; it's supposed to, anyway. But as you know everything boils down to money. If they don't think it's going to make money they don't do it. If you think about it, it's funny because there have been a lot of movies that flopped over the years."

The next person to call in was Wade Bosemen, a guy who drove a cab. He told Joey that he'd thought about trying his luck in the movie business, however, he decided not to when he found out how much it cost to live out there.

Bradley Davenport

"I didn't have that sort of money. There was no telling when I would make money with all of that. The cost of living is high over there."

"Yeah, my best advice on that one would be to try and crash with someone you know," Joey told him. "I'd wish you luck with it."

"That's not a bad idea," the man said. "But now, I like what I have here and I wouldn't change it for anything. Like with everything you have good things and bad. It takes a special breed."

"That goes with everything."

"I've been doing this for awhile. Saw a bunch of crazy things. It just comes with the job."

"I can imagine," Joey told the guy. "In all the time you've done this what was the strangest thing you've encountered?"

The cab driver laughed. "Oh, boy, how much time do you have? I have lots. I can write a book about all of it. I never thought I'd see all the things I had."

"Well, how about two? They don't have to be long ones, just whatever you're comfortable with."

The caller went silent for a minute, then. "This one night I was about to head to the station, clock out, and go home. It'd been a long day and I was done with people. I just wanted to go home and relax."

"I know how that goes," Joey blurted.

"Anyway, I was about three blocks from the station when I got flagged down by two people. I didn't want to but I stopped. They said they needed to go across town when they got in. Now, I was tired but I mustered up the strength. After all, money is money, you know? Told myself I'd try to be as fast as I could. They wanted to go to Moon Dance, you know where that's at?"

"I know where it is, never been inside."

"Asked myself why they wanted to go there but I didn't

Playground
say anything. We pulled into the parking lot. They gave me some money and told me I needed to come in and join them. I told them that wasn't my thing, that I don't get down like that. The guy looked at me strangely and asked what I was talking about. I said I don't do three ways. He told me I was way off, that he wasn't talking about that at all. He was talking about joining them for a meeting."

"A meeting?"

"It seemed they were there for a meeting with the guys running the Church of Modo, and they wanted me to sit in."

"Did you?"

"I did. Told them I had to take the cab back to the station and I'd be back in my car. After all of that, I got my car and came back. It lasted for a little over an hour."

"What did you think?"

"It was odd, I have to say. There were about twenty of us in one of the party rooms. It was this guy, Luke Reeves, giving this talk about what he and his friends were starting. He had a few people with him. The whole thing was pretty strange. Guy started talking about the end of the world, and how we all needed to better acquaint ourselves with God and Jesus before it was too late."

Joey said, "Yeah, I've heard some things from him."

"Really?"

"Yeah."

"He went on to talk about his father, and how he was finishing what his father started. He was quick to tell some of the people that it wasn't a cult."

"That's funny. That's what his father always used to say."

"Yeah, it's a good way to suck people in."

Joey asked Wade if he joined. The cab driver said it

didn't feel right to him, and that he wouldn't join no matter what they told him. A few days after the meeting Luke showed up at his house. Wade told the guy if he didn't leave he'd be forced to call the cops. Wade hadn't heard from him or any of his people since.

"And it seems he isn't going anywhere," Joey told him. "It's crazy to me that he wants to start this whole thing up again. I'd think given what happened before he'd want to steer clear of any of that."

"Never know what goes on in people's minds," the cab driver said. "You think you have it all figured out, but then you realize you don't know anything. That's why I like driving a cab, I just get behind the wheel of this machine and cruise. I liked picking up people and getting to know them, sharing the brief time we had with each other. A good way to make money. Don't get me wrong, there are the odd, crazy ones you give rides to."

"That's the world we live in... We get our share of strange callers."

"Join the club, buddy!"

The two men talked a little longer about Luke, then, Wade started to talk about this girl he gave a ride to one night, and about her pimp who tracked the cab down and told both of them he was going to kill them. The whole thing turned into a crazy adventure where the pimp and some of his friends chased the two around the city.

"What happened to the pimp?" Joey asked.

"He got arrested a few days later for shooting some guy."

"And her?"

"She got a plane ticket and got out of here."

"Where'd she go?"

"Didn't ask where she was going. Honestly, I wanted nothing more than to see her go. I gave her a few bucks and turned my back. Because of her I almost died. Hope

Playground
everything worked out for her. But if she showed up today I'd turn my back and walk away."

Joey said, "Oh, man, now we're getting to it. You had a thing for her, didn't you? She might still drop you a line."

"Nah, nothing like that. I was just doing the right thing. I could never see myself going for that type of girl. I never understood how someone could get into that line of work."

"Someone has to do it, I guess. I've had a few approach me before. That's one thing I'll never pay for."

"I don't blame you."

Joey laughed.

Wade told the host about the night he gave a homeless guy a free ride. It was a little cold that night and Wade was afraid the guy would die if he didn't get out of the cold. The guy didn't look that healthy, to begin with. The homeless guy said it was nice to walk the streets and look at all the different people roaming around. He said you shouldn't have too many expectations from people, that in most cases they let you down. After awhile, you get used to everyone betraying you. He told Wade that you're left by yourself in this life. All you can do is hope the next one isn't too bad.

"That's an interesting way to look at it," Joey said.

"I mean, I guess. Typically, I don't listen to homeless people when they say stuff like that. Half the time they're off on some rant about how society had done them wrong, cast them out like garbage. I don't want to hear that stuff. Sure, some of that might be true but if that's all you're going to talk about just leave me alone."

Joey told the man he understood. Wade said he had to get off the line, but before he did he told Joey what a great job he was doing, keeping all the night creatures company. He looked forward to the show every night.

Bradley Davenport

"Thanks for that," Joey told him. "When I hear people say stuff like that it makes it all worth it."

Wade told the host that they needed to hang out sometime. Joey thought that was a little strange. He didn't want someone turning into a freak and trying to kill him. He had that happen from time to time, people would suggest they needed to meet up, go out to dinner or a party, or something like that. He'd just brush it off as another creep.

28

When they took another break Joey leaned back in his chair. "I'm surprised they hadn't fired me yet."
"Why'd they do a thing like that?" Bruce snorted.
"Hell, they'd get rid of me before they do anything to you. Anyone can do what I do. They can't say the same about you. You bring in the listeners, you connect with them. I can't do that. I don't think I have the attitude for any of that."
"Don't say that. Anything can happen. If you want something bad enough you can make it happen."
"That's easier said than done, I'm afraid."
"Hell, man, it'll happen one day. Just keep on doing what you do best."
"I just ask myself if they even care about what I do here."
"You keep thinking about it too much," Joey told him.
"Maybe."
 When they came back from break a few people called to talk about strange occurrences: One guy who went by Norman talked about his first experience with a demon, or, what he thought was a demon. There was no other way to explain it. He was nine or ten years of age when he awoke from his sleep one night to the sound of two demonic voices arguing outside his bedroom window. A minute after Norman opened his eyes one of the voices said, "Kid, get back to bed."
 Norman blinked his eyes and became confused because he was still lying in bed. The next day he told his brother what happened. As it turned out his brother heard the voices as well and he got out of his bed and walked into the living room to investigate.
 Since there was snow on the ground they figured if there had been someone outside their windows there'd

be footprints; there were no footprints. Until this day they have no clue what that was outside that night. For the next few nights, Norman heard sounds outside his window. No matter how many times he told his parents they didn't believe him.

Joey said, "And have you heard the voices since?"

"No," Norman said. "I never heard those voices again. We moved out of that house about a year later. I think if I heard them today it would freak me out too much."

"Sure, I can understand that. I think that'd freak anyone out."

"It sounds odd, but in a way, I want to hear those voices again. I don't know, I just need to know. I'd like to know something, a confirmation of some kind."

"What year was that?"

"1988 right here in Bancroft. We moved just to come back in '93."

"Why'd you move?"

"My father worked for the railroad and got laid off both times. We've been here ever since."

"Oh, that's nice."

"Yeah, I've always enjoyed this area. It's what I'm comfortable with. I've done a lot of things over the years here, you know?"

"When I graduated I moved away for a few years, but I moved back because things didn't work out."

"That's how it goes sometimes. You try things, sometimes they work, sometimes they don't. You just have to make those steps. No one gives us a road map."

"You got that right."

They talked for a little longer before Norman said he needed to go. Joey thanked him for the call.

The next person to call was Luke Reeves. He was surprised Luke called.

Playground
"How's it going, Luke?" Joey asked. "What's on your mind at this hour?"
"I'm good. Everything is great on this end, you?"
"I'm okay."
"Well, welcome back. I know you were gone for a little bit."
"Yeah, took a little vacation. We all need a little rest now and then."
Luke said, "That's true. One could get burnt out doing the crazy things we do. We must step back and look at this wonderful world we live in. Lots of us, we take all of this for granted."
"Don't have to tell me twice, my man. We all get to that point. You have to find a happy balance."
"I guess so."
"We do what we can."
"At any rate, I'm glad to see you back, and I know others are thankful, too. I got to thinking maybe you weren't coming back. Thought I might've scared you off or something."
"Why would I be scared off?" Joey asked.
"Oh, I just figured you were. I started to think that my church was a little bit too much for you to take. I know, it's not for everyone. I could only imagine what was going through your mind the first time I contacted you. I'm sure when you saw the flyer on your car when you left work that morning you got pretty annoyed?"
"Nothing like that," Joey told him. "I guess I'm just a little curious, though."
"About what? I can answer anything you throw at me. I tell it like it is. I don't believe in beating around the bush or dodging anything. I don't expect to be lied to and I won't do that to others. What kind of man are you if you're going to manipulate the truth all the time, huh? Not anyone I want to be associated with, I can tell you

that."

"I feel the same," Joey said. "With what you guys are doing, what do you hope you're going to accomplish? I don't mean any disrespect but the last time didn't go so well."

"I understand that's always going to be in the back of everyone's mind. I can't change what happened then. Harlan and his friends made a lot of mistakes. But after careful consideration, my friends and I have decided to move on."

"What does that mean?" the radio host asked.

Luke said, "After considering it for awhile we are not going to go through with the Church of Modo. Instead, we are going to open a nightclub and call it Modo."

"Oh, that's refreshing. We can always use another one of those."

"Well, this one is going to be different."

"How so?" Joey asked.

"We have a few surprises for everyone. I can't wait until that day comes. I already bought the land where we were going to build the church, so we're just going to have the club be there. I didn't want to buy another plot of land."

"I don't blame you for that one," Joey said. "So, are you guys ever going to open the church? Like afterward?"

"I gave up on that. There were just too many moving pieces and too many bumps along the way. I wish that wasn't the case, but that's what happened. What are you going to do? Things were out of my hands."

Joey told him he couldn't wait to see it. He told Luke that he liked to hear when people he knew were doing good for themselves. Luke went on to say that if he knew of anyone who needed a job to let him know. He was going to have to hire a lot of people. He told Joey that he could come in as a business partner if he wanted.

Playground

He projected they'd make a lot of money together.

"I'll keep that in mind," Joey told him. "I'm always open to new things."

"Well, I'll let you know when we get closer to deciding that stuff. Right now, it'll probably be six months before we're up and running, and that's going to be pushing it."

"Just keep me posted."

Before Luke got off the line he apologized to Joey and the other listeners. He hoped no one got pissed at the fact he put those flyers everywhere, and that they had to put up with him talking about the church everywhere he went. In the end, nothing was ever going to come of it. But he assured everyone that the club he was opening was going to be something special, something everyone could be proud of. He'd made a lot of bad decisions but he was going to make everything okay again. As he was talking, the thing no one knew was what kind of psycho he was. If they knew Luke killed as many people as he had they would want nothing to do with him. He ended the call by saying he considered everyone a friend, and that he always treated his friends well.

The thing people didn't know was after Luke hung up the phone he walked down to his basement and killed a man. The man, Robert Young, beat a friend of his. Luke just wanted to get payback. After he killed Robert he told his crew to bury the body in the same place they had in the past. They always did as they were told.

29

When Joey got back to his place he was surprised to see Layla there. He didn't have a problem with her being in his apartment or anything, he was just amazed she was there so early. She told him she stayed all night. She wanted to see him. They talked for awhile and ate some food. They headed to his bedroom for some early morning sex. After the romp in the bedroom, they made love in the shower, too. It was clear the two liked each other a lot. Layla wanted to move things forward in the relationship, she just didn't want to end up getting hurt, which was something that happened to her with every guy she had been with. She was always one for falling in love too quickly, making grand plans in her mind with the person she was with. But it was a whole different story with Joey, something about him, something in his eyes, how he treated her, she knew he'd never betray her. And he felt the same about her. She didn't want to mess things up with Joey. On the other hand, why disturb something that was going so well? It was clear they love each other, and shouldn't that be enough? Why would they put it in print, and get a certificate that they loved each other? She wasn't sure about contracts. But she liked the idea of everyone knowing they were together. She knew they had to eventually have that talk, but she'd try to postpone it as long as she could.

Later that day, they were sitting at the kitchen table talking when Layla told him she needed to go.

"Need to go to your place?" he asked.

"No," she said. "A friend of mine, Annie, wants to meet up later. We were just going to hit the town, raise some Hell, you know? She was telling me she wanted me to meet a few of her friends. I'm not sure if you know Annie. I saw her at the store the other day and we made

Playground

plans to meet up today. You might have seen her around. She's stayed overnight at my place a few times. Petite like me, brown hair, blue eyes, glasses."

"Oh, okay, yeah, I remember. That's okay," Joey said. "Hope you have a good time. Think you'll come over later?"

"Not sure. I need to do some stuff back at my place after I get back."

He shrugged. "That's fine."

"I'd love to, though."

"I'll cook for you."

She smiled. "In that case, I'll be over. What are you going to be cooking? How can I pass up something like that?"

"That's a surprise."

"Oh, I like surprises," she told him.

"It's a deal."

"I can't wait."

He smiled. "It'll be worth it."

"I bet, dear."

"You know I do it. I just like to make everyone around me happy."

"That's a good thing."

"I've always been like that."

"Really?"

"Since I was a little kid."

She smiled at him. "Yeah, when I was a kid I was the same way. When people were rude I couldn't figure it out."

"Those people are sad."

They kissed.

He walked her out. She asked what he was going to do. He told her that he thought about seeing if his friends wanted to go out for a few drinks.

30

Layla and Annie met when they both worked at a grocery store, Pinkerton's. They both worked there for six months. When Layla went to the radio station Annie went to a local bank. Layla tried to get her friend to come to work with her, but Annie wanted to make the bank gig a career. They went for a bite to eat. During dinner, they had a few drinks and caught each other up on what was going on in their lives.

"That all sounds good," Annie told her friend. "I'm so happy for you."

"Thanks," Layla said. "What about you?"

"What about me?"

"Have any special guy?"

Annie looked at her and smiled. "Not steady. I go out on dates with guys but nothing lasts."

"Why?"

"Not sure. I mean, I don't do anything that pushes them away or anything. I'd have to think it's them."

"I see."

"I don't know what the problem is. You think I should start dating a different type?"

"Couldn't hurt."

Annie laughed. "I know a few guys I can add to that list."

"Well, there you go."

"That's what I'll do."

Layla asked about the people Annie wanted her to meet. Annie got an excited look in her eyes as she told Layla all about the group of friends of hers, and about the big house the guy lived in. It was out of the city limits with a lot of land, so they could do whatever they wanted without any cops or neighbors around.

"How many times have you been there?" Layla asked.

Playground
"About a dozen times. They always have these badass parties. They're fun. I've hooked up with a few guys from there."
"Really?"
"You can, too."
"I'm good," Layla told her. "I have a guy, thanks."
"But you can always fuck around. Who's going to know?"
Layla laughed. "I don't know, everyone who's there would know."
"Well, they wouldn't know unless you told them you already had a guy."
Layla shook his head. "I'm good. I like the guy I'm with."
"Well, that's you. I commend that, you know?"
"I just do what I do. I've never been the type to cheat on anyone."
"Good for you. I'm not like that, never been and never will."
"Do you think that's very fulfilling?"
"Maybe. It depends on what you're looking for. A lot of times all I want is that intense night of passion. That's just who I am. I can appreciate it if you aren't like that."
Layla asked her what was the guys' name who owned the house they were going to. After a little reluctance, she told her Luke Reeves. Layla knew the name well. Everyone knew the name thanks to Harlan Reeves and everything that happened all those years ago. But all of those people didn't know Luke. There had been rumors here and there about criminal activities. But the ones spreading rumors never had an interaction with Luke. Layla heard the name and the stories, and she knew he had called the radio station a few times because Joey told her about it.
The two women went out to the house and had a great

time. Both of them get drunk and they end up sleeping it off at the house.

The next night at work Joey asked Layla how things went with Annie. She told him everything went fine, and that the next time they went he needed to join.
"Maybe," he told her. "I'll have to see how things go. I'll check and see."
"That's all I can ask for."
He told her he liked spending time with her, and she said the same thing. It was nice to know that they were on the same page.
As it turned out he was about to join her two nights later. She was so happy with him. Layla told Joey they were just a bunch of fun-loving people.
They thought it'd be a good idea to go by the store before going. No one should go to someone else's house empty-handed. Joey didn't want to make a bad impression. For all he knew those people listened to his show. He didn't want to come off as an asshole. They might try to run him out of town. If he had a house they'd burn it down.
They met Annie in the parking lot of the store. They debated for awhile on what they should get. Joey told them the best thing to get was beer. Everyone drinks beer, no matter the brand. They got a few cases and a bottle of whiskey. After they got some snacks they figured that'd be more than enough. Joey didn't know what kind of crowd was going to be there, and he couldn't get too much information out of the girls, which, to be honest, he was a little worried about. He started to think maybe there was a reason he wasn't being told the whole story. Was there a reason he wasn't being told? What was he in for? He'd find out soon enough.
After driving down a road for awhile they turned down

Playground
a dirty road. Joey asked Layla if she was sure they were going to the right place. She said to keep following Annie's car, that if they got lost it would be her fault. But Layla had been that way a few times, and she knew where they were going.

"Hey, if you say so," he told her.

"Trust me."

They came to a big white house on the left with flat land around it. Layla said they were at the house. Joey started up the driveway. People on both sides of the lawn were drinking and having a good time. Big chatter and laughter were everywhere. Joey asked if there was going to be an outside concert or something. There were a lot of people.

"Seems like everyone's having a good time," Joey said. "I guess this is what our night is going to look like."

"Just be glad I talked you into coming."

"I can think of a few ways to give my thanks," he told her. "You'll love it."

"I'm sure I will."

They both laughed.

Annie, who was in front of them parked in a spot on the lawn. Joey parked behind her.

Layla said, "And the fun begins...."

"We'll see," Joey said. "I'm sure it'll be fine. Meeting new people is always fun."

"That's how you have to look at it."

A man rushed to the car and knocked on the window. Joey rolled it down and the guy asked if they wanted any drugs. The guy had a big shaggy beard and wild eyes. He said the only suitable way to enjoy something of that magnitude was to take what he was offering. It would be the most fantastic thing ever. They were in for a real treat.

"We'll have to check that out," Joey told the man. "It's

going to be a night. Plan on being here until the end."

The man laughed. "There's plenty to go around."

Joey nodded.

The man said, "You guys need to get settled. There's nothing but groovy people here. No pigs, nothing like that. It's all about having a good time, you know? I can't say enough how much you guys are going to love this place. Yes, indeed!"

"Sounds good."

"The cops, they are probably somewhere eating their donuts," he laughed. "Maybe they're fucking hookers they arrested."

"Maybe."

"Right, right, right, the great protectors of the world! They need to save us from ourselves."

"I can see that sure," Joey told the man.

"I've never been a fan of those dirty pigs, those dirty motherfucks."

"Some are okay."

"Guess I don't know those," the guy laughed. "You guys feel free to do whatever you want here. The owner, he doesn't give a single fuck."

"That's good to know," Joey told him.

The man looked at Layla. "Yeah, I know you. You were here the other night with that one girl. That kicked ass. Tonight is going to top that."

"Yeah," Layla said. "I told my guy he had to check this place out."

The guy looked at Joey. "You guys together."

"Afraid so," Joey told him.

When the guy found out Joey and Layla were together he lost interest in her. He told the two to have a good time, and that if they decided to pass out at the house the sofa in the den was his.

"We'll keep that in mind," Joey said.

Playground

When they got out of the car the guy handed Joey some pills. "These will fuck you up, buddy."

After Joey gave him some money, the guy told them if they wanted anymore that he'd be at the house until the next day. They said they'd keep that in mind.

Annie got out of her car, and as soon as she did the guy ran over to her and asked if she wanted any of the drugs. She told the guy she'd get some later. She was going to have to pace herself.

"Smart move," the man said. "You have to take your time sometimes, I can dig it. Whenever you want, just come find me."

Before Annie could say another word to him he was off in another direction, chatting with someone else about the same thing.

Annie looked at Layla. "Well, that guy's sure excited to tell everyone what he has."

"I guess he's on the moon, far from any of us."

31

All sorts of charters were hanging around, stumbling, dancing around the place. Loud music came from the house. People walked up to them and offered drugs and booze. Joey didn't know who owned the house but wanted to find out. He thought it was more than a little odd the girls didn't tell him. They wanted him to find out on his own. He and his friends could start promoting the parties if he knew who owned the place. It could turn out to be very profitable for all concerned.

"Who owns the place?" Joey asked.

Layla shrugged. "You'll just have to see."

"You aren't going to tell me?"

"That's right, it's a big mystery."

"Well, whoever it is, they have good taste. This house is pretty nice."

"You'll have to tell him that."

"It's a guy?"

"Yeah."

"Oh."

They knocked on the door.

The door opened a short man was on the other side. He wore a leather jacket and a black hat. He gave Joey a strange look.

"Welcome to my home," he said.

"Who are you?" Joey asked.

"Oh, I'm sorry," the man said. "I'm Luke Reeves and this is my house."

"Luke?" Joey said.

"The one and only... Good to meet you."

"I'm Joey, we've talked a few times."

"We have? My memory fails me sometimes, sorry. Who are you?"

"Joey Ryder," Joey said. "You've called my radio show

Playground
a few times

"Glad to meet you in person. This is my paradise. You can probably see why, am I right? I got the impression you wanted to meet with me. Layla told me you talked about it."

"Strange how that happens. Well, there are only so many people in the world, we were bound to run into each other at some point. I wanted it to be sooner rather than now but what can you do? Things don't work as planned sometimes."

"I know what you mean, buddy. Crazy world we live in."

"I know."

Luke told Layla how nice it was to see her again. He asked where Annie was. Just as he asked Annie ran over to them. She'd been talking to this guy who wanted to take her out on a date. When they asked if she was going to go she said she wasn't sure. She didn't want to come off as mean of anything, it was just how things had to be. She explained she had to take a break from the dating world for awhile.

Luke laughed. "Us guys, we'll do it to you. It's a game we're always playing. You win some, lose some. You just have to keep playing the game."

Annie gave him a frown and asked where his better half was.

"She might be in the backyard," Luke said. "Lost track of her a bit ago."

Annie said, "She needs to pick up a new man."

"Okay, that was a little rude," Luke told her.

"Yeah, you know I love you, buddy."

"Sure, I've heard that before
e, dear."

Annie told Layla she had to join her so that they could walk around to the backyard. They ran off in the sea of people.

Luke told Joey to join him in the kitchen.

"Nice place you have," Joey said.

"Thanks. I got it at a pretty good price."

After they got a beer Luke gave Joey a tour around the house. He told the radio host that he needed to buy one of the houses in that area, which there were three houses along the other side of the tree line near Luke's property.

"You'd love it," Luke said. "It's a great area. We don't have the cops come out here often. You can be as loud as you want. No one is going to bitch about the noise. Hell, we have parties like this all the time. If people do complain just threaten them, that'll shut those people up. And, just continue your party. The fuck else are they going to say?"

"All the time?"

"Well, most nights."

"Sounds nice," Joey said. "where I live now, it's close to the radio station. As for now, I'm good. I'll keep this in mind. though. I'm not the biggest fan of the place, it's still an apartment. But I have to make due for the time being

"Yeah, man, I called up there, to see if I could interview on someone's show. I guess you were the only one who'd talk to me. I didn't know what the deal was."

"What did they tell you?"

"Said they couldn't."

"Why?"

The man shrugged. "Not sure, honestly. I don't know, maybe they thought it would've been bad for business or whatever? I've had things like that happen before."

"Not sure," Joey said. "Maybe you should've told them you aren't going to open the church anymore. That's something people don't want to forget."

"It was before I'd decided not to reopen it."

Playground
"Get back in touch with them, then."
Luke brushed it off, saying it was a fight for another day.
"People change," Joey took a swig of beer.
"I know, I know. You think that could convince them?"
"I could talk to my managers about it."
"Thanks."
"Think nothing of it."
Luke looked at his new friend, laughed, and asked the radio host what he thought during their first phone conversation.
"Honestly," Joey said, "I was a little shocked you call. When I asked myself why you called, that was when you started to talk about your reason for calling. I'd known of your family name for awhile. Back when I was a kid, when all of that stuff happened I didn't realize how what it was."
"I've heard a few people say that."
"I remember I was watching TV that night when they showed Harlan being led out from the compound in cuffs."
"How did that make you feel?"
Joey shook his head. "Nothing. At the time I didn't know what it was all about. I knew from how excited the reporters were talking about it that it was something big."
Luke went on to tell Joey that his father started the Church of Modo all those years ago with the best intentions, or, at least that was what Harlan told him. Harlan told his son he was doing the work of their creator. When Luke asked how Harlan came to be in the cage he was in, his father told him that power and ego got the better of him. The idea was simple; help those who needed it. A lot of the people who decided to live at the compound were young adults who felt lost in the world,

Bradley Davenport

like everyone had turned their backs on them and they needed a way to stay alive. After awhile, some of the people who joined knew things had started to take a turn for the worse.

Harlan wanted everything his way with no exceptions. As the days passed the rules he'd make were unbelievable to a lot of them. When things didn't go to Harlan's liking, that's when his temper would show. Those who lived told their tale in court.

After having a lot of time to think about it, Harlan wished things could've been different. It was when he was alone in his prison cell that he finally saw the error of his ways. There were a lot of drugs flying around and he just became a maniac back then. He was forced to pay the price. He'd lost everything, family, friends, and his freedom. His son saw him now and then, but it got to be too much for him and the visits stopped. A few years later Harlan told Luke that he needed to continue the mission. Still, at that time, people around the city and elsewhere had bad memories of Harlan and what he did, and the lives he ruined. There was nothing he could do to repair the damage he'd done. The only thing he could hope for was that everyone would forgive him in time. He understood some could never forgive. They aired a special on TV back in 2001 where they interviewed survivors and their families. One of the guys interviewed for the program, an older man, told the reporters he wished Harlan would be able to walk the streets as a free man just so he could shoot him between the eyes with his shotgun. After all of that Harlan still wanted to start things up again. He contacted his lawyer, and the lawyer contacted Luke to set up a meeting.

Luke was faced with the daunting task of starting his father's business again. He wasn't sure how he was going to achieve what had to be done. He knew he didn't want

Playground

to follow the exact steps of his father, stealing to raise money. But when things didn't seem to be going his way he decided not to start the church back up. He still wanted to do something, and that was when the idea of the club came to his mind. Everyone else liked the idea.

 "And you're in luck, " Luke told Joey. "You'll get to meet my dad. I know that's something you want. You can report it on your show and be the topic of conversation the next day. They might put you on the news. Shit, everyone wanted that interview. He was locked away and they never would allow it. I think they didn't want to have him celebrating the things he did. I don't know, it all seemed crazy to me. They always interview all those serial killers that are behind bars, those sick fucks. Those garbage people never belong on TV."

 "I was going to ask about that, I thought he was in for life?"

 "He made a deal. He gave them some information they needed."

 "About what?"

 "I don't know all the details, but it had something to do with going undercover on some top-secret stuff. He didn't tell me what it was about. Guess the cops told him if he told they'd throw him back into a cell. Honestly, I think he might have told a few people about things that happened on the inside. I mean, shit, those places are very violent. I'm sure bad things go down all the time. It's just another day to them."

 "Damn," Joey muttered.

 "He didn't want to talk about it."

 Joey said, "I bet it's been good having him back?"

 "It's been good. Been nice having him back. He'll be here a little later."

 "I see."

 "It's just been a big transition for him, for both of us.

But we got him in his room upstairs. It's just a nice little family here."

"I can imagine."

Joey asked what Harlan said when he found out the church wouldn't be opening. Luke said he didn't mind, which surprised him given the fact he wanted it so bad. But when Luke told him why he wasn't going to open it Harlan was a little annoyed. But he understood.

The two kept talking as people were parading in and out of the kitchen, drinking, hollering, and going crazy. Joey told Luke again how much he liked the house.

"I'm glad you like the place," Luke said. "I put a lot into it. I don't know if they told you, I own a few other homes."

"That so?" Joey asked.

Luke shook his head and said he'd been very lucky. He said that one of the best things to have was good lawyers, they could steer you in the right direction when things come up, when buying a piece of land, when signing a contract, or when you have to sue somebody. Nobody wants a lawsuit, but when you are in one you want a great lawyer. Joey agreed, saying they are good to have. He had a few legal battles of his own over the years.

While they talked, Layla and Annie came through the back door. They both were having a blast. They wanted to know what the guys were talking about. Luke continued to talk about the club, about how they were going to have events every night the first week. They told him it all sounded good, and that they couldn't wait to see how it went.

Luke said, "My investors and I put a lot into it. I mean, there's still a lot of work to do. Things are running

Playground
smoothly so far. I just hope it keeps up."
"How many investors?" Joey asked.
"Three, including me."
"You aren't worried about having too many hands in the pot?"
"I don't know, hadn't thought about it."
"Might want to consider it," Joey warned.
"Nah, not my guys, I trust them. We already agreed to split everything evenly. Greed isn't going to be a factor. If things go down like that we'll just have to fight it out. If something like that happens I'll just have to kill someone."
"You'd kill your friend?" Joey asked.
"I have before."
"Really?"
"Sometimes the situation calls for it."
"I see."
"Oh, fuck 'em," Luke said. "I have to get them before they get me."
Layla looked at him, then laughed. "You're joking. You've never killed anyone."
Luke said, "You want to bet? I can tell you where some of the bodies are buried."
She got a serious look on her face and told him that wasn't a nice thing to joke about. Again, he told her he wasn't kidding. He told her just to ask some of the people at the party if she didn't believe him. He laughed and slapped her on the shoulder. She backed away from him.
"What?" Luke said.
She giggled. "I don't know. I guess I'm a little buzzed."
"Well, fuck, that's a good thing. That's what it's all about. Why the fuck are we here?"
"You're right about that, buddy."
Joey gave the man a strange look. He didn't want to be rude to his host, so he didn't say anything to him. But he

Bradley Davenport thought Luke was crazy. He couldn't believe Luke just told him what he had. He wondered how many there had been.

Luke told Joey that he'd never go to prison. He remembered visiting his father when he was a kid, and he never wanted to end up in that place. He told his mom that he'd die before he went to that place. Luke couldn't believe that they could just take someone's freedom like that. When everything with his father and the church fell apart he was still pretty young and didn't understand what happened. His mother, Tiffany, never liked talking about it. She'd tell her son it was what was in the past, and it should remain there. All Luke could ever get over of her was that it was very bad and wrong. They were young and things got out of control. Luke knew whatever happened involved violence.

Luke asked Annie how many dates she agreed to go on since she'd got to the party.

"Fuck you, dude," Annie told him. "It's no business of yours who I sleep with. You're just mad I haven't slept with you yet."

"Yet?" Luke replied. "So, eventually, we are so why not make it tonight, babe?"

"You have a girlfriend," Annie told him. "She'd be pissed at you, man."

"She wouldn't care."

"Why?"

"We have an arrangement."

"Oh, you don't say?" Annie thought about it. "Maybe another night. I don't want to do that tonight."

"Come on, babe."

"Another night."

"Why?"

"I told you."

Luke took her hand. "You sure about that?"

Playground

"Yes, I am. Sorry about that. Eventually, I've told you that."

"I guess I can wait. Even though I don't want to, I guess it'll be okay."

Annie smiled at him, then, she told Layla that they needed to go to the backyard and see what was going on outside. The girls told each other they wanted to get drunk that night.

Both guys told the girls they'd join them in the backyard. Luke told Joey that he'd love the setup they had in the backyard. It was just a good thing the weather was nice out so they could enjoy it. And the backyard was also where Mindy was. Luke's better half was busy drinking and talking to all sorts of people.

White lights were strung up throughout the back on small pillars. White patio furniture was lined against the privacy fence. The lawn was level and smooth. A little bar was tucked away in the corner. There were big blankets in the center of the lawn.

When they found Mindy she was telling one of the bartenders he needed to run to the store and buy some more beer. She gave the guy some money and told him to get a few cases.

"No problem," the guy told her.

Mindy walked over to the group and gave Luke a big hug. She said it was nice to see everyone, and that she wanted everyone to have a good time.

"Thanks," Joey told her. "You guys have a nice place."

"Nice of you to say," Mindy said to him. "Have you not been here before?"

"This is my first time."

"Oh, okay, I thought you'd been here before," she laughed. "Guess I was thinking about someone else. I can't keep up. Too much shit, you know?"

Joey agreed. He knew all too well what she was talking

Bradley Davenport

about. He'd been there many times. Hell, he was on his way there that night. Why not? When everyone else was drinking and smoking weed, you might as well join them, right? You never wanted to be the odd man out. Someone rolled a joint and started to pass it around. After a little bit, Joey noticed two other joints joined the rotation.

"When is Harlan getting here?" Joey asked Luke.

"Should be anytime," Luke looked at his watch. "Well, it's just now after midnight. I'm sure he's on his way."

32

About twenty minutes later the backdoor opened and an older gentleman walked through. The man was dressed in black slacks and a blue button-down. His graying hair and wrinkled face told a tale of a man who'd lived a long and rough life. Luke called him over to where they stood and introduced him to Joey.

"I've heard a lot about you," Joey told him.

"That so?" the man said. "I hope nothing but good things, yes?"

Everyone laughed.

Instantly, Joey had a list of questions he wanted to ask the man. But he figured they'd get into that stuff soon enough, plus, he didn't want to come off as rude and upset the man. He had to play it cool. The man told them he would've been there sooner but the cab he got a ride in was pulled over and the driver got arrested. They'd been stopped for a traffic violation. After the officer ran the driver's name it was discovered he had outstanding warrants. Harlan was forced to walk the rest of the way to Luke's house.

Luke said, "You should've called. You know my number?"

"It's a little hard to do that when you forget your phone."

"You forget it here or there?"

"Here."

"Oh, that can be a problem."

"Tell me about it. Hell, I miss the days when there were payphones everywhere. If you got into a jam you could just drop in some change and give someone a call. If it were up to me I'd still have those things. But it wasn't up to me to get rid of those. Nobody consulted me."

Luke let out a laugh. "I'm afraid those have become a

relic of the past."

Harlan said to Joey. "It amazed me, all the things that changed in the years I was in prison. I mean, when we were inside we knew things were changing but I didn't realize how much."

"I bet that was crazy," Joey replied. "Yeah, I miss some of that stuff. Well, hell, even some of the stuff from the early 2000s, you don't see anymore."

"Seems like the world's going to Hell," Harlan said. "Somebody is going to have to answer for all of this."

They continued talking as people were coming and going from the backyard. Some people at the party treated Harlan like he was some sort of celebrity or something. Joey couldn't understand it and didn't want to.

Luke offered his new friend another beer. He thought it was pretty funny that the beer they brought was all gone. They still had the whiskey, and he was okay with him. After the beer, he started on the bottle. Layla came over and said she wanted some. They took a couple of swigs then each lit a cigarette.

A man with big brown hair, Ronnie Williams, told Joey he listened to the radio show all the time. Ronnie told him to keep up the good work. He told Joey he'd love to be on the show sometime. When asked what they'd talk about, he didn't know.

"Well, think of something," Joey told him. "I'm not that picky. My bosses give me a lot of freedom to do what I want. They just don't want dead air."

The man said, "If they don't see your vision they can fuck themselves. You let them, they'll run all over, man. You got to take a stand somewhere, you know? Can't let them win. They get their way, might as well give up the whole thing, get out while you can."

"I have a good thing going on," Joey told him. "I plan

Playground
on being in the business for a few more years."
"You may think that now, sure. But then you'll wake up one day just as they kick your ass to the curb, my friend. Mark my words, they aren't loyal."
"Interesting point."
"Yeah, you have to watch your fucking back out here. No one's going to do it for you," Ronnie smiled. "Someone like you, what you need is a big ass motherfuckin' gun. Don't know when some sick fuck will want to kill you. We don't need anything like that happening to you. You're needed on the radio. Hundreds of people listen to you every day."

Joey laughed. "Thanks for that. I'm good. Nice of you to say that. I just think of it as doing a job. I'm nothing special."

"That's what they all say."

Luke came over to see what the two guys were talking about. He knew how Ronnie was, that people can be easily annoyed by him. And he didn't want any of his guests scared off by the guy.

Ronnie said when he got on the show they could discuss the genius which was Luke Reeves. They could also talk about guns. Joey, after meeting Luke, didn't think he was a genius. He didn't have anything against Luke, he just didn't know him that well. Just to be polite he nodded and told Ronnie he'd look into it.

Ronnie hit Luke on the shoulder and said they needed to go to the movies some night.

"That'd be good," Luke told him. "I'll give you a call sometime."

"That's what I'm talking about," Ronnie said. "If nothing else we can always get some drinks somewhere."

"Sounds good."

Before Ronnie talked away he offered the guys some drugs. They were cheap. The guys thought about it and

Bradley Davenport
told Ronnie they weren't interested.

A guy with a bushy beard named Mike ran over and told Ronnie they needed to leave right then because a guy they were going to buy cocaine from was about to leave and they needed to handle their business.

"You bet!" Ronnie said. "We need to go, go, go, now, buddy! He might be all out soon. Everyone wants a taste. That shit is fucking hot. We need to buy everything he has. No one knows what'll happen later, man."

They asked Joey and Luke if they wanted to join. The two told them they were okay, to go without them and have fun.

The two men left.

Luke didn't know why the guys were so excited about buying stuff. They had plenty at the party. It was just their dumb luck that they didn't think to stop and look around. It was everywhere.

The homeowner pointed his beer bottle in the direction of the door. "Those two guys, I bet you one of these days they're going to get their asses locked in a cell. And who are they going to call for bail? Where are they going to turn when I don't pick up the phone?" he took a swig of beer.

"You never know with people," Joey told him.

"But a broken clock is right twice a day. They have their good points. I'd want them on my side when shit goes down."

"How often is that?"

He scratched at his brow. "More often than not. Seems I piss off a lot of people. Make enemies wherever I go, that's what I do. I don't know, think they're jealous of me? Most of them are unstable. I just try to be a nice guy."

"Sounds like a problem."

"Not really," Luke said. "I don't care for that many peo-

Playground
ple. But you have to act like you care."

"I just ignore them."

"That works sometimes. You can't always ignore things. If someone fucks with you or someone close to you, you have to fuck them back. You have to fucking kill that motherfucker."

Joey said, "I don't know. Guess you'd have to take it on a case-by-case basis."

"But why take a chance? Luke said. "If someone wants to hurt someone, they don't care about people, feelings, whatever. Might as well put them down before they beat you to the punch."

They talked awhile longer about the subject. Joey felt awkward talking about that sort of thing with him. It was a little too creepy. The thought of running out of there and reporting him to the nearest police station crossed Joey's mind. He'd already admitted to killing. He seemed fully capable of doing it again. Honestly, he didn't want to find out.

Mindy came over. She asked the two what the hell they were doing. She ran inside. When she came back down she was carrying a big bag of grass. She told Joey there was a pound in the bag. She smiled and said they needed to get high. Layla and Annie went over to Mindy and told her they needed some of that good stuff.

"That's what it's all about," Mindy told them. "Having a good time, never know when it's all going to fade away. You have to live life for the moment."

Layla said, "I love your outlook, girl. It's so true."

"I'm one of the truest bitches you'll come across," Mindy laughed. "And those are some big facts."

"Can't argue with that. So tell me, I long have you guys lived here? I meant to ask the last time I was here."

Mindy cocked her head to the side for a minute. "About three years now."

"Really?"

"We almost didn't get it. Luck for us the guy who sold it gave us a discount. We still had to take out a pretty big loan, though."

"Yeah, prices for everything are outrageous these days."

"It's a shame. And things are only going to get worse. But we all have our health, that we can be thankful for."

Joey looked at Luke. "Hope things work out the way you want with the club. You know, if you still want, I can talk to my station manager a give you that interview. You can promote the club. Let them know you guys aren't doing the church anymore."

"Really?"

"I'll ask if I could do it."

"Anything helps. Promoting something, anything can be expensive."

"I know. It's fine. I'll ask when I go back to work, and I'll let you know something."

"Thanks, dude."

"Don't mention it."

"It means a lot to me. Not many people know what it feels like to take nothing and make it something. I mean, just having a vision isn't enough, sadly. It takes planning and preparation. We knew not everyone was going to be happy when they found out about the land the church used to be on. But my lawyer told me if they talk bad about me in the papers we'll sue the hell out of them. There were a few instances. When we told them what would happen they retracted their statements."

"That was smart of them."

"It was that or pay a chunk of money. They chose wisely."

"How many were there?" Joey asked.

"I can't say, that was one of the terms of the deal. Going after me was one thing, but after awhile, they started

Playground
dragging Harlan's name through the mud. He didn't need that kind of shit. He had the stuff he was dealing with. I can never forgive them for that."

Joey said it all was a shame. Luke told him to forget about all of that stuff, that there were still some people he needed to introduce him to inside.

"Okay, then."

They went back inside.

There were a few people on the couch; John Fox, Rex Dalton, Jane Stevens, and Sara Miloe. They all gave Joey a wave as they were introduced. Luke said he hoped Joey liked to meet new people. He had all sorts of connections. Luke had a person for everything. He could call them up at any hour of the day and they'd come through. It was good to know those in high and low places. He just didn't have an inside man at the radio station. But he did with Joey. It was always good to have connections, and people in your corner. You never know when they'll come in handy.

Rex said, "Hey, man, stick around awhile. We're just doing that thing we do, party until the sun comes up."

"I'll be around, sure," Joey told him.

John said, "Yeah, sometimes we go for two, or three days. might as well do it now, know what I mean? You only get one shot at this motherfucker. When I kick, I want to be remembered as someone who enjoyed life. Can't be afraid of it. Holy shit, this is it, buddy! It's all about being in the moment, you know. Fuck what they think about us. The powers that be, they try to tell you what to do. Fuck, man, we're adults. We aren't fucking kids or anything like that. If I wanted to, I could walk outside and blow someone's face clean off. I don't care who knows it."

"Of course," Joey said. "I'm always down for a good party. Guys seem pretty good. I don't kill people, though."

"You should," John told him. "You don't know what you're missing. It's very liberating."

"Guess I'll just have to take your word about that."

"Oh, man, we can go out later tonight and get someone, if you want?"

"I'm good. I'm not here for all of that."

"Your girl, maybe?"

Joey shook his head. "No, she wouldn't be into anything like that. What is wrong with you," Joey squinted at him. "What is wrong with you?"

John said, "No, no, no, I was just kidding about that stuff. Just pulling your leg. I don't do anything like that. Don't mind me, I'm a little too high. I don't have a clue what I'm talking about."

Rex said, "Don't worry about him. He needs professional help."

"Seems like it," Joey said. "Think he needs to quit while he's ahead."

"I tell him that all the time," Rex threw his arm around John. "He never listens."

"It happens," Joey said.

John asked Joey about the radio station, and what he was planning for the future. Joey told him that he didn't have anything special planned. Just the same old thing. John asked if he could be a guest sometime. He had some crazy stories to tell, and he wanted to make sure they got out there through the right form of media. At one time he considered starting a blog. He always told himself he was going to do big things, but did nothing. He was lost and needed to be found.

"I'll look at everything and see if I can fit you in," Joey told him. "I can't promise anything."

"That's good," John told him.

Rex came over and asked how long Joey and his lady

Playground

were going to be at the party.

"Not sure," Joey told him. "Might stay here. We've already drank way too much."

Rex said, "Just stay here, wake up in the morning, and start drinking again. Fuck it. Lots of times you need to walk around in a twenty-four-hour drunken haze."

Joey thanked the man and told him he'd take that under advisement.

Joey and Layla went back to the backyard and continued the party. It was nice out and everyone was feeling fine. There was something in the air, something you really couldn't put your finger on. As the hours passed they drank more. Things, bright and dark danced around.

33

Joey opened his eyes to a bang. He blinked a few times, then, another bang came. He wasn't sure if he'd dreamt the sound or not. He picked his head up and didn't recognize the room he was in. It took him a minute to remember where he was. He looked over and Layla was asleep next to him. He got out of bed and let out a stretch. He couldn't remember how much he drank, but he stopped counting after the half bottle of whiskey. It had been one hell of a night. He stood there and tried to remember but there was nothing. After a minute he heard muffled yelling coming from outside. He walked over to the window and looked out the blinds. Luke was standing in the front yard with a few people on either side of him. Three people were knelt in front of them, while another was face-down on the ground. The person face-down wasn't moving. After more yelling Luke took out a gun and shot all three men in the face. The three fell over.

Joey stepped away from the window. He didn't want Luke or any of the others to see him. They'd march up to the room and shoot him. He didn't want any of that. He looked at Layla and shook her awake. After she woke he told her they needed to leave as soon as they could.

"What are you talking about?" she looked at him. "What's the problem?"

"Come on, babe, we have to go."

She got out of the bed. "What's wrong? Are you okay? Are you still drunk?"

"I don't know," he said. "I just saw something I can't come back from."

"What was it?"

"I'll tell you later."

She reached out and touched his face. "You sure you're okay?"

Playground
"I'm not sure. I just know we need to get out of here." After they got ready they walked downstairs. As they walked around the corner Luke was standing there with a few other men. Luke introduced Joey and Layla to Tick and some of his other guys. They invited Joey and Layla to stay for lunch but they declined. Joey said they had things to do; a lie.

"We'll have to do it next time," Mindy told them. "It's a shame, though, I'm a good cook."

"I believe you are," Layla told her.

"Awe, thanks for the compliment."

"I'm not the best cook, so I praise anyone who is. I know, I need to learn how to do more."

Mindy said, "Well if you want, I can show you a few things sometime?"

"Okay, sure, that sounds good."

"I have a lot of cookbooks."

"I love cookbooks."

"They come in handy when you're looking for something new."

"You have to try new things now and then."

"You're right about that," Mindy said.

"Where did you get them?"

"The cookbooks? Oh, when my parents split I got them as a gift, along with some other old shit."

Layla asked when they got a divorce. It had been two years and Mindy was over it. That was strange for her at first, but she got used to it.

"Hell, Mindy, I'm an asshole for bringing that up. I didn't mean anything by it."

"That's fine."

"I know, but I'm sorry anyway."

Mindy smiled and told Layla to give her a call whenever she wanted to get a lesson. When they walked out of the house the bodies Joey saw earlier weren't there anymore. He didn't want to ask what happened, he knew better than that. Joey only knew he and the love of his life had to get out of there.

When Joey and Layla were a little speck down the road Mindy asked Luke if everything had gone as planned with the guys they killed that morning.

"They aren't living anymore," Luke told her. "If they start walking we have a problem."

"I'd say so," she replied.

Tick asked Luke why he thought Joey and Layla left like they did. Luke said not to worry, that they didn't know anything.

"You better hope that's the case," Tick told him.

"What makes you say that? Did they say anything to you?"

"No, not to me. I'm just saying if you keep having them come around they might start asking questions."

"Like what? The only thing they know about me is that I have some business around here and that I'm into a little bit of everything. Trust me, we have nothing to worry about from them."

"But what happens if they do find out?"

Luke sighed. "Well, we'll cross that bridge if it comes to that. Something tells me that won't happen."

"What makes you so sure?"

"I just have a feeling about it."

"You need to make sure of it."

Luke was about to tell him something else when Layne walked through the door. He looked tired and had beads of sweat on him. Layne asked what the guys had done to deserve to be killed. Luke told him not to ask questions like that, and that he needed to mind his own business if he knew what was good for him.

34

"I don't know about those guys," Joey said over breakfast.

Layla said, "What makes you say that?"

"Something about that Luke guy struck me as odd."

"Maybe he thought you were odd, you think?"

"Maybe."

She said, "I'm sure it'll all be okay. I'm sure your next time will be better. You'll know what to expect."

"We going back?"

"Yes," she said. "Don't you?"

"I'm sure it'll be fine. I think I just had something else in my mind. Don't know what."

"I think you nailed it."

"Thanks. We'll see. Everything will come out in time. I get the impression he thinks he needs me for something."

"Can you blame him? I mean, even if I didn't need you for something I think I'd just make something up so I could talk to you."

"Thanks for that."

"It's true. You're one of the best things that ever happened to me."

"My magic worked on you?" he laughed.

"Oh, you're a funny one."

"I do what I can."

"I see that."

Layla got up from the kitchen table and asked Joey if he wanted more coffee. As she filled both cups she asked if he wanted to go shopping with her. She needed some groceries and other things for her place.

"Sure," he said. "Don't have anything else going on. Don't have to be at the station until tonight."

"Good," she took his empty plate. "Maybe later we can

catch a movie or something, sound good?"
"Sure."
"Okay, then."
They got ready and headed out. After they got the groceries and took them back to her place they went to the movies. They saw Wild Times, a coming-of-age drama about a group of teens in New York. The title is a series of novels; five in all. Layla hoped they made the other books into movies. As they watched the movie Layla quietly told her man things like, "That's not the way it happened in the book," or, "They needed to explain that more."
When the movie ended and they walked out she asked him what he thought of it. He liked it. He had heard of the books but had never been interested.
Layla said, "If you want, I have all the books at my place if you want to borrow them sometime. The next one is coming out in a few months."
"Book or movie?" he asked.
"Book. I hope they make the others into movies."
"You never know until you know, you know?"
She laughed.
He told her he'd start reading the books, saying he's always up for reading new authors. She said that was good, that it was important to expand one's horizons. They went to dinner at Spouts, a burger place down the road from their apartment complex. The place had good food. They spent most of dinner discussing the movie they'd just seen. Layla told Joey it would be great if they could get Ethan to do the adaptions of the other books in the series.
"That's an idea," Joey told her. "I could run it by him, and see what he says."
"That would be pretty cool," she said. "And if he needed any help, we could be the ones to help him."

Playground

Joey shook his head. "I could put in a call to him, but I think he was planning on getting out of the business."

"Was he being serious about that?"

"I think so. He had said he was going to move back here."

"Well, people write and make movies in Arkansas."

"You make a good point."

"And if we played our cards right he might even put us in the movies."

Joey said, "Guess I need to read the other books."

"You'll love them."

"I'm sure I will."

"Just trust me. You'll thank me later, babe."

Joey told her the movie business would be an interesting thing to get into. Lord knows it would pay more than they were making at the time. They could move into a house or get one built. Their lives would change forever. He remembered how Ethan told him it was an addiction, you make one and you'll want to make more. Before you know it you'll have a dozen scripts on your desk. It'll turn into a job. Joey thought about it as they talked. Layla told him they could promote the movie on the radio show.

"We could," Joey agreed. "You can reach a lot of people that way."

"You can even get your new friend, Luke, involved."

"I'm not sure about that. Somethings tells me we'll end up fighting more than anything."

Layla said, "He could cut you into his crime stuff."

Joey laughed.

They paid their bill and walked out into the night. A thin breeze crept through everything. Layla said how beautiful the night was. There were people out walking around, making small conversations with one another. Joey and Layla got into her car and went back to his place. Layla told him she liked staying at his place. She felt comfortable and protected at his place. He didn't mind.

"Fine with me," he told her. "Any place is better with you."

"Awe, thank you. That was sweet of you to say."

"I'm just nice like that."

They opened a bottle of wine and drank the rest of the night away.

The two were lying in Joey's bed. Layla was cuddled next to him with her head on his chest. They talked before drifting off to sleep. They were in love with each other.

They spent the next day with each other before Layla went to work. He did nothing but watch TV before going in. It was a typical night at work, and that was the way he liked it. In his line of work, he had odd calls but that was it.

The next few days went without incident. One morning he walked out of the station to go home. He was tired and just wanted to get some rest. As he looked at his car from a distance a man got out of his car and met him before he got into his car.

"Joey?" the man said.

As Joey got closer he recognized the man as Layne, the strange guy who Layla said was bothering her.

"What are you doing, Layne?" Joey said.

"Nothing. I was just at home, thought I'd take a drive out here."

"Why?"

"To talk to you," Layne cracked a smile.

"It couldn't wait until I got to the complex?"

"I thought about that, and I told myself it wouldn't be a good idea."

Playground

Joey said, "What's so important? You okay?"

"I'm good."

"Well, let me go home, get some sleep and I'll get with you later."

Layne shook his head. "That won't work."

"What do you want?" What is this?"

"I hope my being here isn't disturbing to you, is it?"

"Why should it be?" Joey eyed the man suspiciously. "Trying to scare me or something?"

"Nothing like that. I was just hoping we could talk man-to-man about a few things."

"What's on your mind?"

Layne walked closer to Joey. "I need you to stop seeing Layla."

"Why? What business is it of yours?"

"She doesn't want to be with you."

"That so?" Joey took out a cigarette and lit it. "She told you that?"

"She's just placating you, waiting for the perfect time to dump your sorry ass."

"Why would she do something like that?"

"She wants to be with me."

Joey said, "That's funny. She told me you were creeping her out, how you wouldn't leave her alone."

"You know how women are? She was just playing hard-to-get."

"I didn't have a problem."

"Come on, I told you why that was. I bet all the girls do that to you?"

"Can't say that's ever happened."

Layne snorted. "Sure about that?"

Joey took a big drag off his cigarette and exhaled. "The fuck is your deal? You can get any girl you want."

"I know, and I want her."

"Well," Joey said, "you aren't going to get her."

Layne stared at him for a minute. "I've heard you've been hanging around Luke Reeves."

"And? You going to tell on me?"

"He's had people killed, you know? He's killed people. He just got rid of a few people the other day."

"What's your point?" Joey took the last drag off his cigarette and smashed it on the ground.

"Just warning you. Maybe one day you piss him off, what then? Layla will be bringing flowers to your grave."

Joey chuckled. "Thanks For the information."

Layne walked in front of Joey's car door, so he couldn't get in.

Joey said, "You going to more?"

"I'm sorry, you need to get inside your car?"

"Can't get anything passed you, buddy."

Layne gave a hard sniff into the air before he backed away from the car. Joey told him not to try and act like such a tough guy before he opened the car door. He fired up the engine and backed out of the parking lot. After he got gas and smokes at the gas station down the road Joey told himself he might have to talk with Luke about Layne. He didn't want the guy to turn into a problem. Layne looked and acted like he was a few donuts shy of a dozen. Joey paid the clerk and walked back out to his car. He was about to get in when he noticed Layne's car parked across the street in an empty fast-food parking lot. The place wasn't even open. He shrugged it off, figured the asshole was getting high or something.

He was about a mile down the road when he noticed Layne was following him. As long as he went his own way when they both entered the apartment complex.

When Joey parked in the parking lot Layne parked a few spaces away. Both men got out of their cars at the

Playground
same time.
Layne called out. "Hey, Joey, we're home now."
"Very observant," Joey muttered. "And your point?"
Layne walked over to Joey. "It's time to see what you're made of."
"I'm not going to fight you."
"You a pussy or something?"
"You're right about that," Joey walked to his apartment door.
"Hey, what's wrong with you? You're going to fight."
Joey turned to him. "I don't think so."
"Yes, you are."
Joey waved off the man and told him to go home and sleep it off. Just as he put the key in the keyhole Layne said he had something for him. Joey turned back around to see Layne holding a handgun.
Joey said, "You plan to use that?"
"Thought about it. Might have to."
"You're just going to stand there, threaten me like that? What the fuck is wrong with you?"
"Oh, you have no idea."
Joey looked at the gun for a minute. "You fire that thing and someone will call the cops."
"I'm willing to take that chance."
"What do you want?"
Layne said, "I told you what I want, buddy. I want you to stop seeing Layla."
"That's not going to happen."
"Why don't you get out while you still can."
"Well, I'm not going to do something like that."
"You stupid?"
"Maybe. Haven't been tested lately."
After a few more words Layne said he'd be seeing Joey again real soon, then he just walked away. Joey turned back around to enter his apartment when he was attacked

from behind, being tackled to the ground, and hitting his head on the lower part of the door. Good thing for Joey that the door was made of wood. Layne hit Joey in the back of the head with his fist. Joey was able to elbow Layne off him. When he picked himself up Layne was on the ground. They continued to fight for about ten minutes, both threw punches and kicks. During the confrontation, Layne's gun fell on the ground. When Layne saw it on the ground. He reached to pick it up but Joey kicked it away. Layne hit him in the face. Joey came back with a right hook. A man who was about to go for a run rushed over to try and break the fight up. It took another guy interfering to stop everything. One of the guys said if they didn't both walk away he'd have to call the cops. As they were going their separate ways Layne called out to Joey that he'd better watch his back.

When Joey got back to his apartment he called Layla but got no answer. He thought about leaving a message but decided against it. She called back an hour later, saying she was with some friends of hers and she had just noticed he'd tried to call. She was going to be back at her place soon, and she wondered if he'd want to get a pizza with her and watch some movies. He told her that was a fine idea.

That night they watched movies and ate pizza. She told him it was the perfect evening. All she needed was him and good conversation. As they talked he told her all about Layne, and what he told him.

"That guy is crazy," she said. "No telling what someone like that would do. You should start carrying a gun."

"You think?"

"He could come at you again."

"Oh, I'm not that worried about him," he told her. "That guy, he's nothing but talk. He had that gun but didn't use it. He was just trying to scare me."

Playground

"Trying to? Shit, you guys got into a fucking fight! I think it was a safe bet he wanted to hurt you. You're lucky he didn't use that gun."

"Maybe," he told her. "If he shoots me next time all I ask is that you give a little speech at my funeral. You can talk about what a great guy I was."

"I'll be sure to do that."

"Thanks, babe."

they continued talking and watching movies. They liked spending time with each other. As far as Layla was concerned Joey was the one for her, the one she wanted to spend the rest of her life with. She trusted him with her life.

35

A few days later Annie wanted them to come back to Luke's place for another party. She told them it'd be well worth it. Joey, he didn't want to but Layla talked him into it. She told him that he'd get used to it, and all the new people even if some of them were a little strange. He just hoped Layne wasn't going to be there to start anything. He wasn't in the mood for any of the bullshit. He wanted to spend as much time with her as he could, so he agreed. At any rate, he figured he could get material for the radio show.

They told Annie they'd meet her at Blu Pig, a fast-food joint about two miles from their apartment complex. When they got to the place they had a couple of burgers and fries while they waited for Annie. They both had been starving, and it seemed like two days since they had eaten anything. About ten minutes after they finished their food Annie drove into the parking lot. She wore a black blouse with a dark red skirt.

"How's it going, guys?" Annie said. "You guys eat without me?"

"Sure did," Layla told her. "We couldn't have waited forever, girl! Hell, we're hungry people over here. Where were you, anyway?"

"Had a few things at work I had to take care of. My boss got his dumbass fired this morning. The owner found out he stole some money."

"How much?" Layla asked.

"A few grand," Annie got wide eyes. "And I even heard he was sleeping with two of the bartenders."

"Really? That's crazy."

"But everything is copacetic once again. We just had to figure out some of the mess he made with some of the paperwork."

Playground
"Well, I'm glad it all worked out."
"Not for him, they didn't."
They laughed.
Annie went on to explain there should be a lot of people at the gathering, more than the other night they were there.
"Sounds like a good time," Joey said. "I'm always up for meeting new people. You never know about this crazy world we live in, some are good and others aren't. The ones who aren't, just move to the next one. It happens to the best of us, you know?"
Annie gave him a thumbs-up. "Never thought about it like that before."
"It helps," Joey went on. "You always hope for the best. It doesn't always work out the way you want. You live and learn, you know?."
"Sure, sure."
Layla said, "You guys think we should bring anything, beer or something?"
"Good thinking," Joey said. "We can hit up the store on the way."

They followed Annie to the store to get some beer. They got a couple of 12-packs. When they got to Luke's house there were all sorts of characters on the front lawn drinking and taking drugs like before. Joey asked the crowd where Luke was. This one guy introduced himself as Huey, wore a cowboy hat, and hollered into the night that everyone at the moment in time should be getting drunk and stoned. He told Joey he'd just sent the host a text, telling him to bring out some more drugs.
"We're getting low out here, brother," Huey told him. "We plan to go longer. Hell, it's all a party! You have to get straight with what's going down."
Joey said, "I hear you. Have to do what you have to,

fella. When it all comes to an end you want to make sure you're fully loaded."

"Yes, sir. You don't want any part of that mess."

Huey told Joey he would give him a discount on anything if he needed it. He just needed to ask and his wish would be granted. Joey told the man he'd keep that in mind, and that it would come in handy later.

"I'll be around," Huey said. "When you need me, just ask where the coolest guy at the party is."

"I'll keep that in mind."

A guy came up to Annie and they started talking. He wanted to get with her, but she wasn't having any of it. He called her some bad names and stormed away.

Annie said, "Damn, I get tired of losers who want nothing but to sleep with me. I have more to offer, you know?"

Luke came to the door and welcomed his guests. He was so glad they came. He told them that they had been missed the past few nights when they had parties. Joey looked at Luke and told him he had to make money at somehow. No one was going to give you anything, or, that had been his case all his life. He couldn't speak for anyone else. Luke laughed. Joey didn't know what to think. Luke wasn't born into a rich family. And he spent more than half of his life without his parents. With Harlan in prison and Tiffany off doing whatever, he knew he couldn't count on them for anything. While Joey didn't care for the type of empire he was building.

Luke led Joey and Layla through the maze of people having a good time. Luke liked the fact people had good times at his house. He knew eventually they'd all want something from him. He liked the idea that not everyone knew him, what he was going to do, what he was thinking. He learned long ago not to let people know what you were thinking. When asked how could they afford these parties every night, Luke said it was from a private fund they set up. Joey didn't want to know and dropped it.

Bodies were scattered everywhere. They went outside and it was the same thing. The layout of the backyard was the same as before; the bar, furniture, and big blankets laid out on the ground. Joey asked what the blankets were for. Luke told him they were for relaxing.

"Whatever makes people feel good, I guess," Joey told the man.

"Yeah, it's a nice place to be. It's important to me I take care of all my guests. I want this to be a place where people like coming to."

Joey told him it was a nice idea to have a place people liked to be around. It's a refreshing thing to have friends who want to be around you. Joey still wasn't sold on Luke and his friends. If anything he wanted nothing to do with any of them. He was slowly finding out what Luke was all about, and he didn't like it at all. The only reason he agreed to hang out with the crowd was because Layla and Annie liked them, and he wanted to make his girl happy. Even though he told Layla some of the things Luke had been up to she didn't seem to mind. Joey didn't understand why she didn't seem to care. When he told her all the stuff about Luke he left out the part about seeing him murder people. He didn't want to worry her.

As they greeted people and started drinking Joey wondered how many nights they'd have to spend at Luke's. But at any rate, he was always one to enjoy a good party.

The night crept on and conversations became drunk Harlan Reeves walked over to Joey and told him they were going to be having a special ceremony.

"What kind of Ceremony?" Joey asked.

"You'll see. It's something they've been doing a few

times a month. Now, I can join in the fun since I'm out."
Joey nodded. "Must be a good feeling, huh?"
"It feels great. I never want to go back to that fucking place. Man, honestly, I'd rather die before I went back there. The best way to do that is not to get caught."
"Well, that's what you need to do then."
Harlan said, "One way people always get caught is others tell on them. I couldn't have any of that."
"I can tell you, you won't have to worry about me. What people want to do is their own business. Who am I to say what's best for anyone?"
"Glad to hear you say that."
Joey nodded. "And I've learned over the years it's not wise to talk about people behind their backs."
"You're right about that. Some people don't mess around with stuff like that."
The two continued to talk. Joey asked Harlan if he had any plans. Harlan had a friend who wanted him to start driving a truck. Harlan wasn't too sure about doing something like that, spending all that time on the road.
Joey said, "Yeah, there isn't enough they can pay me to do something like that."
"I said the same thing. I have my freedom, I don't want to spend it on the road all the time. It might be good money, but there's more to life than just paper."
"I know what you mean."
Luke came over to the two as they continued to talk, telling Harlan he needed to talk to him in private. They went off to discuss something. Joey asked himself what they needed to discuss, but he figured it was none of his business.
Awhile later the two came back, and Harlan was wearing a white robe. They told everyone to finish their drinks and gather around the blankets. Layla and Annie ran over and told Joey to join them at the gathering spot.

Playground

Once everyone was around the blankets Luke and Harlan walked in the middle of everyone.

Harlan looked at everyone. "Ladies and gentlemen, thank you for joining us tonight. Luke and I trust you are enjoying the festivities. We want everyone to have a memorable time. We just want you guys to have a good time. It's all about peace and love."

Luke said, "Just don't ask if the house is for sale, it's not. I'm sorry if I just shattered your dreams. For those who haven't heard, Church of Modo, it's not going to happen. Instead, we're opening a nightclub, Modo. It should be up and running in about eight or nine months. It's going to be on the site of the old Church of Modo. We need to thank all of you guys. If you want to donate any kind we have boxes inside."

A few claps and cheers came from the crowd. Some laughed and joked around.

Harlan said, "I wanted the church but it wasn't meant to be, I guess. You know, everything happens for a reason, right? But a nightclub is a good time! When I was in prison I knew I wanted to do something big when I got out. At first, I didn't know how anything would go. I was inside for too long. I'm just glad I got out when I did."

Someone in the crowd yelled out how glad they were Harlan was back, and that they'd better not take him away again. If they didn't happen to take him away the guy said he'd bust him out. Harlan laughed and thanked the guy, saying there was no need for that. It was something that wasn't going to happen.

As Harlan continued addressing the crowd Joey looked around at everyone. He was amazed at how intently they were listening to him. He must have put some sort of spell over them or something. It looked like Harlan could use a radio show all his own. Out of the corner of his eye, Joey saw Layne approaching. He wasn't in the mood for a fight, so he hoped Layne would stay civil. There were certain people out there who were ready for a fight no matter where they went.

Layne walked over to Joey. "The fuck are you doing here? You come for a beating? If that's what you want, that's exactly what you'll get. I don't care. I'm always ready for anything."

Joey said, "Don't strain yourself. I don't want a fight."

"I'm afraid you stumbled into one."

"Just calm down, buddy. I'd hate to have to embarrass you in front of all of these people."

"You have that backward," Layne chuckled. "You should be glad you aren't on the ground right now. Most of the time, that's exactly where you'd be, son. But I like you. I like that radio show of yours."

"Trust me, I thank my lucky stars."

"You should," he looked over at Layla. "What about it darling, want to go home with a real man?"

Layla smiled. "Already have one of those, but thanks," she clapped her hands together. "Oh, were you talking about yourself? Sorry about that. Yeah, man, I hate to tell you but that'll never happen. Plus, from what I hear you aren't a real man."

"Sure about that?" Layne walked closer to her. "I'll be the best lover you ever had. You'll keep coming back for more. We can get to it right now, drop this loser. It's about time for him to get tired of you anyway, isn't it?"

"Fuck off."

"No, bitch, fuck you," Layne pushed her back. He balled up his fist like he was going to punch her.

Just as Joey got between Layla and Layne, Luke looked over and saw what was going on. Luke told Layne to come up next to him. "Come on, Laybe, what are you doing that for? We don't want that bullshit around here."

Playground

After the commotion died down Harlan kept talking to the crowd. He told them they still needed to stick together even though they weren't reopening the church. They were going to be developing a new faction. They needed to keep the dream alive.

Harlan said, "We need to be as one. All of you are here because you're friends with me or Luke. We were very careful who we selected. Trust is important in this thing. We need to make sure you guys don't go rogue, and try to knock down the world on your own. When the time is right we'll strike."

Luke said, "And part of the reason we brought you guys together tonight is to test you. How are we going to test you? Here's the thing, we're going to be a big family here. As I'm sure you know one of the elements about being in a family is that we have to trust each other, trust that we will do the right thing by each other."

A few in the crowd agreed.

Luke continued. "Part of being in our family is about sharing, you have to learn to share. Share everything, information, supplies, and our bodies. We aren't going to go at it small tonight. We are going to ask only one girl to participate in the sharing tonight," Luke scanned the crowd. He pointed at Annie and told her to stand beside him.

Annie got a puzzled look on her face. It took her a moment to realize what he just asked. After a few minutes, she walked over to Luke. He told her to take off all of her clothes and lay on one of the blankets.

"Take everything off?" Annie asked.

"Yes," Luke told her.

"Why? What for?"

He pulled a handgun out and pointed it at her head. "Fucking to it or die."

She took off her clothes slowly as a few tears rolled

down her face. He told her she had a beautiful body. He ran his hands over her pale breasts. After he was done he moved his hand down to her vagina and stuck it in. After she let out some light moans he took it out. He looked at the crowd and asked if Annie was beautiful. A few people muttered things. Some were surprised at what was going on, others weren't.

Luke held his gun to Layne's head and told him to undress. After he had all of his clothes off they were both told to lay on the blanket and have sex. They had to or Luke was going to kill them both. The two had sex in front of everyone. When they finished Luke had them stand. Luke told everyone he was sorry things had come to this, and he pointed his gun at Layne and shot him two times, dropping him on one of the blankets. Luke turned the gun on Annie and shot between the eyes.

Luke made it clear to everyone that if anyone even thought about going to the cops they'd be very sorry. He'd have no choice but to kill the person the same way. A few people yelled and screamed. Everyone was in shock. Luke and Harlan instructed some of the guys to clean up the mess.

Harlan said, "Sorry, we know that must've come as a shock to some of you. We had to let all of you know we meant business, that if you disrespect people in any way that's what is going to happen. And honestly, I couldn't stand Layne. He was always a little fucker. He was given a lot of chances to redeem himself and he kept messing up. I just hope you guys learned something from this."

Someone asked why Annie was killed. Luke said he just felt like it, plus, from what others said he tried to get her to have sex with him one night and she wasn't having any of it.

Luke pointed the gun in the air. "Anyone else what any of this?"

Playground
No one said anything.
"That's what I thought," he lowered the gun. "I trust you guys won't go running to the cops, telling them a bunch of lies. If I hear any of that going on you'll have to pay. Now, I'd feel really bad about doing that. But sometimes you have to do shit you don't want to."

Harlan said, "And if they find out about this they'll lock me back up, you don't want that to happen, do you? If that does happen, mark my words, after I'm in the cell you'll get a visit from my son or someone else. And you'll be dead," he looked up into the sky, then looked at everyone. "Luke told me these two had to go. Said they'd become a problem and couldn't be contained anymore. Now, I don't know. I knew Layne but didn't think much of him. Luke did the world a favor by getting rid of him. And the girl, I didn't even know her. Luke wanted him gone for whatever reason."

There was some scattered chatter from the crowd. Some of them still couldn't believe what happened. Layla looked at Joey and asked why that happened to her friend. He didn't know. She hugged him tight.

Mindy came over to everyone. "You guys all should get another drink. Get it while you can. It could be all gone soon. We just want everyone to enjoy themselves."

Harlan said to everyone. "Here's the thing, if you want to be part of us we need you to be loyal to us We can't afford any of you to go astray. If you ever need help I suggest you get with one of your fellow members to help you," he paused. "Here's the thing, the times are changing, and moments are upon us. The world is going to end soon. We don't know exactly when that'll be. We need to be ready for anything."

Someone asked what they were going to do.

Harlan continued. "I think most of you know my history, yes? Before I was arrested at the compound all those years ago I believed the end was near. Now, as you guys know, that didn't happen. I was recently visited by God again, we need to stick together. We need to survive and continue the human race. We won't be here much longer. They will invade, and we need to live among them. Yes, ladies and gentlemen, I'm talking about aliens. God told me they'd be contacting me any day now. When they arrive they want us to shed our Earthly bodies and continue in their skin. All of you here, all of you are for a reason. You were chosen."

Someone asked when the aliens were coming. Harlan said he didn't know, but they had to be ready for anything. Harlan told them when they open Modo that they'll be able to hang out there. Until the club was ready they'd have to party at Luke's place. That was fine with all of them. They liked Luke's place. The idea of living a carefree life was something that attracted most of them, the spectacle of it all.

Another guy from the crowd, Calvin Webb, approached Harlan and told him that he wasn't comfortable with what happened to Layne and Annie. He said he might have to go to the police about it.

Harlan looked at the man intently. "I guess you need to do what you think is best."

"Two people were murdered here, you aren't going to do anything about that?"

"Why should I?"

Calvin said, "What are you doing here? What the fuck is going on. They didn't deserve to die."

"And they told you this? Who are you to make that determination? Did you know them outside of this house?"

"I didn't even know them. You can't just go around killing everyone you want."

Harlan nodded. "That's an interesting way to think about it," he took out his gun. "Now, if I shoot you in the

Playground
face nobody here will give a flying fuck. I mean, yeah, they might talk about you for about five minutes but that'll be it. You'll be forgotten so fast. No one will even care. We'll just put you in the ground."
Calvin gave a hard swallow. "Fuck you!"
Harlan raised his brow, turned his back on the man, took a couple of steps, turned back around a shot the man in the head and chest. Calvin fell to the ground.

Luke told everyone if anyone else had a problem they should say something. They didn't want any unpleasantness down the road. The crowd said nothing. After the bodies were taken away and everything cleaned up Harlan told everyone to go home. The sun slowly started to come out. As everyone started to file out of the backyard Harlan told everyone not to talk about what happened. If they did they'd be sorry.
On their way to the car, Layla told Joey she didn't feel good. She just wanted to go home and forget the horror that happened.
"I understand," Joey told her.
"Thanks."
As the sun fingered itself across the land they got into the car and drove away. On the way home the silence was deafening. Joey wasn't sure what to tell her that would make everything okay. But nothing he could say or do would suffice. The only thing he could hope for was that time would help things get easier.
"So, do you want to come back to my place?" he asked.
"I do."
When they got into his apartment Layla ran to the restroom and cried. Joey told her if she needed anything to let him know. When he asked if she was going to be okay she said she didn't know. He felt bad. Layla walked out of the bathroom but didn't say anything. He cooked

some food and offered her some and she declined. She went back to her place.

36

When he went back to work all he could think about was Layla. He wanted to be there for her. He'd tried her on the phone a few times but never got an answer. He continued with his job, talking, answering phone calls, and drawing up theories about the world. He told himself that after his shift he would go home, get some sleep then knock on her door. And he figured if she didn't answer he would write her a little note and put it outside the door. He needed to make sure she was okay.

After a few hours of people calling in with their rants and rambles, he was finally off work. When he got home he stayed up a little while watching television and thinking. The next thing he knew he woke up. He looked at his phone and realized six hours had gone by. He rubbed the sleep from his eyes and picked himself up off the bed. Birds were chirping outside his bedroom window. Somebody in the distance was mowing their lawn. He looked over at the nightstand and grabbed the pack of cigarettes and a lighter. He took one of the smokes out and lit it. After giving a deep sigh he stood. He walked to the bathroom to get ready for the day. A hot shower was just what the doctor ordered.

When he was out running errands he thought it'd be a nice gesture to pick up some flowers and candy for Layla. He didn't understand the philosophy of buying flowers for people when they were just going to die, the flowers that were. Yes, you could replant them if you were dedicated enough, but she wasn't the type who would do such a thing. He thought he'd pick up some of her favorite coffee, too. Nothing was quite as comforting as coffee. He knew she was upset about her friend being killed. As much as he wanted he couldn't do anything about that pain. All he could do was be there for her.

Bradley Davenport

He needed to make sure she was going to be okay. He walked over to her apartment door and knocked. No answer. He knocked a few more times and still no answer. A nervousness crept over him. He knocked again. After a minute the door unlocked and opened. Layla was on the other side. She was dressed in a dark blue t-shirt and white sweatpants. Her hair was messy and she looked as though she'd been crying. In a soft voice, she told him to come in.

The place was immaculate, top to bottom was clean as could be. The television was turned on but the volume was cut off. They just stood there for a minute looking at each other.

"How've you been?" He asked.

She shook her head. "Okay, I guess."

He handed her the flowers and chocolate. "These are for you."

"Thanks. You didn't need to do that."

"I wanted to."

She smiled. "It means a lot."

He told her he wanted to make sure she was okay.

"I've done a lot of thinking," she said. It's been hard."

They sat on the couch in the living room

"I can only imagine what must have been going through your mind," he told her. "I was pretty shocked, myself. I think most everyone there was."

She offered him something to drink. She rattled off a list of beverages she had available. He told her he'd take what she was having. She got a couple of sodas and handed him one.

"Thanks," he cracked the can open.

She opened hers and took a drink. "I have to apologize for being so distant. I know you were thinking it, so I thought I'd just come out and say it."

"I wasn't thinking much of anything," he looked at her.

Playground
"I didn't know quite what to do or say. She was a good friend of yours
"for the past few days, I've had endless thoughts race through my head. I couldn't help it, thinking about everything, tossing and turning at night. There was a point that night I thought they were going to kill us."
"Really?"
"I didn't know what was going to happen."
"I can't presume to know what you were thinking about."
They lit cigarettes.
She said, "I hope they pay for what they did. That shouldn't happen to anyone."
"No, it shouldn't. Their day will come."
She took a drag off her cigarette. "And isn't that Harlan guy on parole? His ass needs to go back to prison. They need to keep him there."
"I don't even know why he's out. I know Luke had said something about how he had useful information that the cops needed, something like that."
"Like he told on someone?"
"I guess."
"Still, that's fucking crazy. Didn't he kill people?"
"That's what he went away for. I mean, he didn't get arrested for starting a cult, for doing strange things. A lot of people do strange things who aren't behind bars."
"That's more than a little strange."
"Yeah, I agree with you," he said.
She blinked. "I thought about going to the police. I didn't. Had a nightmare they found out and came after me. But you'd think someone else there would talk, don't you think?"
"I don't know."
She said, "We'll maybe we can call the cops, you know?

"We'd have to use a pre-paid phone. They'd be able to track our phones. That'll turn it into a whole other thing."

"I guess you're right."

They went to the store that afternoon and bought a cheap throw-away phone. She called the police and disguised her voice as best she could. She just told the officer that she heard gunshots in the area the other night, and they might want to go out to the house and make sure everything was okay with whoever lived there. After they made the call they threw the phone away so there'd be no trace. After they got rid of the phone they went to grab a bite to eat.

A few days later, Joey was wrapping up his radio show. It had been a frustrating shift, to say the least. It seemed most of the people who called up the station that night had been more interested in talking about the fair that was going to be in town the week after than wanting to discuss the topic of the night. When Joey closed the show he took off his headphones and told his producer that the show that night had been a piece of shit.

"Hell, I should've just stayed home if this was all I was going to get out of people," he said.

Bruce laughed. "It happens. Nothing we can do about it. The price we pay for being servants of the people. Something different is in the air these days."

"You won't get any argument out of me."

"It's the way of the world. No one can fully understand it. You can try, spend all the time on it, the only thing you'll get is twisted in your mind."

"Right."

"But what the hell do I know? I'm just an old son-of-a-bitch who's been doing this gig for far too long. Shit, half the time I wake up amazed to still be alive. Figure the man upstairs would take me in my sleep."

"I think that would be the best way to go, no pain."

"Exactly. No fear of anything. One night you go to sleep, next day you just don't wake up. Everything just ends."

They did some things around the studio before they left. The morning crew came in as they were finishing things up. They talked for about twenty minutes. Everyone wished each other a nice day, and that was that. The morning crew didn't want to hold them up too long. They knew the hours were rough at times.

When they got to the parking lot Joey and Bruce went in separate directions. As soon as Joey got into his car someone knocked on the driver's window. He rolled it down and looked. He was surprised to see it was Luke and Harlan Reeves. What did they want? They told him that they needed a quick word, and asked him to get out of the car. Joey opened the door and got out.

"Sorry to bother you like this," Luke said. "I guess you had a long one?"

"Wasn't too bad," Joey said. "I've had worse. What can I do for you guys this morning?"

"Oh, we were just in the neighborhood. Thought we'd stop and have a little chat with you."

"That so? What about?"

"We had a visit yesterday, a somewhat unpleasant visit from the police."

Joey raised a brow. "Oh, yeah? Someone gets arrested or something?"

"Nothing like that," Harlan told him. "No, not this time, at least. They were checking up on a call they had earlier. It seems someone had reported hearing gunshots from our place the other night, the night we had the last party."

"That so? What did they say?"

"Just said they got a call about shots fired that night."

"Oh?" Joey gave the man a puzzled look.

Harlan continued. "We told the cops that someone must've been out hunting that night."

"You guys have deer out there? I never noticed."

"I've only seen deer out there once. The thing is, no one goes out there hunting for anything. After the cops left Luke and I were thinking about that night, about how we never saw any cars that weren't supposed to be out there."

Joey said, "Maybe you guys just missed them?"

Harlan looked at Luke, then back at Joey, and shook his head. "No, that's not it. We took an inventory of everyone who was there that night and started narrowing down who could've called. whoever it was didn't give their name," he snorted. "Who would be so fucking stupid to do a thing like that? Did they think we were never going to find out? You and your girl were there that night and know what happened. You know what those shots were."

Joey shook his head. "I do. What are you saying here?"

"Were you the one who called the cops?" Luke asked.

Joey looked at both men for a minute. "Listen, I didn't call anyone about anything. If you guys don't mind I would like to go home. I've worked a tiring shift and I'm exhausted. If you want, we can continue this conversation later this afternoon?"

"That won't work," Harlan told him. "We have other things to do then. A full plate. The world doesn't stop just for you, you fuck."

Joey said, "Well, okay, you got my answer, now what? Are you still going to keep asking me the same thing?"

Luke told him in a cold voice that if he was Joey he would've made the call. If he was Joey he wouldn't want to be mixed up in anything having to do with murder.

Playground

Harlan pulled out his gun. "This thing here, if we find out you were lying to us I'll have to shoot you. I'd rather not do that. If someone tells on me I go back to prison. No more parties for me. They'll leave me there until the day I die. Hell, they might put some of the poison in me and get rid of me quickly. But before I go I'll tell Luke to kill that bitch of yours and everyone in your family. They'll all just disappear. I don't want to do that. Don't force my hand, you won't like it. I like you."

"Understood," Joey told him.

Out of nowhere, Harlan punched Joey in the belly, dropping the radio host to the ground. Harlan told him to consider that a warning, and if he found out it was Joey who made the call the punishment would be worse. They knew where he lived and worked. They told him they were holding a meeting at Luke's place two days later and he and Layla had to be there. If they weren't there they'd be hunted down and killed. No nice funeral or cemetery, they were just going to be thrown in a dumpster or a ditch somewhere.

Joey got up off the ground just to be hit down again. After they threatened Joey some more the two got into the car they came in and sped away.

When Joey got back to his place he collapsed on his couch. He was in pain but nothing too bad. Luckily, he didn't need to get medical attention. He fell asleep and woke five hours later. He felt like shit and figured a shower might make him feel better. After he got out of the shower he called Layla and told her what happened. She came over to his place. They talked about what they should do. If they went to the cops they'd find out and kill them. If they didn't continue to go to the meetings they'd be dead. It looked like there was no way out. How did they get themselves into this situation?

Layla brought up the idea of going to the cops, saying that they wanted to stay alive. She had a lot more life to live.

Joey said, "I wouldn't be surprised if they had someone watching this place and tailing us, making sure we don't do anything we shouldn't."

"I doubt that, babe. Who would be crazy enough to spend their whole day tailing people?"

"Really? You've met these people. I wouldn't put anything past them, those crazy fucks."

They spent the next few hours running down their options. Layla told him they should just leave the area, and go across the country. Hell, they could go stay with Ethan in California. They could start fresh. Joey considered it then said he didn't want to.

"So, you just going to wait here till they hurt you, babe? Come on, don't be foolish. We can spend the rest of our lives together. We stay here, we'll have to always look over our backs. That's no way to live."

"We won't have to do that."

"What do you mean?" she asked. "They'll never stop."

"I'm thinking if we go along with it for a bit, that might be our best bet here. After some time we'll just tell them we want out."

Layla didn't want to go through with being a member, however, that looked better to her than death. She agreed to join. Anything to stay alive.

37

They went to the next gathering Luke had. They told Luke and Harlan that after thinking it over and debating for some time about it, they decided they wanted to be a part of the cult. They'd do anything that was asked of them.

"We're glad you two decided to join us," Luke told them. "It means a lot. And you'll see what we have to offer is beyond anything you could imagine."

Harlan and Luke looked at everyone who'd gathered in the backyard. They were impressed with the amount of followers they had.

Harlan said, "We see everyone's enjoying the food and drinks we've provided. We want everyone to feel comfortable here. If there's anything else we can do, just let us know and it'll be taken care of. Think of us as family. Every single one of you has something to contribute to the group. We don't believe in leaving anyone out," he paused. "On that token, we will not tolerate anyone who denigrates anyone else. Don't be cruel to each other. Everyone is equal here. If you see it fit to break this rule, that's your choice, just know that you'll be punished. When we go see those from beyond we want to have pure souls. I don't think that's too much to ask for, do you? If you have a problem with anyone here just come tell either Harlan or myself. I'm sure we can figure things out."

After Luke was finished talking he walked over to the bar for a drink. His wife, Mindy, told everyone she so so happy to see them. She told everyone that the gatherings meant a lot to her. She never really had a family to call her own, and she loved how everyone got along. When being in a cult one of the worst things was being around people you didn't like. But it was just one of those things about life you couldn't control.

Harlan said, "Tonight, we're going to have another performance for you. We want to give all of you a communal experience. You have to remember, these are just the bodies we're using for now, and only that. When the aliens beam us up we'll get new bodies. Frankly, the ones we have now are nothing but trash, am I right? I know it might be hard to understand, but it's true. I wouldn't steer any of you wrong. We're all about peace and love over here."

Someone in the crowd asked about his prison time, and if he regretted killing the people he had.

Harlan said, "Yes, I do regret some of the things that happened back then. But I can't go back and change any of it. There were a lot of drugs floating around back then. Because of what happened I missed things, things I should've been here for."

The guy with the question asked if he heard from any of the victim's families. Harlan looked at the man and said he never heard from any of them at the time. But when it was released to the press he was getting out he heard from all sorts of people. They wrote all sorts of letters to the warden and parole board. None of it mattered. The powers that be had already made up their minds. When asked if he would be a future threat, Harlan said that he had no reason to hurt anyone, that it wasn't him, it was the drugs. That poison got in his head and made him do those things. Harlan told the board they had nothing to worry about. Yes, he had information the FBI needed, but if it meant they were going to turn a maniac loose they'd pass.

"I'm glad to be here," Harlan told all of them. "I spent a lot of my hours on the inside thinking about what I was going to do on the outside if I ever got released. That day came, and I was more than happy about it. Luke

Playground
picked me up and the first thing we did was stop for burgers. I was a free man. Later that day we had a party here, a homecoming," he gave everyone a big smile. "I don't want any of you to go through what I did. If something comes up, you do something to get yourself compromised with the law, all you need to do is come see us and we'll figure it out. And if some people have to go, well, that'll be dealt with."

No one said anything. Joey told himself that would've been a great time to have recorded Harlan and get him on audio saying what he had just said. He could've turned it in to the police and they'd handle the rest.

Harlan told all the women to stand on the blankets that were in the center of the backyard. Layla was a little confused about what they were doing, but she went along with it. She didn't want to become a problem. She joined the rest of the women. Harlan walked over to the guys. He picked three men to join the women. He told the first guy, a tall man named Sanders to pick the woman he wanted to have sex with. Sanders looked at all the women for a minute, all ten of them. For a minute he was going to pick Layla but decided on the girl next to her. The second guy picked the girl who was standing on the other side of Layla. The third guy walked up to Layla and looked her up and down. He asked what her name was. After she took a hard swallow she told him. He got a smile on his face. Layla saw Joey, and she knew as soon as the guy picked her he'd attack the guy. Just as Layla bit her bottom lip the guy turned his head to the front of the line, saying he was going to pick his wife. He walked over to her. An ocean of relief washed over Layla. The only guy she was interested in was Joey. After all three men were with their chosen woman Harlan instructed them to take off their clothes and have sex with them. When they finished they had to move to the next girl who was chosen. After each guy got two turns with each woman Harlan told them to stop.

Later that night they were back at Joey's place. They couldn't believe what happened, and that they had to watch.

"You have to make me a promise," Layla told him.

"What would that be?"

"You have to promise me that when you get chosen, feelings won't be involved whatsoever."

"Of course," he said. "I love you."

"It'd be easier if you didn't have to do it at all, but I know that can't happen. If you don't do what they say they may kill you."

"I know they'll kill me," he told her. "It'll just have to be one of those things. We're just going to have to see how this thing plays out. There's no way around it."

"That's the sad truth."

"Afraid so."

They made something to eat and spent the next few hours watching TV, not talking about the evil that loomed over them. Joey told himself that they had a long way to go to get out of the mess they were in.

Two nights later they attended another party. They inducted a few new members. Someone asked Harlan how many more people they needed. Harlan said they could use as many people as they could. He told them a war was about to take place, and they needed as many souls as possible to go beyond this life. Harlan couldn't say for sure how long they were going to be on the planet they were going to. As he put it, the head alien would appear in his dreams and give him the information. The being told him that there were things that couldn't be revealed to him at that point, that in time everything would be ex-

Playground

plained. Harlan told them, the followers, that the higher beings would only talk to him. They considered Harlan the leader, and they didn't want to waste their time talking with anyone inferior.

Harlan said, "We have to be very cautious, as I'm sure you can imagine. But if you know of anyone with whom you can trust, feel free to tell me and we can work on getting that person to join. After all, we're trying to help people, not hurt them. Those who have already been hurt, it was because they mistreated another. We can't have that. We need to respect one another," he took a pause and looked at everyone. "We need to learn how to trust each other. And that's one of the reasons we have these sex episodes. We need to learn to become one, and I include myself in that."

Twenty minutes later Harlan was still rambling on about the importance of this and that when Luke said they needed to get on with it. Harlan looked at Luke and laughed. Luke knew he was one of the only people who could get away with pulling a stunt like that.

Harlan said, "My kid is funny. Oh, man, I've enjoyed spending this time with him. You can never get lost time back. The only thing you can do. It's been something, I can tell you."

People in the crowd told him that was a good thing, and that it would be in his best interest to stay out of prison.

After more talks and laughter Harlan told everyone it was that time of the night, that time when they got wild and free, when two became one. He picked a few women to join him in the center of the yard. One of the women who went to the center was Layla. She was nervous. Harlan told the women to get naked. Layla did as she was told and undressed like the others. She ran her hands across her pale breasts. Her nipples were as sharp as knives. Everyone saw that her crotch was nicely shaven.

Bradley Davenport

Harlan told a couple of guys to join them. The first guy that got to the center went right to Layla. The other guys got to fight over the other women. When everyone was ready Harlan told them to start having sex. They did a few rounds. Layla ended up having sex with 4 different guys. After they were all done they got dressed and rejoined the crowd.

The next group of men and women were called to the center, Joey was among them. After everything was done he had sex with three women. The whole evening was a mix of excitement and awkwardness. Everyone was glad it was over.

Joey and Layla looked at each other. They didn't know what to say. When they got back to their apartment complex they went to their separate apartments to take hot showers. They both felt like shit. Later when Layla went to Joey's place they agreed never to discuss what happened.

"I think that would be best," Layla said. "This is turning into something I don't like. It's completely fucked up and dark. I don't think I can do it anymore."

"You can. I know you can. It won't be for much longer, I promise. Do it for me."

Layla nodded. "Yes, babe, I'll fuck other men for you. Lucky thing, you get to watch. Must get you harder than a rock seeing me with another guy, am I right?"

"I didn't enjoy it. I hated to see you have to do that. I'm very sorry."

"But you didn't do anything about it."

"What did you want me to do? I had nothing, just my two hands. They would've killed me before I knew what happened. I hated it as much as you. I'm sorry for everything."

"I don't know," she sighed. "I just wished that had never happened."

Playground
"I know."
"Do you? I bet you don't know what was going through my mind, you a mind reader now?"
"Among my many talents that's not one of them, no."
"Thought so."
He brought her in close and hugged her.
They kissed.
They did their best not to talk about what happened ever again. But in the next two weeks, they would be forced to have sex with a dozen people each.
Joey began to get the feeling that the excuse Harlan have for the orgies was bullshit. He liked to amuse himself, telling everyone it was get get emotionally closer to each other. Harlan liked to get off by watching others in the act.
At one of the parties, while Joey was watching the show with the others at the house, he felt a tap on his shoulder. He turned around and saw Mindy. She was dressed in a black blouse and mini skirt. Her thin-framed glasses and red lipstick went well with her complexion.
"Hey," Joey said to her.
"Having a good time?"
"It's okay."
She nodded toward the people having sex. "Enjoying the show?"
"Not really."
"Really?"
"Normally, I'd prefer being the one having sex."
She laughed. "Well, the night's still young."
"Good observation."
She smiled. "Want to get a drink? They're going to be at it for awhile."
"Sure."
She took his hand as they walked to the bar.
"It's a lovely night, wouldn't you agree?" she asked.

Bradley Davenport

"There's just something so calming about it."

"I guess so."

They both got a beer and two shots of whiskey.

She said, "I know you don't want to continue watching the show. Let's go inside to my bedroom."

"What about your husband?"

"Oh, he won't care."

"Sure about that?"

"We have an open relationship thing."

"Those can be tricky sometimes."

"With certain people, I guess."

He let out a chuckle. "I just don't want anyone kicking my ass."

"He wouldn't do that. He'd have to get through me first."

"I feel so protected."

"You should."

"Thanks for that," he told her.

Joey looked at the people having sex one last time before they stepped into the house. Before heading upstairs they grabbed some more drinks.

"Let's boogie," she winked at him. "I've been waiting for this since we first met."

When they got in the bedroom they drank all the drinks. They undressed each other and became one.

38

"What the fuck are you doing?" Luke had a shotgun trained on Joey. "Answer me!"
Joey blinked three times. "What?" he picked himself up from the bed. "What are you doing?"
Joey cocked the gun. "You want to die, motherfucker?"
"Hadn't planned on it," he looked at the other side of the bed, and Mindy was gone. "Hey, where'd she go?"
"She's downstairs."
"That would explain it," he looked at Luke. "You mind getting that gun out of my face? It makes me a little nervous."
"As it should," Luke lowered the gun.
"Thanks," Joey said. "My head's still a little foggy."
"Well, did you enjoy yourself?"
"I did, thanks."
"It won't happen again. You're lucky I didn't shoot you between the fucking eyes."
"Why?" Joey said. "She told me you wouldn't care. You guys looked like you were having a good night."
"Oh, we did."
Joey glanced out the window, then back at Luke. "Where's Layla?"
Luke ran his hand across his gun. "She's busy in Harlan's room."
Joey gave him an ugly look.
"And when she's done there she's going to see me," he laughed. "Hey, if you want to go another round with Mindy be my guest. She won't have a problem with it. Hell, you can take her home with you. That girl of mine, she's good at what she does. Trust me, you'll want to keep her. When we're done with Layla we'll send her your way. Not sure when that'll be. Judging by how long they've been in Harlan's room. Hell, man, when he's

done with her Tick might even spend time with her."

The anger in Joey started to build. He balled up his fists and lunged at Luke, knocking him to the ground. One on the ground he hit Luke in the face a few times. Luke kicked the man off him, sending Joey across the room.

"Oh, man, you just made a terrible mistake," Luke snorted. "You just signed your death certificate, motherfucker," Luke charged at him, throwing two punches, making contact with both. Joey was able to knock him away again. He charged again and was knocked to the floor. Joey stood over him and kicked him in the belly a couple of times. All of a sudden Joey was tackled from the side. He looked up and saw Tick.

"The fuck is going on here?" Tick shouted. "Have you lost your mind?"

Luke stood up and staggered over to the shotgun laying on the floor, cocked it, and pointed at Joey. "All I have to do is pull this trigger and end you."

Joey said, "You don't want to do that."

"Why not?"

"My guys will come after you," Joey said.

"Your guys?" Luke laughed. "And tell me, you think your guys could hurt me?"

Footsteps came from down the hall.

Harlan appeared in the doorway. "What's going on here?"

Tick said, "I came in and this guy had your boy on the ground. He was kicking him over something. I'm not sure what the fight was about."

Harlan told Luke to lower the gun.

"Why should I?" Luke protested. "He started it."

"What's wrong with you?" Harlan asked. "You in elementary school? Did he take your lunch money? Drop the gun."

"I'll drop it on his fucking head," Luke snapped.

Playground
"No you're not," Harlan walked over and put his hand on Luke's shoulder. "I'm sure this can be sorted out. You don't want blood on your walls and carpet. Come on, let's just have a little conversation. If you don't like what you hear, there's always the basement."

Joey apologized to the men. He let his emotions get in the way. Luke understood and told Joey he was sorry for his part, and that the whole thing was a big misunderstanding.

Joey said, "Since we're on the same page again I need a favor."

"What would that be?" Harlan asked.

"After heavy consideration, I've decided this thing you guys have going on isn't for me. I mean, don't get me wrong, I appreciate everything you guys have done. But Layla and I want out."

Harlan said, "Have you thought about it long?"

"I have."

"I always say before you make a big decision to think about it long and hard. You don't want to be too rash."

"I've thought about it, yes."

"And just before we were going to start charging you a fee? Harlan said. "You decided just in time. Okay. You have my blessing. Go ahead. I wish the both of you the very best."

Joey said, "Just so you guys know, I won't ever say anything about things I've seen here. You have my word."

Luke told him he better not say anything. If you did Luke was going to have to use his gun on him.

"Understood," Joey said. "I'd never do anything like that. You can trust me."

"I hope so, for your sake."

Joey asked where Layla was. They led him to Harlan's room, where Layla was putting her clothes on after taking a shower. When she saw Joey she ran over and gave him a big hug.

On the drive home, they decided to stop and get some breakfast. They stopped at a diner called Sunrise Skillet. They got eggs and coffee. Joey was in a much better mood, all the ugliness from before was in the rearview. He smiled at Layla as they talked about everything that happened.

"I can't believe they weren't mad when you said you wanted out," she said.

"I thought they'd put up more of a fight about that, honestly," he told her. "I told Luke I wouldn't say anything about what I know."

"Why'd you tell him that?"

"Well, I figured if I told him that we might not end up dead."

"Good thinking. Still, I'm thinking we should tell someone. Who knows what they'll do next? It might save someone's life. They don't have any qualms about killing people. Seems like Harlan taught his son well, how to get rid of someone that disagrees with him."

"Seems like it."

She took a drink of coffee. "And our tip could very well send Harlan back to prison. They'll need to lock him away for good. No parole, no nothing."

Joey nodded. "Yeah, the world doesn't need him around."

"Exactly."

The two sat across from each other and enjoyed the rest of their breakfast. Joey told her that the whole ordeal had messed with his nerves. He didn't know when he'd be normal again. She told him that she understood, that she felt the same way. Something like that, a sane person just wouldn't walk away from and be normal. It was going to take some time for the both of them.

Playground
"It'll just take time," Layla told him.
"But look on the bright side, at least we got out before we had to give them money."
"Yeah, that's true. We can use that towards a vacation."
"That sounds good."

39

Ethan Bursott called Joey one day and told him he was moving back. He was moving back for good this time, no matter what they dangled in front of him.

"I had enough," Ethan told his friend. "I know they'll have someone who'll try to get me back. I'm just going to have to put my foot down. I think I've done everything I can out here."

"Good for you," Joey told him. "So, when are you going to be here?"

"I have a few things to take care of before I leave. I was going to drive over there sometime next week."

"I could come out and get you, make a road trip out of it?"

"Thanks but I'll be fine. The quiet will do me some good. I'll get to take in some of the land, you know?"

"Okay, then."

"But it's going to be a party when I get there. It's been too long."

"You're right about that. Is Emily going to be with you?"

"We broke things off a few weeks ago. Guess she liked sleeping around town too much, I don't know."

"Sorry to hear that, buddy."

"What are you going to do? That's life."

"I know that's right."

Ethan asked how everything was going, and if there was anything new going on. The two friends talked for about an hour.

After they ended the call with each other Joey called everyone and told them the good news. They were all excited to have their friend coming back to Arkansas. Doug said that they'd be able to party like they did before he left as nothing changed. It would be fantastic.

Playground
They'd pick up like no time had passed.

Doug said, "We could rule the world if we wanted. I see only good things for us, don't you? I can see it now, guys."

Everyone told Doug he was crazy like they always did. In a lot of ways, they looked up to Doug, the one who was loyal to the bitter end, the one you could call day or night about anything, the one you always wanted on your side in a fight. He was a man who was always true to his word. Yes, he could be wild at times, but who wasn't? He was just a fun-loving guy, someone who loved making people laugh, and a lot of times that's all you needed.

The first night Ethan was back in town they hit a few bars to celebrate. They drank and talked like they didn't have a care in the world. Doug and Quinn were interested in getting Ethan a new girl when they discovered he was single again.

Quinn said, "I think the problem is this, these women, they don't know how to handle guys like us. I mean, look at Foug and myself, we keep trying with women but they always leave after a few months, and I think we can put you in that group, Ethan."

"That's a good way to look at it," Ethan told his friend. "I don't know, they're all different. I don't think you can put your finger on just one thing."

"I get that, sure. Do you know what we should do? We should start a group for single men. We could meet on the first Tuesday of the month, something like that."

Doug laughed. "Well, boys, I hate to tell you but I'm going to be off the market soon. You guys with have to fight over where you sit in the meeting without me."

"You have a special someone?" Ethan asked.

"No, not right now. But I think it'll be any day now. All I have to do is walk into a place, it'll all be over. The

Bradley Davenport
women will start running."
"They'll run the other way," Quinn quipped.
Doug flipped him the bird.
Ethan asked the guys if they wanted more to drink. Joey told his friend that was a crazy question to ask, knowing that they could drink the full inventory of a liquor store and not think twice about it. They called over the pretty blonde who was waiting for them. They told her everything they needed, and as she wrote it down on her note pad she told them that was a lot. It was clear she didn't know who she was dealing with. When she was finishing up writing the list on her pad Doug told her to put her add her name to the list. She found that to be very amusing.

"What are you doing to do now?" Doug asked him.
"Not sure," Ethan said. "Just need some time to relax. Not really in the mood to jump back into something."
"I see."
"I mean, I have enough money to hold me over for a good chunk of time. But I want to start writing a book at some point. Figure that's the next best thing to writing a movie script. In a lot of ways a book is better, you can go into more detail if you want. And if you don't, you don't have to. I've always been writing. Actually, at one point out there I was going to release a book of my short stories. My agent told me he thought that'd be a bad idea at the time. He told me my movie career would take a hit. I didn't think it would, but what do I know?"
"Sounds like a plan," Doug said to his friend. "I'd like to read some of your stories. Bet you have some good ones, yeah?"
"I tend to think so. You know, I wrote everything for myself first, then, if others liked it that was a plus. I think that's how everyone should approach it."

Playground
Doug shook his head. "Yeah, that makes a lot of sense. You need to love what you do. People will see how much you enjoy it, they'll hopefully feed on your energy "That's one way to look at it."

They sat drinking for a few more hours. At one point Ethan bought two rounds for everyone in the bar. A lot of the patrons proclaimed him as the hero of the night. He told them he'd wear that honor with pride. He knew the only reason they said that was because he bought their drinks. They didn't give a fuck. They would've said that to anyone who did what he did. They were all drunks numb to the world.

"I'm glad to do it," Ethan told all of them. "Wish I could do more."

One of the patrons said, "You should open your bar."

"Not sure. I'm not in the market for anything like that. You should do it, man."

The guy said, "Nobody wants that. I'll end up crashing that place to the ground so fast. I'd have to burn it down one day for the insurance money."

Ethan hoped he was joking. If he heard of a new bar being burnt he knew where to point his finger. But he didn't want to have anything to do with that sort of thing. They'd probably throw the book at him just for knowing something.

The guy laughed. "A friend of mine did that to the bar he had. It was a shit box that started losing money. After he closed one night, my friend took a torch to the place. They did an investigation and found out how it burnt to the ground. My friend eventually confessed and told the cops what happened. They threw the cuffs on him. After a judge heard what happened he got three years."

"Damn."

"He just got out a few months ago."

"I'm guessing he won't do that again?"

The guy laughed and shook his head. "That guy, that stupid fucker said he'd do it again. I told him he'd get caught like before."

"I'd have to agree with you there."

The man told Ethan and the others to have a good night.

Wayne gave a toast to his brother and said how nice it was he was back where he belonged. Back when he'd decided to go back to California after leaving the first time, it hit them all pretty hard. They didn't know how badly they would miss their friend until they were faced with that reality. They learned that you needed to value the time you had with your loved ones. You never know what the future holds.

As they continued to celebrate a strange feeling crept over Joey. He wasn't sure if he should tell his friends about what happened to him and Layla. He thought they might've just thought it was funny or something. After all, he was more than a little embarrassed about what happened. He didn't know how they'd react. He didn't want them to get upset, go over to Luke's place, and do something they'd regret. No matter what those people had to be stopped. They'd discussed Luke and Harlan a few times, and none of them thought Harlan should've ever been released from prison. It was Wayne who said that the police should've killed him when he first got arrested.

"Sometimes the justice system lets us down," Wayne would say. He'd go on to say how his judgment day would be here soon, but it wasn't fast enough.

After some more drinking, Wayne told his friends they should go back to his place. He had more booze back at his place, and they could get a good card game going.

40

The crew was back together and that was all that mattered. Ethan spent the first two months at his brother's place until he found a house to buy. When he got the new place he threw a big party. As the party was dying down, as most of the people had left, the crew was on the front porch drinking and talking, enjoying each other's company, when they noticed a dark car creeping down the road. No one knew who the car belonged to. At first, Ethan thought it might've been someone who lost their way looking for his house.

As the car slowly came by the house the passenger window rolled down. But they couldn't see who was in the car. The streetlight reflected off the car. The only thing they could see was the outline of a shotgun coming out of the window. They scattered as the bullets blasted from the window.

Luckily, no one was hit. Due to the gunfire, the cops showed up. They said one of the neighbors called. They took down everyone's information and statements, but they couldn't tell them a thing. They knew nothing. The cops told them they'd be on the lookout for anything. They were told if anything happened in the case they'd be the first to know.

"Thanks," Joey told the officer. "Our friend just moved in, that's why we were celebrating."

The officer said not to worry about a thing, that it was a good bet they wouldn't try that stunt again.

"You might consider getting some cameras installed out here," the officer told them. "You don't want a situation that's going to continue."

"No, we don't."

After the officers had everything they needed they told the group to have a good one, and then they were on their way, crime fighters who made everyone feel safe. Some days were rougher than others

Ethan made coffee as the others were talking about what happened.
Quinn said, "Nobody recognized the car?"
"It was too dark," Doug told his friend. "I don't know what the fuck that was until it was too late. I wish that wasn't the case, you know?"
Wayne said, "Damn, at least they could've yelled out something before they started shooting. What the fuck? I mean, give us some kind of clue. I have no clue who that could've been. As far as I knew we are well-liked by everyone."
They asked each other who could've done it. Again, everyone around the room said they didn't know.
"I could ask someone who might know," Joey told them.
"Who?" Ethan asked.
"Luke Reeves. Couldn't hurt to ask."
"Can you trust him?"
"I think I can."
"Let's go see, then."
They stayed at Ethan's house that night and drove out to Luke's the next day. Joey didn't want to show up unannounced, so he called first. Considering what happened between them Joey was a little reluctant about asking the guy for his help. But he figured if Luke delivered that might go a long way to repairing bad feelings.

41

When they pulled up to Luke's house they didn't know what to expect.
Doug said, "Damn, he has a nice place. What does he do?"
Joey told him he didn't know.
They walked to the front porch and rang the doorbell. A little while later Tick came to greet them. They entered the house and walked down the corridor to the kitchen. Luke and Mindy were sitting at the kitchen table talking and drinking coffee.
"Hey, guys!" Mindy said. "Good to see all of you."
Luke eyed all of them. "Welcome Joey and Layla. This place brings up good memories? he stood. "I see you brought some friends. That's good."
Mindy said she'd make them coffee.
Joey said, "We need to talk to you about something."
"I know, that's what you said on the phone," Luke walked over to them. "I take it you guys are doing good?"
"Everything is good," Joey told him. "Well, except what we came here about."
"Is that so? I'm here to help any way I can," he looked over at Layla. "And dear, I owe you an apology. The last time you guys were here things got a little out of control. We do that type of thing often, but I can see where something like that can be unsettling to new people."
Layla was silent at first, but then said, "Yeah, that was something that took me by surprise. I wasn't expecting anything like that."
"You'll have to forgive us for that."
Joey looked at Luke and told him they needed to keep it in the past. They didn't need to go through all of that again. Their friends asked what they were talking about,

Bradley Davenport
but were told it wasn't important.
"So, what can I help you guys with today?" Joey asked. Everyone moved into the living room. Mindy brought everyone a cup of coffee. They thanked her. She told them no one should go without coffee.
Luke said, "To be honest, I didn't think you guys would be back. I know things got crazy. Things usually get out of hand on those nights. We're just a bunch of maniacs, what can I say? So, what can I do for you guys today?"
Joey said, "The other night we had a party at Ethan's house, that's what we need to talk to you about."
Luke nodded at Ethan. "You're the one who just moved back from California?"
"That's right," Ethan said.
"That's a place I've never been. I bet that was a lot of fun, the movie business and everything?"
"It wasn't bad. Like everything else it had its moments."
"I can imagine. Any business, no matter what can be ruthless at times. You can only do what you think is best. You win some, you lose some. The world keeps turning. You just have to keep going. It's anyone's guess."
Ethan said, "Have you seen any of the movies I've worked on."
"I haven't had the pleasure yet. I'll get around to it one of these days."
"Fair enough. There's fourteen of them in all."
"That's very productive, I must say. You only live once, might as well do what you can while you're still here."
"That's right," Ethan said.
"You just get tired of the movie thing?"
"Something like that," Ethan told the man.
Luke asked them what the issue was.
"Anyway," Joey said, "we were having a party at Ethan's new house the other night. It was good, every-

Playground
one was drinking, getting high, getting fucked up, it was great. At the end of it, as some people were going home we were on the front porch talking, and all of a sudden a car crept up, the window came down and a shotgun started blasting away."

"Oh, shit," Luke said. "Sounds like someone got pissed about something. Did anyone get killed?"

Joey told him that thankfully no one got hurt or killed, just got a big shock. He went on to tell Luke that the police came out but weren't much help. They said that things would be checked out.

Luke chuckled. "That's the cops for you, they can fuck up the simple things. Unless they're invading a donut shop they're useless a lot of the time. My friends and I need to teach them how to put in work."

Ethan said, "We were wondering if you might know who was behind it?"

"The fuck would I know about that?" Luke looked at Ethan. "I don't know what happened. I didn't have anyone shoot your place, friend. I don't even know where the fuck you live. What is this? Think I had something to do with it?"

Joey said, "We were hoping you could check around, and see if someone said something about anything. We thought your connections could help out."

"Connections?" Luke asked.

"Yeah, to all of the criminal shit that goes on around here."

"Oh, I see. Well, because I like you guys I'll see what I can do. It might take time. People, most of them, don't like to advertise what they did. But I'll check around. It might cost a little money. You guys can just pay me back when I get something. Things like this, it takes detective work to figure things out."

"Thanks."

"What do you plan to do with this information when you get it?" Luke asked.

"We just want to know who and why. Why did they pick that house? We don't have a problem with anyone," Joey paused. "If there's a problem with anyone I'd like to resolve it."

Luke shook his head as he put down his coffee. "I understand. You have my word, I'll get to the bottom of it. I hate when things like that happen for no reason. It's bullshit and should never happen. Now, let me ask this, if there is a problem do you want me to get rid of it? I can do that with no problem."

"I don't think that'll be necessary. I would just like to know why they did that. Did we do something to someone? I don't know, I just need answers."

Luke told all of them that if they wanted to join in the investigation they were more than welcome to do so. He warned them that it could get violent. After talking it over a little both Ethan and Joey said they'd like to join the hunt.

Joey was glad to hear it. He joked that he'd get Ethan and Joey to join his gang. Joey told them it was hard to find people who don't mind getting their hands dirty. You had to pay your dues if you wanted to climb the ladder, and that went for the criminal world, too. Some made it, others didn't.

"There are certain skills you develop over time," Luke explained. "With someone like me, I'll steer you guys in the right direction," he nodded at Ethan. "I'm sure your friend here has told you about me?"

Ethan said, "A little. Just a few things. But don't worry, I know how to keep my mouth shut. I'm not stupid."

"That's good," Joey told him. "And I'm sure you've heard about Harlan?"

Ethan shook his head, saying he had. He was a little interested in meeting the man. He thought it was interesting they let someone like that out of prison. If they were willing to do that with a murderer, what would they do next? The whole idea of letting violent criminals out of prison was crazy to him. As they continued talking Harlan came down the stairs. When he saw Layla she blew her a kiss.

"How are you?" she asked.

After telling her he was fine he asked Mindy if there was any coffee left.

"I'm not sure," Mindy told him.

They spent the rest of the afternoon at Luke's place drinking and shooting guns. The rest of Luke's crew came over and they had a ball. Mindy and Layla made lunch for all of them. At the end of the day, they thanked Luke and the others. Luke told Joey and Ethan to come out to the house the next day, and they'd start the hunt. Luke told them they'd need to move fast. He was too fucked up to do anything that night.

The next day when they were driving out to the house Ethan asked Joey if he still wanted to press the issue, and that it was okay if they just forgot about it.

"We can't do that," Joey told his friend. "What if they come back? What if they hurt someone the next time? That wouldn't be good for anyone."

"You have a point. I didn't think about that."

"I mean, if you want to back out that's fine."

"Oh, no," Ethan told his friend. "I'm still in it until the end. People fucked up my house. I'm having to pay to get it all fixed."

"How much would that cost?"

"A couple grand. I have the money to take care of it, but that's not the point."

"Yeah, I know."

42

When they got to the house Tick and some of the other guys were out front talking. They greeted Joey and his friend. Tick asked Joey if he was ready to beat some people.

"I hope it doesn't come to that," Joey told him.

"You never know. Don't want to be unprepared."

Joey asked what they were doing. They told him they were debating whether or not to start a meth operation. Tick said one of the guys, Bobby, already had the things they needed. They just needed a place to cook. Bobby said he knew how to cook, and that he'd already done it for a few other people.

"There's good money in it."

Ethan looked at the man. "Good money if you don't get yourself blown up."

"No, man, I know what I'm doing. That won't happen with me. And the best part, I have connections to people who want to buy it."

"Seems like you have it all figured out," Joey said.

"We just need a place out of the way to set up shop. I was thinking about constructing a little shack on the side yard. Nobody will bother us out here."

"There you go," Ethan said. "Sounds like a plan."

Just then the front door opened and the man they all called Hammer came out. He was drinking a beer, saying it had already been a rough one. He told Tick they needed to pay a visit to the guy who slept with his wife. Hammer said they needed to teach him a lesson that he'd never forget."

"Yeah, we'll take care of it," Tick told his friend.

"One thing I thought, I thought you could put a bomb in the motherfucker's car. Show him how you got that name. You be up for that?"

Playground
Tick shrugged. "That could be arranged, sure. That'd take planning. Wouldn't you just want to blast him away with a gun?"

"We'll have to get her, too. Can't risk her saying something."

"That goes without saying."

Joey went on to ask them how the club was coming along. The club, Modo, it was going to take a few more months before everything was ready. Joey said he couldn't wait to see the place, and that if they needed help with anything to let him know. He knew his way around things like that. They thanked him but said they had it under control. He'd just get in the way.

Joey and Ethan went to the front door and let themselves in. Luke was at the kitchen table reading something. When they walked into the kitchen he looked up and greeted them. Luke asked the two if they were ready to hit the town. Things could get a little rough, so they needed to make sure they wanted to go on. Some of the people Luke knew weren't that nice, rejects and scumbags society forgot about. some chose that way of life, while others fell into the cracks of a floor that was already broken.

Luke offered them something to eat or drink. They declined.

After Luke was ready they headed out. Most of the seedy bars were open by then, and Luke told them they may get some sort of answer, depending on who was there. Tick and Hammer joined them.

Hammer said, "If they see all of us coming they might run. All of us at once, they'll be sorry."

The first place they stopped was Trappers, a little dive place that had cheap drinks. They opened the front door to a dark room that smelled of stale cigarettes and beer.

Bradley Davenport

They walked to the bar and looked around. They ordered a beer from the short bartender. The man's name was Scott and he owned the place. He told the guys they could stay if they promised not to fight. If they fought they were out, simple as that. The man didn't want to put up with anyone's funny business.

"Won't have a problem from us," Joey told the man. "We aren't here for trouble."

"Good thing for you guys."

Luke looked towards the end of the bar and nodded at a guy. "See that guy at the end of the bar, Joey?"

"What about him?" Joey said.

"He might know something about what you guys need to know. Name's Culler, Ronnie Culler."

"What's his deal?"

Luke shrugged. "He's working his way to the big time. For now, he just sells pills and a little coke."

"I see."

They walked over to the guy. He was a short fella with long brown hair and facial hair. He wore a blue ball cap. He looked like one of those guys who had trouble growing a full beard. As they walked closer he lit a cigarette and looked at them. "And what's this?"

Luke said, "How are you doing these days, Ronnie?"

"I've been good, I guess. Better than some, worse than others. How's your world?"

"It's been good, been good. You should come out to the house sometime. How long has it been?"

"Too long."

"You're right about that."

Ronnie took a drag off of his cigarette. "Good to see you still around. Figured someone would've taken care of you by now."

Luke laughed. "What makes you say that?"

"It just comes with the life," he looked at the guys

around Luke. "What's the deal with your fan club?"
Everyone laughed. They moved to a table. They told Ronnie why they were there, and if he knew anything about it.
"I was your first stop?" Ronnie asked. "That feels insulting."
"Don't read anything into it," Luke told him. "We're just trying to get to the bottom of this."
"Well, I'm sorry guys, I don't know anything about that. The guys who work for me, I think they're smarter than that."
"You sure about that?"
"Anything is possible. I mean, I'm not their parent or anything but they know what the rules are. If they get out of line they're out."
Luke thought about it for a minute. "Any chance of anyone going rogue?"
"My guys?" the man smiled. "They know better. If they ever did they'll have a tough fight on their hands."
"So, you don't know who it could've been?"
The man shrugged. "Have you talked to Ned Finch?"
"Isn't he still on the inside?"
"He got out a few months back."
"Interesting."
"Might talk to him," Ronnie took a swig of beer.
"I'll do that, thanks."
"I assume he still has his old crew. Last I talked to him, about a month ago, he was talking about getting out of everything. Said he couldn't go back to prison. But I've heard people say that before. Won't believe it until I see it."
"Yeah, guys always say that shit. They can't give up life, though, that's the thing. What else are they going to do? Half of them don't have any skills, that's how they found themselves in this, to begin with."

"Can't disagree with that. There was a time when I thought about getting out, then, I thought about it hard. What else would I do? I was never that great at anything. Hell, I'm surprised I haven't been killed yet doing what I do."

"Think everyone's thought about that a few times."

Ronnie didn't know exactly where to find Ned, but Luke had a few ideas. He wasn't going to let the issue go unchecked.

The next three bars they stopped at gave them nothing. On the way to one of the bars they even stopped at Ned's house but he wasn't there. They stopped at a place called, Fletch's Place, for some beer and a few games of pool. It had been a long day of running around, and it didn't feel like they got anything accomplished.

As they were sitting at a table drinking they were approached by a few men. They knew Luke through some mutual friends. They heard he was looking for Ned, and said he should be arriving in about an hour.

"You sure?" Luke asked.

"Talked to him about an hour ago," the one guy said.

Luke told him and his friends to stay for a drink. He was buying. They'd be fools not to take him up on the offer. You should never turn down free drinks. The guy, Eddie Mane, thanked Luke, saying any man who will buy people beer is good with him.

Eddie said, "We've been hanging low for awhile. Myself, I just got out of the joint six months ago. Was on a five-year rap but my lawyer worked some magic."

"What were you in for?" Luke asked.

"Robbery. This guy I did the job with told on me. He'd got busted for drugs a few weeks after we did the job. He admitted what he did, and to cut a deal he gave them my name."

Playground
"Oh, man, you have to hate when things like that happen?"
"You can say that again. When I find him, let's just say he's not going to have a good day. I'll rip him apart."
"You have any idea where he might be?"
"Heard a few things, nothing solid."
"Hate when that happens."
One of Eddie's guys, a fella by the name of Clyde Cooke, said the guy was going to end up dead when they saw him. Clyde had a lazy eye and was a little slow. He'd suffered some brain damage after he was beaten up outside of a bar two years before. He was a nice guy, though. It didn't take long after the beating for Clyde to get his revenge. Needless to say, the guys weren't ever seen again. Some say if you walked through a certain area of woods in southern Arkansas you'd find the shallow graves beside a little creek.
Clyde said, "We'll flip him off the roof. Guy goes down, what's the big deal, right? Everyone gets fucked with. It's a strange life we have here."
Eddie said, "Oh, man, you guys are all something else, I tell you," he looked at Luke. "I heard you were opening a club."
"Where'd you hear that from?" Luke asked.
"A friend of mine, Rant, was at your house."
Luke started to tell him about the club when Ned and a few of his guys walked through the door. As soon as Ned saw Luke he walked over to him. Ned was the type of guy not to mess around. He didn't want anyone to think he was weak or anything. Guys who knew him wondered if he ever enjoyed himself. He was short with a sharp jawline. A thick black mop rested on his head.
"It's a pleasure as always, Luke," Ned pulled up a chair."
Luke said, "It's been awhile, how have things been?"

Ned shrugged. "I'm still here, that's what matters most. Everything else, it can all be figured out in time."

"I guess you're right."

"That's the way I see it."

Over a drink, Luke explained to Ned the problem he had, and he asked the man if he knew anything about it. When Luke gave him the address he told everyone he'd only been in that area a few times because it was another person's territory.

"I know my place," Ned said. "I don't want to start a war with anyone. I've bought stuff from over there but I don't want to expand into that area. There's plenty for us all. Greed only gets you killed, that's one thing I've discovered over the years."

"That's true."

"In the past, yes, I've been known to be a little greedy. But that's not me anymore."

Luke sat back. After a bit, he looked at one of Ned's bodyguards. The man's name was Simon. He was dark and lean. Luke ventured the idea that maybe someone went behind Ned's back to try to take over territory that wasn't theirs. It was suggested that the bodyguards were behind it. The other bodyguard, a mean-looking man by the name of Dusty, gave Luke a "fuck you" look. Luke sighed at the man like he knew something about the man no one else had.

Dusty said, "You got a fucking problem, man?"

"Why would you say that?" Luke responded. "I'm just sitting here thinking why you guys are bodyguards, you know?"

"What do you mean?"

"From the look of you two, you should have your crew. You look like you could run something really good."

Dusty looked at his friend, then back at Luke. "Thanks, but we're fine. We aren't trying to do all that."

Playground

"Is that so?"

Ned said, "They're free to do whatever they want, no matter how fucking stupid it was. Everyone wants what they don't have. It's a shame."

Both bodyguards denied everything. They didn't know who would tell anybody false information like that, and they didn't want any part of it.

"I don't know who told you we were involved," Simon said. "Tell me who said it and I'll take care of it."

"You're telling me everything I need to know," Luke told the guy.

"What does that mean?" Simon asked. "We're telling the truth."

"I'm sure someone will believe that. Can't pull the blanket over my eyes."

"Bullshit."

"Hey, I'm not the one trying to pass a truckload of lies."

Simon said, "You want to go outside? We can sort this out. Believe me, you'll be sorry. And if you want this to go another way, I can always call a few people."

Ned told the man to calm down. The guy kept on about how he didn't do anything. Ned told him it would be in his best interest if he didn't threaten anyone. A threat to somebody like Luke was no joking matter. If you didn't watch yourself something like that could be a death sentence.

"We did nothing," Dusty told them. "This whole thing is pretty fucked up. You guys don't know what you're talking about. Show me proof. You won't because you can't. You need to talk to someone else about this. We don't even know these people."

Ned told the two that it wasn't the best time to branch out and that they had to pay their dues. And they should be glad to still be alive.

Dusty said that even if he wanted to go out on his own

he wouldn't shoot up that neighborhood. He had more sense than that. He went on to explain how he thought that section of Bancroft should be burnt to the ground, all the buildings and houses. None of it was any good.

Luke had to let on like he didn't believe anything the guys were saying. He pointed his finger at the guy. "You're in trouble. Don't try to talk your way out of it. You know what you did. You fucks tried to take over something that you had no right to take. But you ended up just shooting up a house and making a fucking mess. How did you guys even get to be bodyguards? I wouldn't trust you with anything. Well, you guys are going to pay."

They asked how much. Luke laughed and told them that it wasn't money they'd have to pay.

"I don't know what to tell you," Simon said. "We can try to track down the real shooters if you want?"

Ned shook his head. "Afraid we can't do that. We'll just be wasting time doing that. It'll be the same story, and you guys will be crying the blues about how you can't do anything about it. No one wants to do that," Ned glanced around him, then back at the two men. "Don't get me wrong, I know why you guys want to start your own thing, really I do. You want to be more than just bodyguards, and that's a commendable thing. You aspire to be more. I was the same way. I wanted it so bad that I'd do anything, any dirty deed anyone needed to be done. I worked my way up. I know Luke can tell you the same thing. But you can't do it like this. Yes, there are times you have to make a point but that's not it."

Simon spoke up and said he agreed with what Ned was saying, about how to get ahead in the criminal world, however, they still had nothing to do with the shooting. Dusty asked what the big deal was. Whoever did it, nobody got killed.

Playground

"That's not the point," Ned told him.

Dusty looked at Ethan and Joey, and he told the both of them they didn't know who it was, that they had to believe it wasn't them.

"Dusty," Luke said, "how much longer are we going to go down this road? Honestly, this is getting tiring and we have other things to take care of after this."

The man started to say something else. Luke stopped him and told both of them to wait outside. They were told to go outside to the back of the building where their cars were. Some of the guys followed them out, to make sure they didn't run off and do something stupid. Luke and Ned had to discuss what to do about the situation. After the two discussed it everyone went outside where the men were. Before the men could say anything Ned and Luke took out their guns and shot them. They couldn't have people like that going rogue.

They drove out to the forest by Luke's place and buried the bodies.

Ned said, "You guys might need to get a new place to bury people. You need to start charging for plots, make some money out of this."

"We might get a lot of cash out of it," Luke said. "Hey, any way to make a few extra bucks is good with me. We've talked about it."

"Could be something new to get into."

"You're right about that."

They asked Ethan and Joey if they wanted a few drinks. Luke told them they needed something hard to deal with what they had seen. The first few are the hardest, but then, after awhile, you become numb to it.

Everyone went into Luke's house and had a few drinks. When they left the house Luke thanked Ned for playing along. The truth was, they didn't have a clue who did the shooting. Luke knew they just wouldn't let it go until they had a name. Luke just gave them what they wanted. If you asked him he didn't feel like he'd done anything wrong.

On their way back to his place Joey asked Ethan what he thought about what Luke and Ned did.

"Disturbing... I don't know, someone needs to do something about them," Ethan said.

"Like what?"

"The cops."

"I've already been there. Luke threatened me once. Said if I went to the cops about him or any of his guys he'd kill me."

"Damn."

"Think our best bet would be just to steer clear of them."

"Would they let you do that?"

"We'll see, I guess."

"That's crazy."

Joey explained to his friend all about Luke, about how he wanted to continue things that Harlan started. Joey told him that he decided to open a nightclub instead of a church.

"Why isn't he doing the church?" Ethan asked.

"I think it was a money thing, mainly. Think he tried to get investors, but they wanted nothing to do with him."

"Can you blame them?"

"I'd rather shoot myself in the foot. Layla and I went to a few parties at Luke's place, and they were strange. They started nice, and the more the booze crept into the night, the more bizarre things got. We were all out of our minds."

"I know what that's like," Ethan laughed.

They talked the rest of the way back to Joey's. When they got back Ethan didn't feel like driving home, so he just crashed on the couch.

Playground

By the time Joey woke the next day, Ethan was already gone.

Later that day Joey got a call from Luke, asking if they could do that interview at the radio show. Joey didn't want to but he agreed. He'd been promising Luke an interview for some time and he felt obligated.

When Luke and Harlan got to the station. The hardest rule they were going to have to follow was not to curse. After they started the interview Luke explained to the listeners who he and Harlan were for those who didn't know. They knew those who lived around the area during the time Harlan's church was running, they probably didn't think very highly of the man. And then when he went away to prison, they didn't care for him. He knew he had to rebuild his public image. After they talked about themselves they told everyone about the nightclub. They were going to have the best drinks the city had to offer. There was going to be live music most nights. And in a section of the club, they were going to have dancing girls. After they talked about the club for awhile they started to talk about the aliens, and that the basement of the club was going to act as a meeting place for those who wanted to join the aliens. Until the place was built they were going to have the meetings at Luke's place. Luke told the listeners that if they were interested they should get in contact with him. They'd sort out the details. He didn't want just anyone to know where he lived. He had to keep some things secret from the outside world.

Luke said, "I know my listeners find all of that very interesting. I'm sure you'll get a lot of people calling."

"That's what we hope," Luke said. "We want everyone to rejoice in the splendor of life outside of this world. We're all seekers, just having fun on this strange trip. I

Bradley Davenport
can't wait to see what the next adventure holds."

Harlan said, "Over the past year I've been communicating with a few aliens. They come to me in visions. One thing they told me, they told me that all of our human sins will be erased once we join them. They told me everyone will love it where they live. From what they tell me, we need to find a new place other than Earth to live. Who am I to defy aliens? I'm sure they know more than I do. I urge everyone to join us."

Luke said, "We know this whole thing might seem crazy to you. When Harlan first told me I thought he'd lost it, gone off the deep end. I thought I was going to have to call the crazy house on him. I'd heard of alien things before but never actually knew any of the people who made those claims."

Harlan continued by saying he didn't know what they were going to do with the planet after they left. His thought was that they'd blow it up to help humanity, so it couldn't harm anyone anymore. For all he knew they might even construct a planet for them.

Joey asked Harlan if he trusted the aliens. Harlan had no reason not to believe them. He said he didn't think they would do something like that. They were very kind beings. They said that they didn't mean to bring harm to anyone on any of the planets.

They said the planet they'd be taking everyone to was just like Earth, everything except the fact that it wasn't dying.

A few people called and asked both men some questions. Most of them wanted to join and asked about the meetings.

"Does this cost any money?" one of the calls asked.

"No, not at all," Harlan said. "They don't need money. I don't fully understand how it all works. There are still things I need them to explain to me, then, I'll let all of

Playground

you know. I don't want to see things go bad in this. If this doesn't work I don't know what's going to happen next. But what am I saying? Everything is going to work out. When I was a kid my parents always told me I worry too much, I guess that hasn't ever changed. I started smoking weed because I worry too much. When I was in prison I worried every day."

Joey told him that was understandable.

The interview ran for another forty-five minutes. After they finished Luke told Joey that he and Layla needed to stop by his place for another meeting. They shook hands and parted ways.

Joey and Layla ended up not going to another one of their parties. They talked it over and didn't want to get sucked back in.

43

Six months down the road Modo finally opened. Joey and his friends went by to check it out. The place was packed. They were surprised by how busy it was. Joey told himself that if everyone knew what Luke and his father were really up to that they wouldn't be there. They'd be far away and wouldn't give them a second thought.

A band called Shadow Kings was playing. They did a pretty good job. They had the crowd cheering and hollering. Joey and his friends walked over to the bar and ordered some drinks. Luke walked over and greeted all of them. He told them the drinks that night were on him, so they needed to drink up. It wasn't every night someone was willing to buy you drinks.

"It looks like business is going good," Joey said.

Luke said, "Yeah, it's been okay. You know, there's been a few bumps down the road. It always works out in the end."

"That's life," Doug said. "Thanks for the drinks. Tonight's the night to get a little crazy, man. I can see it all over."

They talked a little more, then Luke invited them all to come to the basement of the place. A warning started to go off in Joey's head. He knew from the history with this guy what might be waiting for them down there.

The basement had been converted into a living area equipped with carpet, couches, game tables, and TVs. There were about sixty people scattered among the two big sections. Yes, it looked like Luke and Harlan were up to their old tricks.

Harlan got up in front of everyone and did his song and dance, telling people that they had to come together as one, that they needed to be ready when the aliens came

Playground
to get them, and that the time was approaching for them to ascend. After his father finished Luke addressed the crowd with some more strange talk.

The crew was in the basement for about an hour when they had to get out of there. They had enough of it, enough of the madness. It was as if they were all twisted on drugs and didn't know what they were even talking about, saying things like they all had to wear certain clothes before they go, that they all had to drink this special drink that would help them with the transformation.

The crew, after going back upstairs, stayed at the club for another hour or so. They had some more drinks, watched the dancing girls, and played a couple of games of pool. When they left they talked all about Luke and Harlan. Joey finally told the others what happened to Layla and him with the cult.

44

It was first reported by WAYZ2, one of the other radio stations in the area, that Bancroft police responded to a call about the nightclub, Modo, on Leverett Ave.

The caller said they attempted to enter the establishment but the door was locked. A few others tried and failed. Finally, someone contacted one of the managers to come down and unlock the door. The manager, Sean Moore, knew something was odd. They were supposed to be open at the time. They had a band scheduled for that night. Sean, after unlocking the door, walked through the entire place with two police officers. Everything looked fine, nothing was out of place or anything, then, they walked to the basement where they discovered the horrific scene. Thirty-five bodies were found throughout the basement. After tests, it was determined they all took a lethal dose of drugs mixed with soda. Upon further investigation, it was discovered that Luke Reeves and Harlan Reeves were among the dead. After interviews were conducted they learned that everyone who died belonged to the cult Luke and Harlan started.

For the next month or so the community was still in shock. They couldn't wrap their heads around it. How could something like that happen? They talked to Joey, Layla, and their friends about the situation. But they were all careful not to say anything that implicated themselves. By everything they were saying to Joey and the others they wanted someone to take the fall, someone they could point their fingers at and blame. Of course, some people pointed their finger at the prison system, saying that if Harlan had never been released it could've never happened, others disagreed.

Playground

A few months later they tore down the building Modo was in. No one wanted to move into the building after what happened. No one could blame them. People started to say sometimes at night you could hear voices over there, laughter and music. Some people even said they've seen ghosts in the area. The thought of ghosts roaming around struck fear in some. They wouldn't even go near the land. In the passing years, local teenagers would dare one another to stay on the plot of land through the night. Only two teenagers over the years stayed a whole night. A lot of the other kids would say the reason you didn't hear any voices or see ghosts, was because they were all somewhere in outer space with aliens. Who knew? The only way they'd know was if they came back and told people. Those who remember Harlan Reeves back when he had the Church of Modo believed he had all of those people kill themselves for no reason.

After a few weeks, things in Bancroft went back to normal. Everyone continued with their lives like they always had.

Playground

Part 2

1

Logan Mekenzi sat at her big wooden desk. She was smoking a joint and texting on her phone. Brown hair draped around her. Occasionally, she brushed dangling strains of hair from her face. She wore faded blue jeans and a light blue sweater. To finish the wardrobe she had on a pair of boots. She looked up from her phone, reached into her big pink purse on the desk, and took out a little mirror. She finished the joint and looked into the mirror, hazel eyes looked back at her. She ran her hand along her face and smiled. She loved her smile; it was one of her favorite features. People often told her she had beautiful eyes and an amazing smile. After a bit, she put the mirror back in her purse and sat back in her chair.

The next few days were going to be long, and that day was the first. But it was something that needed to be done. It was something that was going to test her sanity. Luckily, there was a big bag of grass on her desk to get her through the days. When she opened her purse and saw the bag a smile crossed her face. She knew everything was going to be okay. She took out the bag and rolled another fatty. From the first inhale she went to a place where she was calm and relaxed, a place where no one had to depend on her for every single thing, a place she wanted to stay, a place far away from where she was. When was it going to be her time? When was someone going to come by and ask if everything was okay? The idea of helping others, she loved it more than anything. But she needed help now and then, too. But all of that would have to take a backseat for the time being. After all, it was her job to make sure things ran smoothly for everyone else. She had to uphold the responsibility of the job. She was God and it was a massive job. The thought of asking the council for a vacation crossed her mind a time or two. Everyone needed a vacation now and then. She could go to another planet, somewhere she'd never been before. There were millions of places she could go to.

The intercom on her desk cracked: A woman's voice asked if she could come in. Logan said it was fine. The door opened and a pale redhead, Heidi Lee, walked through. "Good morning. How are you, ma'am?"

"I'm doing good. You?"

"I'm good," Heidi walked over to Logan's desk, a fat manila folder in her hand. "I had a magnificent weekend."

"Glad to hear it," Logan looked at her. "I take it you had a gentleman caller?"

Heidi plopped the folder on the desk. "Oh, girl, you know I did. It was nice. It wasn't like he stayed all weekend or anything, but it was beyond fantastic. That was just my Friday night. The whole time away from here was just relaxing, you know?"

Logan laughed. "It always is," she threw her arms out in front of her like she was hugging the air. "Man, I'm so glad to see you today. Good thing you didn't decide to stay home or anything. I needed you."

Heidi smiled. "That makes me happy you'd say something like that. It means a lot to me. You smoke one without me?"

"Well, a girl's gotta do what a girl's gotta do. It was calling my name. I had to. I couldn't resist."

"Good point," Heidi said. "Well, if it calls your name you have to obey. Don't wanna go against the forces."

"I agree," Logan told her. "Next time I'll let you know."

"Thanks for thinking of me."

"Don't mention it. That's what friends do for one another."

Heidi took the chair in front of the desk. "I was thinking

Playground
about you this morning."

"How so?"

"I know it's going to be stressful," Heidi crossed her legs. "Just know no matter how things go it'll be okay."

"Nice of you to think of me. Not really. I mean, sure, it'll take time but it won't be that bad. I just wish I could throw the case in the trash. But doing it over a few days, it's a lot better than trying to get it all done in one day."

"You're God, ma'am, the boss, the head honcho around here. You can do it."

Logan smiled. "Can I elect you to help?"

"Not a chance. If I had the job I'm afraid I'd become a drunk."

"Maybe I should do that, you think?"

Heidi shook his head, "No, no, no, no, you don't wanna do that. It'll only lead you to dark places. Just stick to the grass. I have faith in you."

"Thanks."

"But if you do want to start, I have a whole cabinet at home full of bottles."

"I might take you up on that."

"If you want, we can dip out real fast?"

Logan sat back in her chair. "Maybe later. I need to stick around here. Heidi, how long have we known one another?"

"Let's see," Heidi shifted in the chair. "I came to you in 1991. Thirty-two years, something like that. It's been a long time."

"It has. We've been through a lot over the years."

"Glad I was here for it all. Sorry, I couldn't have been here before then."

Logan ran her hand through her hair. "Oh, believe me, there was talk about it."

"Really? When?"

"It was long ago. You were ten years old at the time."

Bradley Davenport

"How would it have happened?"

"There was a few ideas. None were very good. There were a few of us talking about how to do it. We couldn't figure out anything so we just waited. We just thought it'd just be a random act. There were a few local gangs around where you lived."

"That's okay. I like it here," Heidi thought about it. "My parents loved that house, I remember. By the time they sold it, they were happy to see it go."

"Why?"

"For the reason you said. The gangs were getting out of control. When they first bought the place it wasn't anything like that. My parents looked into all that stuff when they. Then, the crime rate wasn't that bad. But as time went on the violence just blew up. I mean, it was crazy. Just the thought of people not hesitating about ending someone's life... It's funny, though, when you think about it because I did get shot, after all," she laughed. "You won't get any complaints out of me, though. I love it here. Plus, the guy I was dating at the time, Sean, I think he was sleeping with other women. I hope there was a part of him that felt guilty. But, yes, I'm glad to be here. If that hadn't happened we would've never met. But I guess if it was in the cards something else would've happened to me."

"Glad to hear you say that. I couldn't have done it without you. I always knew you were a good person. All that business on Earth 3 with you and that gang member, you were just running with the wrong crowd. It happens. From the looks of it, you tried."

"Yeah," Heidi said. "And I got killed for it. Is he dead yet?

"No, he's still walking around like nothing ever happened. That's just a day in the life for those punks."

Heidi said, "You know, over the years, I've thought

Playground

about going down there, haunting that little son-of-a-bitch until he went crazy. Would have served him right. Right after me he went and shacked up with a girl he almost got another woman killed. He was just bad news."

"Indeed."

Heidi told God the same thing would happen to that girl that happened to her. Heidi said all men were the same, they will always play you for a fool to get what they want.

Logan laughed, "Well, I'm afraid that's how it happens. If you run in those crowds it's bound to be your downfall. I don't mean to laugh, but invariably somewhere down the road that's going to be the outcome. It's a dangerous life."

"Very true."

"Yeah."

"And when you think of it, it's just such a waste."

"You don't have to tell me. You started to walk down that same path."

Heidi smiled. "Is that your way of saying you were helping me by having me shot?"

"Something like that."

"Thanks."

"Hey, what are friends for?"

"Looking back on it, for me, I fell in love with the excitement of that life. And I thought he was sexy."

They laughed.

They liked one another. When Heidi first got to Heaven she was a little sad and upset. It took her awhile to be okay with everything that happened. She was mad at the person she thought loved her. She wanted to ask him why he put her in the situation he had. Did he want her out of the pictures? She wanted to confront him with that question and a lot more. Why? She never got the chance to ask him. She figured when he died she get her chance to find out.

When she first met this guy, Sean Hawke, all she knew was that he was in a local band in North Brown Ridge, Arkansas. Later she discovered he was in a criminal organization. But she didn't leave when she found out. In the back of her head, she thought that if she tried to leave he'd kill her. She found the sad irony in the fact she was shot because of Sean. He got mixed up with bad people because he wasn't man enough to take care of her. What did she ever do to him? She was nothing but loyal to the guy. At the time she was ready to take their relationship to the next level. The plan was to talk to him about her feelings after the show that night, but she got shot and never got a chance.

When Logan introduced herself Heidi was shocked. It took awhile for her to digest what was going on. Maybe it was a dream? Maybe it was just a big joke. She couldn't believe God was a woman. Things happened a little too fast for her. Heidi had a truckload of questions for Logan. Some were answered, others weren't. One of the main things the girl wanted to know was if she could go back as a ghost. She remembered seeing Ghost with Patrick Swayze and wondered if she could come back to her loved ones, watch over them, and try to protect them the best way she knew how. She wasn't happy to find that she couldn't do that and that she'd have to wait a certain amount of time before she could. She was going to have to learn to live in Heaven.

Logan looked at the woman who sat across from her, put her finger on the folder on her desk, picked it up, opened it, shuffled through the pages then and it down. "What a shame...."

Heidi said, "Is everything okay, ma'am?"

Logan sighed. "Everything's just perfect. From what this says I'm not liked on Earth. I don't answer enough

Playground

prayers? What's that all about? Would it help if they knew it wasn't all me? I'm not the only one who works on these things. It's a group effort. I'd love to tell them about the game that goes on up here."

"I don't think anyone knows that, no," Heidi told her boss.

"But I'm the one they all blame."

"Sorry about that," Heidi said. "I'm sure if you could explain things to people they'd understand. Sit people down, tell them how things go."

"Maybe."

"You could do a press conference, you think?"

"I can't do that. People aren't ready for me yet," Logan said. "They say they are, but they can't handle the truth. That would be a big mess. You'd have hundreds of people rioting. They'd freak-the-fuck-out."

"I hadn't thought about that."

"That's the only way some people there cope with things they don't like or understand. See, the other planets, have no problems with it. For some reason, those guys on Earth 3 can't take any of that. They all do too many drugs to pay attention to anything. And I'll go on record with that."

"That's crazy," Heidi told her. "I know when I was there it was like that at times. It's a shame they don't know you. The last year I was there the people I was hanging around weren't the best representation of the planet."

"Hell, a bunch of them don't even believe I exist," Logan said. "Well, the position, I mean. The ones who do believe, they're always trying to get the others to believe. Most people claim that others are too pushy when it comes to that. You just can't win. I do my best to get to as many prayers as I can. You always piss someone off. I just wish it wasn't the way it is. Everything sets off a chain reaction."

"That's true. I wish I could help."

"Don't worry about it. Things like this always happen. You can't change it. This was something I was tasked to do. But I think the troops should be aware of this. Might motivate them to do a better job."

"Couldn't hurt."

Logan said, "I can't have this getting in the way of my job this week. I need to stay focused."

"If you want, I could just go see them, and let all of them know about the numbers. See what can be done about this?"

"That's okay," Logan told her. "I need to go. They need to see my face."

"I think that would be the best thing," Heidi said.

Logan picked the folder up and smacked her open hand against it. "Those fuckers!! Those stupid motherfucking fuckers!!!"

Heidi said, "Don't feel bad about any of this. If they make you feel bad tell them to go fuck themselves."

"Yeah, I shouldn't feel too bad," Logan shook her head. "And I can't help but think a lot of this is Trent's fault."

"I figured that."

"Yeah, he doesn't like me, that's for sure. It amazes me that after all this time he holds anger for me."

"You ever talked to him about it?"

"Tried to."

"And?"

"Does no good."

"Oh."

The two walked out of the office, down a long hallway, beyond a row of offices to an elevator. They stopped at the sixty-third floor. When the elevator doors opened they walked down another long hallway. After a few more twists and turns they found themselves standing in

Playground

front of a metal door. Logan punched some buttons on a keypad, placed her hand on the scanner and the door opened. They walked passed twenty cubicles, hung a left, and walked another hallway. They got into another elevator that took them horizontally for two miles. The elevator door opened. A lot of guys in suits were at desks working at computers.

  Logan and Heidi walked to the back of the room. They walked over to a tall man who was making copies at a machine. The tall man was bald with a dark beard and a black suit. He was wearing a yellow tie. He was a thin with a sharp jaw.

  "Devin?" Logan said.

  The man turned around. "Oh, hey! Good morning, Ms. Mekenzi. Charming to see you. How have you been?"

  "How's everything here today?" she asked.

  "I'm just glad to be here, you know what I mean?" he said. "Just making the dreams happen."

  "You have to do what you're best at."

  "That's right," Devin said. "They want something really bad they call me. They think everything is a pressing matter. A good chunk of time you look at something and it's not that important. They find it hard looking at the big picture," he picked up his copy that came out of the machine and looked at it. "Well, damn, that's not good."

  "What?" God asked.

  Devin looked at her. "This guy, Josh Bryant, in Arkansas, was walking down the street on the way to the store when he was hit by a car. Trent's the one who ordered it. They took the guy to the hospital."

  Logan took the paper and looked at it. "Our numbers are a little low, can we make him pull through?"

  "A little?" Devin raised his brow.

  "A lot," she said.

  Devin told her he could work his magic and see what he

could do. But as he looked into her eyes he told her he couldn't promise anything. He wouldn't be the only one who was going to work on it. He explained to her that they needed to get rid of some of the workers in his department, that they weren't performing to the best of their abilities. She told him not to worry about that at the moment, that she was going to make a lot of changes. Some he'd like, others he wouldn't. But she was used to the fact not everyone who worked for her liked her all the time. She didn't care what they thought.

Devin sighed. 'I'll personally work on it. I can't promise anything."

"That's all I can ask," Logan told him. "As much as I like to come here and see how you guys are doing, there was another reason we came here."

"What's that?" he asked.

Logan gave Heidi a nod, telling her to hand Devin the folder.

"What do we have here," he opened the folder.

After Devin read the first page he looked at Logan and suggested they rip the folder apart so no one knew. If there's no paperwork, there's no problem. She told him they couldn't do that. The ones who were above her would find out. They wouldn't be happy with any of them.

Logan asked if they could discuss the matter in his office.

Devin said, "Well, ma'am, pardon me for saying so but don't you have enough pull?"

She smiled. "Oh, don't even get me started on that. There are some people I just have to give up on. I guess the other side has to win some. I know it sucks. I don't like it. If it were up to me I'd win all the time." Logan laughed. "You do one thing for someone, something else suffers. Finding that balance, it's harder than it looks."

Playground

Devin said, "At least we're up a little from the last quarter."

"True," Logan said.

"It could be worse."

"You can all do better."

"We can always do better, yes, I agree. But it's important to look at all the good we've done. We've done a lot for a lot of people. I mean, sure, we aren't perfect but we do our best. We need to clap ourselves on the back now and then. What we do, what we all do is inspire life. Every time we answer a prayer it gives people hope."

Logan said, "It's up to us to do better. We owe it to everyone to do better. Some of us might say it's a waste of time, some people may think we're all crazy to devote our time to those beings down there. We do it because that's what is asked of us. We have a job to do and we always have to keep that in the front of our minds. They depend on us. They don't know what goes on up here."

She went on for a bit longer, explaining to anyone in the office that they couldn't let evil win. Trent couldn't win the ultimate game. No one could utter a word. They were impressed with what she was saying and how she was saying it. They loved her passion, her drive, her commitment. Her point was that they could all do better. After she finished a few of them stood up and cheered. A few felt bad they let her down. They told her they were sorry. She told them to calm down, and that everything would be okay.

"We can do better," Devin told God. "But I have to say, we don't have enough people working, doing all the good deeds. Look, if we had everyone we need we can make anything happen. I can't help if people don't want to do this job."

"I realize that. We can't just have anyone working on

this, though. They have to pass the test. Last I checked there were only forty from the last group who even qualified. I can't just break the rules, and bring someone in here with no training. People have to know what they're doing."

"I didn't know that," Devin said. "It's been awhile since I was over that way."

"Looks like you should go over more often."

"Guess so."

"I'm sure they'd love to see your face," Logan told him.

"Don't know if I'd go that far."

"Why?"

"Oh, I never told you?" Devin asked.

"What?" Logan inquired. "I hadn't heard anything."

"Well, then, I have a story for you."

"Please tell."

Devin had been seeing this girl, Angie Blackwell, for about five months. They'd worked together for years in Heaven before they started dating. Things started to change, as they always did for Devin, but then, after a few arguments, he realized how crazy Angie was and broke things off. Most people in those circumstances would just walk away, and move on to something better. Angie wasn't like most people. She tried everything to get Devin back, pulled every punch she could, and asked favors from some friends. Nothing worked. She thought maybe stalking him was the answer, to hopefully try to get him to fall back in love with her. She would stand by his desk at work and try to talk with him, follow him in her car when he left the office, and stand in the bushes outside his house. He tried to explain he wanted her out of his life. She wouldn't listen. She wanted him back. She started spreading all sorts of nasty rumors about him, hoping that would make him take her back.

Heidi said, "I've heard some things."

Playground

"Like what?" Devin asked. "Hope it wasn't anything too bad?"

"There was a rumor going around you have a small member."

"That so?" he smiled.

"And you gave her an STD."

Devin told her that was untrue. Heidi told him about a few other things Angie told her. Devin denied it all. He told her Angie was full of it, and that was part of the reason he broke things off with her. She was too damn crazy.

Devin asked the two ladies if they wanted coffee. They told him they were fine. After he poured himself a cup he glanced at the calendar on the wall, then looked at Logan. "Well, I see today's the day, right? Busy around the clock."

"Don't remind me," she told him.

"Guess the case isn't an easy one?" he continued.

"He started a cult," Logan said. "We're talking about someone terrible, beyond redemption."

"Oh, one of those? Those are fun, aren't they? If he's that bad why don't you just end him? Just make a few adjustments. No one will ever know. What's his name again?"

"Harlan Reeves," Logan said. "He's always been a bad seed."

"Name sort of rings a bell. Think I remember him asking for some miracles," he raised a brow to Logan. "He asked for the bad miracles. See, those things are tricky. Some say they compromise other people's miracles, others say it turns into a positive thing. If we could all see into the future we'd know the right move to make. But you have to think, if we could see into one's future we would've already prevented that which we were looking into. It's all a big mystery."

Heidi said, "There are way too many of those on Earth, too many people asking for things."

Devin shrugged. "We've been doing this for awhile. Hell, you do this for so long that they all start running together. Now and then things stick out. But, you know, I don't think I have to tell you guys that, do I?"

Heidi said, "Not at all."

"Times like these I need to be on vacation," Logan laughed.

Devin took a drink of coffee. "I feel for you, really I do. You know, being here, doing what we do, I get so aggregated sometimes. Do these people even know what we do for them? You know, they always say they're grateful but you have to wonder. Think they just say that half the time because they've been programmed to do so."

"Well, they can think on their own," Logan told him.

"We drop hints around them at times. They don't always pick up on everything."

Devin told the two ladies if they needed any help they knew where to find him, that he knew the pressure she'd be under for the next few days.

The two thanked him.

After talking some more they left.

Logan and Heidi walked back to her office. When the two got into the office they smoked some grass. Logan didn't want to have to play host to whomever they were going send over from Hell. Reviewing cases wasn't her favorite part of the job, but it was something that had to be done. Heidi assured her that if she needed anything while she was working on the case she'd make herself available.

"I feel bad for you," Heidi said.

Logan looked at her. "Why did you say that?"

"It's just... You know, when you have to overlook these

special cases you always get cranky. I hate to see you like that."

"Well, thanks for saying that. It's something I don't wish on anyone. But I have a job to do. This isn't my first time, won't be my last. I just especially don't care for this case."

"How long will it take?"

Logan thought about it. "Hopefully, just a few days. At most, it'll be a week. There's a lot of things to go over. The thing is, yes, he did bad but we also need to look at the events he set in motion, and what happened to some of the people along the way."

"Oh."

The two women were good friends outside of work. They had apartments across the hall from one another in the Heavenly Delight building. When Heidi first got to Heaven Logan was a big help to her, showing her around, introducing her to people, and explaining things to her. When Heidi got to her new home she was nervous, not knowing how to feel or act about everything new to her. When she was brought before the council and given the job of Logan's secretary she was excited. She made it clear to them that she'd do her best. They told her they did not doubt that she would.

A few people over time told Logan that she couldn't trust the people she worked with and that she couldn't be friends with those she worked with. She told all of them that she was no better than anyone else. The thing she told them was how was she able to trust them and keep up a good rapport with everyone if she couldn't be their friend outside the office. She wanted to show everyone what a fun person she could be, and that doing that, would make people want to help her more. The council still had their concerns.

Logan told herself she probably wasn't the first God

that the council didn't agree with. Thousands came before her and thousands were gonna come after, so she didn't care what they had to say. Hell, if they told her she had to give up her title that would be okay with her. She never even wanted the job.

Logan passed the joint to Heidi. "Heidi, my dear?"

"Yeah?" Heidi hit the joint and handed it back.

"You still gonna see that guy, Jim?"

"No."

"Why not?"

"Nothing. We were fuck buddies for a month, but that was about it."

"Why?"

"I dunno. As time passed I realized I couldn't see having a long-term thing with him. He filled a need at the time."

"That's a shame."

"Why do you ask?"

Logan said, "Just to ask. I love you, girl. I care about your ass. I just want to see you happy."

"Awe, well, thank you. Well, if you must know I did think about it, but then, I gave him a hard look and told myself I wanted something more in a guy. He was immature."

"I can't fault you for that," Logan laughed.

"You know what I'm getting at? I can't hang with that mess. I wanna date an adult not a little boy."

Logan took a big hit. "Hey, you have to have standards. If you didn't have that you wouldn't have anything."

"Don't get me wrong, he was great in bed, that wasn't an issue at all."

"That's always the best part."

"If you want I could give him your number?" Heidi offered. "I'm sure he's single."

"No, that's fine. I don't need help in that department."

Playground
"If you say so. Got a long list, do ya?"
"You're such a bitch!" Logan laughed. "I do pretty good for myself."
"Oh, girl, how dare you."
"It's nothing like that. I just know what I want. Call me picky. I guess I've just had so many bad relationships in the past. It just makes me want to settle down even more. But like anything else, I can wait until I think I've found my soulmate. It's funny like that. But to your point, if I just wanted to go out and get some wild sex I could get some with no problem."
"That's what I'm saying," Heidi told her. "We need to go to the bar sometime."
"I'd be up for that, sure."
Heidi shook her head. "Sounds good."
"It'll be fun."
Heidi told Logan she needed to go out to her desk, and that she had some paperwork to finish. Logan told her to let her know when the guy from Hell came for the review. She wished she knew who it was going to be. She didn't like to be in the dark about such matters. Heidi, with a smile, said she'd let her know when he came and walked out of the office. An hour later Heidi called Logan's phone and told her the guy was in the lobby
Logan said, "Okay, thanks. Give me a few minutes then tell him to come in."
"Anything you want," Heidi said. "Are you okay?"
"No, no, I'm okay. I just need a little time."
"You got it."
"Thanks."
Heidi put down the phone.

"Is she ready?" the man asked.
The man was tall with a baseball hat on backward. He

Bradley Davenport was wearing a pair of khaki pants and a white T-shirt. While he talked to Heidi he took off his hat for a minute, exposing the light brown mop on his head before putting it back on.

"It'll be a few minutes," Heidi looked at the man. "Sorry, she has been pretty busy lately."

"Oh, that's okay. That's understandable. I can't only imagine. I don't have anything else to do."

"Can I get you something while you wait? Coffee? Soda? Water?"

"I'm fine right now, thanks. Might need something later. I'm gonna be here awhile."

"Yes, sir, of course."

The man took a seat. "Should be fun."

"That's what she said."

He gave her a hard stare. "I can't believe I never ran into you before. It's clear I need to come this way more often."

"Perhaps," Heidi giggled. "We're always here. I take it this is your first time reviewing a case?"

"I wanted to sooner, but Trent had told me I wasn't ready."

"Oh, I see."

He looked around the room. "Got a nice place here. Much nicer than our offices. Should ask my boss for a transfer."

"Think he'd go for that?"

"Probably not."

"It's worth a shot."

They talked awhile longer. Heidi thought he was very friendly and handsome. She debated asking if he had a girl. She told the man he could go in. He thanked her and said he'd see her again soon.

Heidi got a big smile on her face. She looked at the clock and wished it was later in the day. She wanted it to

Playground

be lunchtime; it was one of the best parts of the day. She turned on the little radio that sat on her desk and continued doing her paperwork.

The man entered Logan's office. He introduced himself as Cambry Dee. Logan was taken by his young face and voice. He took a seat across from her as she instructed.

"I've seen you before," she told him. "I've seen you a few times over here, but never got a chance to talk to you."

"That's quite okay, ma'am. I know a few people over this way. They keep me pretty busy, so whenever I get a chance I like to see friendly faces."

"I'm sure you guys do stay pretty busy. We're big fans of having friends over here. I don't know how your boss feels about things like that."

Cambry said. "If I can say so, I don't think he's too nice of a guy. He has people around him he talks to all the time, but he's a real asshole."

"You won't get any argument out of me," she laughed. "I could tell you some stories, that's for sure."

Cambry said, "Yeah, I heard the two of you shared a past."

"Really?" Logan asked. "What things have you heard?"

"A few people were talking about it over in Hell one day, we were looking at some lives and Trent came by. After he left they were saying you guys came here together. By what they said you guys were an item. And when you got here you went your separate ways because of the jobs."

"Yeah, something like that. You're talking about something that happened a long time ago," Logan shook her head. "Yeah, those were crazy times for me."

'That so?"

"Booze and drugs. Glad I'm not around that anymore."

"Was that what brought you here?"

"In a way, yes."

"I'm sure there was a story there," he said.

"It was a car accident, everything happened so fast." He nodded. "Yeah, I can understand that. Mine was similar."

Logan got Heidi on the phone and asked for a fresh pot of coffee.

Logan looked at the man and continued. "We do quite a lot here. People down on Earth 3, never understood. A lot of folks down there think this is all a joke, and some don't think I even exist. People always fight to try and get their point across. They give so much credence to the church. Shit, the church can be anywhere."

Cambry chuckled. "When I was down there I didn't think about any of that. I mean, I'd go to church as a kid but I didn't put much thought into it. Mostly, I just remember being bored. I came here and a new world opened up to me."

"I had that, too," Logan told him. "I thought everything, God, Heaven, Hell, were just myths, stories people came up with."

They went back and forth on their thoughts for awhile longer. Heidi's voice came through the intercom and said she was going to bring them coffee and cookies.

Soon after, she came in with the coffee and a big plate of cookies.

"Since we're going to be spending the next few days with one another, why don't you tell me a little about yourself? I'm sorry, I don't get a chance to meet the ones he creates all the time. Trent and I've been at odds for awhile, so I don't go over there much."

"Understood," Cambry said. "That happens sometimes. Relationships, they're a tough thing."

"Well, there's more to it than that."

Playground
"There always is."
Heidi came into the office again and had papers Logan needed to sign. After God was finished with the papers, Heidi asked both of them if they wanted anything. Logan told her that they were fine. When Heidi left Logan asked Cambry to continue with what he was telling her, about his life. She liked hearing people's stories.

Cambry Dee had two other lives: The first time he was born was in 1960. The parents he had at that time, Tim and Mary Locke, named him Kevin. A few years down the road Tim left and started a family. Kevin had always been a good kid, always polite and friendly, willing to do what he could to help anyone. He was good in school. His teachers would always tell Mary she had a smart son. During the 1970s Kevin started to become a handful for his mother. When he was seventeen he started smoking weed. Mary found out and didn't seem to mind. She was just glad it wasn't anything harder. She didn't like any of that cocaine stuff, and she'd heard nothing but bad things about it from friends and television. Kevin befriended a few older people who liked to party and smoke weed. One of the guys in the group, Ben Hooper, who was ten years older than Kevin, got him into dealing drugs. The two made some good money. Kevin didn't have a care in the world. He had all the money he wanted and the women were plentiful. On June 3rd, 1977, he got a call from a guy who wanted a pound of weed. Kevin met the guy in a vacant parking lot to make the deal. Little did Kevin know the man intended to do more than just buy the pound. When Kevin asked to see the money, the man brought out a gun and shot him two times in the chest. Kevin fell to the ground and died on the scene. A few weeks later the guy who shot Kevin was arrested.

The first time Cambry was reincarnated, he came back

Bradley Davenport

as soon as Kevin took in his last bit of air. His name was Charles Hunt, and he had a pretty good childhood. He had two older brothers and a sister came along when he was five years of age. He had a good life while growing up, always with friends and family. He always had a huge love for music, and when he was sixteen he formed a band. The others shared his deep passion for music. Charles' parents would let him and his friends practice in their garage. They called the band Bash. They did pretty well for themselves, playing local bars and surrounding areas. They got picked up by a label and re-ordered their first album. Everything was perfect. They went out and toured all over America. They were in the middle of talks to go to Europe when things took a turn for the worse. April, 5th, 1999, Charles was running simple errands when he crashed his car. He passed away a few days later due to his injuries. The rest of the band went their separate ways and formed other bands.

It took a little while before the soul would find the man who'd be named Cambry Dee. The powers that be couldn't decide if they wanted the soul reincarnated or not. No one quite knows what all the deciding factors are when deciding to reincarnate a soul, and how many times. When the soul is not reincarnated, the soul comes to either Heaven or Hell in the body of its former vehicle.

Cambry Dee was born on September 13th, 2000, to Zack and Linda Dee in Mountain Oak, Texas. Cambry's childhood was a pretty loving one, both of his parents had stable incomes and were well off. Zack was a realtor who had his own company, H&R Group. Linda owned a successful retail store, Middle, which had two locations; one, in the town they lived in, and the other, in the next town over. When Cambry was old enough he started working at the Middle, the location in their town. He did

Playground

pretty well and was told by his parents they were surprised he took on the responsibility with the greatest of ease. At the end of his run at the store, he went to the local college. He wanted to be a teacher. After taking a lot of the classes he needed, one day, he decided he didn't want to teach. He saw how students talked and treated their professors, and he told himself he didn't want to have to deal with any of that mess. For awhile, he was unsure what he wanted to do.

  He and the girl he took up with just drifted through life, seeking out whatever came their way, experiencing everything life had to offer. After he turned twenty-one he decided to start making beer. He figured he could sell his brew and make some good money. He told himself at some point he'd open his bar. After he finished making his first batch of beer he decided to call it Cambry Breeze. Those who bought it couldn't get enough. They came back for more. He convinced some of his friends to help him out. He explained that if they made more they could sell more, and that would turn into a profitable business for them all.

  He had grand plans. Everything was going well until March of 2020. The world shut down due to a pandemic. COVID-19 turned the world into a more chaotic place than it already was. With the pandemic, a whole new list of rules were forced on everyone. Because of the shutdown Cambry was forced to dial back his business plans. None of his business partners could be around one another. Facing an uncertain future he racked his brain on what to do.

  After a few days, he decided the best way for him to get money was to steal it—that wasn't the best thing to do, but the way he saw it there was no other way. He told some of his friends about the idea. He knew there was a lot of risk, but he was smart enough not to get caught.

Bradley Davenport

He broke into a few cars and made good cash. After a few more small cash grabs he told some of his friends they needed to get bigger. They started breaking into houses. The first few homes went off without a kink, no one got hurt and they got what they wanted. On a hot night in July of 2021, a friend of his told him about a house where the occupants were on vacation. The two broke into the house and were shot. Both men died in the house. As Cambry drifted away all he could think about was how he thought the house was supposed to be empty.

"That's quite a story," Logan said. "I don't think I reviewed that case."

"Why didn't you?"

"Couldn't tell you that," she said. "I was probably off that day. I can't do everything around here."

Cambry laughed. "I know what that must be like. Me, I'm good not being the boss. Most likely I'd mess things up anyway."

"I don't think that's true."

"You'd be surprised."

Logan smiled. "Don't put yourself down like that."

"Thanks."

After she told him her story he just sat back in amazement. He was interested in her. He wasn't sure if she felt the same about him. He told himself he'd find out in time.

2

On a December night, in front of a place called Binco in Lewis, Ohio, snow started to fall. At first, it was light, then, it came down in fat flakes. Logan walked out the back of the place and sat on the metal steps. She was dressed in black with a long black coat. She was staring at a blue dumpster at the edge of the property. She lit a cigarette. The music from inside the club was muffled, but she could still hear it great.

The band that was playing was a group of guys who called themselves Cool Kids. They had been asking if they could play for some time, so Logan and her boss finally caved and let them. All they asked was that they put on a good show—if they did that, they'd be asked to play again. Cool Kids just recorded their first album and were working hard to promote it. From what Logan could tell everyone in the club loved the music. She didn't care for the band. She thought the music was okay, but all of the guys were total assholes. It was just something she had to put up with. Even if she didn't want to admit it they were making the place money. Half the bands that played the club, within a few months, split up. She always thought that was a little funny, almost like playing Bingo made them break up. But she'd never been a superstitious person, and just thought it could be something else. After all, keeping a band together can be a struggle, some make it, others don't.

She looked up at the light pool beside the dumpster as snow cascaded down. How pretty it was, she thought. She wanted to wake up the next day to a white blanket covering everything. She loved the snow. She liked everything about snow, like how sound traveled in it, the crunch your footsteps made. She remembered when she was a little girl, she would play in the snow and have so much fun with her friends in her hometown of Bigalow, Ohio. The only thing she didn't like was when the snow melted—it left water and slush everywhere. If only the snow could just vanish without a trace, wouldn't that be nice? But she'd never get that lucky. She always liked the cold weather because it gave her an excuse to wear thick sweaters and coats. It's the perfect time for hot cocoa and blankets, curled up on the couch watching movies.

She stood and started walking to her car, which was beside the light pole. It had already been a long night and it wasn't over yet. She needed something to get through it all. halfway to her car, the back door to Binco opened. She looked back to see a man standing outside the door. He was tall with dark hair and a thick beard. He had a bottle of booze in his hand.

"Hey, sweetness," he called to her.

"I love you, Trent!" she called back.

"I love you more."

"To the moon and back?"

"Of course."

"Good."

He walked over to her. "To the moon a billion light years away. It's pretty rockin' in there. The crowd, they're eating it up. It's a pretty good scene. What are you doing out here?"

"That's sweet of you to say. Had to come out for a smoke. I was just about to grab my other pack."

"Oh, I see."

"I had to get a break from there."

"I don't blame you there. After awhile, it stops being music, just loud noise. It tends to get all fuzzy. There's only so much you can stand, you know? Overheard one of the guys say they were doing three more songs."

"What a joy," Logan muttered. "And we're left to listen

to it."

Trent chuckled. "That's what it amounts to."

She nodded at the bottle of booze. "Need help taking that down?"

He walked closer to her. "What's mine is yours."

"You're too kind."

"That's the only way to be."

"It's one of your better qualities."

"Never thought you'd ask."

"I'm a woman of many mysteries."

He handed the bottle to her.

She took the lid off and took a gulp. "That's some good stuff. Just what I needed to make the night right."

"You can't go wrong with it. Only the best for my baby."

"Ah, a man after my heart. I love it," she smiled.

"Well, what can I say?"

"Why are you so sweet to me?" she asked.

"It's just what I do."

"And you do a very good job at it."

"I couldn't imagine it any other way."

"Good."

He reached out and ran his finger down the side of her face. "You are truly spectacular."

"I have to say, the same about you."

He held his arms out to hug her.

She fell into him.

Trent said, "You're perfect."

"Oh, I don't know about that."

She felt safe in his arms. She knew no matter what he would always do his best to protect her, to make sure no harm would ever come to her. It made her happy to know someone cared about her so much. A lot of her friends were stuck in relationships that had fallen apart, and she didn't want to be like that. Sure, it wasn't perfect all the time but nothing ever is. All they could do was be the best they could be—that's the only thing you could ask from anyone. Logan and Trent had a love story for the ages, there was just one small problem. She wasn't sure if she wanted to get married to the guy. She just didn't want anyone controlling her, and she knew he'd do that if they got married.

Trent said, "I just wanna get outta here, get some more smoke and a bite to eat, get some time in bed with you, and call it a day."

"Wish it was that easy."

He sighed. "Gonna be another late one?"

"Pretty much."

"Always exciting times, don't you know?" he grabbed the bottle and took a swig. "Another night, same tale. It never changes."

She smiled. "Oh, yeah, it's always what I dreamt of."

"Yeah... When I was a little boy I told myself I always wanted to work at a shit club for crappy pay. Everyone's goal in life, right?"

She laughed. "Awe, come on, it'll get better. It's not that bad. Could be a lot worse."

"You're right."

"Look at it like this, you get to spend time with me."

"And that would be the biggest plus."

"Hey, everything has perks! You just have to find what that is."

"I like the way you think," he told her.

They kissed.

"I like that," she said.

They passed the bottle between them until it was empty. Trent threw the bottle in the dumpster. He told her they needed to go to the store and get another bottle of that stuff on their way home.

"Sure," she said. "We can always do that."

Playground
"Might have to get two."
"Or three?"
Trent laughed wildly. "That could work."
"Might as well make a party out of it."
They each lit a cigarette. Logan said how much she loved the snow. It was supposed to get heavier as the hours continued. She kind of hoped it'd be enough to give her an excuse to call out of work on her next scheduled shift.
"Why can't we just go?" she asked.
"I'm afraid we can't do that, babe."
"Fuck! This shit's fucked," she muttered. "Sometimes I wonder why I ever got into this job, you know?"
"Oh, I know."
She looked out the window. "To be somewhere else... I need to be home relaxing."
"Me, too."
"It's total bullshit we can't do that."
"Well, we can. I mean, we might not have our jobs in the morning, but... moving on is always good, too. There's a lot of things we can do."
"I couldn't do anything like that. It would put John in a bad place. I'd feel bad. He'd eventually get over it, but I couldn't live with myself if I did that. I've never been the type to just walk out on something. I just have to suck it up."
"I can understand that. Yeah, you're right. You're a better person than me."
The owner of Binco, John Hayes, bought the place in 1970. Before John moved in it was a clothing store called Strip Stripe.

When Logan got the job at Binco she started as a waitress. After six months she was promoted to manager. She felt good about herself but wanted more. There was

Bradley Davenport

no doubt in her mind she could handle anything that came her way. She wanted to run her place. The only thing she didn't like about her job was when she had to book bands. She liked everyone she worked with, for the most part. It's nice to work at a place where she got along with the people she worked with. Everyone loved working with her. They'd always say what a wonderful person she was to be around, that she brought joy to wherever she was. All sorts of guys would ask her out but she was a little picky when it came to that department. She wanted someone she could grow with, and not just some guy who was interested in a little fling.

 John Hayes liked Logan. He liked her attitude and work ethic. He told her many times she could go anywhere she wanted in life, and all of those places would love to have her. She had a good head on her shoulders. At one point John asked if she'd be interested in opening another Binco club. She didn't feel she could take on something like that. She thought maybe someday, just not at that time. When she told Trent about it he laughed and said it would be a bad idea, that she wouldn't like it. Everything would fall on her shoulders. But she reminded him she wanted to open her place one day.

 Trent said, "Well, sweetness, the difference would be that it would be your place when you open it. Going to another Binco location would still be working for the same company."

 "You have a point, babe," she told him.

 Trent McCoy and Logan Mekenzi met one night at a party. A friend of Logan's, Misty Feed, invited her to a party. When Logan got there she ran into lots of people she knew and some she didn't. She noticed Trent talking with some people. She was taken by him right away. He was taller than her with dark hair, a great smile, and a

Playground

soft voice. She asked someone who he was. After she found out his name she walked over, introduced herself, and he did the same. They started talking and found they had things in common. They had a drink and continued talking. As the party was coming to an end someone mentioned that another party down the street was in full swing. They all left and went to the party. Everyone had a good time. They ended up having sex that night. It was clear they enjoyed each other very much. They wanted it to last.

It didn't take Trent long to ask her out on a first date. That first night, it was a fantastic event. Trent was a little nervous at first but that quickly subsided. He took Logan to dinner and a movie. After the movie, they stopped at a coffee shop and spent a couple of hours getting to know one another more. They talked about their pasts, loves, losses, and things they wanted for the future. They dug each other. Logan told herself it was wonderful to meet a polite guy.

She had a history of guys who weren't so nice to her. She was very happy. But she'd been down that road before, and she knew even though things may seem to be going great at first they tended to devolve as time marched on. It wasn't until date number five that Logan started to think Trent might be a serious boyfriend. He just seemed more mature than any of the other guys she had been with. She loved the way he looked into her eyes and said her name. He told her she was beautiful all the time, and he meant it. They couldn't get enough of each other. They always wished each other a good day. When they weren't together you would catch them on the phone with each other multiple times a day. Before they knew it they were living together. All of their friends told them the next step was to get married. Logan wasn't so sure about that step.

Logan was looking out the windshield as Trent was telling her they needed to start their own business. He told her they needed to open a bakery.

"A bakery?" Logan said. "Did you forget about the fire in my kitchen two months ago? I can bake but I don't know about doing it as a job. Doing something I love day after day, I could get tired of it. I don't wanna get tired of baking. I'd have to teach you how to, too. I'm not going to be the only one slaving away."

"It's not like we're opening tomorrow or anything," Trent said. "Still have to get the money together, find a place to set up, all that leg work. I'm not sure how long that'd all take."

"We can always go to the bank for the loan."

"Oh, well, guess we need to do that. How long does it take, you know?"

"No clue," she told him. "They'll have you do paperwork and stuff. They do a background check."

"Oh, we have time."

She looked at him. "Of course you do. Babe, why the fuck would you wanna open a bakery? Why that? It's sort of a strange thing for a guy to say."

Trent Shrugged. "Why not? It'd be a way to make money, to be our bosses, to do whatever we wanted. It'd be simple."

"We can make money doing a multitude of things. What's up with you and the bakery? You gonna put on your little white chef's hat, cook, and just bake away?"

"What are you talking about? Everyone loves baked goods. And don't forget man, we can make weed cookies and brownies," he laughed.

"Those are good."

"Yes, they are. I remember the first time I ever ate one."

"You gotta tell me that story."

Playground
"Before we met, years ago, I was at a party with friends and they started making some. I never had any before. One of my friends said I should eat one, so I did. We continued to party and have a good time. I got high but I really couldn't tell a difference. Had to work the next day so I went home. Woke up about two hours before I was supposed to be at work, got a shower, got dressed, and whatever. I walked out of my apartment, lit a cigarette, and started across the parking lot and it hit me. I got high all over again. I got to work, saw my friend Carrie and she just laughed. She told me that was exactly why she didn't eat one."

Logan giggled. "That's funny."

"She laughed at me and said I was a dumb shit for eating that cookie. I told her she probably was right."

Logan said, "I can see that, sure."

"We ended up smoking a blunt at lunch. When we got out of work we smoked another one. It was a pretty good day."

Logan said, "Sounds like it. Wish I could've been there for that. Were you two dating?"

"Who? Carrie and I? No, no, nothing like that. We were just friends."

"Oh, I see."

"I'd thought about it. After some debate, I decided not to. Didn't want to have to still work with her when things started to go bad."

"Good call on that. When things like that don't work, it's not good for anyone. Now, as for you and I, it works. We have our groove going on."

"I couldn't see it any other way."

"You got it, babe."

Trent said, "Well, I just think it's important. I'd never get tired of you."

"Thanks."

The two got out of the car and walked back into the club.

After the band was done playing everyone left. After all the employees left for the night Logan and Trent started the inventory. As they were doing the count Trent poured them a few beers. They drank as they worked. The owner, John, allowed them to drink under the condition they didn't get too drunk and start acting crazy.

Trent worked there as a bouncer. He liked the work. He never liked when he had to kick people out or call the cops. He just wanted everyone to have a good time and get along. He got into a few altercations with people. He never wanted to fight anyone, but some people would get too rowdy. He wasn't concerned with working his way up the ladder. He was content with his station in life; a good woman, a good job, and good money. The future was still in front of him. He wanted to marry Logan and buy a little place.

Along with drinking, the two had sex in Binco. When Trent joked they should have sex on the bar she laughed. He told her they could smoke a blunt and do it.

"Maybe next time, big guy," she smiled. "We need to get this done. I promise we can do that later. I just wanna get this done and go home."

"I guess I can wait."

"I would've thought you got your fill?"

"Well, yeah, but you can never have enough of that, can you?"

She laughed. "How can I argue with that?"

"I'm just telling you the facts."

"You're too cute, man."

"That's what they tell me."

Logan said, "They're right."

"Hey, I'm just an amazing guy. Few can do what I can. You can try to tell them but I don't think they'll get it."

Playground
"Probably not," Logan told him.
"I should teach a class or something."
"You should."
They finished the inventory around 4 am. When they walked out the door she told him she'd drive and they could come back the next day for his car. Snow had stopped falling from the sky. Trent told her since they'd both been drinking they could get a cab, but she told him she'd be fine. She told him she'd be careful and that he had nothing to worry about. Trent had his doubts.
"You sure?" he asked.
"I'm fine," she told him.
He stared at her for a minute. "I can drive if you want?"
"That's okay, I can handle it."
"Just making sure. I don't want anything to happen to you."
"It'll be fine," she told him.
They walked over to her car and got in.
Logan buckled her seat belt. She told her man to buckle his. She was always told to buckle whenever she got in a car for a ride—that had always been a piece of advice she'd always held on to from childhood. Trent told her he'd be fine without it.
Logan said, "Why don't you want to?"
"Hell, babe, you're a good driver. I trust you."
"Even though, you should still do it."
He waved off the idea. "I'll be fine."
"Have it your way."
"I'm tough."
"That might be so, but you should use the buckle. I'm not worried about us as much as I'm worried about the other drivers. I mean, I trust myself but not them. People, they're crazy around here."
"I know."

"And you still won't do it?"

"Nope."

"Okay, then," she started the engine and pulled out of the parking lot.

She didn't feel like arguing. She was too tired. They had about a thirty-minute ride ahead of them.

He looked out the window.

She cranked the radio on full volume.

Trent looked at her. "Gotta keep it rockin', babe! Fuck yeah!!"

She just smiled at him. She wanted to get out of the work head-space and get to that place where she could relax.

About a mile down the road Logan stopped the car to let a brown dog cross the street. She was an animal lover at heart and she couldn't ever imagine hurting anything. When someone would tell her chickens and cows were animals, too, she'd just laugh and say their job was to be food for humans. It wasn't like she'd ever own a pet cow or anything.

"You wanna stop at a drive-through somewhere?" Trent asked. "I bet you could use a bite, no?"

"You wanna stop somewhere?"

"I need something to get by on."

"You got it, babe," she told him. "I can use something, too. I guess burgers it is!"

"Only thing you can get at this time. We need an all-night pizza place around here."

"I couldn't agree more."

"That would be cool, babe."

"I just think all food places should be open all the time."

They came across a World of Beef location and got some burgers, fries, and drinks. It was one of the only things that was open 24/7.

Playground

As they continued down the road Logan started to get a little tired. She had to keep her eyes open until she got home. Just a little more to go. When she got to her place she could crawl into bed. She looked forward into the darkness. She wondered what was beyond. She started to think about the possibilities of aliens hovering above them, collecting information to use in their invasion, because that was bound to happen at some point. She and Trent had to be ready for whatever came their way. She could probably persuade them to let her live, to help them any way they needed. She liked to help. She could help repopulate if need be. Trent could help, too. They could be the new king and queen of the world. What if they were already here? When would they let everyone know? The mind can go all around, through galaxies of the mind. She was always wondering what the future held. But she didn't know if she wanted to know anything. She glanced over at Trent, who was staring out the passenger's window.

"Trent, babe, you doin' okay?" she asked.

He looked at her. "I'm good. Just over here thinking."

"About what?" she asked.

"Ever think about what things are gonna be like in the future?"

"What do you mean?"

"I mean, you know, what's gonna happen with everything?"

"With what? You mean about the world blowing up?"

"Is that gonna happen?" he asked.

"Hopefully not anytime soon."

"That's comforting. I still have stuff to do before that happens."

"I have things I'd like to do," Logan told him.

"Like what?"

She went on to tell him about some of her plans, about how she wanted to get a nice two-story house and start doing some writing and painting. She wanted to do a lot of things. She was young and had a lot more years in front of her than she did behind. They were both young and loved one another. She told him how she'd like to go to New Zealand and Ireland one day. She told him that she often thought about the future. She didn't believe all of that mess about flying cars and that robots would run everything someday. Why would robots run everything? You still needed humans to repair and program the robots. If people had to do that why would they build such things?

"Those are all good things," he told her. "When would you wanna start that stuff?"

"I'm not sure," she said. "Have to figure some things out first. What about you?"

"What about me?"

"What things do you think about?"

"Me, you, everyone. Sometimes I wish I could see into the future, you know? Just imagine if you could do that, watch your life and future as you glide through the clouds. You could see everything that was gonna happen—if it was something you didn't want, you know, you could warn yourself so you could do something about it."

"That's interesting. I'm sure everyone thinks that," she said. "If you could see into the future you could plan things perfectly."

Trent asked her about marriage. He wanted to spend the rest of his life with her, and he was pretty sure she wanted the same. He asked when she wanted to get married to him.

"I dunno," she told him. "That's a pretty big step, don't you think?"

Playground

"Yeah, it's a big step, is that your only point?" he asked. "What do you mean?"

"I just want to make sure."

"I'm sure it'll be okay. Things seem to be going pretty well. We're a perfect match. We have a good time together. You're what I've been searching for. You say the same thing about me. It might be a step, but it'll be a step in the right direction. We're strong and can beat anything that's thrown our way."

"It's just— I don't know. I don't wanna get into it now. It's been a long one and we are both tired."

"I can take it. You don't have to spare my feelings," he looked forward. "That's one thing I'm good at."

"Oh, come on! I'd just feel more comfortable telling you another time."

"Telling me what?"

"Don't get mad, I just think we should wait."

"Until when?"

"I'm not sure. I love you, but I think we should give it some more time."

"I love you, too. I don't understand, if we both feel the same why don't we just commit?"

"Just wanna make completely sure, don't you? I'm sure you don't wanna be a year into marriage, wake up one morning, and say, 'Oh, my, what have I done? now I'm in this thing that's not that easy to get out of.' I don't want you to be disappointed with me. Do you know how much a divorce costs? You could feel differently down the road."

"Disappointed in you? That would never happen."

"You say that now, but you'll find something that'll change your mind. Sooner or later it'll be something."

"How can you say that? I'd never think that. I've never thought about that in the whole time we've been together. I love you. I love everything about you. We have that chemical thing going on, babe. It can't be helped. It's just how we were made. I mean, we can try to fight it but that force will always win. All of it, it's about human nature."

"You promise?"

"Cross my heart."

She smiled. "That's a sweet thing to say."

"But it's still the same answer?"

She laughed. "You picked a strange time to talk about this. But, yeah, you're talking about a big leap. Even though I love you very much I can't do that—not right now, at least."

"What are you afraid of?" he asked.

"Me? I'm afraid of nothing. Why does something always have to be wrong? I just feel the way I feel. Don't give me a hard time about it. Just do me a favor and respect my feelings, can you do that for me? I've always supported you."

"I'm sorry, babe, I'm just trying to understand things. I thought we had a good thing going here. Thanks for finally telling me how things are. This whole thing has been for nothing."

"Don't be like that. Come on, let's just get home. We can talk about this later. We're both tired. It's been a long day."

"Whatever."

"Don't give me a hard time," she told him.

"Just doesn't make sense."

She glanced at him. "Listen, I'll just talk to you tomorrow about it."

"Tomorrow is gonna be another excuse. You can never be fucking happy with anything. What the fuck? I should jump outta this car right fucking now. Shit's fucked."

"Why would you jump out of the car?" she asked.

"Fuck you," he growled. "I can't believe you."

Playground

They sat in silence.

Trent looked at his love. He loved her and didn't want to fight. He couldn't figure out why she was acting the way she was. It didn't seem like her. Something was wrong but he didn't know what it was. Was it another man? That was the only thing Trent could think of. But he knew Logan would never cheat on him. He was at a loss, not knowing what to do

Logan didn't want to marry him but she didn't know how to come out and say it. She loved him but she didn't want to spend the rest of her life with him. She didn't want to be tied down to any one person. She was still young and had a whole lifetime to experience. She didn't want to deny herself anything. It was all about living life, and she wanted to do as much of it as she could. She wasn't going to let anyone control her. She didn't know if Trent would ever understand.

Trent broke the silence. "If you feel that way, I guess I need to move on."

"I figured you'd say something like that."

"There's no reason I should put my life on hold if this isn't going anywhere."

"You're right," she said. "I'm not going to hold you back. Do what you want."

"Glad that's settled," he snorted. "And you the same."

She smiled. "So, you got any bitches lined up?"

"Maybe."

"Ah, I see how it is."

"What about you?" he asked. "I'm sure you've had those beautiful eyes set on others."

"Guess you'll just have to wait and find out."

"What's that supposed to mean?"

"I don't think I stuttered."

"Oh, okay, it's like that?" he shrugged. "I'm not your boss."

Bradley Davenport

They came to an intersection. When they turned right another car slammed into the back of them, spinning Logan's car around, and launching Trent through the windshield.

Everything went black for both of them.

In an instant something very bad happened, something neither of them could walk away from.

Maybe it was all meant to be.

3

Logan was standing on a marble floor. She looked down at herself and thought she had to have some sort of injury, she was just in a car accident. She called out for Trent but got nothing. She looked at the white walls and wondered where she was. A few feet in front of her was a big spiral staircase. She looked up to see where it went, but it was too high to tell. She glanced around and couldn't locate a door of any kind. She didn't know how she got there, or how long she had been there. Panic crept into her mind. She didn't know if she was in danger or not.

She called out but no one answered. She called again. Nothing. She closed her eyes for a minute and heard her name being called. Her name was called again. It was like a dream. She didn't think any of her friends were there to greet her. When she opened her eyes she saw a man and woman dressed in white robes walking down the staircase. She gave a hard swallow. Both the man and woman had long blonde hair and blue eyes. Both had pale skin. They were about the same height. The two had an ethereal quality about them, glistening and sparkling in the light.

"Greetings," the man said. "I'm Ziggy," he pointed to the woman. "And my friend is Siz."

"Welcome," Siz said.

Ziggy went on. "We hope you find this place to your liking?"

"Where am I?" Logan asked. "Who are you? What do you want from me?"

"We know you must have questions. They all have questions when they first get here. I promise all will be revealed."

"Get where? What is this place?"

Ziggy said, "Heaven, of course."

"Heaven?" Logan muttered.

"Yes."

"What happened? Last I remember I was in an accident."

"Yes, the car accident," Ziggy said. "We understand your confusion. Perhaps we need to explain, yes? It happened so fast. Neither of you knew what was coming. I'm sorry, dear."

Logan shook her head slowly. "Yeah, that would probably help if you guys explained things. I don't know what this is."

"We don't mean to scare you," Siz said. "You have nothing to be afraid of. You can relax. We're about peace. Everyone reacts the same at first. We wish that would change, be we can't make it so."

Logan said, "What happened to my friend? What happened to Trent?"

The two looked at each other.

"Your friend," Siz said, "went to the other side."

"The other side?" Logan asked.

Ziggy said, "We refer to the other side as Hell."

"Hell?" Logan said. "Isn't that down there," she pointed her finger to the floor. "I don't understand."

"That's a common misconception," Ziggy told her.

"In what way?"

"It's just the other side of the place. Both Heaven and Hell are run by the same group. There have been a lot of misconceptions over time. For instance, you've always heard Hell referred to as 'down there' and Heaven as 'up there'?"

"That's right."

"That's incorrect," Ziggy said. "There's a long story behind that. Would you like to hear it?"

Logan cocked her head to the right. "I'm not doing anything else, I guess. I'd like to hear, yes. I'm sorry, I'm not sure what to make of this place. It's amazing."

Siz said, "I think we should continue this discussion upstairs."

"I'd love that," Logan's eyes went to the stairs.

The three started up the staircase.

When they got to the tenth step Siz snapped her fingers and they were in what looked like a living room. There were couches and chairs, and two big-screen televisions in the room. A coffee table sat in front of the couches. Everything was bathed in white.

Everything was neat and clean.

They told her to take a seat on one of the couches.

She sat.

They sat across from her.

They asked if she was comfortable.

She was.

Ziggy said, "Like I was saying, you were always taught that Heaven and Hell were separate places. All of that, it's just been propaganda conjured up by those who wrote the Bible. Great efforts had been made to rectify this misinformation over time—sadly, it hadn't worked. Even though people don't know the truth they'll believe something they've heard multiple times from their friends. Humans are funny creatures when it comes to things like that."

"I can see that," Logan said, as she leaned back on the couch.

"It's quite a strange thing. Can't say I blame them. People are flawed. They're all the same. Everyone thinks they know the truth when nobody does. They believe one another. I used to be the same way, I'll admit it."

"At least you admit it."

They laughed.

Logan continued. "With that being said, how do I know

you're telling the truth?"

Ziggy told her she made a good point, and that wasn't something he had considered. But he assured her he and Siz were telling the truth. At that point, Logan had no choice but to believe them. Something told her she wasn't going back to where she was anytime soon.

Ziggy said, "The ones we've told before, they didn't believe us either. I know you're searching inside yourself right now, looking for something to cling to, telling yourself you need to run. But you shouldn't worry, like Siz said, you don't have to be scared. We understand what you must be thinking. We've been where you are before. Sometimes it takes some longer than others to understand. The only thing we can do is try to ease your transition."

Logan said, "Will I ever see my family again?"

"I'm afraid not, dear. Your life has changed forever. Your soul has passed. You don't have to worry yourself with the troubles you had on Earth any longer. It may not be what you wanted, but it's who you are now. I know you never asked for this. No one ever knows until the end—and then, once you find out you can't tell anyone on the planet you just left. Each time your soul is sent back, it's a clean slate, impossible to conjure up past lives. Most of those past lives, depending on who you are, are played out in dreams. For years people have tried to understand the meaning of dreams, but that's a mystery they'll never get an answer to. A soul's past life processing through itself...."

"What am I here for?" Logan asked. "I'm sorry, this whole thing is just a little too crazy."

Siz stared at her for a bit and told her that she was special. When Logan asked what that meant they told her they couldn't tell her. Logan shook her head like everything was fine, but inside she didn't know what to think

Playground
or say. Someone had to have been playing a cruel trick on her. She told herself if Trent was behind it she was going to kick his butt.

Ziggy said, "We feel that it would be irresponsible of us to tell you. We leave that job for the council."

"The Council?" Logan asked.

"Yes, made up of fourteen people."

"Are they God?"

"No."

"I see," Logan said. "Who are they?"

"Think of it like Congress in Heaven. I guess that's the best way I could explain it."

Siz could still sense something was wrong with Logan. She took Logan's hand into hers. "Trust me, it'll all be okay. We understand. Take comfort in the fact you're here instead of with the others. It'll be okay. You came to us at the perfect time."

Her voice comforted Logan.

Everything fell silent. Logan continued to scan the room.

Ziggy pulled Siz closer to him

"So, are you guys a couple?" Logan asked.

"A couple of what?" Ziggy asked. "We're a couple of crazy ones. It's always a blast when we're around! You can count on that. We own it all!"

Both women laughed.

Siz said, "To answer your question, yes, we are a couple. We've been together for five trillion years."

"That's a long time," Logan placed her hand on her knee. "What's the trick? How have you guys been together for that long? I can't seem to keep a guy for more than a year."

Ziggy said, "The day we met, we died the next day. A true romance... It was a crazy couple of hours. I wasn't planning on doing anything big that day, but things have ways of changing."

"Really?" Logan said. "I'd say they do."

"It's all a mystery, I have to say. We're all just floating around, just waiting for a moment when something glorious happens. She always talks in riddles and landscapes."

Siz said to him. "I love the way you look at things, babe."

"Always," Ziggy told her. "It's the way they painted the picture, a true masterpiece."

Logan smiled at them.

Ziggy said, "We met through some friends of ours. My friend called me up one day and asked if I wanted to go to a cookout. They were grilling burgers, drinking beer, playing cards, and having a great time. Just another day to relax and enjoy life. Told them I had things to do but I'd be there by noon. I ran around town for awhile and did my business. I got there about two hours later and everyone seemed to be having the time of their lives. That stuff always made me smile. I talked to a few people, shot some jive, and caught up on things with friends. Some of them had been out of town. Funny how things get away from you sometimes, you know? I'd been there for awhile before I met the most beautiful woman I've ever laid my eyes on. We talked for a long time. We had a lot in common."

"That's so sweet," Logan said.

Ziggy continued. "I was interested in everything about her. I asked if she wanted to go to another party that night. She was something else, something special. I'd never met anyone quite like her. For the next few hours, we drank and had a lot of fun. It was one of those days where everything felt right with the world, you know? She told me she liked me. That made me happy. I knew I couldn't rush things and scare her off."

Playground

"Oh, babe," Siz said, "I was all in. I was ready to see how things were going to turn out."

Ziggy and Siz went to the other party. It was a good time, with booze and drugs everywhere. In those days Ziggy was dealing drugs. He was making good money at it, and that was the main thing that kept him doing it. Ziggy and Ziv ended up getting shot that night by drug dealers. The only reason Siz was killed was because she was the girlfriend. For a long time after they died he would apologize to her daily.

Logan looked down, studied the floor for a minute, then looked at the two of them. "Are you God?"

"Not hardly," Ziggy laughed. "That's a good one. They asked me the other day if I wanted the job. I passed."

Siz said she wasn't God either.

Logan said, "I don't understand. Are you saying it's a job title?"

"They usually do the job for twenty, thirty years at a time," Ziggy said. "There's been a few cases where people wanted the person to stay for longer. The longest anyone ever did the job was by a guy named Adam Hook. He ended up doing it for a century. He got tired of it, retired, and went to another planet. He has never been back. He was a pretty good guy."

"That's a long time doing the job," Logan told them. "Who has the job now?"

Ziggy said, "We're currently in between people right now. We haven't had one for over three decades."

"Why?"

"They can't find the right person to do it. The last person we had just got tired of doing it. He did it for over nine hundred years."

"What does he do now?"

"He spends the day watching movies and playing his

guitar. He wanted to start a band. He came to me at one point. But I never had any musical talent."

"I see."

"Yeah, it was something I just never good at. He taught me a few things but I forgot. It's been awhile."

"Well, it's never too late," Logan said.

"I know, I know," Ziggy said. "We only have time here."

"In that case," Logan told him, 'you have all the time you want to learn."

"You're right."

"Well, if the guy is still here why doesn't he just go back to doing the job?"

"He doesn't want to. A lot of people have asked. He doesn't want anything to do with it."

"So," Logan said, "if no one is doing the job then who's been granting miracles?"

"We have a guy, he's been filling the spot. Someone always has to keep the game going, the fighting over souls. As it stands right now our side is winning."

"That's good, I guess."

"It's always been a give-and-take thing. We win some, lose some. But in the end both, sides have to work together. Sometimes I get lost in it all. Being good and bad, it's a very fine line sometimes. It can get blurry. But that's the game. The world is their playground."

Siz said, "This all must seem crazy to you, huh?"

"A little," Logan told her.

"We're used to that happening. Normally, when you get to Heaven you're met by Dirk. He's been on vacation for the past two weeks. But seeing as how we knew you were going to be joining us we thought it best to come meet you," Siz smiled.

"How did you know I was going to be here?"

They told her they watched her from above.

Playground

Logan got a confused look on her face. They explained that they could watch people on all of the planets. Logan asked how many planets there were. The answer she got was more than a billion.

The two took Logan around and showed her everything in Heaven. There were a lot of people walking around, no cars anywhere. Ziggy told her that Heaven was a big city.

"This is just Heaven One," he told her.

"How many are there?" Logan asked.

"Two thousand."

"Really?"

"Yeah, and there are more being constructed."

"That's a lot."

"It is, isn't it? Well, this Heaven is just for Earth 3 and 4."

"What do you mean by that?"

"There are many Earths. You were on Earth 3."

He told her about how Earth 1, the first one ever created, had blown up due to an alien war in space. The wars lasted a long time.

On the sidewalks of Heaven people were talking wildly to one another. Everyone was happy and smiling. Ziggy told Logan he hoped she liked the place because it was going to be her home. She said it was good because she'd always wanted to live in a big city. Both Ziggy and Siz were happy for her.

Logan asked about her loved ones, the ones who came to Heaven, where they were. Siz told her they were around somewhere, and that they aren't notified about everyone who comes there. Logan nodded and said she couldn't wait to see everyone. Still, she wondered what they meant when they told her she was special. Sure, she'd always heard people telling her that when she was

Bradley Davenport

on Earth 3, but she didn't know why they were saying such things about her in Heaven. As the three talked Logan thought it all had to be a dream.

They walked passed big skyscrapers and small shops and restaurants. She was impressed with how cozy everything was, how everything seemed so normal. People were walking around smoking marijuana and drinking beer.

"Can you do that out in the open like that? Logan asked.

"You can do whatever you'd like," Siz told her. "You just can't harm anyone else. We're all about peace here. You can't go around killing people—if you do that, you go to the other side. Trust me, you don't want that. They run things differently there. In the past, yes, we've had to transport people to the other side. It's happened more than I'd like to admit. You just can't control everyone."

"Hell?" Logan asked.

They told Logan that over in Hell you can murder people all you want. They're always sending souls over to Hell.

Ziggy looked at Logan. "You break the rules and a price has to be paid."

They stopped in front of a coffee shop.

The girls wanted a cup. They walked through the door of the shop. The place wasn't too busy. People were scattered at tables making small talk. The music playing overhead was a jazz piece. Logan smiled as she sat at a table with coffee in hand. She looked around at everyone and asked if all of those people were dead.

Ziggy said, "All of these, all those people outside, they've all reached their reincarnation limit."

"There's a limit?" Logan asked.

"The number is different for everyone. There are many variables to consider."

Playground

"I imagine a lot goes into that."

"It keeps them pretty busy over there," Ziggy took a drink of coffee. "I couldn't do it, to do what they do. I was asked. I told them I didn't want the responsibility. Some of them try to talk their way into another life, but that goes against the rules."

"And there are those who only get one life," Siz added. "For one reason or another, they are denied another chance. Usually, those cases are reserved for murderers and other very bad people. But like everything some things have slipped through and additional lives were granted. Misplaced paperwork led to embarrassment over time. No one's perfect."

Logan asked what Ziggy and Siz's numbers were. Ziggy's number was four, and Siz's was three. They told her when you got to Heaven you could watch all the lives you had lived play out. But you don't know how many lives you've lived until you arrive there.

"How do you find that out?" Logan asked.

"You can find out from the Council."

They talked more as they finished their coffee. There were a lot of things Logan had to learn about the place. She asked if she could visit Hell.

Ziggy explained to Logan there were alternate universes, and that when he and Siz died together that was the only time they were in the same universe. He told her about how most universes had the same historic events with small changes. The first time Ziggy died was during the First World War when he was shot in the chest; the second, when he was ten years of age in 1972, he was playing with a friend on the roof of a five-story building when he fell off of the building. The two had been playing football before dinner. The parents spent the rest of their lives in a deep depression. Their sadness became too much and they took their own lives four years later. They couldn't live with the pain any longer. The third life he led, in 1987, he was murdered when he was involved in a drug deal gone bad. He was with a friend of his when they were making the deal. And because of the fact it was his first time, he was very nervous, which made the guy they were doing the deal with nervous. The guy pulled his gun quickly and shot Ziggy and his friend. The both of them were pleased to learn the guy who shot them, Joe Dicco, was arrested for killing a couple six years later. The fourth time he died was when he and Siz met.

When he was shot in the chest in World War 1, even though he was on Earth 3 he was in the Tikan dimension. A planet has thousands of dimensions in it. A person can live their whole life without seeing any of the other dimensions. The layers are inviable to the naked eye.

When he fell off the roof in 1972, he was in the Montayi dimension. His last two lives were in the Coli and Spitrex dimension. When Ziggy and Siz got to Heaven they were told they had to stay, that they wouldn't live another life. At first, they thought they had done something wrong but were soon told the rules that limited lives. It took them awhile to be okay with all of that. Ziggy asked if he could go back as a bird or something, but he was told he couldn't. He thought it would be awesome to fly everywhere, or, if he came back as a fish so he could swim underwater, and explore where few humans have gone.

Siz, before the last time she died, had been in a plane crash in 1985 on the planet called Urantia. All of her other lives were spent on Urantia. After they both died and came to Heaven they were a lot like Logan, not having a clue as to what was going on. As they got their feet

Playground

about things the council asked if they would help make others understand things better, to make the transition easier, or try to. Everyone goes into it differently. Some require more adjusting than others. The thing that surprised Ziggy and Siz was how many people believed in the things that were written in the Bible. It amazed them how misled all of those people were, that they hadn't even heard the truth. All those guys who called themselves preachers, how they didn't know much of what they were talking about. Yes, as far as they knew everything in the book was correct. People before them were told the same thing they kept rattling off to others. Truth was, all those stories in the Bible were fiction—conjured up by authors, good ones. But they were all made up. To give credit where it's due, they were good storytellers with fantastic imaginations.

For awhile, they questioned everything they thought they knew. If they were lied to about those stories, what else were they lied to about? How can you prove anything? There was no way they could go and let everyone know the truth. All they could do was watch people believe in the lies.

At one point, Ziggy scheduled a meeting with the man who held the title of God. They wanted the truth about everything. God told them they needed to keep quiet about all of it, and just do what they were both told. They didn't understand. They were confused. How were they supposed to get others to understand if they didn't, themselves? When they asked why they had been given the task all they were told was that the two of them were special. They were brought to a big white house and told that was where they'd live. Siz loved the place. She'd never lived in a place quite like it before. She was happy when she thought about all the decorating she could do. And if they didn't like it they'd have to kick her out. She didn't care. She knew they wouldn't do that. They were needed. They had no way of knowing what the job was going to be like.

Over time they got to where they loved their job, guiding souls through every corner of Heaven. There were a few others who helped guide souls. The story about Paul at the gates of Heaven wasn't true at all. Those who came up with that story, Ricky Styles, had a distant uncle named Paul he wanted to pay tribute to. Paul had been in a wheelchair all of his life.

After some time God called for Ziggy and Siz to meet with him. When they got there they saw God had a few other people with him They were all drinking and smoking weed. God was telling them how he needed to go to a bar and hear live music.

Over the next few hours, they told the couple all of the secrets. When they got ready to leave God told them they couldn't go around telling what they knew. God told them it was important they didn't divulge what they just learned. If they told before the time was right they were going to Hell never to be seen again. They made the two swear.

Siz looked at Logan. "I'm sorry, but we can't tell you everything we know."

"Understood," Logan said.

"But after some time we discovered that even we were misled about a few things."

"I guess they had a good reason?" Logan suggested.

Siz shrugged. "Maybe. Who knows? We might get the real truth one of these days. See, all of those people on the planet you came from who run around, saying they're God or Jesus, when they get up here we're instructed to not tell them anything, like a punishment. But most of those lunatics are sent to Hell," she gave a smile. "It's a crazy place around here. They do it to themselves.

Playground

We can't say anything. We just have to sit back and let it all happen. Believe it when I tell you, we know what you must be thinking. We felt the same way at first. Unlike us, though, you are very special to this whole thing. We were told we couldn't tell you under any circumstance whatsoever. In time I hope you'll come to terms with all of it."

Ziggy said, "Maybe we aren't made to know everything? Hell, I wish I could give you an answer on that one."

Logan asked the two where she was going to stay while she was in Heaven. Ziggy told her they had an apartment for her. The place was across from the building that housed the council. The apartment building was a big red brick affair. Logan liked the sound of that, an apartment all her own. When she was on Earth all she had throughout the years were roommates. Now, she had a place all her own. She was so lucky. She'd be free to do whatever she wanted.

They walked through the front electric sliding doors of the apartment building. People were coming and going. People were sitting in the lobby talking about whatever. A few were sitting in the bar area drinking the day away. They walked to the front counter. The guy behind the counter knew who Ziggy and Siz were. They told the guy Logan was here and they knew what to do.

"Miss Logan," the man slid her the apartment key. "If you need anything at all don't hesitate to ask. We hope you enjoy your stay with us."

"Thank you," she told the man. "How much does it cost?"

"Cost?" the man said. "You don't have anything to worry about, ma'am. It's all been taken care of."

"Oh, okay. Thanks."

"It's what we do. We just hope you like all of our accommodations."

"I'm sure I will."

The guy smiled as he thanked her again. He was a pale man with black curly hair and a beard. He told Logan his name was Sherman.

"Nice to meet you, Sherman," Logan told him.

The guy said, "The pleasure is all on my end."

Logan smiled at him. "Thanks."

"No need."

Ziggy nodded to the guy. "And they told me to tell you they owe you big on this one, and that they won't forget it."

The man shook his head. "Well, I think that's a few they owe me for. But who's counting, huh? It's just good to be useful. It makes me feel like I'm doing my part in something big."

"I know what you mean. At any rate, my friend, they still wanted it said. And they said for you to stop by whenever you want."

"I'll keep that in mind. What do you think will be in it for me?"

"I can't tell you that," Ziggy said.

"Think I should ask for a promotion?" Sherman asked.

"Couldn't hurt. We all need one of those."

The man laughed.

The three walked to the apartment. When they got inside Logan was surprised that it was so nice. The place was already furnished. There was even a big-screen television in the living room. They walked into the kitchen. The cabinets and the refrigerator were fully stocked with food. They went through the apartment and there were all sorts of supplies she'd need. She didn't have to buy anything. She asked about her stuff in her place on Earth. She told them about this one particular blanket she had, and how it was one of her favorite things ever.

Playground

She told them about how comfy it was. Logan went on to tell them about a few other items; a bong, albums, some clothes she liked, books, and other stuff she wanted. Ziggy said he could get those items for her, and that it was no problem. With a snap of his fingers, Ziggy was gone. A minute later he was back surrounded by the items.

"Thanks," Logan told him.

"Think nothing of it," he looked over the things. "Anything to make your stay comfortable, it's part of what we do."

She nodded. "I like that. I need to learn how to snap my fingers like that."

"How's the apartment?" he asked.

"I love it."

Siz said, "We're glad you like it. We had hoped you would. If you ever want to change anything just ask one of the guys downstairs."

Ziggy and Siz started talking to each other about other things that needed tending to. Logan asked both of them if they knew anything about what happened after she died. They told her that after they got in the accident it didn't take long before help arrived. The two told her they watched the funeral from Heaven. It had been a very sad event, everyone was crying and was sad. A few of Logan's friends and family members gave eulogies.

Logan sniffed as a few tears rolled down her face.

Siz placed her arm around her. "Come now, there was nothing that could've prevented this. Don't feel bad. In time you'll understand. I'm sure if your parents knew your true purpose they wouldn't have minded you leaving their world. You were loved so much by your friends and family. You'll be able to see them all again one day. Try not to cry, my child."

Logan asked what happened to the person who crashed

into her car. They told her the people she got in the accident with, Billy Price and Alana Jones, were both drunk. Billy was the one who was behind the wheel. They were both arrested. They spared Logan the other details. They didn't want to upset her more than she already was.

Logan walked over to the kitchen and got a glass of water. "How long was I in that room before you guys called my name?"

Ziggy said, "I know it must not have seemed like it to you, but you were there for over an hour."

"What?" Logan said. "An hour? Oh, gosh, it didn't seem that long. To me, it seemed instantly."

"I know, I know," Ziggy shook his head. Your soul was motionless for awhile. We kept an eye on you and made sure you were going to be okay. Everyone seems to have a different reaction. Some of it has to do with how they died. If it's sudden, like yours was, the soul goes into shock. And there's no way of knowing how long the shock lasts. I've seen it last for up to twenty years before. I know the first time I saw that I didn't know what to do. I had to go get someone for help. That's when I first heard about that."

"Damn," Logan exclaimed. "Glad they told you about that one."

"Tell me about it."

Logan walked over and sat in a chair at the dining room table, and sighed. "This has all been a lot to process. It's like a dream or something. I'm not built for this.'

Ziggy walked over and took the chair across from her. "In time you'll learn everything you need to know."

"Can't I just go back?" she said. "I mean, just tell them I never came here, can't you do that? Tell them I went rogue or something."

"We can't do that."

Playground
"But I wanna go back home. I don't know this place."
Siz pulled up a chair and joined them.
They talked for what seemed like four or five hours. Logan had some doubts about the place they called Heaven. She asked if they were playing a cruel trick on her. They told her once she talked to the council she'd change the way she thought about the place. There was something they weren't telling her, and that didn't sit well with her. She'd been down that road too many times with people. It was hard for her to trust anyone.

Logan sighed and said she wished Trent was with her.

Siz told her it'd be okay, but, she was sorry Trent couldn't be with her.

"Why?" Logan asked.

"Because he's over in Hell."

"And? The two don't mingle? He wasn't a bad guy. He's a sweet man who'd never hurt anyone. I don't understand. Why was he sent there?"

Siz said, "When everything's settled I'm sure you'll get a chance to see each other. You'll be able to see one another a lot. We can't say anything more. We made a promise."

"About what?" Logan asked. "It doesn't sound right. I'm getting the feeling something bad is at play."

"We can't say," Ziggy told her. "And I'm a man of my word. I keep my promises. You'll come to understand things soon enough. Both of you have been chosen for something special. We don't want either of you to be compromised."

"He's been chosen, too?" Logan asked. "I'm excited to see what it is. I have to tell you, if it's anything involving cooking I'm not the one for the job. I'm an okay cook according to friends, but I'm not the best by any means."

Ziggy laughed. "Trust me, it has nothing to do with cooking skills."

"Good to know."

He continued. "It's better than you can ever imagine."

Logan liked the sound of that. She was going to be able to see Trent again. She loved him so much.

After they talked some more Ziggy told Siz it was late, and they had to go. Both of them told Logan they'd see her again soon. Ziggy snapped his fingers and they both disappeared.

Logan spent the rest of the night walking around the apartment thinking. She turned on the television and rolled a joint. She loved the fact you could enjoy weed in Heaven. She started to think about Trent and hoped he was doing okay. She couldn't figure out why he was sent to Hell. He was a nice guy. He was a heavy party animal, but they were both guilty of that.

She walked out to the balcony of the apartment and stared at the clear night. She was lost in the stars, counting them one by one. As she took a big hit off the joint it occurred to her that the life she had once known was no more. She was a little sad about that.

4

The next day Logan woke early to watch the sunrise. After she got something to eat she got ready for her meeting with the council. She was still a little nervous and didn't know what to expect.

She walked across the street to where the council was. She walked through the sliding doors of the building and was met with astonishment. Everything was so beautiful and nice. Everything was marble. People came and went in a rush. A busy place, she thought. She hoped the meeting wouldn't take long. If she had time she might take a walk around the city. When she walked over to the counter she was met with a big smile from a guy named Mike. Logan told him why she was there and who sent her. Mike picked up his phone and dialed someone. He had a brief conversation with someone, telling whoever it was that she had arrived. A few minutes after Mike put down the phone another man came down from the elevator. He walked over to Logan and introduced himself.

"Hi, Logan," the man said. "I'm Jerry."

They shook hands.

"How'd you know my name?" Logan asked.

"I didn't mean to alarm you. I apologize. The people upstairs, they've been expecting you. They told me who you were."

"How long have they been expecting me?"

"For a long time."

"Oh."

He smiled at her. "They knew you had been the one they'd been waiting for all this time. They thought a few people were suitable, but they didn't work out in the end. I hope your stay so far in our city has been to your liking, yes?"

"Everything's been good so far. A little confused,

though."

"I understand," Jerry told her. "There is a period of adjustment. The period of transition is different for everyone."

"Really?"

"I've been doing this for several years, and I've seen all types of people come live with us."

"I see," Logan said. "Well, so far I haven't had a problem."

"That's good. If you should have any issues with anything just let us know. We want everyone to be comfortable."

She thanked him.

"I hope you're not afraid of elevators," he gestured to the elevator. "Are you ready?"

"As ready as I'll ever be."

The two walked onto the elevator and went to the thirty-second floor. The doors opened to an open office space. A long table was in the center of the office with twelve people sitting around it. They all introduced themselves to Logan.

"What's this about?" Logan asked.

The man who sat in the middle, Val Lune, asked Jerry to get everyone a drink. He went on to explain that he was glad she met with them. She said that it wasn't a problem.

Val said, "You don't have anything to worry about. We mean you no harm."

"Seems I've been hearing a lot of that lately," Logan said. "I guess everyone thinks I'm scared of everything, something like that. I guess they think because I'm a girl I'm helpless in this place."

"We understand that," Val said. "The thing is, what we have to talk with you about, can seem to be scary to someone. Some people we've told this to, they wanted to

Playground

go back to Earth. Can you believe they wanted to go back to that place? That place, it's a dump. It's full of rubbish these days. It was once a good place, but now... It's going to take a long time to get that place back in order. If you ask me I think they just need to bomb the whole place. They just need to start from scratch."

Logan said, "It's something else, that's for sure."

"At this point, we just keep it around to amuse ourselves. So much craziness goes on down there. It's humoring to us. Things need to be regulated more."

"You won't get any objections from me," Logan said.

"If you ask me they should've blown it up years ago, but they never listen to me. I told the others and they voted me down. Not much I could do about it after that. They all were just insistent that it would get better with time. I went along with it. I figured if I placated them they'd see the light at some point. Oh, I was wrong. And now they have that huge disappointment on their hands."

Logan laughed.

Everyone around the room laughed.

"But," Val continued, "I'm not even sure why I care. I just wanted everything to run like it was supposed to."

Another guy, a bald guy named Daxton said, "Can we get on with this? We have a lot on our plate."

Val turned to the guy. "I think we can spare as much time as we need. After all, the job we're going to ask Logan to do is important, very important to everyone in the universe. I think you and everyone else can appreciate that."

Everyone agreed.

"And what job would that be?" Logan asked. "I'm flattered."

"We need you to be God," Val told her.

"God?" Logan gave him a strange look.

"That's correct."

"What? Why? I don't under— What are you talking about?"

Val said, "Yes, God. That God. I'm sure you have a bunch of questions for us. We have all day to talk through this. We'll take as long as we need."

Logan looked at everyone around the table. "I think this is gonna take a little explanation. I honestly don't know what to say to all of you."

Daxton said, "See, you guys, I thought we'd decided on that other guy," he looked at Logan. "No offense to you, ma'am."

"No offense taken," Logan told him. "What guy were you talking about?"

"I forgot what his name was. A lot of times I don't pay attention to memos I get. We get so many of those damn things around here."

"Why?"

"I'm not sure. Most of it, it's just so lame. I dunno, maybe I'm just burnt from all this shit."

"You might be on to something there," Logan said. "A vacation always did the trick for me."

"If I took one of those I may not wanna ever come back."

"Change of job" Logan suggested.

Jerry came back with the drinks and handed them out.

Val explained to Logan exactly what was expected of her. They told her the origins of God. The person who created the universe was the first one who proclaimed himself as God. His name was Dillon. The way he originally planned it, the person who was elected to be God had that position for ten to twelve years, and then he/she would give up the duty to another. The past three people elected to be God had to run over their term because they couldn't find the right person in time. When they were told they had to do the job some of them refused,

Playground

and then the council was forced to ship them to another universe. And when they got shipped out they weren't allowed to return.

They told Logan she'd been fed false information all her life. The council went over everything Ziggy and Siz already told her. They told her that pretty much all the stories in the Bible were false. Everything.

There was a guy who was a carpenter named Jesus, but he wasn't anything special. They told Logan that Jesus was a childhood friend of theirs. He was a good guy but that was it. He was always getting himself into trouble; stealing, robbing, getting into fights, and having sex everywhere with any girl he could. Val told her Jesus built his first house. Jesus did walk around a lot. He was the type of guy who was always thinking up stuff to do. In his later years, Jesus would run around and act crazy, telling people dirty jokes and cussing at them. When he started hanging around Mary Magdalene, that didn't help things any. She was crazier than he was. The two of them were always getting in trouble and having sex.

Val told Logan that the reason Jesus was put on the cross was because he murdered two men. Val's memory was a little fuzzy on the details but he told her it had to do with the two men betraying him. He went on to tell her that, yes, he had a few people who followed him around, but they were just friends and liked hanging around one another. Val said that Jesus and his friends were just a bunch of hoodlums, lunatics, and just a mischievous bunch all around. Jesus and his friends were people you just wanted to be a part of. Val told her about the time Jesus stole a few items from two men. They confronted Jesus about the matter a few days later. He and a friend attacked the two and beat them with rocks. A few days later people discovered Jesus and this other man did the crime. Val told her some other stories about Jesus. He told her the reason people wrote good things about Jesus was to pay tribute to him as if to say those were things he could have done. All of his friends knew he had greatness in him. Jesus' madness got the better of him.

Val and the others continued to explain to her how everything worked. She still had a whole lot of questions. They were patient with her and answered anything she had for them. They needed to make sure she was comfortable with everything. Before they knew it ten hours had gone by.

Daxton looked out the window, then at Logan. "Where does the time go, huh? Time has a way of running away. You try to hold on, but it flutters away in the wind."

The others around the table agreed.

Logan didn't say anything.

She asked how long she was going to stay at the apartment.

"As long as you'd like," Val said. "If you don't like the place I'm sure other arrangements can be made."

"Oh, no, no, I like it. I just wasn't sure if you guys wanted me to stay there or not."

They told her she'd start her new job the next morning. They told her someone would be by in the morning to take her to the office.

"Sounds fun," she said. "I can't wait."

"We can't either," Val said. "It's going to be interesting around here."

After the meeting, she left the building and crossed the street to her new place. There were still things she wasn't quite sure about.

The next day started early, a little before five. She liked everyone in the office—which was good because she

Playground
was going to have to spend a lot of time with all of them. And you never wanted to be the one in the office no one liked.

As time went on Logan grew to like the job. When she first found out how things worked she was a little shocked by all of it. She liked the idea of having ultimate power over something. And she liked the fact she got to relax a lot.

She spent a large portion of her time in meetings, deciding who should go to Heaven or Hell, or, who should be reincarnated. The job wasn't an easy one. Most days would end with her throwing her hands up in a moral conundrum. Who should get what? Every time she looked into a file to decide a representative from Hell had to be a part. After all, everything had to be fair. Over the years she won some, lost some, had arguments about why certain people deserved what she wanted to give them, and gave passionate speeches to make her point. When she was over-ruled she kept on, not letting anyone know what she thought. She felt bad for people a lot of times, knowing their prayers weren't helping, knowing they had to compromise with other prayers. The quest to make everyone happy wasn't an easy one. And all she could do was hope people would understand. But she realized most wouldn't understand until they made it to Heaven or Hell.

As luck would have it she worked with Trent on many cases. As time wore on she grew to dislike Trent and the manner he did things. It got to the point where she couldn't stand the sight of him. After discussing the case of Cody White she threw up her hands and told Trent to go fuck himself. She was mad about that case for awhile.

Cody White came from a good home in Jones, Alabama. All through school he was known for being very smart, liked by all his teachers, and an honor student.

Bradley Davenport

When he graduated he had plans on going to college so he could teach. He liked teaching people things. The summer before he went off to college everything changed. A friend of his introduced him to cocaine. At first, he told himself he'd just do it to have fun. He got a pretty good summer job fixing computers, so he could afford the powder. He was having dinner with some friends one night when they told him he should think about selling the drug to pay his way through school, so he didn't have to take out any loans. A few months later he was on a morning run when he was hit by a car. He was thrown into a ditch and died.

Both Logan and Trent decided Cody was to be sent to Hell. The main reason he was sent to Hell was because one of the guys he sold cocaine to, a guy by the name of Eddie Crawford, shot a cop who pulled him over for speeding after he did some drugs. Eddie was afraid the cop would arrest him. Because Eddie killed the cop, the cop's brother went crazy and took his anger out on everyone he saw. The brother ended up in prison for killing a man. Eddie went away to kill the cop. Four days later Eddie was beaten to death with a pipe by an inmate.

After they decided on Cody's fate Trent told her that he told Cody to start selling the drug.

Logan swore she wouldn't talk to the asshole ever again. She told him from that point on she'd deal with his trusted minions instead of him. She knew he needed to win some but she didn't like it. She thought he had a pretty shitty attitude throughout the whole thing. And when he knew he was winning he proudly flaunted it. She told him to go back home.

5

Trent found himself in a blue room. Everything was blue; walls, floor, ceiling, and the door. The room was complexly empty except for himself. He looked around but nothing happened. He called out for Logan. He got no response. The last thing he knew was that a car slammed into them. After a minute the blue door opened and a tall man with white hair walked through. He was dressed all in black. Trent could see the hallway beyond the open door, everything was blue.

"Hello?" Trent said. "Where am I?"

The man walked closer to him and introduced himself as Killroy. He told Trent there was nothing to worry about. He could be at ease.

"Who are you?" Trent asked.

"I told you. I was asked to come over and get you."

"For what?"

"I think it would be best if we discussed this someplace more comfortable."

Trent was at a loss for words. He didn't know quite what to think of this guy. He had to keep his eyes peeled. For all he knew this guy was trying to play a trick on him, lead him to a dark room somewhere where he'd rob and kill him. They could've drugged him, who knows?

Killroy got a big smile on his face. "Come on, you can trust me. You have nothing to worry about. I was instructed that you should be treated special, not like the others."

"Special?" Trent asked.

Killroy nodded. "That's what I was told. I think once you find out why you're here you'll agree. And, I don't kill anymore. I got all of that out of my system years ago. We have a lot to discuss, my son."

"Well, I'd always tell the ladies I was special."

Bradley Davenport
"I don't doubt it."
"I'd just tell them that because I wanted to have sex with them."
"You don't say?"
"Pretty cool, huh?"
"I guess," Killroy said. "How often did that work in your favor?"
"Sometimes. Can't win them all, though."
"That's one of the more important things I learned during my life."
Both men laughed.
Killroy said, "I've been greeting people like this for years, seen souls come and go, seen a lot of interesting people come in. You always have to play nice, but some of those people don't deserve it. If it were up to me things would be different around here. Anyway, you Trent, you have what they want."
"How can you tell that? Who are you talking about?"
"I've seen it in your mind."
"In my mind? What are you, a witch or something?"
Killroy laughed. "Nothing like that. I can understand how you could come to that conclusion, though."
"What are you?"
The tall man sighed. "I'm just an old man, trying to help people like you understand all of this. Give it time, let it all sink in. I know it all may come as a shock at first. Things are about to change for you."
"Is that a good or a bad thing?"
"Depends on how you look at it."
"Look at what?"
The man said, "I really can't tell you more than that."
"You haven't told me much," Trent said. "Who can tell me what I need to know? Who are you? What is this place?"
"My name is Killroy," the man said. "I'm a man with

Playground

many regrets. I've hurt a lot of people. I've been a product of chaos for years, that's who I am. I'm someone who's worn many faces. Some have called me a bad guy. But I was just doing what I had to."

"Sounds intriguing."

"Not really," the man said. "Come now, we have places to be."

Trent nodded.

They walked out of the room, and down two long corridors. Trent was turning things over in his head, not knowing what anything was. He'd asked the man a direct question but got no answer. He didn't like things one bit.

A few twists and turns and they were in a living room. Everything was dark red, purple, and black. The floor was red. The man told Trent to take a seat on one of the black leather chairs that were scattered throughout the room. The man pressed a button on the wall and a fully stocked bar appeared.

"We have everything you can dream of here," the man said behind the bar. "What will it be, Trent?"

"Whiskey, if you have it?"

"Of course," the man said. "What sort of bar doesn't have whiskey?"

"Is that a riddle?"

The man laughed. He filled two glasses, walked over to Trent, and gave him one. "Hope you like it."

"Should we toast?" Trent asked.

The man held up his glass. "To you, Trent. To your future and everything it'll bring you."

They clanked their glasses together.

Trent took a drink. "It's good."

"Thanks," the man said. "We only get the best here. The guys on the other side, they'll tell you the same about their stuff. Don't get me wrong, no matter where you go it's always good stuff. This is the time of your life here. Feel free to do whatever you want. Nobody is going to stop you. Hospitality is key here."

"Nice trick with the bar," Trent took another drink. "You practice magic?"

"Me? Not a chance. I wouldn't even know where to begin. I've known those who have, though. They keep their secrets close by."

"Like when you tell a girl you wanna get with to come over to your place, next thing you know she's naked in bed with you?"

"Something like that."

Trent laughed. "Yeah, those make for some good times, know what I mean?"

The man said, "I guess I should tell you, it's not like you're going anywhere any time soon. Welcome to Hell," the man threw his arms out. "We are pleased to have you."

Trent said, "Hell? That's something, isn't it?"

"Yes, it is?"

"Why am I here?"

Killroy unloaded on Trent, giving him a bunch of information. He told him the nature of Heaven and Hell. The two rambled on for a few hours.

Trent asked about Logan.

"She's in Heaven," Killroy told him.

"Why? Why am I here and she's there? Is she better than me or something?"

"Couldn't tell you that," Killroy said. "I was just told to come over and greet you, explain things more. All they said was that she was over there. I didn't ask any more questions. They wouldn't have told me anyway. Honestly, I'm not sure why. Maybe you could ask them that?"

Trent nodded. "I see. I tell ya, I'm gonna need some information on this one. This doesn't sound right to me."

Playground
"That's to be expected."
Trent seemed more than a little concerned about what he was being told. He couldn't wrap his head around Heaven and Hell being the same place. He thought it had to be some sort of joke. Nothing quite prepared him for the conversation he was having. He told Killroy he was always taught the two places were separate. Killroy said a lot of people thought the same thing.

"Then, where where did the disconnect come from?" Trent asked.

"I'm not sure. I've asked the same thing for years. Someone down on Earth, they misinterpreted the Bible, told others and they ran with it. No one thought to get any sort of clarification, so for years and years that's what people had thought."

As the host continued to talk the door to the room slowly opened. A little chubby man with long hair limped into the room. He was dressed in a nice white suit. He greeted Trent and said that he was sorry for the interruption but it couldn't wait. He limped over to Killroy and told him there had been a change of plans. The people that were supposed to talk to Trent about things couldn't do it. Things came up and they wanted Killroy to do the honors.

"I can do that."

"Good," the little man said. "I'm sure they'll be appreciative. If there's anything you need they said to let them know."

"Okay, then. Just let them know. We have a lot to discuss."

"Understood."

"And I'm not sure how well it'll go."

The little guy laughed. "I know how that goes. It's a total mind-fuck. They'll most likely still want to talk with him, run a few things up, and see how it goes."

Killroy nodded. After the little man finished speaking to the guy he went over to Trent and told him how much of an honor it was to get to him him. And he looked forward to working together. After they shook hands the man staggered out of the room.

6

Killroy took out a joint and handed it to Trent, saying he might want to smoke it while he told him what he was about to do.

"It'll calm the nerves," he explained. "I got more if you need it.".

Trent took the joint. "Sounds good to me," he dug in his pockets for a lighter. "Not sure what happened to my light."

"No worries," the man displayed a lighter and lit it.

"Thanks," Trent told him.

"No problem. Your lighter flew out of your pocket in the crash. It shattered. But not to fear, you can get more at a store here. Everything you ever need is within walking distance."

"That's convenient."

"It's one of the bonuses about the place. And given your status you can have everything delivered. Truth is, this whole place is just a huge city. I can take you along, and show you some sights if you want?"

"Sure," Trent took a big hit of the stuff.

Killroy got them some more drinks from the bar. "Now, what I'm going to tell you next might put you in shock."

"Why? What is it?"

The man handed Trent his drink and sat across from him. "You've been chosen for a great purpose."

"And what would that be?"

"You've been chosen to be the Devil."

"What?" Trent almost dropped his drink. "Say that again?"

"Yes, the Devil."

"That's what I thought you said."

"I understand that was a big shock."

"You think? It's not every day somebody gets news like

that."

They talked some more before Trent asked to see the city. Killroy snapped his fingers. The two walked down the crowded sidewalk as they talked. Trent couldn't believe how many people were just walking around.

"Who are these people?"

"Occupants of Hell," Killroy said. "All of these are souls that can't return as other lives."

"Why can't they return?"

He told Trent the rules of reincarnation. Trent looked interested as he was told about the different planets and dimensions. He asked Killroy if he was on some heavy drugs because that was a fantastic story. The man assured him that, no, he wasn't on any drugs. Everything he told him was true. And if he didn't believe it he was free to ask any of the other people in Hell.

"Man," Trent muttered, "I don't know what to say."

"Over the years we've tried new techniques to ease the news. Nothing has ever worked."

"I think you're doing a good job."

"Thanks," the man said. "At least someone appreciates what I do around here. Most people overlook things like that. They only care about the work they do."

"I know people like that."

They continued walking down sidewalks, crossing streets, and looking at the sights. Killroy introduced Trent around. They walked over to an older man selling hot dogs, and they bought some. Trent was a little leery at first, but it was a good hot dog. He was surprised no one used money. They were just giving everything away for free. It was great. Why couldn't they've done that on Earth? When somebody took something another would appear in its place. They never ran out of anything. Killroy told Trent that a lot of problems happen because of

Playground

money. Some people end up committing suicide due to money problems. Trent had to talk to someone about getting that memo to Earth that a person should kill themselves over money.

They passed a man with a floppy hat playing guitar, strumming away like he was begging for a job. The songs he banged out were good. Trent told him if he ever started a band he'd leave a spot open for the guy. The guy thanked him and asked if he played.

"A little," Trent said. "Got to a point where I had to put it down. Had to focus on other things. I wasn't good at making money with the guitar."

"Well, come on by sometime. I've been talking with a few other guys. We can make it work, man."

"I'll keep that in mind," Trent told the man.

"Sounds great, man. We can make some fantastic things happen. It's all about good music, know what I mean? I just sit out here playing groovy tunes. Everyone seems to like it."

"That's good," Trent told him. "I'll have to get back to you about playing sometime."

"Right on!"

Trent wondered if the guy had been a musician before he came to Hell. He didn't recognize the man. But that wasn't saying much, when he lived in Ohio he spent most of his time on drugs. They stopped and talked with a few other people until they came to a door with a big X on it.

"What's this" Trent gestured to the door."

"Oh, you'll love this," Killroy said, as he opened the door. "You might have too much fun here."

When they walked in people were walking around with mugs of beer. Some were at tables laughing, joking, playing cards, and just being loud. A stage was erected in the center of the room with three women in bikinis dancing around. Music was blaring from speakers above. One of the girls, a blonde, wore a thin black suit. The other two girls, both had brown hair, one wore tan and the other blue. Trent wanted to rush the stage and have fun with all three. Killroy looked a him and laughed. "Can you get with that kind of action?"

"You bet I can."

They walked to the bar and got some drinks. The bartender asked if they wanted anything else. Before Trent could say anything Killroy told the bartender to show his new friend one of the non-food/non-drink menus. The bartender handed one to Trent.

"And all of that is free," Killroy patted the new guy on the shoulder. "The best part is you can't overdose. You're already dead."

Trent shook his head, and looked down the list, "All of this?" he looked at Killroy. "They have every drug in history on here."

"And every drug not in history, too," Killroy said. "Those on the list you've never heard of, those are wonderful. You should try some."

"You sure?"

"Have I steered you wrong yet?"

"No."

"Well, then, take some. We have all the time we need."

Trent said, "I think I'll just go with something I know."

"That's okay, too."

Trent told the bartender he wanted a small bag of cocaine.

"What a nice choice," the guy told him.

After a minute he was back with the bag. Killroy got some meth. The two walked away from the bar and got a table.

Trent made a line of cocaine and snorted it.

Playground
"Good?" Killroy asked.
"The best. You need to try some. It's really good stuff."
"We have the best of everything here."
"I can see that."
"We like to have fun here."
Trent looked over at the dancers.
"You can have any of them you want," the man said. "And you don't have to worry about sexually transmitted diseases."
"That's good."
The man continued. "You'll come to find that many of the restrictions that were on Earth don't exist here."
Trent did some more cocaine. He offered some to Killroy, but he said he'd get his own later. Instead, he gave some meth to Trent.
"Have you ever had any of this?" Killroy asked.
"I've known people who have cooked and sold it, but no, I've never had any. Before I died."
"I see."
Killroy asked him how he liked the stuff.
Trent started to ramble, telling him that was the best stuff he'd ever had, that it was a lot better than the stuff he was doing. He told the man he wished he could feel like that forever.
"That won't happen," Killroy said. "The first time is the best. All the other times you're trying to reach that same high, that's the biggest reason it's so addictive."
"I didn't know that."
"See, if I weren't here you wouldn't have known that."
"Maybe."
Killroy laughed, "Something tells me I'm right."
"If you say so."
The two drank and looked at the dancers. Tent thought back to the one time on Earth when he took a dancer home. That was a good night, and he wanted more nights

like that.

"We're gonna be hanging around each other a lot," Killroy told him.

"That so?"

"Trust me, this is a place you want friends in. You have to share in the memory. From now on think of me as your right-hand man."

"Do I need that?"

The man explained that he was there to help Trent with anything he wanted. He was there to serve and consult with Trent in any matter when it came to the business of Hell. Killroy loved the job. It wasn't glorious all the time, but nothing was supposed to be.

"There's a lot to oversee," Killroy told him. "It's not all fun and games."

Trent looked at the man. "There's always a catch somewhere."

"Afraid so. But once you get the hang of everything, it'll come naturally. I mean, you don't have a choice in the matter. Might as well deal with it the best you can."

Trent thought about that for a minute. "Yeah, whatever it takes. If it can be done I'll always do my best. Look here, I'd like to look around for some old friends, would you know where I should start?"

The man shifted in his seat. "This is a big place. What are the names?"

Trent gave some names.

"Well, you can try the outskirts, I think some of those junkies are over there."

"Really?"

"You know who else is over there?"

"Who?"

"Jesus."

"Jesus?"

"Yeah," Killroy said. "I know, everyone down there

Playground
where you came from, they have always had this misconception he was this good guy; that's not entirely true. Yeah, friends of his wrote some good things about him in that book everyone takes literally. And, yes, I guess some of it was true depending on how you look at it. But he wasn't magic by any means. He was just an ordinary guy just like you and I. The whole thing with him being nailed to a cross, was because he robbed and killed two guys—well, he didn't do it alone. All that shit about him being the son of God and a martyr was a bunch of bullshit. His friends got a kick out of it. That planet you came from, if they only knew the truth. How do you think they'd react if they knew the real story? Storm the gate? Rage war on everyone they saw?"

Trent said, "There's no telling. They'll go to war over anything."

"A bunch of fools," Killroy muttered.

"Still, that's interesting," Trent told the man. "Changes everything I thought I knew."

The man took out another joint and lit it. "Seems we have a lot to discuss. It might come as a shock to you. It'll all make sense in the end."

"But do things end? I've always thought of it like a river."

"Could be. That's one of the fundamental questions of life, one of those that you think about in the silent hours."

"I mean, I was never one to study stuff like this," Trent said. "I'd think about it now and then, sure. I was never one of those guys talking crazy to everyone, yelling at them because they didn't agree with every word I said."

"There are a lot of those."

"Yes, there are. Just a bunch of guys running their mouths, hoping people will stop and listen to what they have to say."

Bradley Davenport

A voice broke through the music being played, introducing a new girl who was coming to dance on stage. Her name was Sissy Sex Machine. She wore a red number that she ripped off as she came on stage. She started dancing and then jumped on the pole in the center.

Trent nodded to the stage. "I need to take that girl."

"It can be arranged," Killroy told him. "But first, we need to get to the business of things."

"Okay."

7

Killroy's birth name was Roy Dillon. He was born in Laxum, New York in 1922 on Earth 2. Roy came from a loving family. They taught him how to be helpful and respect people; two things that are important no matter what planet you live on or who you are.

Roy and his dad would play ball in the backyard on most days. His parents loved the fact their son had something to do instead of drugs and getting into trouble. He and his friends would have kickball games. They had a few teams going. It was just something fun to do. Nobody took the games that seriously. In one of these games, when it was Roy's turn to kick the ball, he gave the ball a strong kick and it went a great distance. His parents came outside to see what was going on.

"You killed that ball, Roy," his father said. "You see how far the ball went, Roy? You keep that up and you'll go all the way."

His father kept calling him "Kill Roy" when he would do a good job in whatever sport he was playing at the time. He'd tell Roy that he was a killer.

"Killer Roy," his dad would call him.

The name stayed the whole time Roy was in high school. And it didn't end with sports.

Soon after, his mom and friends started calling him the same thing. His father asked Roy's football coach to put "Killer Roy" on the back of his uniform. The coach told them they couldn't put the word "Killer" on the uniform. At first, Roy was more than a little mad they couldn't put that on his uniform. But his thought was that he'd put it on something else.

When Roy turned twenty his mother and father told him that there was going to be a war over on Earth 3 and that they were asking everyone for help. At first, Roy kept saying he didn't even want to fight in a war that had nothing to do with him. He had a good point. Who would?

His father said, "I'm going. I think we can do some good."

"You're going?" Roy said.

"It sounds like they need help over there," his father told him. "And if I can, I wanna do my part."

Roy said, "I've never fought in a war before. I've never even fired a gun. I'm not sure what to do."

"If things get really bad for them, who's to say the bad guys won't come here?"

Roy saw his father's point, but he still had doubts. There were things he wanted to do, and places he wanted to go. He couldn't do any of those things if he was dead.

His father told him that it would be okay. He told his son they had time to train, that they weren't going to have to fight until the first half of the 1940s, Earth 3's timeline. He told his son he'd be with him every step of the way.

"I don't understand," Roy said. "If their fight hasn't happened yet, how do they know it'll happen?"

"Our rulers," his father told him, "saw it in the future. They can see into the futures of many planets. They've already had one big war, and they thought that was going to be the end of everything. It wasn't. They still have a long way to go."

"If they can see into the future, though, why didn't they tell the people about the war?"

His father sighed and told him that they tried to warn Earth 3 many times. They told the people who ran Earth 3 about a man, a very bad man, who would try to rule the world. Many times they tried to get the people of Earth 3 to understand. Finally, after about twenty years of being told, they said they'd accept help.

Playground

For the next ten years, Roy and his father trained for combat along with a dozen or so of their neighbors. It was tiring, long days and hours. At one point, Roy asked if it was even worth it. Roy wasn't sure why they had to help. He didn't want to die.

They brought in big space crafts to transport all the guys. On their way to the planet, they outlined what they were going to do. They were told that this guy named Hitler was behind the whole war and that the main goal was to get rid of that guy.

When Roy was given his orders he wasn't sure he could do it. His father had orders to be a few miles from him. Roy was scared. He wanted his father. He killed a few people. He didn't care if the people he killed had been good or bad. One of the guys he killed had a pen and notepad on his person. He guessed the guy had used it to write his fellow soldiers' messages. Roy took the pen and notepad and wrote "Killroy was here." He was going to put "Killer Roy' but decided against it.

His thought behind this was that if his father came across the message on the notepad he would know Roy had been there. He was sure his father would remember when he called him that. As time went on Roy got no confirmation his father ever stumbled upon the message. When he killed someone he just kept writing the message, hoping he would hear something. He was scared and wanted to leave, to go back to his planet.

A few of his solder buddies saw what Roy was writing and would ask about it. Roy would explain it to them. The guys thought he was crazy, that he had lost his mind. Maybe he had lost his sanity. But in times of war, you have to do anything you can to distract your mind. It surprised him just how many people carried pens on their person. After some time passed Roy got a little more creative, drawing pictures along with the messages. The pictures usually depicted a cartoon-like figure with a big nose looking over a wall. He started hearing from guys that they'd seen messages like Kilroy's all over the place. Some of those messages accompanied a little cartoon sketch. He thought the whole thing was pretty funny. He'd told a few people the real reason he did it. But he didn't know why other people decided to do it. Later in life, he learned that the whole thing became something of a mystery on Earth 3. He got a big laugh out of it.

After the war was over Roy discovered that his father had been killed a few hours after they landed to join the fight.

He didn't know what to think. He was heartbroken. They did their good deed and helped those people, and all his father got in return was to get shot and killed. Roy decided right there that he'd never help anyone ever again. When he and the others were getting ready to go back to their planet he figured that he had nothing to go home to, that he was lost. He didn't want to go home and live a life of horrors. Before they started the ship to go back he told a few of the guys to tell his mother he was sorry. With the guys around him, he put his gun in his mouth and pulled the trigger. When he got to Hell he was told the reason he was sent to that Hell was that he died on Earth 3 so he was sent to the corresponding afterlife.

"That's quite a story," Trent told the man. "Do you regret any of it?"

"No. If I had to do things over again I'd do things the same way. I shot myself because I wanted to be with my father again."

"What about your mother?"

"I figured she could get along okay without me."

"What made you think that?"

Playground
"Not sure. She had always been a strong woman."
"That's a good thing. But don't you think she would've wanted to see you again?"
"I don't think so."
Trent finished his joint. "Man, I still gotta say, that was a crazy story. Hell, you can't make that shit up."
"I know."

Killroy put his hand on Trent's shoulder. "There are still some things we need to discuss."
The man told Trent all about the genesis of Hell and Heaven. He told Trent how the fight between God and the Devil had been blown out of proportion. Since Heaven and Hell were in the same area, God could've created Hell just to throw Satan into it. Both parties just agreed to stay on opposite sides. Yes, it was true Satan thought he was all-powerful and challenged God to a fight, but God wasn't having any of it.
He told Satan if he didn't want to work together he could just go away. As luck would have it they would have to work together all the time, and they would have to find ways to get along if they were going to be effective at their jobs. Everyone on the planet depended on them, even if they didn't know it.
When Trent asked why he was chosen he didn't get a clear answer. He was told it was what the people wanted. As with the others who came before him, Trent had a bunch of questions about his role, about the game, about the expectations. Killroy was patient with him, answering everything he asked, and taking time to make sure he understood.
Trent stood from the table. "So, if this is going to be my job where's my office?"
Killroy gestured to the back of the club. "Back there. Mine's back there, too. A few others have offices back

there. It's a good spot. Our offices used to be in the place we just left from."

"Oh, okay, sounds pretty good."

The two walked to the back. All the offices were big. They were all furnished with couches, desks, and televisors

Killroy told him if he ever wanted anything to just ask.

"When do I start working?" Trent asked.

The man told him he could start as soon as he wanted to.

Killroy told him he still needed to see some of the sights, and there was someone he wanted to introduce to him. They walked out of the bar and about two miles down the sidewalk. There were some abandoned buildings where people in shaggy clothes were hanging around. Killroy pointed out a particular man in a black beanie, shoulder-length brown hair, who wore flannel with jeans. As the guy turned Trent saw the guy's jeans had holes in them.

"That's the guy you want to talk to," Killroy said.

"Him?" Trent raised a brow. "Who is he?"

"Oh, come on, you'll like him. He's a pretty nice guy."

"If you say so."

As they approached the man, Killroy said, "There he is! What do ya know, JC?"

The man looked over. "Hey, man! How the fuck are ya, Killroy?"

The two shook hands. Jesus said it had been awhile since he saw Killroy.

"I know, I've been busy. You know how that goes, huh?"

Jesus nodded at Trent. "Who's this guy?"

Killroy looked at Trent, then at JC. "Trent, I'd like you to meet a very good friend of mine. You might know him as Jesus Christ."

Playground

Trent was speechless for a minute. He didn't know quite what to say to the man.

Jesus said, "What do you guys have going on today? Wanna get high?"

"That sounds like a great idea," Killroy said.

They walked back to the bar. They spent the rest of the day getting drunk and high. Jesus told him some stories about himself.

Jesus said, "There's been a lot said about me over the years. Good and bad. I told certain people to only say good things about me. I got a kick out of it. Someone gave me a copy of that book."

"What did you think of it?" Trent asked.

"It was okay. I don't think it captured my wild side enough."

"That so?"

"So, I'm working on my own. I just started writing it. Don't even know what I'll call it."

They told him if he needed help with it to let them know. The three of them spent the next few days getting drunk and stoned. They invited a few people over at some point and continued to party.

Trent told Jesus he wanted to work together, and that he could be one of Trent's helpers.

8

Logan told Cambry, they had a lot of work to do. After leaving the office they made a few twists and turns until they got to where the archives were kept. The place was huge, rows upon rows of files. All files were accompanied by videos from the person's life. The two greeted the couple in charge of overseeing the department, Angie and Melvin Watts. The couple had been married on Earth for twenty years before an illness claimed them both. Whoever was in charge of their determination chose to keep them together.

Logan and Cambry walked to the "R" section. Logan found a file marked "Harlan Reeves: Church of Modo guy." She smiled and said she didn't like the ones who claimed to have talked to her, that it was an insult.

"I don't blame you," Cambry told her.

"Oh, please do. They say they talk to me all the time—if they did that I wouldn't have any time for anything else. If they knew me they'd know I don't want to be associated with that evil. They all say it's all in my name, but it's the furthest thing from that. As many times as I sent those folks signs over the years, you'd think they'd catch on. Some people, you just need to beat it into their heads. Even then, they don't want to listen. I don't understand it at times. Honestly, sometimes I don't know why they decided to start all of this all those years ago."

"Oh, I know how that goes. It comes down to sheer decency, having respect. From what I've seen most of them on Earth refer to you as a male."

Logan laughed. "I know. It cracks me up."

"If they only knew, right?"

"Yeah."

"When I was on the planet I didn't believe in any of that. For me, it was hard to believe in something I

Playground
couldn't see or feel. People kept telling me to just believe in the stuff. I'd go to church and at a certain point I asked myself what I was doing. I just found it boring."

"I've heard a lot of people say that over the years."

"And the preacher guy, he would get up and give his sermon, everyone would listen so intently, swallowing everything they were being fed. I'd just think it was strange how all those people could listen to what this guy was saying and take it as truth. And he didn't have a clue what he was talking about."

Logan shook her head. "Whatever it takes to get the crowd hooked, right?"

"You can look at it like that."

"Many of them are just full of it, making people praise them. It's a good ego booster."

The two walked across the room to a smaller room, a room for reviewing the videos.

Cambry took one of the chairs in the room. "This one is going to take more time than I thought."

"Yeah," Logan said. "Harlan made a good mess for himself and a lot of others," she took the seat beside him. "He's one of the worst out there. I hate him," she put the files on the desk in front of them.

"He's still alive?" Cambry asked.

"He was in prison. He was supposed to die in that place, but it looks like that isn't going to happen."

"Who would let something like that happen?"

"Trent probably had something to do with it. He made some sort of deal, and he's doing some work with the cops in the area. Undercover work to get some other bad people, something like that. I think it's total bullshit, but what are you going to do, you know? Sounds like he's just doing what he can to stay alive."

"Oh, I see."

Logan looked at the clock that hung on the wall, then at him. "If you need coffee or anything feel free to get some. We can call the two over there. They can get us food if you're hungry."

"Might come in handy later."

"Yeah, I love coffee. Don't know what I'd do without it."

Cambry liked the sound of that.

Logan slammed her hand down on the file. "It's fuckers like this who give people a bad name. If it was up to me I'd destroy him right now. All we need to do is push a button."

When the council gave her the job they told her she had to be fair, that she couldn't just end the life of anyone she wanted. She had to play nice with anyone that was helping her with a case.

She opened the file, placed it on the desk, picked up the first page, and read it to herself. She gave the pages to Cambry. She joked again about how she should go down to Earth and tell them all about her.

"How would you go about that?" he said.

"Not sure yet. Need to think about it more. If it's something really big they'll think it was the aliens. Everyone wants to believe in aliens."

"I heard they have a problem with that."

"Among other things."

"Well," Cambry said, "if you need any help you can call me."

"Thanks."

"Glad to help. I'll do everything in my power. I hope after this I'll get a promotion."

"I'll be sure to put in a good word for you."

Cambry looked at Harlan Reeves' file.

9

Harlan Gene Reeves was born on June 11th, 1946 to Doyle and Amy Reeves of Bancroft, Arkansas. The couple were proud of their boy. Both parents tried their hardest to give a good life to their son, a life that they never had. When Harlan was fourteen his parents divorced. His father became a drinker and his mother wasn't going to stand for it. After she kicked him out Amy moved in with a man named Ricky. At first, Ricky seemed like the man of her dreams but soon turned into what Doyle was.

Ricky Tull was a slender guy with black hair. He was forty-five years of age. He owned a garage in Bancroft called Tull's Garage. It was a pretty good living. Some days were better than others, but when you owned your own business that was to be expected. He had a reputation for being a shrewd businessman. There were even talks that he was involved in illegal activities, of course, no one would ever come out and say anything for sure. No one wanted any problems with the guy.

Harlan and Ricky got along okay. It took both of them time to get used to one another. Some say they never got along. Ricky didn't want to mess things up with Amy, so he did his best with Harlan. When the kid was old enough Ricky let him work at the garage. Harlan was thankful to his stepdad for the job. He didn't want to let Ricky down. Things were fine for awhile. But eventually, Harlan fucked everything up and got fired. He came into work drunk one day and tried to fight one of the other workers. A week later he got into a fight with Ricky over Ricky's car. Harlan had taken it joyriding with friends without asking. They were drinking, smoking weed, playing loud music, and speeding. The car ended up in a ditch. The other people in the car were too drunk and high to care. Cops were called. After awhile, they discovered who owned the car. They called Ricky and said he could come pick his car up the next day, and that they were going to hold everyone overnight.

When he got off the phone Ricky didn't know quite what to do. The only thing he knew was that the kid needed to learn a lot of respect for other people's things. He told Amy he was going to teach her son how to act, something his father needed to have taught him if he were around.

The next day Ricky and Amy went to get Harlan and the car. When Ricky saw Harlan he told him they were going to have a talk when they got home.

When they got home Ricky and Harlan started to fight. Harlan's mother told him to leave, that she thought that's what they both needed, that he was growing older and needed his own space. She told him she and Ricky needed their own space, too. Harlan needed to become a man

"What's the problem? Don't you love me anymore?" he asked his mom.

Amy said. "Of course I love you. We're doing this for your good, son. You need to go out into the real world. We can't have you acting like this anymore. You'll understand one day."

"Whatever!" Harlan snapped at her. "I understand you don't want me around anymore."

"I've tried with you, son. You don't want things to work. You don't want to live by the rules. You're lucky you aren't in jail."

"You don't know what I want."

"Don't be so dramatic, Harlan," she pointed her finger at him. "I can't deal with your shit, not anymore."

"Fine."

After some more argument, Harlan left the house. He needed to forget about everything.

Playground

Amy felt she'd spent enough of her time being a responsible adult. She felt her job of trying to mold a boy into a man was done. She wanted time for herself—which, Harlan knew meant she and Ricky wanted to stay stoned and have sex with each other. They didn't want to worry about a kid getting in the way. Ricky knew Harlan was going to be thrown behind bars for good before too long.

"Don't say things like that," Amy told him. "It's just a phase he's going through. Give it some time. It will be alright."

"How naive can you be, honey?" Ricky said to her. "He's rotten."

Amy said, "Don't say that."

After talking about it Ricky decided not to press charges for the car. His thought was that if he wanted to give the kid another chance.

Harlan went to his father, but Doyle wasn't in any position to take care of anyone. After a few days of being with each other, doing drugs and hookers, Doyle sent his son on his way. He gave Harlan twenty bucks and told him to spend it wisely.

"You'll do good, son," Doyle told him. "I don't know what you expected out of me. I was just living my life with your mom then you came along. It's time for you to go your way. I can't teach you anything."

"Okay. But why can't I stay with you for awhile?"

"I have things coming and going. I don't have time to keep track of anyone."

"You won't have to look after me."

Doyle looked at his son. "Think I already told you once. Now, I suggest you start moving on. If you don't want busted-up you need to get out of my sight. I'm not a role model."

"The hell with you!" Harlan flipped him the bird.

He and Harlan argued a little more. Doyle pushed his son.

Doyle said, "Take a swing if you want."

"I don't wanna hurt you," Harlan said.

"Get out of here with that mess. I don't wanna have anything to do with you."

"Fuck you!" Harlan yelled.

Doyle squinted at him. "You need to leave."

Harlan told him to go have sex with himself. His dad got a gun and said he'd kill him if he didn't leave. He couldn't believe both parents would treat him in the manner they had. He was under the understanding they were supposed to do whatever they could for him. He wished he'd been told earlier. He was devastated, to say the least. Everything he'd known was no more. He wandered the streets for a few hours, then called a friend of his.

Harlan crashed with friends until he got enough money together to get his place. He found a place in the paper. It was small but it was his place. He could do whatever he wanted. He was known for being loud, and having parties at all hours. Finally, after many complaints, the manager of the apartment evicted him. Soon after he hooked up with a girl and stayed at her place. It was about that time he started to steal. At the time he was out of work and needed fast cash. Every job he got he got fired from. The last guy that fired him broke into his house and stole a bunch of tools and cash. After he sold the tools he figured he and the guy were even. Harlan continued down the wrong road of stealing and getting into trouble.

He'd always go on about how people were out to get him, that it was never his fault. He started stealing cars. Some of his friends started stealing cars and told him about all the money he could get out of it. He always

Playground
wanted things he could never have. The first car he ever stole, he did it on a dare. He liked the feeling it gave him, the adrenaline rush it gave him. The money, the money was pretty good. He was surprised at how easy it was to steal.

After months of not seeing each other, he made a surprise visit to his mother's house. She told him that she heard what he'd been up to and she didn't approve at all.

"How do you know?" Harlan asked.

"I have eyes and ears all around," she said. "You can't get anything passed me."

"Must be nice."

Amy said, "You need to stop doing what you're doing, son. You don't want things to go bad for you, do you?"

Harlan shook his head. "I never plan on getting caught."

"Things don't always go as we plan."

"You don't have to worry about me, I'm good at what I do."

"Good at what you do?" she said. "You may think that, but everything comes to an end one way or another. And I don't wanna see you go down like that."

"I see your point. Look at it like this, though, every new thing you get into, there are gonna be bumps in the road. You have to make mistakes so you can learn from them. But I'm not gonna make any mistakes. I'm better than that. And it's good money. Ricky might wanna get in on this."

"No way he's ever doing that."

"Just think about it. I could even talk to him about it."

"You'll do nothing of the sort. I don't need him to become a deadbeat like your father."

"Oh, I see how it is. You guys aren't together anymore so you think you can talk shit about him?"

"I talked shit about him when we were together."

They talked awhile more before Ricky got home. Harlan told Ricky about his idea. His stepdad yelled at him a little before kicking him out. Harlan threatened to set their house on fire.

Harlan went to his father's place. Instead of fighting, the two men got drunk and got some hookers. After a few hours of fun, he floated the opportunity to his dad. His dad didn't want anything to do with it, but he wished his son well.

As he continued to steal cars and everything he was getting deeper into life. He was surrounding himself with dangerous people. At some point, he decided to only steal cars on the weekends and break into houses during the week. Things went well for awhile.

A few weeks later he was arrested for breaking into a house. Considering his past he was sent to prison for a few years. After he got out, that was when he started the Church of Modo with his friend Denny. When Harlan was sent to prison after the cops and FBI took down his compound, he elected that his son, Luke, take over the business.

The first file Logan looked at was titled "Chad Baker's Story."

Cambry asked who Chad was.

"One of the guys that Harlan encountered and turned upside down."

"Oh."

"He wasn't part of the group that lived in the compound."

"What, then?"

"He worked at one of the banks the guys robbed."

"They robbed banks?"

"For awhile," Logan told him. "It was this whole thing.

Playground

They went on a road trip, trying to recruit as many people as they could."

"I see."

"Yeah, he did anything to get followers."

"That's pretty messed up."

"That's pretty sad."

10

When Harlan's crew went to New York and robbed the National Bank & Trust, after the cops came and went, after everything calmed down, Chad Baker, the bank manager went home to his wife. He told his wife about the day he had. He was surprised to learn the robbery hadn't been on the news. With all the crime daily, the news outlets can't report on all of them, he guessed.

His wife, Ruth, was just happy he was alive. She wouldn't know what to do if something were to happen to him. He was the love of her life. At the time they'd been married for five years and planned to spend the rest of their lives together.

Chad had been the one who opened the safe for the robbers. As he was taking the money out Harlan had a loaded shotgun pressed against the back of his head. Chad Prayed to God he'd survive. He thought it was the end of the line, that there'd be no more tomorrows. With the gun to his head, all he could think about was Ruth. He wanted to see her again. Her voice ran through his mind. He had to make it through. As quick as it all started it was over. When the cops got there and took everyone's statement Chad started to calm down. It was music to his ears when the cops cleared everyone to go home. He was thankful to be alive and go home. He'd be able to grow old with his wife, and that was the most important thing to him.

That night he had one of the best nights of sleep he ever had. The next morning Ruth made a big breakfast. They had to close the bank for a few days to dust for fingerprints and collect any evidence they could. When the bank re-opened it was business as normal. People who came in to do their transactions asked the employees all sorts of questions. Everyone wanted to know who the

Playground

robbers were and if they were still on the run. While the other people were open to talking about it Chad wasn't. He didn't know why everyone wanted to know so badly—it was odd to him like they were making him relive the event. Why were they so curious? Did one of them play a part in it?

But they were still out there. They were still roaming the streets, the people who almost killed him. He didn't know if they'd ever be caught. He couldn't do anything about it. They may find out where they live and come get them. Before he and Ruth would go to bed at night Chat would load his shotgun and place it by the nightstand. He didn't want to use it, but he would if he had to. When they got married he made a promise to Ruth to always protect her no matter what, and he was going to do what he said. He was the man of the house.

When Ruth was fast asleep Chad was wide awake. Every time he closed his eyes they popped open when he heard the smallest sound. They lived in a brick two-story with wood floors that was built in the 1940s. Ruth talked about how she wanted to remove the wood floor and get something else, but they never had the budget for it. Chad didn't care just as long as they were living together.

The next day Chad woke up to pancakes and bacon running through the house. He got out of bed and went to the kitchen. Ruth was over the stove cooking. He walked out to the porch to get the morning newspaper. When he got inside he went to the kitchen table and started in on the paper. He was looking to see if they caught the robbers. He'd called down to the police station a few times but they kept telling him the same thing, that they had no leads and when they did they'd let him know. He didn't believe they'd tell him anything.

Chad muttered, "There's nothing about it," he put the

paper on the table. "I don't understand. Surely someone saw something."

Ruth brought his plate of eggs and bacon to the table and sat it in front of him. "Oh, Ron, I don't know what to tell you. Maybe they know but they aren't releasing it for some reason, you think?"

"I don't know," Chad said, as he picked up a piece of bacon and took a bite. "It makes you wonder about the world, about what's going to happen."

"Now, dear, you don't need to think about things like that."

"Yeah, I know, I know... So, what are you planning to do today?"

Ruth took a drink of coffee. "I need to go to the store shortly. We need milk and butter."

"Going to make something?"

"A cake for Brooke's party."

"Oh, that should be nice."

"I just hope it comes out better than the last cake. We can't afford for the house to burn down."

They laughed and continued eating.

Before Ruth left for the store she reminded her husband he needed to mow the lawn, that it wasn't going to mow itself.

"But it's Saturday, Ruth," he protested. "Come on, I still have tomorrow to do it."

"I don't want you doing it tomorrow. We have the party tomorrow night and I don't want to see you all worked up.

He waved his hand at the idea. "You worry too much, that won't happen. I know my limits."

"Sure, sure."

He gave her a dirty look. "Don't be like that to me."

She joked that if he didn't do what she asked she was going to knock him on the head with a frying pan.

Playground

She laughed.
He stared at her.
"I was kidding, honey," she told him.
He continued to stare.
"I said I was kidding."
He pointed his finger at her. "You need to stop."
She laughed again.
He shot out his hand and hit the side of her face, making her fall against the wall and dropping to the floor. He walked over and kicked her two times. "You're lucky I don't take the belt to you, bitch," he kicked her again. As he walked away he told her to get up and go to the store.

11

Ruth was on the floor for about ten minutes before she managed to sit up. Chad was nowhere in sight. She struggled as she got to her feet. She walked across the kitchen floor to the living room. She called her husband's name but got no response. She couldn't believe what happened. What made him do such a thing? Was it something she said? Ruth made it to the front door and opened it. She squinted as the bright light washed over her. After stepping outside she saw Chat sitting on the front steps. He turned to her.

"I'm sorry," Chat told her. "Are you okay?"

She put her hand to the side of her face. She had a bruise but it didn't break the skin.

"Why'd you do that?" she asked. "Don't you love me anymore?"

He got to his feet and went to her. "I'm sorry. I lost my temper."

"And that's supposed to make it okay?"

"No," he said. "I know it was wrong."

"Then, why?"

"Can we go inside to talk about this? I don't want to do it out in the open."

She agreed and they went inside. As soon as they got into the house he asked his wife if she needed anything. She shook her head and said she was fine. They sat across from each other at the kitchen table.

"I think I have a problem," he said.

"You think?"

He let out a big sigh. "It's that robbery. I keep thinking people are out to get me."

"What people?"

"The robbers," he told her. "I'm afraid it might happen again. At night, after you go to sleep I walk around the

house with that loaded gun."
"You do, why?"
"I have to protect what I have."
"Nobody is going to get us here."
"You don't know that."
"You don't know it either, hon. The people who robbed the bank, don't know where we live. Do they even know your name?"
"They don't."
"If they don't have any information about us, Chad, what makes you think they'd be after us?"
"I don't know. I'm afraid it'll happen again. Yeah, they don't know where we live but they could've figured we're in the area. They could be out there right now looking us up. asking people around town."
"I highly doubt if they robbed a bank that they'd come back here. None of them want to get caught."
"You can never be too careful these days. We have to be ready for anything that comes our way."
"For anything?" her eyes got wide. "Nobody is going to hurt us. If they wanted to they would've done it already."
"Maybe so. Who knows? Guess time will tell. I'm afraid something is out there."
"I understand. I'm not going to press charges. No one got seriously hurt. Let me help you. We can get through this together."
"Okay."
She told Chad maybe he should talk to someone.
"Who?" he asked.
"A therapist. They could help you get your feelings out."
"How would they do that?"
"By talking."
He shook his head. "I don't know about that."

Bradley Davenport

She smiled. "Well, honey, I'll tell you this, if you don't go it'll be over between us. I won't be able to deal with these violent outbursts for much longer."

"Okay, I'll go."

The next day Ruth looked in the phone book and got a number. She called and made an appointment.

The man she loved was almost killed by a maniac with a shotgun. And for all she knew the guy was going to track him down and finish the job. She was a little worried. But she didn't want to stir things up with Chad so she didn't say anything. She wasn't as paranoid as her husband, but it was in there somewhere. She didn't know what to do with it, so it just stayed inside.

A few nights later, the nightmares started. He would wake in a cold sweat, screaming and yelling. It would wake Ruth and she would talk to him until they both fell back asleep.

He woke early the next day. He felt good. He told himself he needed to stop this feeling he'd been having. Not everyone was out to get him. Maybe the doctor could help him? Nothing else seemed to work. If nothing else he needed to do it for Ruth. He loved her a lot. He told himself he needed to go for a drive to clear his head.

He got into his blue Honda, turned on the radio, and pulled out of the driveway. As he drove down the street he kept looking in the rearview mirror to make sure he wasn't being followed. Nothing was going to get him again. It was a bright sunny day and he was thankful to be alive. There was no real destination. At one point a black SUV was in the rear view. He told himself whoever was in the car was after him. The SUV looked like it was on Chad's bumper. He increased the speed to shake the SUV. His forehead and palms started to sweat. He kept switching his attention between the road and the SUV. He had a gun in the glove compartment but hoped

Playground
he wouldn't have to use it. But he would if he had to. He wasn't the biggest fan of guns but had it if he needed one. He decided he was going to go for the gun. He popped open the compartment and grabbed the gun. The thing already had bullets in it. He rolled down the window to stick the gun out. Just before he pulled the trigger the SUV turned right, to get off at the next exit. Chad tossed the gun on the passenger seat. Was he going mad? Had it come to this, pulling guns out in the middle of traffic? Things could've ended very badly for both of them.

When he got back to his house he was still sweating. He was motionless for about ten minutes. He took a cigarette from his pack and lit it. After he finished the smoke he walked into the house. He was a basket of nerves and needed to calm down.

12

The next afternoon Chad found himself in a boring waiting room with brown chairs. Twenty minutes later the girl at the front desk told him the doctor could see him. The doctor, a sexy blonde who introduced herself as Vicky Mitsel, told him he had nothing to worry about. She was one of the best in the business.

He took to the black couch in the office. She took the black chair across from him. Her office was plain, tan carpet, one dying plant, and nothing on the wall but a map of America and her framed diploma on the wall.

Vicky said, "Since this is your first visit tell me a little about yourself, if you don't mind? Why are you here? I got a fast once over when your wife called, but I need to know more about who you are."

Chad told her a little about himself and his history. He told her about the bank robbery and how it affected him.

"I see," she said. "I'm sure that was quite an experience."

"Oh, it was, trust me. Not something I wanna go through again. I wouldn't wish that on anyone."

"No one can blame you for that."

Chad glanced around the room. "See, the thing is, this thing has made everything seem deferent. I'm not sure if it's normal or not. It feels normal but I'm not the expert. I've never dealt with anything like this before. I just can't help but think it'll happen again. Not sure if I could deal with something else like that. I think about Ruth and what would happen to her if I died."

Vicky placed her hands on her lap. "That's an experience I've never had, however, I can try to help you get through it. Good for you, you took the first step in a long process."

"Is it gonna take long?"

Playground

"Depends on the person. Everyone handles trauma differently. Some people want to be around others more often, then, some shut out the outside world. They take up with imaginary people and do things by themselves. They push away those who try to get close. One of the main reasons people who were the victim of robbery are paranoid, it's because they are afraid the person will come back and do the same thing, if not worse."

"That's me," Chad told her. "And I don't need that. Given my job, I have a big responsibility. I can't do my job if I'm scared all the time. The feeling I have all the time, I can't take it. I can't be a proper husband to my wife. If I don't get help for this she may take up with another guy, know what I mean?"

The doctor shook her head. "I can understand that, sure. I think that's a common thing in couples when something like that has happened. subconsciously, the person's partner may blame them for what happened and the effects it has. Since you're a man she might ask why you let this develop. Why didn't you put your life on the line to stop it?"

The man looked down at the carpet, then at her. "I couldn't imagine. She'd never mess around on me. Think if I ever caught her doing something like that I'd kill her."

"Oh, come on, Chad, you don't mean that. It'd be crazy of you."

"But it'd make me feel better."

"That so?"

"I don't want to be made a fool of."

"But violence isn't the answer."

"Maybe. It's like this, I think about the day of the robbery and get mad. I just want to find them and show those guys justice. I assure you they won't do that to anyone anymore."

"You'd get arrested. You wouldn't be around to be a husband, you think of that?"

"She wouldn't care. Hell, she'd probably tell the judge to add a few more years. Without me in the picture, she'd be able to go lay with other men."

"Has she ever cheated before?" she asked.

"There's a first for everything. I mean, anything is possible. If she went out without her wedding ring I bet she'd have numbers from half a dozen guys," he laughed. "Nah, you don't want to hear all of that."

She smiled.

Chad felt more at ease as they talked. She told him to take things one day at a time. Healing isn't something that happens overnight. It could take weeks, months, or years in a lot of cases. Chad had an issue and needed to solve it soon, needed to do something about it no matter what. He understood all those stories about people falling in love with their therapist. And it helped that Vicky looked really good. But that would be unprofessional of him to do anything. She probably had guys fantasizing about her all day. They'd just go home, and tug at themselves before their wives put dinner on the table.

When they finished he told her it was nice to meet her, and that he'd see her next week. Even though he'd never say anything, he was skeptical of her ability to help him. And he wasn't sold on the idea of spilling all of his secrets and feelings to a stranger. He wasn't sure.

13

When he got home Ruth asked him how it went.
Chad looked at her. "Okay, I guess."
"I'm glad to hear that, hon. You sure need it. Oh, hope everything works out. Well, would you do something for me?"
"Anything."
"Just try your best. I know how you can get sometimes."
"Really? And how do I get, Ruth?"
"You're stubborn half the time. You're someone who never wants change. People have to force it upon you."
 He told her to mind her own business and go cook something. He didn't want to hear any of her bullshit that night, or any night again.
 Ruth made some chicken for dinner and they spent the evening eating and watching television. Ruth told him how lucky they were to have each other. She wouldn't know quite what to do if she didn't have him.
 The next morning Chad woke around 6 am and started his routine to get ready for work. As he was getting his hot shower the idea of not going to work crept into his mind. But he knew he couldn't, too many responsibilities, too much at stack. He didn't want to throw it all away. Ruth would never let him live it down. She'd nag him to death, and after he was dead she'd nag some more. Ruth, with only one income, wouldn't be able to make it. And not everyone in the world was lining up to hire her. She hadn't had the best work history.
 When Chad got to work he told himself it was going to be a good day. The first thing he did was make coffee—that was one of the best parts of his day, coffee.
 He had a good thirty minutes until they had to open for the day. He spent it making sure everything was running

smoothly, talking to the tellers, making sure they were ready for the day. He gave them a little pep talk, telling them he wanted everyone to have a great day, and that the reason their branch was still in business was due to them. They made him look good. Everyone in the office loved Chad. He was one of the best bosses anyone could ask for.

When they opened Chad told them he was going to his office to do some paperwork and make some phone calls. Just another day at work. The first few hours went without fail until Chad got a knock on his office door. He told the person knocking to come in.

It was one of the security guards, a pale blonde man named Philip.

"What do you have for me today, Philip?"

The man said, "Sir, sorry to disturb you. I think you should come out here. There's a lady who has an issue. She's getting belligerent with a few of the tellers."

"Really? Shit!" he got out of the chair. "Can you tell them I just quit?"

The man laughed.

Chad followed him out of the office.

When they got to the front a big woman in a flower dress and brown curly hair was yelling at the teller. Chad recognized the woman as Beth Duran. They'd had a few issues with her in the past.

"Can I be of any assistance, ma'am?" Chad asked her.

She turned to him. "Are you the Manager?"

"Yes, I am," he said.

"Well, I hope you can help me out here. These other people don't seem to understand anything."

"What seems to be the problem?"

"Well, I came here today because I had money taken from my account and I don't know why. Now, I have a lot on my plate today and don't have time to spend too

Playground

long here."

The teller went on to explain to the woman the reason the money was taken out was due to a loan she had with the bank.

"It would've been nice to have gotten a call or something, telling me the payment was due. You didn't need to just take it from my account."

Chad said, "Ma'am, the terms of the loan were clearly outlined in the paperwork we gave you. We did our part. You should have read the terms closely. We have the right to obtain the amount due by any means. You signed the paperwork," he showed her the signature.

She got a mad look on her face. "Well, I needed more time to make the payment."

The teller told her they tried contacting her by phone, but couldn't get anyone. He went on to tell the woman they gave her a few chances and sent her a couple of letters. If she needed more time to pay she should've called the bank about the situation.

"I meant to call," she said. "Is there any way you could put the money back in my account?"

"Sorry, we can't do that," the teller said.

"Why? All you have to do is take one of those little slips of paper, fill it out, and put the money in my account. What's so hard about that?"

"We can't do that."

"That's bullshit," she barked.

Chad put his hand in front of himself. "Listen, ma'am, we're trying to be nice about this but you're pissing me off. You had the information. You knew the rules and you decided to ignore them. How the fuck is that our fault? We were nice enough to grant you a loan and this is the thanks we get? What the fuck is the matter with you, lady?"

Her mouth dropped. "That's not professional at all, sir.

Bradley Davenport

I'll be contacting the corporate office about this. I'm sure they won't be happy with you once I tell them what was said."

"We're going to have to ask you to leave," Chad told her. "We're asking nicely."

"And what if I don't?"

"We'll have to call the police."

"On me? Shit, I'll tell them what you did. And they'll arrest all of you. You guys are nothing but stupid fuckers!"

As Chad stood listening to her rip them apart he wanted to hit her. He wanted to hit her to the ground and kick her in the head. He thought she needed to pay for what she said to himself and the others. He clenched his fist. The idea of striking her hard in the face crossed his mind. She needed to be taught some manners. Who did she think she was? She didn't make the rules around there. She was lucky Chad was working on his anger. She threw her arms in the air as she yelled at the teller and security guard. She said they were all going to be sorry for messing with her, then she stomped out. She jumped in her car and sped away.

The craziness was gone, they were glad for that. They talked about what a silly thing it had been. Chad told everyone he was heading back to his office. Just when he was about to open the door to his office the woman burst through the front door. She told everyone that their day had come, and they needed to pay for what they had done. She took a gun out of her purse. Without thinking Chad calmly walked over and punched her in the face, knocking her to the floor. As Chad stood over her he wanted to choke her to death, instead, he called the cops. When she came to the cops placed her under arrest. The rest of the day went without incident.

14

On his way home he couldn't get the woman out of his mind. Had he been too harsh with her? Was that completely necessary? Was there something else that could've been done?

As he rolled by his neighbor's house he saw the guy outside and gave a wave. The man didn't return the wave.

Chad stopped the car and rolled the window down. "Hey, dick," he called out to the guy.

The guy turned around. "Chad, what do you say, you fuck? Want to come in for a beer?"

"I do," Chad turned into the man's driveway.

The man, Jack Riley, was sixty-five years of age. He was a rugged man with no family. Chad only regarded the man as his drinking buddy. He tolerated the man but didn't like him. He often told Ruth that the man was a loser.

The two went into Jack's house. Jack was glad Chad stopped by. He was excited to tell him about this new girlfriend he had.

"How long is she going to stick around?" Chad laughed.

"Laugh all you want, kid. I think you'll be surprised."

"Hey, man, I have faith in you. If you want it bad enough it'll happen."

The two walked down to the basement, where they shot a few games of pool and drank cold beer.

A few beers later Chad said he had to go home. Ruth was going to yell at him for being gone for so long. If he would've thought about it he would've invited her over. She liked to drink.

When he got back to his house Ruth started on him, demanding to know why he felt the need to go to Jack's and not tell her. After another heated argument, they had dinner and went to bed. Before Chad fell asleep he thought about how nice it would be if Ruth wasn't at the house anymore. He'd be free to do whatever he wanted. He wouldn't have anyone telling him what to do.

The next day was a Saturday and they were going to spend it shopping. One of the places they were going to stop, a place called Fresh Face, had a huge sale going on. Ruth had her eye on this blue dress. She'd wanted the dress for a few weeks but felt guilty about buying it before. Chad, who always wanted to make his wife happy, said it was okay with him. If nothing else the purchase would keep her quiet for awhile. In return, she told Chad he could buy anything he wanted. He didn't need or want anything. He just told her to hurry. He wanted to go home. The idea of spending the whole day shopping didn't amuse him. It was a Saturday after all, and he didn't want to be in public any longer than he had to. Since the robbery, he didn't like going to stay out too long. It was one of the things he had to work out with his therapist.

Along with the Blue dress Ruth bought a few others. Chad figured since she was spending money he should, too. He picked up a case of beer, two bottles of whiskey, and a bottle of vodka. They headed to the registers. A couple, a few people ahead of them were having an issue checking out. After some back-and-forth, the cashier threw her hands up and called a manager over. It seemed the couple's credit card wouldn't process. When the manager came over the two kept saying they had more than enough money in their bank account.

"Well," the manager told them, "our system is saying there's insufficient funds."

"That can't be," the man said. "You have to run it again. You guys have a scam going on here or some-

Playground

thing?"

"Sir, we're not in the business of doing that to our customers. I suggest you go to your bank and deposit enough money in your account. You can come back and make the purchase."

The man looked at his card, then at the manager. "This is a bunch of bullshit. We've been coming here for a few years and never had a problem."

"You most likely had enough money on your card then."

The man looked at him. "You know, every time we come in here it seems there are always different managers around here, why is that?"

"They're always moving us around. I'm sure you understand, right?"

"There has to be another reason."

"You can always call corporate and file a complaint."

The guy shrugged. "You guys are all incompetent. Guys need to learn how to do your fucking job," he slammed his fist down on the area by the register. "This whole fucking place is nothing but bullshit!"

"Sir, I'm going to have to ask you to calm down and not raise your voice. If you continue acting the way you are I'll have to call the police."

"Call them! They need to know how you screw people over."

The man's wife told him to calm down, that they could just go to the bank and get it sorted out. The man said he wasn't going to leave, and he was going to explain his case to the cops if he had to. Another manager saw what was going on and came over to help. They continued talking over the matter but nothing got resolved.

Chad and Ruth were behind people with frustrated looks in their eyes. They just wanted the man and his wife to move on. When Chad had enough he approached the guy.

"And what do you want, fella?" the guy asked Chad.

"Come on, buddy, you're holding up progress. All these people, need you to move. We can see what's going on here, now, it's just time to go."

The guy laughed. "You don't worry about what we do. If you were me you'd be doing the same thing."

"Maybe," Chad told him. "But we're here and you're there, and these people need you to get this show on the road. Believe me, I haven't been in the best mood lately, and I don't want to get into it with you."

The guy stepped closer to Chad, "Mister, get the fuck out of my face!" he pushed Chad into the register stand. "How do you like that, you fuck?"

Chad sprung back and knocked the guy square in the jaw. Both men got a few good punches in before they were broken up. Unfortunately for Chad, the cops walked through the front door just then. Both men were arrested and taken to the local jail.

The whole way to the station Chad insisted it wasn't his fault. According to him, the other guy was responsible for it all. When they got to the station they took Chad's fingerprints. They had to make sure Chad and the other guy were separated in the big holding cell. They didn't want a fight on their hands.

A couple hours later Ruth bailed her husband out. When they got to the parking lot Ruth told him he needed to do something about his anger.

"I was thinking about it, you need to get some help before I'll have to make a change."

"What sort of change?" Chad asked.

"With us. I won't be able to do this with you anymore. I can't be around this."

"I'm seeing that doctor, isn't that enough?"

"You have to apply yourself more if you want results."

Playground

"If you say so."

When they got home they started arguing. She asked him what his problem was, that he couldn't just go around picking fights with people. He would regret it one day.

"Honey, I'll be fine," Chad told her.

"Doesn't look like that to me. Good thing you're going to the doctor tomorrow. You'll be thankful for her one day."

"Hell, I don't know about that."

"Why?"

"I don't need someone who doesn't even know me telling me what my problem is. I'm okay."

"No, you're not. Anyone can tell you that, buddy."

He told her to shut up. He didn't want to hear anything from her. She knew she should've left the first time he got violent with her. She loved him and wanted to help in any way she could. She told herself there was a lot of good in him. He was just going through a difficult period. Everything will go back to normal soon.

Chad and Ruth had been in relationships with other people when they first met and started their affair. At the time it was easy for them to fall into each other's arms. It was one of those things that weren't planned. But things like that happen all the time. You can't help where your heart goes, can you? It was exciting for the both of them, sneaking around, going behind the backs of their loved ones. They laid together every chance they got.

When their secret finally got out they had no one else but each other They were both dumped by the person they were with. Chad and Ruth had each other and didn't care what everyone else thought.

They figured there wasn't any point in having a big wedding, and went to the courthouse downtown. Five minutes later they were husband and wife. They honeymooned for a week in Florida. The beach was a nice place to relax and forget everything for awhile. When they got back the days turned to years, and before they knew it ten years had passed. They got into a boring routine. At that point, they questioned whether or not they were still in love with one another. All the things they used to do, they didn't do any of that. Even though they slept in the same bed they hadn't had sex in ten months. Chad nor Ruth had any interest in going outside their marriage. There was a woman who Chad worked with at the bank who was interested in him, but he told her that he was a married man and he didn't do that sort of thing. If he had it to do over again he would've taken her up on the offer.

The next day he went to see his doctor. When she asked how everything was going he told her there was nothing to worry about, that everything was under control.

"Is that true?" she asked.

"Of course, it is. I wouldn't have said it if it wasn't true."

"I'm not so sure."

"Look, I know I've only been here a few times but I'm cured."

"Something tells me that's not entirely correct."

"Well, that's what you may think," he told her. Hell, keeping me here is putting more money in your pocket."

Vicky told him that wasn't true at all, that she wanted to help all of her patients. She told him they still had a lot of work to do. He waved her off and said he didn't have time to sit around and talk about his problems. She said he'd regret it one day.

15

The next day started like any other day, they got up and got ready for work. It promised to be an outstanding day, with the warm sun bathing everything in sight. While they were on their way out of the house Ruth asked her husband if everything was okay. Something was off about him, and she couldn't quite figure it out. He seemed quieter than normal. She'd hoped he wasn't going to have one of his outbursts. She almost told him to stay home and take the day off. But she knew they needed the money and didn't say anything.

He told his wife everything was fine, that he was okay and not to worry.

"You worry too damn much, honey. Everything is good."

She didn't feel like getting into it so she dropped it. After all, he was an adult and had to learn how to cope eventually. They kissed and wished the other had a good day. But in the back of her mind, she knew something was wrong. She figured she'd call him at work later that day to see how he was. It was a Monday, the first day of the new work week, a fresh start in a complicated game. Who'll win, who'll lose? Some weeks you are ahead of the curve, others you are limping in last place.

Ten minutes into his commute Chad got stuck in traffic. There had been a two-car crash that had traffic at a stand-still. He was going to be late. His first instinct was to drive fast, pushing everyone off the road. He turned on the radio and got a tight grip on the steering wheel. The police on the scene eventually started to reroute people. The alternate way wasn't where he was going. It was only going to make him later. There was no other choice but to take the route. He could just picture beating the cop in the face when he was told about the inconvenience. He didn't need any of it.

When he finally pulled into the parking lot at the bank he looked at his watch, he was an hour late. Better late than never. He walked in, greeted everyone, and explained his tardiness. He went to his office and started working, which for the first two hours consisted of making and returning calls. The rest of the day went without incident, just the same bank business as any other day.

On his way home he decided he wanted something with alcohol in it. He drove over to the liquor store to get some booze. Something told him Ruth would have a problem with him drinking. He didn't give a damn what she thought of him anymore. The way he saw it, she had her thing and he had his. Who was she to tell him he couldn't drink? He was a man and could do what the fuck he wanted. She didn't know what was best for him.

After spending about twenty minutes of deciding what to buy Chad grabbed a couple of bottles and walked up to the counter. No one else was in line, so that was a plus. And the way his life had been going he took it as a win.

"How ya doing, sir?" the clerk asked.

Chad nodded. "Good, I guess."

"That's the only thing you can hope for these days."

"I know what you mean."

"Hell, you can't even find good news in the paper anymore."

"That's just the way of the world, I guess. I'm afraid the good old days are in the past, my friend."

"Got that right."

"We can always dream, can't we?" Chad chuckled.

The clerk rang up the bottles. He asked if Chad needed anything else.

"No, that'll do it."

"Okay, come back and see us again."

Playground

In a flash, Chad was out the door. He drove around a bit, not wanting to go home to face his wife. In a lot of ways, he'd grown tired of Ruth and her ways. He didn't exactly know how to tell her how he felt. The days of joy and happiness had forgotten him. The past year with the robbery and everything that followed, just went to show him what a weak person he had become. When he was a little boy he was always taught to treat people the way he wanted to be treated; this hadn't been what he'd seen. He was constantly surrounded by mixed signals. He didn't know what to believe. He wanted peace of mind and not to be scared anymore.

He drove out to the Skaggs bridge. On most nights you would find any number of young adults hanging out there, getting high, drinking, and making noise. The police normally got called out there at least three times a week to break a crowd up; on that night, however, no one was there. It was silent. When he parked his car he killed the engine and got out with one of the bottles in hand. He walked the bridge while he drank half the bottle. He looked at the water. He thought of how everything moved through the world like water, flowing one way to the other, always moving. He wanted to move like water, to another place far from there, to a place he could never be found. He wanted to jump into the water, to sink to the bottom. He finished the bottle and threw it, making a splash. He considered getting in his car and heading to one of the local bars. He could get a woman if he wanted. Hell, who was he kidding, what woman would want him? He was a has-been who was passed his prime.

He walked back to his car and drove home. There was nothing he wanted to do. As he expected Ruth started in on him, wanting to know where he'd been all that time.

"Why didn't you come home?" she asked. "Do you

have some sort of problem with me?"

"I do," he told her.

"And what would that be?"

"You're boring."

"Boring?"

"Yes."

"In what way?"

"All the ways."

"What does that mean?"

After they argued for a few minutes he told her he'd be back, leaving her in the living room as he walked to the bedroom. When he came back to where Ruth was he was carrying a shotgun, which he pointed at her and fired, putting a hole in her belly. He aimed the gun at her head and fired again.

"Serves you right," he said aloud.

He spent the rest of the night cleaning the scene. In time he'd let them all know what he'd done, but not just then. There was a lot more he wanted to do. And no one was going to tell him he couldn't go through with it. He dragged Ruth's body to the freezer and stuffed her inside. Afterward, he made a couple of sandwiches and sat in front of the TV until he fell asleep.

16

Chad continued to go to work every day like nothing ever happened. It became clear to him and the others he worked with that the perpetrators weren't going to be caught. The police said they were doing all they could to find them, but Chad had little hope. All of them were just glad they hadn't come back. When Chad asked one of the cops if they'd ever find out anything more, it didn't look good. The cop said he didn't know. He told Chad it was a random act of violence. They hadn't hit anything else in the area and they had no leads. If something else in the case happened they'd contact Chad and the others.

When Chad got home after work the mailman was dropping off his mail. Chad looked through the mail, saw there was nothing of importance in the stack, and threw it in the mailman's face.

"The fuck is wrong with you?" the guy asked.

"Fuck you," Chad said. "I'm not in the mood, buddy."

"Whatever."

Chad hit the guy in the face. When he was turned away Chad kicked him in the butt. Chad walked to his car, got a gun out, and fired, hitting the guy in the leg. When the guy was on the pavement Chad shot him in the back of the head two times, finishing the job. Jack rushed outside to see what the commotion was. When he saw the mailman on the ground Chad fired the gun, sending a bullet through his neck.

It didn't take long before the police were on the scene. Someone a few houses down had put the call in. Three police cruisers arrived on the scene.

"It's about time you guys got here," Chad called out as they exited their vehicles.

"Sir, is this your residence?" one of the officers asked.

"Indeed, it is, guys."

They pointed their guns at him and demanded he drop the gun in his hand.

He didn't.

They asked again.

Chad looked down at the gun in his hand, then back at them. "You want it?" he pointed the gun at them. "I suggest you come get it. Before I shoot you guys need to know about the body in the freezer. My wife."

They asked him again to drop the gun. After a few more times of asking and Chad not complying one of the officers fired his gun. Chad fell to the ground.

After they called for an ambulance they entered the house. It took them a few minutes but they found the freezer. They opened it and saw a woman frozen solid.

A few days later, after Chad got patched up at the hospital, he was placed under arrest. He was charged with three counts of murder. He told his court-appointed attorney that he didn't want to live anymore, that he wanted to die. He didn't want to spend the rest of his life in a small cage. Five months later he was beaten to death by inmates in prison.

17

Cambry sat back in his seat after they finished Chad's file. He didn't say anything for a few minutes, then he asked Logan why should Harlan Reeves be blamed for what happened.

Cambry said, "Don't get me wrong, I think what Harlan did was unforgivable but Chad could've gotten the help he needed, couldn't he? It looked like he was getting help. I don't understand."

Logan smiled at him. "That's one way to look at it, I guess. The thing was, Chad knew what the problem was and did nothing to help himself. Because Harlan hurt him, Chad hurt others. That wasn't right. The lives he damaged, they didn't get a say in what happened to them. If anything, both of them are at fault for this one. On the same token, you can say Harlan was responsible for all those shattered lives."

"You have a good point," the man said. "I just don't think you can blame Harlan for this one. I mean, sure, Chad got hurt by Harlan in the bank but Chad knew he needed to deal with his problems. Anyway, you look at it the story was a sad tale."

Logan went on to say the thing that made people like Harlan Reeves so dangerous was that they didn't think about the ramifications of their actions, the chain reaction they cause. They just care about what they want, and they will do everything in their power to get it.

Cambry said, "The thing I don't understand, is if he loved Ruth so much like he claimed you have to wonder why he hurt her, right? She didn't do anything except love him as much as she could. She got killed for her trouble. It's a damn shame."

"I can't say as I understand dark minds like that. It just seemed like he didn't care at the end. He knew he was going to be killed and went crazy. Nothing was going to deter him."

When Cambry asked about whether or not people's lives are mapped out Logan sighed. Truth was, she didn't know a thing about it. There was a time when she thought she had the code cracked, but it turned out not to be the case.

One of the things she asked the council was whether or not everything was already predetermined, and everything just played out like a movie, or, did humans have the freedom to do what they wanted? They looked at her for a few minutes and said nothing. She never got an answer. For years she wondered about the answer. She asked a few other people but nobody knew. Was it all a conspiracy? Why? How long had it been going on? That was one of the biggest things people would pray to her about. She'd hear all those prayers and wonder the same thing. There wasn't a way she could translate her thoughts to them. She wished she could enter people's dreams and implant information. Things would be so easy that way. She'd have to ask if she could do that.

"Do you know how much longer Harlan Reeves has to live?" Cambry asked.

"Oh, I can kill him whenever I want. It's not going to be too much longer. I just got word he killed himself."

"Why?" Cambry asked.

"I'm not sure. He convinced a bunch of people aliens were going to take them to another planet."

"What?" Cambry laughed. "That's insane. Well, hell, I wouldn't let him come back if it was up to me. He might do something like that again."

She told him that was the whole point of them going over the file.

"That's reassuring, I guess. It's still crazy to me they

Playground
even let him out of the cage he was in."
"Some of the people they make policemen aren't the brightest."
Cambry laughed.
Logan asked if he wanted anything.
"I could go for some food."
"What would you want to eat?"
"Anything. I'm not too picky."
"Okay, then."
They got the caterers to make them some burgers and fries with soda on the side, then, they had a couple of candy bars.
"That hit the spot," Cambry said.
"Glad to hear it. We need all the energy we can get. Have a lot of work to do."
"Oh, you had to remind me of that?"
She laughed.
He smiled at her. He told her that when they got done with the case he hoped to get a promotion.
"To what?" Logan asked.
"I'm not sure. I just think I should be due for something. This is a big case, and I know Trent doesn't give just anybody these types of tasks."
Logan said, "If you want something bad enough... After this is over I'll put in a good word for you."
"Thanks."
"Think nothing of it."
They talked a little more before they returned to the files. The next file they were going to look at was a guy named Luther Frost.

18

Luther Frost, when Harlan and his crew were out of the picture, didn't quite know what to do with himself. After the authorities got everything sorted out he went back to his parents. But things were hard for him. After his ordeal, he slept for about twelve hours. He was home but he didn't know he was safe yet. He'd spent so long trying to be something someone wanted him to be. He didn't know how to act. In a lot of ways, he had been robbed of important years of life.

His parents, Tina and Marcus, worked with him to get their boy back to leading a normal life, a pure life before he was taken in by lies. They regretted the fact they'd kicked him out, to begin with. They figured he'd come back in a week or so. They had just wanted to teach their son a lesson. You had to follow the rules. There were years they'd never get back, despite what they did or said. His first couple days home they wouldn't let him leave the house.

They saw their son was going through a rough time and wanted to help. They explained to Luther that Harlan and the others were bad and brainwashed all the followers to do their bidding. Harlan did a good job at making people believe in something that wasn't real, something that wasn't pure. Harlan knew that once he had them he could manipulate them to do and think whatever he wanted. He knew what to say at any given time. He always knew exactly what to say. Harlan knew young minds could be molded. He took full advantage of Luther and the others. One of the things that was always stressed upon them, if they tried to escape or speak out they would be punished. Luther knew the rumors that surrounded Harlan, so he was scared to say anything to anyone. The times he was able to leave the compound he

Playground

had to have an escort. Once Harlan saw Luther could hold his own and could be trusted, he was tasked to do things for Harlan and his crew. He became a spy, letting them know what everyone was doing, making sure no one was doing something they shouldn't.

Luther's parents sat with him at the kitchen table and explained things to him. They needed to make sure Luther knew the truth behind Harlan and the church. They wanted things to go back to normal. Their son deserved the very best life had to offer. They knew it was going to be a process but was something that needed to be done. In a way, they felt guilty about what happened to Luther.

"What do you mean? Why would people do that?" Luther asked his dad, as they were sitting at the kitchen table. "I don't know if that's right."

Marcus said, "There are a lot of evil people in the world. No one knows why people do very bad things. They're just greedy, son. He knew exactly what he was doing. It wasn't your fault."

"He wasn't that bad," he told his dad. "He told me you have to control people when the situation calls for it. He told me that everyone has to have rules and that if those are broken the person has to be punished. Using force gets things done, no matter if it calls for it or not."

Tina looked at Luther with soft eyes.

"No, son, that's not how things should be," Marcus said. "He put things in your mind. He made you guys think a certain way, made you guys twisted in your thinking. You guys were his prey."

"He said there would be people like you, people who would try to tell us things like this. He should know, he had God talking through him. It was what God wanted."

His dad said, "Do you think God wants to kill us? We were created by God."

Bradley Davenport

His mother reached across the table and put his hand in hers. "We love you and will get through this together." Luther said, "You have a point, Dad. If God created us, then it wouldn't make sense he'd want to hurt us. Someone asked Harlan about that and he told them it's Satan at work. He was telling us about how Satan and God were always fighting to get people's souls."

"Do you believe that?" his dad asked.

"That's what Harlan told us."

"And you believe everything he told you?"

"He told us he got it straight from God. And Harlan knew what he was talking about. He just wanted to do good and he got punished for it. The world, it's not a fair place. I don't know, all that stuff was just too wild and crazy. Everything is happening too fast. They say one thing, he says another."

As Marcus and Tina tried to explain their point Luther just looked at them. He told himself that they didn't know what they were talking about. They didn't know Harlan like he did. He was one of the few Harlan trusted. You can't just trust any old person to be a spy for you. The person might double-cross you.

"And let's not forget," Marcus told his son, "he killed those people. No matter what his plans were he needed to pay for the things he did, his sins. If you ask me, I say they need to throw him in prison and throw away the key. If he did it then he'll do it again. I'm surprised he didn't get you. They would be doing everyone a service if they just put bullets in Harlan. Think of everyone he hurt, all the families. No one asked for any of that. He's sick."

Luther said, "They said he did all those things but I never saw anything. He would just tell us they decided to leave the compound and go back where they came from. He would tell us that everyone was a lost soul and that they needed to find themselves. I think people are just trying to pin things on him. They saw that he was trying to do good in the world. They couldn't take it. Someone like that knew all about his past and they wouldn't let it go. Just wanted to keep him down. It's a big shame."

"I'm sure that's what he said to get you guys to believe in him. If I had to guess I'd say he was troubled from the start, that he didn't have any real confidence in himself. You made him look good. I'm surprised he manipulated so many people. Let me ask, why do you think people were blaming him for stuff?"

"They all came there to live because they believed him. I guess someone wanted the power he had. Someone just made all of that up about the murders. All the money people donated to him, they need to get it back if he was so bad like everyone said. And the money I gave him, I need to get that back. I wonder if we can sue?"

"Don't think that would work. He probably doesn't have the cash. They would more than likely go after his relatives for the money. With him in prison, he couldn't pay anything."

"Oh."

His father continued. "And I'd have to think if there were some sort of lawsuit brought against anyone, it would take awhile for you and everyone else to get their funds back."

"That's not good."

"Well, son, that's the sad truth about it."

They continued to talk as they ate. Marcus thought he had his son back, that he set him straight on what Harlan and the others were really about. Luther wasn't sure what to believe. After everything he'd been through Luther was still lost. He was young and needed to find something he wasn't getting from his parents' house.

Bradley Davenport

When Tina and Marcus asked him about school he told them he was going to drop out. He told them that he could always get his GED. His parents wanted him to continue with school, but they couldn't do anything about it.

Things were going well for Luther for awhile. He found a job and met a girl. Her name was Tish Banks and she was stunning. She had brown curly hair and thin glasses. They worked at the same place, a little diner called Hook. Both of them liked working there. The hours and pay were pretty good. Most days after work they spent with one another. He'd go on to tell people that when he was with Tish it was like he was on another planet. As time passed they grew closer. He and Tish wanted to get a place together, but they had to save more money. They were young kids with the world in front of them.

19

Sometimes the newspaper or the nightly news on TV would have a story about Harlan Reeves; his lawyer filed a motion, an interview he was giving about his quality of life behind bars. There were even talks of a book in the works. And with a book always came a movie.

Luther started to think about Harlan and what he did in that place. He had to be pretty bored. He asked his parents if they thought it was a good idea he visit Harlan in prison. They were quick to tell him that wouldn't be a good move. Even though they talked to him at great length about how Harlan wasn't a good person, he still thought they didn't know what they were talking about. Luther told them they shouldn't believe what they wrote about Harlan and his group in the newspapers. He'd tell them reporters would do anything to get good ratings.

Luther called the prison to see when the visiting times were. He caught the city bus to make the ten-mile trip up to the prison. When he entered the building and said what he was doing there they led him to a bigger room with tables and chairs. He was told it would be about twenty minutes. He took a seat at one of the tables. As he waited a few other people were led into the room for a visit. They were scattered all over the room.

He didn't know how Harlan would react to seeing him. Even though he liked Luther harsh circumstances can do strange things to people. But Luther, had to see the man again, even if it was going to be for the last time. He hoped it wasn't going to be their last meeting.

The door to the room opened and two big guards walked in followed by half a dozen guys in tan uniforms. Luther scanned the row of people and nodded at Harlan

Reeves when he came to him. He looked older and grayer. It had been over two years since Luther had laid eyes on him. The officers told the inmates they could go where their visitors were.

Harlan eyed Luther as he walked up to the table. He took a seat. Luther smiled at the man. Harlan was expressionless.

"Looks like you're holding up okay, Harlan," Luther told the man.

Harlan cleared his throat. "Same to you."

"Thanks," Luther told him. "I hope they're treating you good in here, giving you good food."

Harlan scratched the side of his face with his fingers. "I could always do without being here. The food isn't good at all, but it's something. They're sending me back to isolation in a few days."

"Why?"

"For my protection."

"From what?"

The man laughed. "A lot of people in here would love to see me dead. For my protection, they're going to put me in isolation again. But I'm in here for the rest of my natural life, so I don't see the point. If they want to get down to business, we'll see what happens. I've made peace with the fact that I'm going to die in here."

"No offense, why'd they let you into the general population?"

"There are rules about how long they can keep you in there. But for my safety, they are going to put me back. No one here wants me dead on their watch. Yes, they want me dead but no one wants to be responsible for it."

"That's good," Luther said. "You want to live as long as you can."

"That's what I hear."

"It could be worse."

Playground

Harlan asked the kid why he came to see him. The way he saw it, it was like the kid was kicking him in the face when he was down. Luther still looked at Harlan in a good light, despite what his parents told him. He thought they were getting somewhere in the compound when they took Harlan and the others away. Luther asked the man if what they said in the papers about him was true, that he'd killed all of those people.

"What do you think?" Harlan asked.

"I don't know what to think."

"That's the only opinion that matters. People will always say things about you; some good, others bad. You need to look at each case and decide whether you think they're untrue or not. People, they'll start rumors no matter what. They want the attention. In my case, they didn't like my friends or me. They just made up anything they wanted. They never wanted me out of prison, and they were going to do anything in their power to keep me down."

"Why would they do that?"

Harlan shrugged. "Your guess is as good as mine. I think they saw my problems before when I went away and never let it go. Even though I served my time back then they want to punish me forever. It's a strange world out there."

"So, are you saying it's true or not?"

The man shrugged. "What do you think? Everyone has their version of someone."

"I don't think you did it."

Harlan laughed and told the kid he wished that were the case. Harlan told Luther that if he ever planned on killing anyone to make sure he never got caught, and that if anyone knew he'd have to get rid of them

Harlan said, "Can you do me a favor, kid?"

"What would that be?"

Bradley Davenport

"I don't want you to come here anymore."

"Why?" Luther asked.

The man sighed. "You need to forget about me and live your life. You don't want to end up in this place, trust me. And to be honest with you, I didn't treat you right. Get as far from me as you can. I don't like you and never did. My friends and I took advantage of all of you."

Luther didn't understand. He thought Harlan and the others liked him, and that was why they gave him the job he had. But the more he talked to the man he realized that he was used, like an old shoe that got tossed to the side. At the end of the meeting, both men stood and went their way.

On the way home the kid kept turning it over in his head, he thought that Harlan always enjoyed him. After all, Harlan promised him he'd be part of a family, that was why he joined Harlan and the others. Luther told his parents about what Harlan said, and they weren't surprised. They knew what Harlan was all about, and that was what they were trying to explain to their son. Luther, even though he'd developed a trauma due to Harlan, never mentioned the man again. He had trust issues he was going to have to work on.

20

Luther and Tish loved spending time with one another. They liked going out for pizza and bowling—she was always better at the game than he was, however, she felt bad for him and let him in a few times. As they grew closer he got comfortable with her enough to talk about the time spent at the compound.

"I couldn't even imagine what that was like," Tish told him. "I bet you were afraid every day?"

"No. All that stuff they say he did, the murders and things, I never saw any of that. They treated me and the others well. When they were arrested I was in shock."

"I think I'd be, too. That's some heavy stuff for teenagers to see."

"That was when they brought me back to my parents' house. Cops said I'd be better off with family."

"Were they right?"

"I don't think so."

She said, "That's sad. I wish things could've been different for you."

A few weeks later Luther asked her hand in marriage. She said she wanted to but wanted to have more money saved. She wanted to buy a two-story house with a large yard. She didn't know if she could tolerate living with his parents until then. After some debate she agreed, saying the most important thing was that they were together. He just wanted to be her.

He couldn't imagine life without her. He'd never had the feeling before. As a young teen, he had crushes on local girls, but nothing came from it. When he told Tish that he'd only had one girlfriend before her she was pretty understanding. Herself, she had two other boyfriends before him.

Bradley Davenport

After living with his parents for awhile it became clear they needed a place of their own. Luther searched and found a little apartment. It wasn't much, but it was what they could afford. He got a job at a gas station and she found work as a receptionist at a doctor's office. Things were pretty good for the first few months, but then, one day Luther lost his job. He got in a fight with a co-worker and got fired. When Tish found out she wasn't happy at all. It didn't take too long before things changed. He would get mad and argue with her. It got to the point where she told him she'd made a mistake getting a place with him. She stuck it out for awhile but ultimately left. She moved in with a friend until she decided what to do.

21

Without a job, Luther got kicked out of the apartment. He started to roam the streets until he found himself back at his parents' house. He didn't want to be homeless, so he asked if he could stay. His parents told him he could but he had to get a job. He agreed. A week later he ran into a friend of his, Mark Hives. After a small conversation, Mark asked Luther where he was working.
"I don't have a job," Luther told him.
"That so? I have something you might be interested in,"
"What's that?"
Mark led Luther to the trunk of his car and opened it. Bags full of cocaine and pills littered the inside.
Luther said, "You sell drugs?"
"Have to make money somehow."
"There's a lot of risk."
"You have to be careful," Mark laughed.
They went to a local bar to discuss details. Luther was up for anything, anything to get him out of the position he was in. The next few weeks flew by. Luther was making a lot of money, and he was making the supplier a lot of money. Everyone was happy,
Eight months after Luther started selling drugs he was shot to death outside of a nightclub. Someone he was selling to, decided they wanted more than just the drugs and rob him of all his money. When they had the dough they killed Luther.
People who knew Luther were brought to tears when they heard the news. All the neighbors came by the house to pay their respects.
The funeral was nice, a few people got up and said some kind words about Luther.

22

Cambry sighed after Luther Frost's story. He told Logan it was so sad because he was so young.

"Yeah," Logan said, "that's the shame about it all. You see a lot of that down on Earth. No matter what we do they never get the message. If it's not drugs it's gun control, or something else. They don't seem to understand that the things they do are killing them,"

"I was one of those people. Wasn't until I got up here that I realized what I was doing. I had a lot of regrets in those days."

"I think we all had thoughts like that."

Cambry sat back in his chair and asked Logan what they should do about Harlan. Logan told him she didn't feel comfortable letting his soul get reborn in another body. It would only bring more evil into a world that didn't need anymore.

One of the biggest reasons she didn't want Harlan's soul to be reborn was because of the chain reactions he caused. Most of the people he wronged had to live with those scars, and in a lot of cases, it led them to lash out.

Cambry said, "What's going to happen to him?"

"I think the best thing would be to send him to Hell."

"I see."

"And let's not forget all the people in the cult. They were there based on lies. Yes, they had a choice to a certain point. But they were told it was going to be something else. They never went to any alien ship."

Cambry said, "I think if I was one of those people I would've believed him."

When they finished talking they decided it was time to go talk to Trent about all of it.

23

When they got to Hell Logan told Cambry she'd take on the task of telling Trent. She had a few other matters she needed to discuss with the Prince of Darkness. They didn't know how Trent would react to what they decided. When they got outside of Trent's quarters Cambry said he had some things to do, plus, he thought they might want to talk about things in private, given their history with each other.

She knocked on a big black door a few times before it slowly opened. A little man in a black suit and a big black hat walked out.

"I need to see Trent," she said.

The little man looked her up and down. "Oh, it's you! We weren't expecting a visit today."

"I know. I just thought I'd come in person, and tell Trent about this information I have."

The guy stared at her for a minute. "Sure, no problem. He's inside. Just let me tell him you've arrived."

She smiled at the man. "And what was your name, sir?"

"The name is Willy, ma'am. I'm his new assistant. I was wondering when you were going to come by."

"Well, I'm here now."

"That you are."

She laughed.

He told her he'd be right back and shut the door. A while later the door opened and Willy popped his head out. He told her to come inside. They walked down a dark corridor to a den. Trent sat behind a big desk in the corner of the room.

"Hello, Trent," she said.

He stood and walked over to her. "Logan, my dear, you could've just had Cambry bring back the decision."

Bradley Davenport

"I wanted to see how you were. It's been awhile."

He shook his head. "Yes, it has. I'm glad to see you."

As they walked to the dining area she told him that after careful examination she thought it was best to send Harlan Reeves to Hell, that the same thing would continue to happen if he got reincarnated. He told her that'd continue the topic after they finished eating. During the meal they had a nice conversation, exchanging stories of years past, the good days on Earth.

After they finished eating he told her he'd take her side if she'd do something for him. She asked what that something was, but she already knew what he wanted. For the next few hours, they had passionate sex.

After they showed they were sitting in the living area.

"Thanks for that," Trent told her.

"You're very welcome."

He walked over to the bar and poured both of them a drink. She brought up the subject of Harlan Reeves.

He handed her the drink. "Regarding that, you might be upset but I decided to reincarnate him. I already turned the paperwork in."

"What?" she was stunned.

"I think you heard me."

"Why?"

Trent said, "Hell, it was already done before I sent Cambry over to you. I just thought it'd be a funny thing to do."

She smashed her glass on the floor. "I can't fucking believe you. Do you know how much time I wasted? I could've spent that time doing other things What the fuck, you prick?"

"Don't get so mad, baby. I was just goofing around. Look at it like this, the next time he kills a bunch of people we can do this again. You win some, I win some, remember?"

Playground

After yelling at each other for about an hour, she told him to go have sex with himself, then, she stormed out of the room. When she got back to her office she smoked a joint with Heidi.

After awhile, Logan had to go to the bottom floor to welcome some new arrivals.

24

Trent and Killroy were having lunch in the back office of the bar. They were talking about some of the projects going on in Hell when a knock came to the door. Trent went to see who it was. Jesus was standing on the other side.

"Hey, Jesus, what's going on?" Trent said.

"You have a few minutes?" the man asked. "It won't take long."

"I have more than a few, buddy."

"We need to talk."

Trent invited Jesus inside. They offered him some pasta. There was a big pot and red sauce. Jesus told them he'd love to have something to eat. He hadn't had anything all day and was feeling a little empty.

Trent told him one of his girlfriends made it.

Killroy laughed as he poured their guest some wine. "If nothing else, they can cook."

Jesus asked how everything was going. Both men looked at each other and told Jesus there was no problem, that everything was going well. There were a few minor things but it was under control.

"That's what keeps you guys going, you know? Keep everything in line," Jesus told them.

They thank him for the kind words.

Jesus thanked them for the food. He'd been going crazy the day before and it was nice to get something good to eat.

"What seems to be the problem?" Killroy asked.

Jesus sighed. "Well, it's sort of a delicate subject. It has to do with Mary."

"Which Mary?" Trent asked.

"My wife."

"Oh, that one," Trent raised a brow.

Playground

"Yes, that one."
"What about her?"

A guy by the name of Rusty Kane and his crew kidnapped Jesus' wife. He found out where they were keeping her, but he needed help to get her back. He wasn't sure how many guys Kane had with him, so he needed all the manpower he could get.

Trent said, "You know why they took her?"

"Who knows?" Jesus said. "I hate to say it but I think it had something to do with me."

"Why would that be?"

"I made a drug deal with him and didn't make my last payment."

"Why didn't you make it?"

"Was going to. When I was going over there something came up. Was going to do it after. Time got away from me."

Killroy said, "Rusty, that guy's something. We went one-on-one once, and it was a rough go but I won. I always reminded him of it when we would see each other. He didn't appreciate that very much."

Jesus laughed.

"We can't have things like that going on," Trent said. "Right or wrong, you can't just go around taking anyone you want."

Jesus lit a cigarette. "Yeah, that's not a good thing. Everyone already runs around here like a bunch of savage animals."

The two men agreed to help get Mary back. Killroy told Jesus that they wouldn't need anyone else to help. The three of them could take the crew. Trent led Jesus and Killroy to the safe to get the guns.

Jesus looked at the weapons displayed. "Yeah, this should do it!"

Bradley Davenport

They grabbed a few shotguns and handguns.

Trent told him they didn't have to use all of it. And he showed him what the combination was if he ever needed it in the safe and they weren't there.

"We'll show them who you don't fuck with around here," Jesus barked. "Picked the wrong guy to mess with, I'll tell you that."

Killroy said, "You can say that again."

On their way out Jesus told them they were keeping her in one of Rusty Kane's warehouses he had. He didn't know which one, so they were going to have to stop at everyone. It was going to be a long search. Jesus filled them in on the details.

"I hate this shit happened," Jesus told them. "She didn't do anything to them."

Killroy said, "That's what happens in a lot of cases. We'll get it all figured out. Not to worry."

"I just don't want to turn it into a whole big thing," Jesus said.

"Rusty," Trent explained, "is a bad character. I could never trust that fuck. There was a time when he was okay, but that was years ago."

"How so?" Jesus asked.

"He's always been. He's not a fan of mine, I promise you that."

"Well, I'll kill his ass if he did anything to Mary."

"As you should, my friend."

"That motherfucker! Someone should've taken him out years ago," Jesus told them.

"Nobody can argue with that. I thought about it a few times. Think a lot of people have."

Killroy said, "I wanted to once."

25

The first warehouse they stopped at was a few blocks away from the bar. A few guys were outside talking when they pulled up.

"Let me handle this," Trent told them. "I can get the truth out of them."

They got out of the car and started toward the guys.

"Hey, guys," Trent called out to the group. "Nice day out, isn't it?"

The men agreed.

"Which one of you is running this?" Trent asked.

One of the men raised his hand and said he was in charge. Trent walked over to the guy. He was wearing a white shirt and jeans. The guy took off his black hat so his blonde hair could be seen better.

He nodded at Trent. "Help with something?"

"What do you guys have going on today?" Trent asked.

"Not much, you know? Just hanging out."

"What/s your name?"

"Bobby."

"Good to know you. And I think you know who I am, yes?"

Bobby shook his head. "I do."

"Glad that bit of business is out of the way."

"Yes, sir."

Trent eyed the man, then looked at the others. "It's a good time for it, for just hanging out, no agenda for the day. I guess not having an agenda is having an agenda," the man laughed. "Say, any of you see Rusty around today? Need to talk to him about something."

They said they hadn't seen him.

Bobby asked them if they wanted a beer.

They didn't.

Trent asked if he had a look around.

Another guy in the group said, "We aren't doing anything illegal."

"I didn't say you were," Trent replied. "A girl, I'm not sure if you know her, Mary, was kidnapped. We're just checking places out."

"Mary?" the guy asked.

"Mary Magdalene."

"Oh, that girl? You sure she got kidnapped?"

"What do you mean by that?" Trent asked.

The guy laughed. "Well, she's a big whore. Ask anyone around, they'll tell you."

"What's your point?" Trent asked.

"She could've just run off with some other guy. Shit, I like Jesus but he got himself one crazy girl. Someone like that, she most likely moved on, got with another guy. Can't blame her."

"No?"

The guy turned his head from Trent and looked over in Jesus/ direction. "Guess she got bored with that guy. Someone like that always needs something new," he looked back at Trent. "I feel sorry for the poor son-of-a-bitch. Girl did that to me, I don't know what I'd do."

"I see."

Just about that time Jesus and Killroy walked closer to them.

The man with the black hat said, "You guys can search all you want. Have nothing to hide. Nobody's here."

Jesus walked over to him. "Hope that's the case for your sake."

All the men walked into the warehouse. It was nothing special, just a hollow shell with no windows. Bobby explained that when Rusty wasn't using the space for his needs he let him use it for whatever he wanted.

"We were about to leave to bring my car over here," Bobby told them. "It needs some work. Not quite sure

Playground

what it is. Been acting up the past few days. Hell, just might have to sell the damn thing."

Trent told him that they'd be out of their way as soon as possible. They had a look around the place. When Trent told Bobby they were going to search the offices in the back, it didn't sit well with him.

Bobby said, "I don't need to knife you on this one, but we can't let you search our offices."

"Why not?" Killroy demanded. "Do I have to remind you who you're talking to?"

Jesus walked over to Bobby and shoved his gun in his face. "The fuck are you talking about? I can pull this trigger, and blow your fucking head all over everything. Now, you need to rethink what you say."

Bobby stared at him. "Uh-huh... Do what you want, just don't kill any of us."

Jesus looked at him, then slammed the stock of the shotgun against the side of his face. He fell to the ground like a sack of potatoes. Jesus turned to the others and told them the reason he did that was because he disrespected Mary.

"If any of you wanna join him be my guest," Jesus told them. "Honestly, I don't give a single fuck about any of you."

The men looked shocked.

They looked through the offices, and when they saw they were empty Jesus told the men he was sorry for what he told them. He knew he'd better smooth things over before it came back to bite him.

The next warehouse they went to was a few blocks away from where they were just at. After an hour of dealing with the idiots at that location, they found out Rusty was at a house.

They busted into the house with guns drawn. They demanded everyone in the house to go to the living room. When they wouldn't go voluntarily they were forced at gunpoint. They searched the whole house and finally found Mary chained to a pipe in the basement.

Jesus brought her upstairs.

Jesus asked why they took her. After some yelling and cussing Jesus, Killroy, and Trent shot all of the men.

They went back to the bar and had a party. It was clear that Mary was still a little shaken by what happened.

Trent told all of them that they might have a problem with guys who knew Rusty and that they might seek revenge. Jesus said he wasn't worried, that if they wanted a problem they'd find him.

The party lasted for a week. They were so happy to be around one another.